LEGAL ORIGINS AND LEGAL CHANGE

LEGAL ORIGINS AND LEGAL CHANGE

ALAN WATSON

THE HAMBLEDON PRESS
LONDON AND RIO GRANDE

Published by The Hambledon Press, 1991
102 Gloucester Avenue, London NW1 8HX (U.K.)
P.O. Box 162, Rio Grande, Ohio 45672 (U.S.A.)

ISBN 1 85285 048 5

British Library Cataloguing in Publication Data

Watson, Alan *1933-*
Legal origins and legal change.
1. Roman Empire. Law.
I. Title
343.7

Library of Congress Cataloging-in-Publication Data

Watson, Alan
Legal origins and legal change/Alan Watson.
Includes index.
1. Roman law – History.
2. Roman law – Influence.
I. Title.
KJA190.W37 1991
340.5′ – dc20 91-18742 CIP

Printed on acid-free paper and bound in Great
Britain by Bookcraft Ltd., Midsomer Norton, Somerset

Contents

Acknowledgements

The articles reprinted here first appeared in the following places and are reprinted by kind permission of the original publishers.

1. *Law Quarterly Review* (1973), pp. 387-392.
2. *Studia et Documenta Historiae et Iuris* (1963), pp. 337-338.
3. *Edinburgh University Inaugural Lecture no. 36* (1969), pp. 1-15.
4. *Tijdschrift voor Rechtsgeschiedenis* (1969), pp. 351-368.
5. *Tijdschrift voor Rechtsgeschiedenis* (1973), pp. 19-34.
6. *Tulane Law Review (F.H. Lawson Tribute)* (1974), pp. 1122-1128.
7. *University of Pennsylvania Law Review* (1983), pp. 1121-1157.
8. *Journal of Roman Studies* (1972), pp. 100-105.
9. *Classical Quarterly* (1979), pp. 436-447.
10. *Revue Internationale des Droits de l'Antiquité* (1970), pp. 357-367.
11. *Revue Internationale des Droits de l'Antiquité* (1974), pp. 337-342.
12. *Glotta* (1975), pp. 294-296.
13. *Labeo* (1973), pp. 26-30.
14. *Zeitschrift der Savigny-Stiftung (romanistische Abteilung)* (1962), pp. 329-334.
15. *Tijdschrift voor Rechtsgeschiedenis* (1964), pp. 245-254.
16. *Revue Internationale des Droits de l'Antiquité* (1962), pp. 431-436.
17. *Index* (1970), pp. 179-183.
18. *Tijdschrift voor Rechtsgeschiedenis* (1963), pp. 69-91.
19. *Law Quarterly Review* (1963), pp. 87-97.
20. *Tijdschrift voor Rechtsgeschiedenis* (1966), pp. 402-406.

21. *Satura Robert Feenstra*, edited by J.A. Ankum, J.E. Spruit and F.B.J. Wubbe (Editions Universitaires Fribourg Suisse) (Fribourg, 1985), pp. 37-42.

22. *Law Quarterly Review* (1981), pp. 275-286.

23. *Israel Law Review* (1972), pp. 14-24.

24. *Tulane Law Review* (1968), pp. 289-303.

25. *Phoenix* (1983), pp. 53-65.

26. *Law Quarterly Review* (1976), pp. 79-84.

27. *International Journal of Moral and Social Studies* (1985), pp. 21-30.

Preface

Most of the essays in this collection concern Roman private law, but the emphasis differs from those reprinted in my *Studies in Roman Private Law*. Some relate to the making of law, studying aspects of the sources, legal change, legal culture, and law and society. Others deal with very early law or with the origins of legal ideas; and some of these are as much philological as legal.

For each and every one of the articles reprinted here, I received constructive criticism from colleagues and friends. For such great help over many years I want to express my gratitude.

Alan Watson

For Ann and Mick

I

Sources of Law

1

The Law of Action and the Development of Substantive Law in the Early Roman Republic

No one would ever deny the importance of courts and legal process and the control of these for legal development. In a very obvious sense it can even be claimed that, after law has left its most primitive stage, all legal rights depend upon the procedures available to enforce them. But the question must be put whether, apart from that truism, the situation in early Rome justifies the famous dictum of Maine:

> "So great is the ascendancy of the Law of Actions in the infancy of Courts of Justice, that substantive law has at first the look of being gradually secreted in the interstices of procedure; and the early lawyer can only see the law through the envelope of its technical forms." [1]

It appears from the context in which he makes this statement that in so far as Maine was thinking of Rome he was concerned with the time of the XII Tables and subsequent centuries. Most recently, in this *Review*, Birks, who apparently accepts Maine's view, wishes to know the extent to which substantive law was dominated by procedure in 200 B.C.[2] He explains his position:

> "Either we all believe that in beginnings procedure is everything, or dissentients should explode the myth. My understanding of the early primacy of procedure is that the words in which people traditionally make their claims and complaints come long before the lawyers who explain and delimit them scientifically, that those words are the first elements of law as an intellectual system."

As a dissentient I should like to take up Birks' challenge and argue that, whatever merits this opinion of Maine and his followers may have for early law in general or for Roman law before the XII Tables,[3] it does not at all fit the facts of Roman law and procedure at the time of the XII Tables and later in the Republic.

[1] *Early Law and Custom* (London, 1901), p. 389.

[2] In a review of Watson, *Roman Private Law around 200 B.C.* (Edinburgh, 1971), (1972) 88 L.Q.R. 293, 294.

[3] The general validity of Maine's view need not concern us here. But it may be observed that the development of law by the manipulation of procedure does not look very primitive.

To begin with, the XII Tables themselves are dominated by substantive law. Only the first two Tables—as reconstructed by modern editors—are devoted to procedure.[4,5] The clauses which concern private law are not written in terms of the action available to enforce a right, but state the substance of the law without reference to the relevant proceedings. No argument need be given for this proposition since the fact appears from the fragments which have survived on that code.

Secondly, the action available in the mid-fifth century was the *legis actio*. The action itself was heard, of course, in two stages, a formal stage *in jure*, in front of the praetor, then less formalised proceedings *apud judicem*, before the judge. If substantive law is to develop from the interstices of procedure or from the words in which persons traditionally make their claims, then we would expect the substantive law to be created from the formal stage *in jure*. But there is a problem here since the Roman law of the period did not have a large number of forms, each with a narrow scope, which could be interpreted and which might define the substance of the right, but only three forms[6]—*sacramento in rem, sacramento in personam, per judicis postulationem*—each of which could be used in a variety of situations. There seems no way in which interpretation of the form of action will lead to the development (or restriction) of the right. Of course, the wording of the individual *legis actio* will vary according to what is claimed but it is precisely here that we can see most clearly how mistaken Maine is. Thus to take an example from the *legis actio sacramento in rem*: the parties claimed *hunc ego hominem ex jure quiritium meum esse aio secundum suam causam*, an oath was sworn by each party on the accuracy of the claim, and the trial proceeded *apud judicem* to determine whose *sacramentum* was *justum*.[7] Thus, that person will win the action who rightly claimed the slave was his *ex jure quiritium*. Who does have the slave *ex jure quiritium* is a question purely of substantive law, and the outcome will be decided on the basis of matters which are not mentioned in the wording of the action at all, such as the validity of a *mancipatio* purporting to transfer the slave, whether the requirements of *usucapio* had been fulfilled, whether the slave was born to a slave mother belonging to

[4] But see *infra*, pp. 7 *et seq.*

[5] Part of the reconstructed third *tabulae* deals with acknowledged or judgment debtors.

[6] There are as many as three only if we count *sacramento in rem* and *sacramento in personam* as distinct forms. The *legis actio per condictionem* was not then in existence, that *per manus injectionem* was a mode of execution, and so essentially was the *legis actio per pignoris capionem*.

[7] For the form of the action see G.4.13–17.

one of the parties, and so on. In other words the decisive part of the form is the part which is capable of variation, namely that in which the parties state their claim, and that party will win whose claim is judged to be accurate in terms of substantive law. The substantive law is thus logically prior to the action.[8] If there is no right there can be no (successful) action. This appears even more clearly if we look at the *legis actio sacramento in personam*. The plaintiff claimed: "*Aio te mihi decem milia dare oportere*" and here he had to insert the *causa debendi*. The *causa debendi* was the basis of the claim and would necessarily rest on some rule of substantive law such as a provision of the XII Tables. Before the *judex* the real issue would be whether the plaintiff's claim was justified factually and juridically by the stated *causa debendi*. There might well be considerable scope for legal development and this would come from the interpretation of the rule of substantive law stated as the *causa debendi*. "The words in which people traditionally make their claims" could here have importance but only because they showed that the claims were based on substantive law.

A fortiori, in the *legis actio per judicis postulationem*[9] and, when it was later introduced, the *legis actio per condictionem*[10] there was no scope in the wording for substantive law to be gradually secreted in the interstices of procedure, and equally no justification for the view that the early lawyer can only see the law through the envelope of its technical forms.

It may be objected that in the view put forward here I am ignoring the rigidity of the formalism of the *legis actio* system. As one writer puts it: "The formalism of the *legis actiones* was managed with the most extreme strictness. The slightest deviation from the established wording entailed the loss of the action."[11] But this rigidity if it existed—and I do not think it did—would not affect the matter which concerns us. It would mean that the parties had to state their case with great care and that this was an additional factor which had to be watched. But it would not mean that the substantive law would grow out of the formal

[8] As one of his two explanations of the term *legis actiones* Gaius says they may have been so called because they were framed in the very wording of statutes and so were regarded as immutable as statutes: G.4.11. If this explanation is accurate or even if it is based on the correctly recorded fact that the claim was framed in the wording of a statute, then we have a further argument that the substantive law is logically prior to the action.

[9] For the form see G.4.17a.

[10] For the form see G.4.17b.

[11] Kaser, *Das römische Zivilprozessrecht* (Munich, 1966), p. 24: "Der Formalismus der Legisaktionen wird mit äusserster Strenge gehandhabt: Die geringste Abweichung vom feststehenden Wortlaut zieht Prozessverlust nach sich."

wording: as already argued there was no scope for this in the wording.

The traditional view of the rigidity of the *legis actio* procedure is primarily based [12] on G.4.11 where we are told that a man who sued because his vines had been cut down lost his case since in the action he used the word " vines " whereas he ought to have said " trees " seeing that the XII Tables, under which the action for the cutting down of his vines lay, spoke generally of the cutting down of trees. But Daube has, I think, shown that it is more likely the case was lost, not because of actional formalism, but because it could not be admitted that a fresh non-statutory demand concerning the destruction of a vine could replace a statutory ground of action, namely the law concerning the destruction of a tree.[13, 14] Incidentally jurists who hold that the slightest oral mistake in the *legis actio* entailed the irretrievable loss of the action see in this some kind of religious or magical power attributed to the form of words.[15] But in Roman religion itself the ruling was never so strict. From the earliest times a mistake or flaw of any kind, whether in the wording or performance or due to external factors, meant that the whole procedure had to begin again (or a *piaculum* offered); not that whatever was hoped from the prayer or sacrifice was so irretrievably lost that matters could not be put right.[16]

Presumably, the action referred to in G.4.11 was irretrievably lost because of the extinctive effect of *litis contestatio*: the parties proceeded to *litis contestatio* without the mistake in the pleadings being corrected. If the mistake occurred earlier it is difficult to see what could prevent the litigant going back to the beginning and starting again since he would still have his original cause of action.[17]

[12] *Cf. e.g.* Kaser, *Zivilprozessrecht*, p. 24 and n. 4.

[13] " Text and Interpretation in Roman and Jewish Law," *Jewish Journal of Sociology* iii (1961), pp. 3, 4, *et seq.*

[14] When Gaius in G.4.30 says that the *legis actiones* became unpopular because *ex nimia subtilitate veterum qui tunc iura condiderunt eo res perducta est, ut vel qui minimum errasset litem perderet*, he need only be thinking of situations akin to that in G.4.11 and not of a slip of the tongue.

[15] *Cf. e.g.* Kaser, *Zivilprozessrecht*, p. 24 n. 4. In discussing religious formalism, Latte compares it with formalism in the legal field: it would be unjustified, he thinks, to look for priority in one area, and he suggests rather a parallelism which has its roots in the unity of the pattern of thought: *Römische Religionsgeschichte* (Munich, 1960), p. 62.

[16] See *e.g.* Livy, 2.36; Cicero, *de div.* 1.26.55; Macrobius, 1.11.3 (all three texts relate to the same event which Livy dates to the year 491 B.C., Macrobius to 279); *Tab. Iguv.* VI.B.47; (does not concern Rome but a people of similar race); Cato, *de agri cult.* 141.4; *cf.* Bailey, *Phases in the Religion of Early Rome* (Oxford, 1932) pp. 86 *et seq.*; Wissowa, *Religion und Kultus der Römer*, 2nd ed. (Munich, 1912), p. 37.

[17] The point does not really affect the present argument, and need not be considered more fully. Gaius' account is not explicit, and the moment of *litis contestatio* in the *legis actiones* is much disputed by modern scholars: *cf. e.g.* Kaser, *Zivilprozessrecht*, pp. 57 *et seq.*, and the authorities he cites.

No argument for rigid formalism in the *legis actiones* can be drawn from Pomponius D.1.2.2.6. (*sing. enchirid.*). Discussing these actions he says: *quas actiones ne populus prout vellet institueret, certas solemnesque esse voluerunt.* This seems to mean that the forms of the actions came to be fixed and one had to sue according to the form. It does not imply that a slip in reciting the form meant that the case was lost. Nor can any such conclusion be properly drawn from Pomponius' statement in the same text that for about a hundred years the *scientia interpretandi* and the actions were in the hands of the pontiffs.

If I have read him correctly, the sole argument given by Maine for his view of the early ascendancy of the law of actions is that in the XII Tables (which is followed by the Praetor's Edict) and in other early Indo-European codes the rules relating to actions are listed first, before the substantive law. Whatever the significance to be attributed to this fact, it simply cannot by itself support the weight of the conclusions which seem to be rested on it, that "substantive law has at first the look of being gradually secreted in the interstices of procedure "[18] or that "in beginnings procedure is everything." A sufficient explanation for procedure coming first in the XII Tables (and in the other codes mentioned by Maine) would be the practical problem of enforcing the law at an early stage of society. There is no point in knowing the law unless you know how to get the defendant into court and how to proceed against him.

In fact we can take the argument against Maine still further. It is by no means certain that procedure did occupy such a prominent place in the XII Tables as he supposes. The organisation of material in that code is, apart from a few exceptions, a mystery. There is excellent evidence that the XII Tables did begin with the clause *Si in jus vocat*, on summoning the defendant to court.[19] That the clauses on all other aspects of procedure followed it is basically the conjecture of modern editors of the XII Tables who are imposing their own concept of rationality on the surviving isolated scraps of information we have about the contents of the code. On the position in the XII Tables of the form of proceedings *in jure*, that part of the law of actions which might be thought to have an influence on the development of substantive law and which alone concerns us, we have—to put it bluntly—not the slightest information.

What indications there are of the order of the first few *tabulae* suggest a rather different arrangement from that which is customary

[18] I suspect that Maine was indulging in rhetorical exaggeration but has been taken " straight."
[19] Cicero, *de leg.* 2.4.9.

in the editions. Thus, Gaius wrote a commentary on the XII Tables in six books, and it seems reasonable to think that he followed the order of the code especially because he does also deal with summoning to court in his first book.[20] In that book, too, it appears that he discussed the security to be taken from parties to an action[21] and, more important for us, theft[22] and probably the action for cutting down trees.[23] In book two Gaius dealt with postponement of the action[24] and with the *legis actio per manus iniectionem*.[25] From the arrangement in Gaius *ad legum XII Tabularum*, then, the obvious conclusion is that the XII Tables themselves did not deal in the opening *tabulae* wholly, solely, and—in modern eyes—systematically, with the law of actions before proceeding to other matters, but that *furtum* was treated in *tabula II*. From the time of Lenel, indeed, this has been the general opinion of those scholars who have thought about the matter.[26] Maine is inconsistent here. He accepts that *tabula II* dealt *inter alia* with theft, but states only that *tabula III* contained rules on deposit. Yet the very evidence which presumably[27] led him to believe that theft was treated in *tabula II* should also have persuaded him that the clauses which followed that subject reverted to matters of procedure. What mainly concerns us in this is, of course, that if not all the rules of procedure were dealt with in the XII Tables before the rules of substantive law, then Maine's case for the early primacy of procedure is further weakened.

To conclude: I have maintained that for Roman law the view put forward by Maine and his followers that in early times substantive law really develops from procedure is not justified by the argument produced for it even if the facts on which the argument is based are accurately observed; that the supposed facts behind the argument are doubtful; that the form of early Roman procedure is such that substantive law could not develop from it to any significant extent; and that the XII Tables themselves were dominated by substantive law.[28]

20 D.2.4.18.
21 D.2.11.6: *cf.* Lenel, *Palingenesia iuris civilis* i, (1889, reprinted, Graz, 1960), 243.
22 D.50.16.233.2; 47.7.2; 47.7.4: *cf.* Lenel, *loc. cit.*, and nn. 4,5.
23 D.47.7.2.; 47.7.4.
24 D.50.16.234pr.
25 D.50.16.234.1.
26 *e.g.* Lenel, *Palingenesia* i, 243 n. 4. Maine, *Early Law*, pp. 369 *et seq.*; Bremer, *Iurisprudentiae Antehadrianae quae supersunt*, ii (Leipzig, 1898), p. 82; Riccobono, *Fontes Iuris Romani Anteiustiniani* i (Florence, 1941), p. 30 n. 1.
27 Presumably: because as usual Maine does not give the evidence on which he bases his proposition.
28 I am grateful to my friends, Peter Birks and John Barton, for very helpful comment.

2

Usu Farre(o) Coemptione

In Roman law there were three ways in which a woman could come into the *manus* of her husband.[1] These three ways are, so far as I am aware, listed in only four texts – and four texts, at that, of widely differing provenance.

> Gai 1, 110: Olim itaque *t*ribus modis in manum conveniebant, usu farreo coemptione.
>
> Arnobius *Adversus gentes*, 4, 20: . . . Uxores enim dii habent, atque in conjugalia foedera conditionibus veniunt ante quaesitis? usu, farre, coemptione, genialis lectuli sacramenta condicunt? . . .
>
> Boethius II *ad Top. Cic.* 3, 14: . . . Tribus enim modis uxor habebatur, usu, farreo, coemptione. . . .
>
> Servius *in Verg, Georg.* 1, 31: . . . tribus enim modis apud veteres nuptiae fiebant: usu, si verbi gratia mulier anno uno cum viro, licet sine legibus, fuisset, farre, cum per pontificem maximum et Dialem flaminem per fruges et molam salsam coniungebantur – unde confarreatio appellabatur –, ex quibus nuptiis patrimi et matrimi nascebantur; coemptione, cum illa in filiae locum, maritus in patris veniebat, ut siquis prior fuisset defunctus, locum hereditatis iustum alteri faceret. . . .

The lists in all four correspond to a remarkable extent. First, the order is always the same – *usus, confarreatio, coemptio*. It is difficult to imagine this as the historical order of emergence of the ways of obtaining *manus*[2] *and, moreover, it is hard to think of any logical justification for the arrangement. Secondly, the ways are always listed in the ablative. Other constructions, for instance where usus &c* were the subject of the sentence, would have been just as appropriate. Thirdly, the use of *far*, spelt, or *farreum*, a spelt cake, instead of *confarreatio*. Indeed, the ablative of the instrument here is rather surprising. These similarities must be significant and they cannot be explained away on the hypothesis that one of the texts derives from another or that one source,

[1] It is not intended here to enter upon the controversy as to the relationship between marriage and *conventio in manum*.

[2] *Usus* can scarcely have been the first.

perhaps Varro, was common to more than one writer. And the presence of *farre* in two, of *farreo* in the other two is a definite argument against more than two coming from the same immediate source. Not even a common tradition of the exposition of *manus* would be a sufficient explanation – that could account for the appearance of the same order in all of them but not for the other similarities. But clearly all must derive from the same ultimate source. This source must have had two qualities. First, it must have been of very considerable authority – the retention of *farre* or *farreo* in all four, instead of a switch to *confarreatio*, points to a reluctance to alter the wording. Whether *farre* or *farreo* is the original is not greatly important since the other could easily be introduced accidentally in transmission. Secondly, the source must have been very widely known. It is hard to believe, I think, that the qualities could have been combined in a writer, lay or legal, or, indeed, found in an edict. It seems much more likely that the words derive from a statute and, moreover, from a statute of wide importance. That statute can only have been the XII Tables. No other piece of legislation known to us (and one unknown to us could hardly have had the necessary importance) fits the requirements except Augustus' marriage laws[3] and they can be excluded for two reasons. First, there is no place in that legislation for a list of the ways of creating *manus* marriage unless by way of introduction to changes in the law and introductions of this kind would not seem to have occurred. Secondly, *confarreatio* would have been much more likely to have been used at this period rather than *far* or *farreum*. I submit, therefore, that there is a probability that the XII Tables contained a clause on the acquisition of *manus* in which occurred the word: *usu farre(o) coemptione*.

[3] The wording of the *lex Canuleia* is unlikely to have been widely known.

3

Limits of Juristic Decision in the Later Roman Republic

It is to me a great privilege to stand before you today as Professor T. B. Smith's successor. I feel this the more keenly in that my views on the scope of the Chair of Civil Law differ radically from his. I take Civil Law in its traditional meaning: Roman Law. The historical study of Roman Law is still in its infancy, but in Britain at the present moment, under the unquestioned leadership of an Honorary Doctor of this University, Professor David Daube, scholarly standards in the subject are higher than ever before. I appreciate fully the honour of being Professor of Civil Law at this time in the University of Edinburgh. I am happy, though, that the Chair has also responsibilities for Comparative Law and my aim for the Department will be the development of teaching and research in both Civil Law and Comparative Law. Already this year there has been some expansion of teaching for the Honours Class in Comparative Law. Next year I hope we will have an Honours Class in Civil Law and it is my ambition to introduce LL.M. courses in both subjects and a postgraduate Diploma in Roman Law.

But today I want to talk to you not about my interpretation of the duties of the Professor of Civil Law but about aspects of interpretation and juristic decision in the last hundred years of the Roman Republic.[1]

A modern Scots lawyer transported back in time to the later Roman Republic would not find general attitudes to the interpretation of laws, edicts and wills so very different from those prevailing at Parliament House. The basic approaches of those appearing in court were the same. A clause might be interpreted widely or narrowly, according to the needs of the case. The contemporary *Rhetorica ad Herrenium*, a handbook on oratory, gives advice on how to act where the letter of a document and the

[1] This lecture derives from my researches since 1960 into later Republican law: hence the unconscionably large number of references to my own publications.

intention of its draughtsman appear to be at variance. First, the author lists the arguments which he judges to be most effective where one is speaking in favour of the letter. Then he produces the arguments to be used to support the intention.[1] Instances of such arguments in practice are frequent in the sources, the most celebrated being the *causa Curiana* of around 93 to 91 B.C.[2] A testator left a will reading " Let my son be my heir. If my son dies before reaching puberty, let M'. Curius be my heir ". Quintus Mucius Scaevola, the famous consul of 95 B.C., pontiff and jurist—" The most eloquent among the jurists ", to quote Cicero[3]—argued that the will was to be interpreted literally: Curius' appointment as heir was subject to the condition, " If my son dies before puberty "; but the testator never had a son, therefore, the son could not die before reaching puberty so the condition failed and Curius could not be heir. Scaevola's opponent, Lucius Licinius Crassus—according to Cicero, " the best jurist among the orators "[4]—based his case, successfully, on the presumed intention of the testator: the testator wished Curius to be his heir if he had a son who died before puberty or even if he never had a son, was his argument.[5] The court's decision in favour of the arguments of Crassus did not, however, herald a new era in which overwhelming importance was given to the testator's presumed intention against the wording of the will.[6]

Again, the Scots lawyer would find already in existence established principles of interpretation, expressed most clearly, as it happens, in connexion with wills. For instance, the intention of the testator was paramount,[7] but words had to be given their normal meaning.[8] To reach the testator's intention one could look at circumstances known to the testator,[9] or even to facts

1 2.9.13-10.14.

2 The main sources are: Cicero, *de orat.* 1.39.180; 2.32.42; *de inven.* 2.42.122; *Brutus*, 52.194-53.198; *top.* 10.42; *pro Caecina*, 18.53.

3 *Brutus*, 39.145.

4 *Brutus*, 39.145.

5 See most recently on the case, Wieacker, " The *causa Curiana* and contemporary Roman jurisprudence ", *The Irish Jurist*, ii (1967), pp. 151 ff; and my forthcoming, *The Law of Succession in the Later Roman Republic*, Chapter 7.

6 Cf. e.g., Wieacker, *op. cit.*, p. 161; Watson, *loc. cit.*

7 D.33.10.7.2 (Celsus *19 dig.*); 34.2.32.1 (Paul *2 ad Vitellium*); 33.7.16.2 (Alfenus *2 dig. a Paulo epit.*); 34.2.33 (Pomponius *4 ad Quintum Mucium*).

8 D.33.10.7.2; 33.10.10 (Iavolenus *3 ex post. Labeonis*).

9 This was at least the opinion of Alfenus: D.33.7.16.2.

known about the testator.[1] Ambiguities might be cleared by looking at other clauses of the will.[2] A false reason for a bequest did not affect it.[3] Anything so written that it could not be understood was treated *pro non scripto*.[4] A legacy of a thing which could not exist was void.[5]

But I do not want to emphasise the ordinary cases of interpretation or even the principles of interpretation which existed in the later Roman Republic. Rather, I want to concentrate on the unusual instances and extreme limits of juristic interpretation and decision-making—those cases in which to attain a reasonable end the jurists used means which we might not regard as reasonable. The last two hundred years of the Roman Republic were without doubt the most stupendous in the history of the world's legal development. During that time Roman Law attained, in all essentials, the rules and characteristics which have made it dominate all later Western law. The law of the first 250 years of the Empire is, for its balance and maturity, known as " classical law " but by the end of the Republic the creative spirit had already disappeared. As Schulz says: " The heroic age of creative geniuses and daring pioneers had passed away with the Republic ".[6] This expansion of legal science in the late Republic could not have occurred without the existence of brilliant jurists who could see beneath the legal form to the social realities, who could adapt a statute or edict to contemporary needs, and who were not averse to deliberate misinterpretation when they considered it desirable. Their successes—and occasional failures—have lost none of their significance or human interest.

The instances which follow are the most significant[7] which have survived from the last century of the Republic. As it happens, we have none which can be safely dated to the preceding

[1] D.34.2.33.

[2] D.28.5.79(78).1 (Papinian *6 resp.*); 32.100.1 (Iavolenus *2 ex post. Labeonis*).

[3] D.33.4.6pr, 1 (Labeo *2 post. a Iavoleno epit.*); 35.1.40.4 (Iavolenus *2 ex post. Labeonis*).

[4] D.50.17.73.3 (Quintus Mucius sing. ὅρων); 34.8.2 (Alfenus Varus *5 dig.*).

[5] D.33.6.7.1 (Iavolenus *2 ex post. Labeonis*). On the texts cited in nn. 7-14 see now Watson, *Succession*, Chapter 8.

[6] *History of Roman Legal Science* (Oxford, 1953), p. 99.

[7] I hope not to have missed any, but it must be admitted that examples of interpretation will appear more extreme to some scholars than to others.

century though we do know of some early instances of very strange but useful interpretation.[1]

A first example can be chosen from the *interdictum quod vi aut clam*.[2] This was a remedy to compel works which were done on land by force or by stealth to be restored to their previous condition. The wording of the interdict ran: " You should restore to its previous condition whatever has been done by force or by stealth and which is the subject of the present dispute if it is not more than a year since the power of objection arose ".[3] Quintus Mucius Scaevola, the consul of 95 B.C. who, as already mentioned, argued for the narrow literal interpretation of a will in the *causa Curiana*, declared that something was done by force, *vi*, when a person did it who had been told not to.[4] This time his interpretation is extremely wide and must include situations where no one could reasonably say that force had been used. Scaevola must have felt that the scope of the interdict had to be extended. But the jurists still did not feel that the interdict was as wide as it should be. Servius Sulpicius Rufus, a famous jurist and consul of 51 B.C., turned his attention to the word *clam*, by stealth. *Clam* involves deliberate secrecy but Servius says that a person also acts *clam* who does not inform someone who he ought to know will object " lest ", says the text, " the position of fools be better than that of wise men ".[5] This interpretation even changes the basis of liability under the interdict. The interdict envisaged only deliberate wrongdoing, but Servius allowed it also for negligence.[6] Another Republican jurist, Cicero's protégé Trebatius, was ready to give the *interdictum* where there was no *opus* (i.e. no work had been done on the estate), no damage had been caused and the estate had undergone no alteration. He declared that if you carried manure over my field when I

[1] The best known is of the XII Tables' clause: *Si pater filium ter venum duit, a patre filius liber esto*. On this see for all, Daube, " Texts and Interpretation in Roman and Jewish Law ", *Jewish Journal of Sociology*, iii (1961), pp. 3 ff, at pp. 5 ff.

[2] The extreme interpretations of this have already been touched upon by Watson, " Morality, Slavery and the Jurists in the Later Roman Republic ", infra, pp. 263 ff.

[3] Cf. Lenel, *Das Edictum perpetuum*, 3rd edit. (Leipzig, 1927), p. 482.

[4] D.50.17.73.2 (Quintus Mucius Scaevola *sing.* ὅρων); 43.24.1.5 (Ulpian *71 ad ed.*).

[5] D.43.24.4 (Venuleius *2 interd.*).

[6] On all this see Watson, *The Law of Property in the Later Roman Republic* (Oxford, 1968), pp. 222 ff.

had forbidden you to do so, you would be bound by the interdict—that is, you would have to carry the manure back to its prior resting place.[1] But this opinion did not win later support.

These instances of deliberate interpretation aimed at widening the scope of a remedy may be extreme but they are not altogether rare. Another example concerns the *interdictum de cloacis*, the interdict on sewers. This ran: " I forbid force to be used to prevent a person cleaning or repairing the sewer which is the subject of the dispute and which extends from his property to yours ".[2] Trebatius and his contemporary Ofilius declared that the interdict applied not only to the cleaning or repairing of existing sewers but also to the making of new ones.[3] Public utility prevailed over the obvious meaning of the interdict. Again, the Aedilician Edict, dealing with the sale of slaves in the market place, laid down *inter alia* that sellers should declare the existence of any disease, *morbus*, or physical defect, *vitium*, and that if a slave was sold contrary to this provision or contrary to what was declared or promised the buyer could insist that the slave be returned to the seller and the price given back. Slave-dealers were notoriously untrustworthy—they were the used-car salesmen of the ancient world—and there was a tendency to interpret the Edict against them. There was inevitably a great deal of discussion as to what counted as a *morbus* and a *vitium*.[4] But no one else apparently went so far as Servius who declared that a slave who was lacking a tooth could be returned to the seller.[5] Labeo, a jurist of the early Empire, disagreed with him in no uncertain terms.

Of special significance in this connexion is the *actio aquae pluviae arcendae*. This action—which was established by the XII Tables—was the object of more interpretation than any other that we know of.[6] Exactly why it aroused such passionate

[1] D.43.24.22.3 (Venuleius *2 interd.*).

[2] Cf. Lenel, *Edictum*, p. 481.

[3] D.43.23.2 (Venuleius *1 interd.*): cf. Watson, *Property*, pp. 197 f.

[4] For the Republic, see D.21.1.6.1 (Ulpian *1 ad aed. cur.*); 21.1.10.1 (*Idem*); 21.1.12.4 (*Idem*); 21.1.14.3 (*Idem*); Aulus Gellius, *N.A.* 4.2.9, 10, 12; Cicero, *de off.* 3.23.91: cf. Watson, *The Law of Obligations in the Later Roman Republic* (Oxford, 1965), pp. 90 f.

[5] Aulus Gellius, *N.A.* 4.2.12.

[6] Another area of considerable divergence of opinion was the extent of a legacy of *penus*: D.33.9.3 (Ulpian *22 ad Sab.*); Aulus Gellius, *N.A.* 4.1.16-23; cf. Watson, *Succession*, Chapter 12.

interest is not clear and need not detain us at the moment. The action arose where, as a result of work on someone's land, rain water might injure the land of another. The pattern *formula* ran: " If it appears that work was carried out on the estate at Capena, from which rain water injures the land of Aulus Agerius, on which account Numerius Negidius ought to keep the water away from Aulus Agerius &c ".[1] The meaning of *aqua pluvia* " rain water " was much discussed. Trebatius, for instance, who was in favour of making the action as wide as possible was not prepared to give it if a man built a fuller's workshop round a spring and did nothing more to the spring than alter its direction; but if he did anything to alter the spring's character, such as to join more than one channel together or make the water dirty, he would be held liable.[2] Trebatius even gave the action to someone whose land was injured by a hot spring arising on a neighbour's land. The later, classical jurist, Ulpian, disagreed because, as he said, a hot spring is not rain water.[3, 4] Again, despite the wording of the *formula* which demanded *opus factum*, the Republican jurist, Namusa, held that if water flowing even in a natural channel was blocked by filth and flooded higher ground, the *actio aquae pluviae arcendae* could be brought against the owner of the low-lying ground to allow the blockage to be removed.[5]

The strained interpretation—perhaps better, deliberate misinterpretation—might even be of the damages payable under an action. The *interdictum uti possidetis* forbade force to be used, in certain cases, to oust a possessor from land. If a person acted contrary to the interdict, the praetor gave an action against the wrongdoer who was to suffer a condemnation in *quanti res est*, whatever the matter comes to. The jurist of the Empire, Ulpian, declared that *quanti res est* meant " the financial interest anyone had in retaining possession ". He also reports Servius' view that the value of its possession was to be estimated as the value of the thing. This view according to Ulpian must not be accepted: " for the financial value of a thing is quite different

[1] Cf. Lenel, *Edictum*, p. 375 and n. 4.

[2] D.39.3.3pr (Ulpian *53 ad ed.*).

[3] D.39.3.3.1.

[4] On all this, see Watson, *Property*, pp. 155 ff.

[5] D.39.3.2.6 (Paul *49 ad ed.*); cf. Watson, *Property*, pp. 161 f.

from the financial value of its possession ".[1] This attitude of Ulpian seems unobjectionable. Servius' punitive opinion seems directed at ensuring that no one would wrongfully use force against another's possession of land after the Praetor had issued an order to protect that possession. One is perhaps reminded of present day contempt of court.[2]

But ways of changing the law other than by simply extending a relevant remedy or increasing the damages payable might also be found. An irrelevant statute might be treated as relevant. The most interesting example is, I think, to be found in marriage law. There were two kinds of marriage in early Rome. One, the older, put the woman completely under the legal power, *in manu*, of her husband: the other, which was in existence by at least the beginning of the second century B.C., left the wife legally completely independent of her husband. *Manus* in the former kind of marriage could be created in three ways, one of which, *usu*, was independent of the wishes of the parties. If the couple lived together in marriage, the husband acquired *manus* after a year unless the wife absented herself for three nights. *Manus*-marriage gradually became unpopular but remained very common, even in the time of Quintus Mucius Scaevola, presumably because of the *usus* form. Then suddenly, virtually overnight, by the time of Cicero, marriage *cum manu* became rare. The mechanics of the process can be traced in one of Cicero's speeches.[3] He is arguing that a certain woman could not have been in her husband's *manus* and says: " She could not be by *usus*. For nothing can be taken from a tutelage established by law except with the consent of all the tutors ". Here he is referring to a provision of the XII Tables which either forbade the *mancipatio* of *res mancipi* belonging to a woman except with the consent of her *tutores legitimi*, or else prohibited the *usucapio* of *res mancipi* which had been mancipated without the tutors' consent. It did not contain a general prohibition on usucapting the *res mancipi* of a woman where there had been no delivery.[4] Now this provision is lifted from its original sphere in the law

[1] D.43.17.3.11 (Ulpian *69 ad ed.*).

[2] On all this see now Watson, *Property*, pp. 87 f.

[3] *pro Flacco*, 34.84: cf. Watson, *The Law of Persons in the Later Roman Republic* (Oxford, 1967), pp. 19 ff.

[4] Cf. Kaser, *Eigentum und Besitz im älteren romischen Recht*, 2nd edit. (Cologne, Graz, 1956), pp. 198 ff; *ZSS* lxviii (1951), p. 148.

of property to a totally new one, the law of marriage; applied in circumstances (i.e. where there was no *mancipatio*), where it did not apply even in its own sphere; and allowed to operate apparently even where the woman owned no *res mancipi* though those were the object of the original provision. The consequence of this interpretation is that *usus* ceased to be automatic and became dependent upon an agreement made at the time of the marriage. Hence, since *manus* was unpopular, *usus* disappeared.[1]

More is involved here than the simple reinterpretation of a relevant statute. The provision in question never had any relevance. More than that, it had been in existence for almost four hundred years before anyone thought of using it as an artificial device to get rid of *usus*. Yet even these facts were no insuperable obstacle to the new interpretation.

The converse might also occur, and a very relevant statute be so interpreted that it no longer applied. The XII Tables established the *actio finium regundorum*, an action for regulating disputed boundaries. The most curious aspect of this action is that the jurists of the later Republic decided[2] that it did not apply in the city but only in the country. But often, one would think, it would be useful in the city even though, there, frequently the existence of party walls would prevent the occurrence of a dispute over the line of the boundaries. In the Empire indeed, an attempt was made to re-establish the action in city disputes.[3] Why did the jurists of the Republic act as they did? They must have had a reason. A reason can, indeed, be suggested. To judge from a text of Gaius,[4] the *actio finium regundorum* also governed certain activities at the very edge of one's land. One of the provisions of the XII Tables was that there had to be an *ambitus* of two and a half feet, i.e. a space around one's buildings. Thus a building could not be erected closer than two and a half feet to the edge of one's land. This provision is in fact expressly referred to in the Gaius' text. Now in a densely populated city like Rome this gap of five feet which prevents buildings with a common wall

[1] On all this see Watson, *Persons*, pp. 19 ff.

[2] Emerges from Cicero, *top*. 4.23; 10.43; D.10.1.4.10 (Paul *23 ad ed.*): cf. Watson, *Property*, p. 114.

[3] Cf. D.10.1.4.10.

[4] D.10.1.13 (Gaius *4 ad legem XII tab.*).

being erected by adjoining proprietors is obviously very inconvenient and there is evidence that the provision of the XII Tables was never strictly adhered to. Still, the prohibition contained in the provision must have created problems until the solution was reached that the relevant action, the *actio finium regundorum*, applied only to the country. As it happens we can have a good idea when this interpretation occurred since there exists evidence in Cicero of another ingenious, but clumsy and unsuccessful, attempt by Publius Mucius Scaevola to avoid the implications of the provision. This Scaevola was consul in 133 B.C. and the father of the Quintus Mucius Scaevola already mentioned. Cicero writes in his *Topica* addressed to the jurist, Trebatius:[1] " External arguments derive their force above all from authority. And so the Greeks call such arguments ἀτέχνοι, that is, without art. For instance, if you were to say, ' Since Publius Scaevola says that that alone is the *ambitus* of a house, so far as a roof projects for the purposes of protecting a common wall, from which roof the water flows on to the house of him who did the protecting, that seems to be the law '." Thus, Publius Mucius gave *ambitus*—not defined by the XII Tables though declared to be of two and a half feet—such an odd and restricted meaning that in practice it properly could be, and had to be, ignored. Incidentally, this part of Cicero's text has been held corrupt simply because Publius Mucius' definition is so strange.[2] But this is impossible. The very oddity—which is so obvious—is part of Cicero's point. He is discussing arguments which take their force from authority: what could possibly demonstrate this better than reliance on the absurd definition of a renowned jurist ?[3]

Servius appears in a particular case where the application of a statutory provision was excluded by strange reasoning. The XII Tables established an action, the *actio auctoritatis*, which lay for double the price stated in a *mancipatio* when the buyer was evicted from the thing mancipated. Any restrictions in the title had to be stated in the *mancipatio*. In the case facing Servius a testator had given a slave his freedom on condition that he paid ten. The heir sold this slave and declared in the *mancipatio* that

[1] *Top*. 4.24.
[2] Cf. Hubbell, *Cicero de inventione, de optimo genere oratorum, topica* (London—Cambridge, Mass., 1949), pp. 398 f.
[3] For all this see Watson, *Property, pp*. 111 ff.

the slave was to be free when he paid twenty. The opinion was that the *actio auctoritatis* would not lie against the seller for the eviction because in the *mancipatio* he had made an exception of the restriction in title " which consisted in giving ". He did, however, allow an action for damages on the contract of sale.[1] Servius' argumentation seems very odd, since there might be enormous variation between two clauses both of which consisted in giving. But his motive seems plain enough. The condemnation in the *actio auctoritatis*—double the price—was too severe in the circumstances, and the buyer would be adequately protected by the *actio ex empto*.[2]

Perhaps not surprisingly, some of the most blatant instances of disregard for the plain meaning of a statute or will occur where there is not even a hint that questions of interpretation are involved. To take first a case involving a will. Alfenus tells us[3] of a testator who appointed two heirs and ordered them to build a monument for him within a certain time. The will then declared that if either did not build, both were to be disinherited. One and one alone built the monument and he asked about his legal position. The answer he received was " No one can be bound to an inheritance or disinherited by the act of another but as each individual fulfilled the condition so he would be heir although no one else accepted the inheritance ". The wording of the will is unambiguous and the intention of the testator abundantly clear, but the jurist's decision is contrary to both. He makes no attempt to reach his decision by way of interpretation—a strong indication that he was rather at a loss—but justifies it in a very sophistical way. His answer is really in two parts: No one can be bound to an inheritance by the act of another—true but irrelevant. Then, in the shadow of this, no one can lose an inheritance by the act of another—relevant but absolutely false. Presumably the jurist hoped that if the accuracy of the first proposition was accepted, the inaccuracy of the corollary would not be too obvious. Alfenus (or Servius) in fact seems to be caught out giving a decision contrary to the intention of the testator, to the wording of the will and to legal principle. The only explanation is that he made up his mind

[1] D.21.2.69.3 (Scaevola *3 quaest.*).

[2] See on all this, Watson, *Obligations*, pp. 76 f.

[3] D.28.5.45 (44) (Alfenus *5 dig.*).

what the just conclusion was going to be and he did not allow other factors to influence his decision.[1]

A similar example—at least in the form in which the case has come down to us—concerns a statute or edict. D.46.3.67 (Marcellus *13 dig.*) recalls rather strange goings on which were discussed by Servius and Alfenus. Where a creditor was willing to take less than the full amount of the debt and release the debtor, Servius declared that this could be done by the creditor receiving some coins several times from the debtor, returning them each time and then getting them back again. " For instance," the text says, " if the creditor is willing to free the debtor from a debt of one hundred in return for ten, so that when he has received ten he gives the same coins back, soon receives them again and at the end holds on to them." Rather curious behaviour, one might feel, and requiring explanation. Why do the parties go through the motions of giving ten times and returning nine times? A first answer must obviously be that the debtor has no more than ten: that is why he does not give more than ten at any one time, and also why the creditor is prepared to release him from his obligation to pay one hundred on payment of only ten. But then, why does he not hand over the ten once and the creditor release him formally by *acceptilatio*?[2] Something must have prevented the use of this simple machinery. The explanation would seem to be supplied by the so-called *lex Iulia municipalis* of 45 B.C. It seems to emerge from this[3] that at Rome a person suffered *infamia* " who has announced or will have announced to his guarantors or creditors that he cannot pay the whole amount of his debt; or has made an agreement or will have made an agreement with them that he cannot pay the whole amount of his debt; or on whose behalf the sum has been, or will have been, given or paid ". The situation viewed by Servius was one where the debtor could not pay his debt, the creditor was prepared to accept a smaller sum in full payment but, sympathetically, was ready to help in making it appear that the debt had been paid in full, and that there had been no compromise. Servius (and most other jurists) were ready to

[1] On all this see Watson, "D.28.5.45 (44) (Alfenus *5 dig.*)" ***Studies in Roman Private Law*** **(London, 1991), 161ff.**

[2] Assuming, that is, that the debt was contracted by *stipulatio*: otherwise some other means would be utilised.

[3] Lines 108 ff.

accept the dodge as full *solutio*. In the text as we have it, the question of *infamia* is not raised.[1]

Finally among the successes of interpretation let us look at the particular case of the word *glans*. *Glans* in its first meaning has the sense of " acorn ". And whenever the word is used by non-lawyers in the sense of some kind of natural fruit it still means " acorn ".[2] But lawyers came to treat it differently. The XII Tables enacted that it was permitted to collect your *glans* which had fallen onto a neighbour's land. At that time, *glans* would have its natural meaning of " acorn " and of " acorn " alone. Acorns were important as food for pigs. But circumstances changed, a wider scope for the provision became desirable, and the jurists interpreted *glans* more generally as " fruit ". This interpretation—which must have occurred in this context—was so successful that among jurists *glans* came to be used even in other situations as a normal word for fruit of all kinds. Thus, a question was put to Servius:[3] Growing timber for cutting had been sold for five years and the *glans* fell from the trees: to whom did the *glans* belong, the owner of the grove or the purchaser of the wood for cutting? The answer does not concern us but the wording of the question does since we know a number of trees which might be grown for their timber, including several varieties whose fruit also was important: sweet chestnut, peach, hazel, apple.[4] In the context of the question Servius cannot be using *glans* simply to mean " acorn ". And when at some stage an interdict, the *interdictum de glande legenda*, was issued to supplement the XII Tables' provision, it stuck to the word *glans*, though it was now understood as meaning " fruit " in general.[5]

There were, though, some failures where the Republican jurists did not rise to the opportunities available to them. Two instances strike me as particularly noteworthy. The first is a failure of the jurist, Trebatius, which is all the more noteworthy in that he has appeared in this lecture before as a proponent of a wide and vigorous interpretation. A testator provided: " Let

[1] On all this see Watson, *Obligations*, pp. 208 ff.

[2] See the *Thesaurus Linguae Latinae*, *s.v. glans*.

[3] D.18.1.80.2 (Labeo *5 post. a Iavoleno epit.*).

[4] Pliny the Elder, *Naturalis Historia*, 17.20.147, 151.

[5] D.50.16.236.1 (Gaius *4 ad XII Tab.*); 43.28.1.1 (Ulpian *71 ad ed.*). On all this see Watson, *Property*, pp. 120 f.

Cornelius and Maevius, whichever of them wishes, be my heir." Both wished to be heir so Trebatius held that neither was heir.[1] The obvious explanation of this is that Trebatius took *uter eorum* and *heres esto* as meaning that only one of the *heredes scripti* was to be heir. Thus, since both wish to be heir and there is no way of choosing between them, neither is to be heir. This, despite the conjunctive *et*, "*Cornelius et Maevius*" in the text, and not a disjunctive *aut*, "*Cornelius aut Maevius*". This seems a very restrictive and unpleasing decision and was not followed by other jurists.[2]

The second instance is much more serious and represents a general failure of the Republican jurists. The XII Tables laid down the order of succession to an inheritance on intestacy. First, the *sui heredes*, then the *agnatus proximus*, then the *gentiles*. *Agnatus proximus*, the nearest agnate, was understood in a very narrow sense. Only the nearest agnate at the time the intestacy was determined could succeed. If he died before accepting the inheritance or if he refused it, the inheritance did not go to the next nearest agnate, but directly to the *gentiles*. The most likely explanation of this approach is that previously the only heirs on intestacy were the *sui heredes* and the *gentiles*. The introduction of the *agnatus proximus* was a limitation on the rights of the *gentiles* and, not surprisingly, interpreted restrictively.[3] Clearly, though, the interpretation was not a necessary one. Times changed, the *gens* lost some of its significance,[4] and the desire to prefer agnates must have greatly increased. But the meaning of *agnatus proximus* was not reinterpreted, and matters were only put right in the lifetime of Trebatius when the praetor issued an edict, *unde cognati*, which gave all blood relatives, in order of proximity, *bonorum possessio* after those entitled to *bonorum possessio* under an earlier edict, *unde legitimi*. *Unde legitimi* had given *bonorum possessio* to those entitled to the inheritance at civil law but it seems that in it the clause *quem ei heredem esse oporteret* was now reinterpreted so that *bonorum possessio* under it did not

[1] D.28.5.70 (69) (Proculus *2 epist.*).

[2] On all this see Watson, *Succession*, Chapter 4.

[3] Cf. the references given by Kaser, *Das römische Privatrecht* I (Munich, 1955), p. 90, n.2; de Zulueta, *The Institutes of Gaius* II (Oxford, 1953), p. 124.

[4] But it was not so unimportant as is usually imagined. In the first quarter of the first century B.C. intestate succession by the *gens* was still relatively frequent: cf. Watson, *Succession*, Chapter 13.

go to the *gens*. This time a phrase, *agnatus proximus*, had had a particular meaning for so long that the jurists found themselves unable to interpret it to suit contemporary needs.[1, 2]

The conclusions which I want to draw from all this are not that the Republican jurists had no principles and no standards of interpretation. As I remarked at the beginning of this lecture they certainly had, and the great mass of interpretation would be in harmony with present day ideas. But where it seemed socially desirable the jurists of the late Republic were prepared to be ruthless and make original and extreme interpretations. In this they went further than their successors of the Empire who, although they sometimes accepted a wide opinion of the Republic, never again themselves invented anything so extreme. For the purposes of this lecture I have—to a very limited extent—put the instances in certain groupings. This, of course, gives a false impression. Each extreme interpretation stands by itself, is subject to no general principle, and is dictated only by social expediency.[3]

The situations examined seem to give a result very different from the view of many modern scholars that the jurists of the later Republic tended towards strict and meticulous interpretation, were far less free in their interpretation than were the classical jurists,[4] and adhered more to strict legal doctrine.[5] A full discussion of the arguments for that opinion is excluded from this lecture by the time factor, and must be kept for another place. But enough has been said here, I think, to show that any general opinion that the later Republican jurists were bound by strict legal thinking is untenable.

[1] On all this see Watson, *Succession*, Chapter 13. For a different view of the early history of succession by the agnates, which sees here a triumph of interpretation, see Yaron, " Two Notes on Intestate Succession ", *Tijd.* xxv (1957), pp. 385 ff: but contra, Watson, *loc. cit.*

[2] Perhaps the prohibition of gifts between spouses should also be discussed since such gifts were expressly allowed under the *lex Cincia* of 204 B.C. But we have no indication of the mechanics of the introduction of the prohibition though it does seem to date from the late Republic and to have been introduced *moribus*: cf. Watson, *Property*, pp. 229 f.

[3] Unfortunately, apart from the *causa Curiana* there is little evidence of the wealth of argument produced in reaching a decision.

[4] Cf. e.g. Schulz, *History*, pp. 77 ff.

[5] Cf most recently, Ankum, " *Utilitatis causa receptum* " *Symbolae iuridicae et historicae Martino David dedicatae* I (Leiden, 1968), pp. 1 ff at pp. 6 f. p. 6, n.5.

Some of my audience will have reflected that our modern courts can also provide similar examples of the interpretative art: witness the significance and recurring use of " in the course of employment ",[1] the situations which have resulted in a ship being declared " unseaworthy ";[2] and a French court recently very properly decided that frogs were fish.[3]

[1] Cf., e.g. London & North Eastern Railway v. Brentnall, [1933] A.C. 489; Canadian Pacific Railway v. Lockhart, [1942] A.C. 591; Campbell v. Proud's Engineering Co., [1947] 2. All E.R. 97 C.A.; Williams v. A. & W. Hemphill Ltd., 1966 S.C. (H.L.) 31.

[2] Cf. e.g. Owners of Cargo on " Maori King " v. Hughes, (1895) 2 Q.B. 550; Upperton v. Union-Castle Mail Steamship Co. Ltd. (1903) 8 Comm. Cases, 96; MacIver & Co. Ltd. v. Tate Steamers Ltd., (1903) 8 Comm. Cases, 124; Kopitoff v. Wilson (1876) 1 Q.B.D. 377; Moore v. Lunn (1923) 38 T.L.R. 641.

[3] *Trib. corr.* Montbéliard, 28 juin, 1963, *Recueil Dalloz*, 1963, J.544.

4

Narrow, Rigid and Literal Interpretation in the Later Roman Republic

There is a widely held view that the jurists of the later Republic had a rather rigid approach to legal problems [1]). The view appears in various forms. At its most extreme, as exemplified by Schulz [2]), interpretation of statutes and private legal acts [3]) is condemned as inflexible and often miserably literal. A more moderate view contents itself with the assertion 'that the *veteres* were more dogmatical than the classical lawyers' [4]).

Elsewhere I have sought to show that the extreme view is one-sided and that there are many instances of very wide interpretation [5]). The present study will be devoted to a consideration of the evidence for narrow, rigid and literal interpretation in the later Republic [6]).

---

1) In respect of comparison with the Empire a word of caution is voiced by Van Warmelo who observes that Republican materials are scarce and emphasises that the law of the Republic had a different character from that of the Empire. The law of the Republic, he says, is more that of a city state than the law of a world empire, as was later the case: *Die Oorsprong en Betekenis van die Romeinse Reg.* 2nd edit. (Pretoria 1965) p. 64. But it is easy to exaggerate the differences in character between the law of the Republic and the law of the Empire.

2) Above all in *History of Roman Legal Science* (Oxford, reprinted 1953), pp 77ff.

3) Schulz thinks that the interpretation of the Edict was somewhat freer: *Legal Science*, pp. 77f.

4) E.g., Ankum, *Utilitatis causa receptum*, Symbolae David I (Leiden 1968), pp. 1ff at p. 6.

5) *Limits of Juristic Decision in the Later Roman Republic*, University of Edinburgh Inaugural Lecture no. 36.

6) It should perhaps be mentioned that Schulz himself says: 'The materials for

On the interpretation of statute Schulz declares [7]): 'Our evidence as to the republican interpretation of *leges* is very slender. The painfully scrupulous style of the *leges rogatae*, the growing practice of hedging every clause with safeguards, may well suggest the inference that juristic interpretation was growing ever less flexible and more meticulous; but this inference is, of course, not maintainable. Still, the interpretation of the *lex Aquilia* does betray a clinging to the letter: thus *occidere*, in the first chapter, was not taken to cover every case of *causam mortis praestare*, and the difficulty was overcome not by adopting a more elastic interpretation, but by means of actions 'on the case' *(actiones in factum)*, proposed, of course, by the jurists and accepted by the praetor.' Elsewhere [8]), to demonstrate the 'painfully scrupulous style of *leges*' he points to the *lex Silia* of uncertain but early date [9]) which penalized a magistrate for falsifying weights and meticulously added 'or procures their falsification'. This fact, he says, 'permits the inference that procuration would not have been included by interpretation'. Also he says that if, in contrast to the XII Tables, later legislation constantly specifies male and female, 'It is a fair inference that interpretation would not have ventured to hold that 'male' implied 'female''. Now Schulz' inference from the style of statutes is presumably a possible one but it cannot be emphasised too strongly that it is not a necessary one. Two other suggestions are at least as plausible. The first is that the meticulous style is due to increasing bureaucracization or professionalism of the draftsmen and may have nothing to do with increasing rigidity of interpretation [10]). Schulz himself declares [11]) that the 'style shows that the *leges* were formulated not by the proposing magistrates, but by professional draftsmen drawn

---

forming a judgment on the Republican period have not yet been subjected to a comprehensive critical examination'.

7) *Legal Science*, p. 77.

8) *Legal Science*, p. 30.

9) Cf. Rotondi, *Leges Publicae Populi Romani* (reprinted Hildesheim 1966), p. 473.

10) This suggestion was first made to me by Professor Reuven Yaron.

11) *Legal Science*, p. 96.

from the ranks of the senatorial jurists and the secretariate of the archives'. The other suggestion, which I confess seems to me the more satisfactory, is that the meticulous and pedantic style of *leges*, far from being the result of restrictive and literal interpretation is the response to freedom and subtlety of interpretation. Greater sophistication of argument by jurist and orator could result in a narrow or wide interpretation depending on what was most desired in the particular case. To restrain such freedom and to give the law more certainty statutes would be drafted more precisely. Hence the express mention in a statute of both male and female does not permit the inference that the 'male' would not be interpreted to include the 'female'. Rather, the mention of the 'male' alone would enable a subtle orator or jurist to argue that in the circumstances of the situation under discussion, the 'female' was excluded. Sometimes successfully, sometimes not unreasonably. Thus, the XII Tables' provision that if a father sold his son three times the son became free of his father's *potestas* was early interpreted as not applying to daughters or grandchildren. One sale of these was enough to end finally the *patria potestas* [12]).

More attention must be paid to Schulz' specific example of rigid interpretation. In the first chapter of the *lex Aquilia*, *occidere*, to kill, was not taken to cover every case of *causam mortis praestare*, to furnish a cause of death. And Schulz refers to the opinion of the Republican jurist, Ofilius, which is reported in D.9,2,9,3 (Ulpian 18 *ad ed.*). Now the distinction between killing and furnishing a cause of death is frequent in the surviving sources of the *lex Aquilia*. But, contrary to what one might expect after reading Schulz, the distinction is much more important in the Empire than in the Republic. The formulation of the distinction, *occidere*, *mortis causam praestare*, indeed, is the work of the jurist Celsus [13]) (who was *consul* for the second time in 129 A.D.) though admittedly the distinction itself is older [14]). Still of greater

---

12) See, above all, Daube, *Texts and Interpretation in Roman and Jewish Law*, Jewish Journal of Sociology, 3 (1961), pp. 3ff at p. 5; most recently, Yaron, *Si pater filium ter venum duit*, Tijd. 36 (1968), pp. 67ff.

13) D. 9, 2, 7, 6 (Ulpian 18 *ad ed.*).

14) Cf., e.g., D. 9, 2, 9*pr.* (Ulpian 18 *ad ed.*), which gives the opinion of Labeo;

importance is the fact that we have decisions from the later Republic giving the action on the *lex Aquilia* for situations which in the Empire would have given rise to an action on the case, *actio in factum*. Thus, in D.9,2,52,2 (Alfenus 2 *dig.*), two carts were going up the Capitoline hill, one behind the other; the foremost began to slip back, struck the rear one which moved backwards and ran over a slave boy. The Republican Alfenus (or his teacher, Servius) decided that if the men who had been holding up the first cart got out of the way of their own accord, the slave boy's owner could sue them under the *lex Aquilia (lege Aquilia agi posse)*. The killing here is very indirect. The closest situation discussed in a classical text is in D.9,2,7,3 (Ulpian 18 *ad ed.*) where we are told that Proculus (who was active in the first half of the first century A.D.) held that if one man caused injury through being pushed by another, the one who pushed is not liable to an *actio legis Aquiliae* because he did not kill, nor is the one who was pushed because he did not do the injury unlawfully [15]). And in D.9,2,9*pr.* (Ulpian 18 *ad ed.*) we learn of a distinction drawn by the jurist Labeo who was active in the early Principate: if a midwife with her own hands administered to a woman a drug from which she died, the midwife was regarded as having killed; but not if she had given the woman the drug for her to take it herself.

Schulz, however, refers expressly to D.9,2,9,3, and that text must be considered more closely.

> Si servum meum equitantem concitato equo effeceris in flumen praecipitari atque ideo homo perierit, in factum esse dandam actionem Ofilius scribit: quemadmodum si servus meus ab alio in insidias deductus, ab alio esset occisus.

The text envisages two hypotheses, both of which are consider-

---

D. 9, 2, 9, 2, which reports the view of Neratius. In the former text the verbalisation of the distinction, *occidere, mortis causam praestare*, is due to Ulpian.

15) Cf. Watson, *The Law of Obligations in the Later Roman Republic* (Oxford 1965) pp. 241ff. Similarly the scope of Chapter 3 of the *lex Aquilia* was wider in the Republic than in the Empire. We need not linger over Pugsley's interpretation of D. 9, 2, 7, 3: *The Origins of the Lex Aquilia*, LQR 85 (1969), pp. 50ff at p. 65.

ed by Ofilius [16]). The second case is introducted by 'just as', *quemadmodum*, and hence its function is to act as an argument for the first. That is, the second case is the straightforward one while the first is less easy, and so the second case must be looked at first. In this second case there can be no question of the killing not being direct enough. The *actio legis Aquiliae* is refused against the man who led the slave into the ambush not because the fatal blow was not direct enough, but because it was struck by another. This straightforward decision is produced to justify the same decision where the slave is killed by the horse, frightened by the wrongdoer, throwing him into the river. One can perhaps see here the beginnings of the distinction between killing and providing a cause of death, but the basis of the decision is really different. Moreover, any narrowness of interpretation in refusing the *actio legis Aquiliae* is modified by granting the *actio in factum* [17]). But the fundamental conclusion is that if any complaint on this score is to be laid against the Republican jurists for rigidity and literalness it lies with redoubled force against those of the classical period.

We have, Schulz thinks [18]), more material for judging Republican interpretation of private acts in the law, and he suggests that if one confines oneself to 'undeniably authentic texts one arrives at the following principle: if a clear meaning can be obtained by taking the expressions used in the sense of common speech, this meaning must be accepted, even if it in no way corresponds to the intention of the party using them. Rectification of expressions used was resorted to only with the utmost caution. The maxim *falsa demonstratio adiecta non nocet* was still under debate at the end of the Republic, and the doctrines of mistake were in their infancy. A man was protected against his own words only when they had been uttered under duress or owing to fraud; in the

---

16) Shown by the subjunctive, *esset occisus*.

17) Further to the relationship of the *actio legis Aquiliae* to the decretal actions see now Watson, *D. 7, 1, 13, 2 (Ulpian 18 ad Sab.): the lex Aquilia and decretal actions*, IURA 17 (1966), pp. 174ff.

18) *Legal Science*, p. 78.

second century even this much relief had been unknown'. He then lists a few specially clear examples.

The first is where the testator appoints Titius as heir with the requirement that he makes formal acceptance *(cretio)* of the inheritance within a fixed time: if Titius does not do so, Mevius is to be heir. But the testator does not expressly disinherit Titius, and it is held that if Titius acts as heir but without making *cretio*, both he and Mevius share the inheritance equally. The main text is G.2,177:

> Sed si cretio sine exheredatione sit data, id est *in* haec verba: SI NON CREVERIS, TUM P. MEVIUS HERES ESTO, illud diversum inveni*tur*, qu*od*, si prior omissa cretione pro herede gerat, substitutum in partem admittit, et fiunt ambo aequis partibus heredes. quodsi neque cernat neque pro herede gerat, tum sane in univer*sum* summovetur, et substitutus in totam hereditatem succedit.

As Schulz says, this literal interpretation seems to defeat the testator's intention and it was changed by a constitution of Marcus Aurelius (Ulp. *Ep.* 22,34):

> Si sub imperfect*a* cretion*e* heres institutus sit, id est non adiectis his verbis: SI NON CREVERIS, EXHERES ESTO, sed si ita: SI NON CREVERIS, TUNC MEVIUS HERES ESTO, cernendo quidem superior inferiorem excludit; non cernendo autem, sed pro herede gerendo in partem admittit substitutum. Sed postea divus Marcus constituit, ut et pro herede gerendo ex asse fiat heres. Quodsi neque creverit, neque pro herede gesserit, ipse excluditur et substitutus ex asse fit heres.

The difficulty in accepting Schulz' view is that there is not the slightest indication that the narrow interpretation is Republican. That it was accepted in the time of Gaius — on this point there is no sign of dispute [19]) — is not evidence that it existed or was widely held in the Republic. We cannot, of course, exclude the possibility that the narrow interpretation is Republican. Nonetheless, it is surely significant for Schulz' attitude that the first

---

[19]) There was a dispute on a related point in the time of Sabinus: G. 2.178. But there, too, there is no evidence that the subtle narrow interpretation [cf. Buckland, *A Textbook of Roman Law*, 3rd edit., by Stein (Cambridge 1963) p. 314] was widely accepted or even known in the Republic.

instance he cites of a specially clear illustration of narrow Republican interpretation is of a legal proposition fully accepted in the time of Gaius but which in fact is not evidenced for the Republic [20]).

Schulz' second instance is in D.30,63 (Celsus 17 *dig.*):

> Si ancillas omnes et quod ex his natum erit testator legaverit, una mortua Servius partum eius negat deberi, quia accessionis loco legatus sit: quod falsum puto et nec verbis nec voluntati defuncti accommodata haec sententia est.

The decision of Servius, it must be admitted, is puzzling. Schulz is not the only scholar who regards it as very restricted. Kaser also sees in it a narrow-minded dependence on the wording [21]). But it is by no means certain that this understanding of Servius' attitude is correct. There is nothing specific in the wording of the legacy which should lead one to think that children are regarded as accessories. The wording, if anything, is opposed to this — 'slave girls and the children born to them' not 'slave girls with the children born to them'. Indeed, Celsus who disagrees with Servius declares that Servius' decision fits neither the wording of the will nor the intention of the testator [22]), [23]). Intention is more difficult to determine than is the natural meaning of the words. So, if Servius' decision is not easily motivated by the wording of the will it may well be based on the presumed intention of the testator. And it may in fact correspond to what the testator wanted [24]).

---

20) It should be remarked also, that Aurelius' constitution seems to go against the testator's intention.

21) *Partus ancillae*, ZSS 75 (1958), pp. 156ff at pp. 196f.

22) *Et nec verbis* to the end is sometimes held to be an addition to the text: Donatuti, BIDR 34 (1925), pp. 202ff; Himmelschein, *Studien zu der antiken Hermeneutica iuris*, Symbolae Friburgenses in honorem Ottonis Lenel (Leipzig 1935), pp. 373ff, at p. 405. Whether it is by Celsus or a later jurist does not greatly matter for us.

23) Maschi possibly goes too far in the opposite direction when he says that on a literal interpretation one cannot understand why the son of the dead slave is not included in the legacy: *Studi sull'interpretazione dei legati* (Milan 1938), p. 44.

24) Cf. my forthcoming *The Law of Succession in the Later Roman Republic*, Chapter 7.

Schulz' third instance is D.32,62 (Julian *sing. de ambiguitatibus*):

> Qui duos mulos habebat ita legavit: 'mulos duos, qui mei erunt cum moriar, heres dato': idem nullos mulos, sed duas mulas reliquerat. respondit Servius deberi legatum, quia mulorum appellatione etiam mulae continentur, quemadmodum appellatione servorum etiam servae plerumque continentur. id autem eo veniet, quod semper sexus masculinus etiam feminum sexum continet. [25]

Servius gives the legacy the wide interpretation but Schulz says [26] that Servius regarded his own decision as remarkable. Certainly, though, nothing in the text indicates that Servius thought his decision unusual or especially liberal. At the very most tne discussion of the question might suggest that the point at issue was not entirely settled. But this would not be surprising since the point is rather special. This is not the simple straightforward situation of male being interpreted to cover female. A legacy of something 'which will be mine when I die' was apparently not uncommon [27] and its main purpose was to free the heir of the obligation to give the thing if it was no longer the testator's at the time of his death. The matter was of considerable importance in the later Republic since then the obligation of the heir to give the specific object of the legacy rather than its value was more firmly recognised than was later the case [28]. Thus in the situation in the text a person who did have two *muli* made his will and left a legacy of the two *muli* which would be his when he died. Somehow he ceased to own these two *muli* before his death and he did not have others, but he did have two *mulae*. Could these be regarded as having been contemplated by the testator in his will? The problem is, of course, that when he made his will he was thinking primarily of two specific male animals. The nature of the difficulty

---

25) The last sentence does not go back to Servius and there have been suspicions on the genuineness of the text from *quia mulorum*. On the text see Watson, *Succession*, Chapter 8.

26) *Legal Science*, pp. 78f.

27) Cf. Watson, *Succession*, Chapter 8.

28) Cf. Watson *Succession*, Chapter 8.

can be better appreciated if we look at another problem concerning a different legacy of the same type. A testator left to his wife a legacy of choice *(legatum optionis)* of a male slave, Philargyrus, and a female slave, Agathea. After the will was made the testator sold Agathea and later bought other female slaves to one of whom he gave the name Agathea. Servius was asked if this Agathea was an object of the legacy [29]. Of course, in the text which concerns us there would have been no problem if the testator had owned at his death two *muli*. But what would the precise legal decision have been if he had owned three *muli?* Or two *muli* and two *mulae?* Or one *muli* and two *mulae?* Thus, it cannot really surprise us that the question of the legal position was raised when the testator owned only two *mulae* at the time of his death. And it has to be emphasised again that there is nothing restrictive in Servius' decision and no sign that he thought he was being remarkably liberal.

Schulz next asks us to contrast the miserable literalness of the decision in D.50,16,122 (Pomponius 8 *ad Quintum Mucium*) that tutors nominated *filio filiisque meis*, 'to my son and sons', are not tutors to the testator's daughters.

> Servius ait, si ita scriptum sit: 'filio filiisque meis hosce tutores do', masculis dumtaxat tutores datos, quoniam a singulari casu hoc 'filio' ad pluralem videtur transisse continentem eundem sexum, quem singularis prior positus habuisset. sed hoc facti, non iuris habet quaestionem: potest enim fieri, ut singulari casu de filio senserit, deinde plenius omnibus liberis prospexisse in tutore dando voluerit. quod magis rationabile esse videtur.

This time Servius certainly has chosen the narrower of the two possibilities but it is unjust to regard this as an instance of 'miserable literalness'. Servius, in fact, is probably trying to do justice to the testator's intention. Here, too, the situation under discussion is not the simple case. It was just as standard in Roman law to interpret the singular as including the plural as it was to interpret the male as including female [30]. But this time the testator

---

29) D. 35, 1, 28, 1 (Paul 2 *iuris epit. Alfeni dig.*): cf. Watson, *Succession*, Chapter 9.

30) Cf. for the Republic the opinion of Cascellius in D. 50, 16, 158 (Celsus

expressly gave the masculine singular and the masculine plural. Thus, he was not relying on the canon of interpretation that the singular includes the plural. Hence, the argument of Servius seems to be, he should not be taken to have intended that the male includes the female. This is not an unreasonable argument and indeed the latter part of the text which gives the opinion of Pomponius sees the problem as involving a question of fact, not of law. And the question of fact is the testator's intention. We must remember, too, that the decision of Servius does not mean that the daughters will be left without a tutor. The nearest agnates will be the *tutores legitimi* under the XII Tables [31], [32].

The next text cited is D.35,1,40,3 (Javolenus 2 *ex post. Labeonis*):

> Dominus servo aureos quinque legaverat: 'heres meus Sticho servo meo, quem testamento liberum esse iussi, aureos quinque, quos in tabulis debeo, dato'. nihil servo legatum esse Namusa Servium respondisse scribit, quia dominus servo nihil debere potuisset: ego puto secundum mentem testatoris naturale magis quam civile debitum spectandum esse, et eo iure utimur.

This time Servius cannot be exonerated from the charge of giving a very rigid interpretation. A master left to a slave freed by will a legacy of 'the five *aurei* which I owe him according to my account books'. Servius held that nothing was due under the legacy because a master cannot owe his slave anything. Technically, it is true, a master could not own his slave anything. But the intention is clear — indeed, Javolenus' own view expressed at the end of the text simply assumes that we know the testator's intention — and Servius' decision is completely contrary to it.

Schulz sees the case as one where *falsa demonstratio nocet* [33] and, of course, it is his belief that the principle, *falsa demonstratio non nocet*, was still under debate at the end of the Republic [34].

---

25 *dig.*): „in usu iuris frequenter uti nos Cascellius ait singulari appellatione, cum plura generis eiusdem significare vellemus: . . ."

31) XII Tab. 5, 6.

32) Cf. now on the text, Watson, *The Law of Persons in the Later Roman Republic* (Oxford 1967), pp. 115ff.

33) *Legal Science*, p. 79.

34) *Legal Science*, p. 78.

But this cannot be the explanation of Servius' decision; or, at the most, it is a very partial explanation. We do have, in fact, a text which shows that Servius accepted the principle that *falsa demonstratio non nocet.*

D.33,4,6*pr.* (Labeo 2 *post. a Iavoleno epit.*):

> Cum scriptum esset: 'quae pecunia propter uxorem meam ad me venit quinquaginta, tantundem pro ea dote heres meus dato', quamvis quadraginta dotis fuissent, tamen quinquaginta debere Alfenus Varus Servium respondisse scribit, quia proposita summa quinquaginta adiecta sit. [35]

Servius' opinion in D.35,1,40,3 seems in fact not to be based on any principle but to be rather disreputable. The jurists of the later Republic were rather callous in their attitude to the law as it affected slaves [36], and this is one particular instance. Servius is being unfair to the freed slave. He is stressing the social difference between master and slave. The master cannot be in the debt of his slave [37].

If this understanding of Servius' opinion is correct then the decision is blatantly unjust, but it is due to particular factors and cannot be generalised to show that juristic interpretation was rigid and literal.

Schulz now points to what is in fact a very narrow decision by Trebatius [38]:

D.28,5,70(69) (Proculus 2 *epist.*):

> Cornelius et Maevius, uter eorum volet, heres esto: uterque vult: Trebatius neutrum fore heredem, Cartilius utrumque: tu cui adsentiaris? Proculus:

---

35) And in § 1 we are told that Ofilius, Cascellius and the pupils of Servius (*Servii auditores*) held that where a wife brought no dowry and the husband bequeathed "*quanta pecunia dotis nomine, pro ea quinquaginta heres dato*", the legacy was valid. Cf. D. 35, 1, 40, 4 (Javolenus 2 *ex post. Labeonis*). For the social realities behind such legacies, see Daube, *Roman Law: Linguistic, Social, and Philosophical Aspects* (Edinburgh 1969), pp. 102ff.

36) Cf. Watson, *Morality, Slavery and the Jurists in the Later Roman Republic*, Tulane Law Review 42 (1968), pp. 289ff. Infra, pp. 263 ff.

37) See now on the text, above all, infra, pp. 269 ff.

38) *Legal Science*, p. 79.

> Cartilio adsentio et illam adiectionem 'uter eorum volet' supervacuam puto: . . .

The obvious explanation of Trebatius' attitude is that he took *uter eorum volet*, 'whichever of them wishes', and *heres esto*, 'be (singular) my heir' literally and only one could be the heir. Thus, since both wish to be heir and there is no way of choosing between them, neither is to be heir. This, despite the conjunctive *et* 'and', *Cornelius et Maevius*, and not a disjunctive *aut*, 'or', *Cornelius aut Maevius*, in the will. Trebatius' decision is very narrow and unpleasing and was not followed by other jurists [39]).

D.26,2,33 (Javolenus 8 *ex post. Labeonis*) is also brought forward by Schulz [40]):

> Tutoribus ita datis: 'Lucium Titium tutorem do. si is non vivit, tum Gaium Plautium tutorem do.' Titius vixerat et tutelam gesserat, deinde mortuus erat. Trebatius negat ad Plautium pertinere tutelam, Labeo contra, Proculus quod Labeo. ego Trebatii sententiam probo, quia illa verba ad mortis tempus referuntur.

Schulz observes that Labeo and Proculus take the opposite view to Trebatius but does not mention that Trebatius was followed by Javolenus who was prominent at the end of the first and beginning of the second century A.D. [41]). The attitude both of Trebatius and Javolenus and of Labeo and Proculus is understandable. That of the former pair is, of course, the more restricted but it is also the more natural, and hardly, one would have thought, a specially good instance of rigid Republican interpretation.

The final instance in this list of Schulz seems misconceived:

D.32,100,2 (Javolenus 2 *ex post Labeonis*):

> 'Uxori meae vestem, mundum muliebrem, ornamenta omnia, aurum argentum quod eius causa factum paratumque esset omne do lego'. Trebatius haec verba 'quod eius causa factum paratumque est', ad aurum et argentum dumtaxat referri putat, Proculus ad omnia, quod et verum est.

---

[39]) See more fully on the text, Watson, *Succession*, Chapter 4.

[40]) *Loc. cit.*

[41]) Cf., e.g., Kunkel, *Herkunft und soziale Stellung der römischen Juristen*, 2nd edit. (Graz etc. 1967) pp. 138ff.

In a sense Trebatius' restriction of the clause to the gold and silver may be regarded as a case of strict interpretation but the effect, of course, is to increase the legacy to the widow. She becomes entitled to all the clothing, feminine toilet articles and ornaments, whether they were or were not made or acquired on her behalf.

Three texts not mentioned by Schulz should also be discussed.

D.28,5,21*pr.* (Pomponius 1 *ad Sab.*).

> Trebatius ait sic non recte scribi: 'quisquis mihi heres erit, Stichus liber et heres esto', liberum tamen futurum. Labeo et heredem eum futurum recte putat.

In the text 'Whoever will be my heir' suggests that the will had previously appointed an heir and a substitute heir *(substitutus)* if the heir did not take the inheritance. Indeed, Trebatius' decision depends on there being an heir under the will or he could not have held that the slave was free. So the clause of the will quoted in the text has the function of making Stichus co-heir with the previously mentioned heir, and of giving him his liberty. Trebatius' attitude — recognition of one part of the clause but not of the other — is not too easy to explain, but in all probability he is being very formalistic. The first heir named in the will is appointed heir and nothing indicates that he is only to be heir to a part. Trebatius apparently takes this as meaning that he is heir of the whole estate and that any subsequent clause restricting his right is to be treated *pro non scripto* [42]).

D.33,1,17*pr.* (Labeo 2 *post. a Iavoleno epit.*):

> Legatum ita est: 'Attiae, donec nubat, quinquaginta damnas esto heres meus dare' neque adscriptum est 'in annos singulos'. Labeo Trebatius praesens legatum deberi putat [43]), sed rectius dicetur id legatum in annos singulos deberi.

Presumably the will was badly drafted. The very narrow deci-

---

42) See now on the text, Watson, *Succession*, Chapter 4.

43) *Putat* is either a scribal error for *putant* or *Labeo* is an insertion: see now Watson, *Succession*, Chapter 8.

sion of Trebatius (and Labeo) contrasts with that of Javolenus.

D.9,3,5,12 (Ulpian 23 *ad ed*):

> Si id quod positum erat deciderit et nocuerit, in eum competit actio qui posuit, non in eum qui habitaverit, quasi haec actio non sufficiat, quia positum habuisse non utique videtur qui posuit, nisi vel dominus fuit aedium vel inhabitator. nam et cum pictor in pergula clipeum vel tabulam expositam habuisset eaque excidisset et transeunti damni quid dedisset, Servius respondit ad exemplum huius actionis dari oportere actionem: hanc enim non competere palam esse, quia neque in suggrunda neque in protecto tabula fuerit posita.

The text comes from Ulpian's discussion of the edict *ne quis in suggrunda*, but the problem which faced Servius differed in two respects from the situation envisaged in the edict. Firstly, the object actually has fallen and caused damage whereas the edict was concerned with the possibility of future injury. Secondly, the shield or painting had been hung from a booth whereas the edict gave an action in respect of an object suspended from the eaves or a projecting roof. How the first of these differences is relevant cannot be determined. The opening part of the text where Ulpian seems to consider this first difference is badly corrupted due to a careless scribe [44], and any reconstruction must be based on a priori reasoning. And the reason given in the text for Servius' opinion — the reason, too, seems to go back to Servius — is concerned solely with this second difference. Thus, it seems that we should accept that for Servius an object hung dangerously on a booth did not give rise to the *actio de positis ac suspensis* because it was 'placed neither on the eaves nor on a projecting roof'. Thus, here his approach is strictly literal. But any hardship is excluded since he allows an *actio ad exemplum huius actionis* [45].

---

44) Cf., e.g., the editions of Cuiacius, Mommsen, Bonfante etc.

45) In a discussion of narrow interpretation in the Republic D. 35, 1, 40, 1 (Javolenus 2 *ex post. Labeonis*) and 18, 1, 77 (Javolenus 4 *ex post. Labeonis*) should not go entirely without mention though neither is very significant. Perhaps attention should also be drawn to the narrow interpretation of *agnatus proximus* in the XII Tables on intestate succession. This interpretation was early but the Republican jurists did not reinterpret the phrase and matters were put right only in the time of Trebatius: cf. Watson, *Limits of Juristic Decision*, pp. 23; *Succession*, Chapter 13.

Schulz finally turns his attention [46] to the famous *causa Curiana* [47] of around 93 to 91 B.C., which is probably the case mainly responsible for the view that the Republican jurists took a rigid literal view of interpretation. A testator left a will reading something like this: 'Let my son be my heir. If my son dies before reaching puberty, let M' Curius be my heir.' Quintus Mucius Scaevola appeared for the heirs on intestacy and argued that the will was to be interpreted literally. Curius' appointment as heir was subject to the condition 'if my son dies before puberty'. But the testator in fact never had a son, therefore, the argument goes, the son could not die before reaching puberty so the condition failed. Quintus Mucius' opponent in court was the famous orator, Lucius Licinius Crassus whom Cicero describes as the best jurist among the orators [48]. He successfully based his case on the presumed intention of the testator. The testator, he claimed, wished Curius to be his heir if he had a son who died before he reached puberty, or even if he never had a son.

Much has been made by modern scholars [49] of the contrast between the liberal interpretation of the orator, Crassus, who based his case on the presumed intention of the testator, and the narrow interpretation of the jurist, Scaevola, who argued for the literal meaning of the words used. Quintus Mucius Scaevola certainly was taking a very rigid line. But the importance of this for juristic interpretation in the Republic has been seriously overestimated. First, Quintus Mucius — the greatest orator among the jurists, according to Cicero [50] — was giving his opinion in this instance not as a jurist, but as an orator. And an orator has the duty of pleading the case for his client to the best of his ability and

---

46) *Legal Science*, pp. 79f.

47) The main sources are Cicero, *de orat.* 1.39.180; 2.32.142; *de inven.* 2.42.122; *Brutus*, 52.194—53.198; *top.* 10.42; *pro Caecina*, 18.53.

48) *Brutus*, 39.145.

49) For literature and a rather atypical view see Wieacker, *The 'causa Curiana' and Contemporary Roman Jurisprudence*, The Irish Jurist 2 (1967), pp. 151 ff: cf. Watson, *Succession*, Chapter 4 and Chapter 7.

50) *Brutus*, 39.145.

need not be strongly convinced of the arguments he uses [51]). So Quintus Mucius' rigid interpretation in the *causa Curiana* is no sure guide to his true feelings [52]). Secondly, we do have evidence that Quintus Mucius could take a wider view and consider the intention of the testator. Thus, we are told that he knew a Roman senator who wore women's dinner dresses. If the senator left a legacy of 'women's clothing' Quintus Mucius would not think he intended those 'which he himself wore as if they were men's' [53]). Undoubtedly he is here taking into consideration the testator's presumed intention. Again, when a legacy was left of a farm 'with its equipment or with those slaves who are on it' Quintus Mucius declared that the legacy did not include a groom who had been sent to the *villa* by the testator 'because he had not been sent in order to be there' [54]) [55]).

Thus stands the case based on an analysis of decisions for the view that the Republican jurists interpreted statutes and private acts in a narrow and restricted way. It is both grossly exaggerated and one-sided. Exaggerated in that many of the texts pressed into

---

[51]) Cf. *Rhet. ad Herennium*, 2.9.13—2.10.14.

[52]) Gandolfi observes that some of Scaevola's statements are to be attributed to the needs of his defence rather than to his personal opinion: *Studi sull'Interpretazione degli atti negoziali in diritto romano* (Milan, 1966), p. 293.

[53]) D. 34, 2, 33 (Pomponius 4 *ad Quintum Mucium*):

„Inter vestem virilem et vestimenta virilia nihil interest: sed difficultatem facit mens legantis, si et ipse solitus fuerit uti quadam veste, quae etiam mulieribus conveniens est. itaque ante omnia dicendum est eam legatam esse, de qua senserit testator, non quae re vera aut muliebris aut virilis sit. nam et Quintus Mucius [though most mss have Titius] ait scire se quendam senatorem muliebribus cenatoriis uti solitum, qui si legaret muliebrem vestem, non videretur de ea sensisse, qua ipse quasi virili utebatur." Cf. Watson, *Succession*, Chapter 7.

[54]) D. 28, 5, 35, 3 (Ulpian 4 *disp.*):

. . . ut est apud Mucium relatum, cum fundus erat legatus vel cum instrumento vel cum his quae ibi sunt: agasonem enim missum in villam a patre familias non pertinere ad fundi legatum Mucius ait, quia non idcirco illo erat missus, ut ibi esset. proinde si servus fuerit missus in villam interim illic futurus, quia dominum offenderat, quasi ad tempus relegatus, responsum est eum ad villae legatum non pertinere. . . .

[55]) And there is also his extremely wide interpretation of the *interdictum quod vi aut clam*: D.50,17,73,2 (*sing.* ὅρων); 43,24,1,5 (Ulpian 71 *ad ed.*).

service do not show narrow and restricted interpretation by the jurists or not to the extent apparently claimed. One-sided in that the more numerous texts which show very wide interpretation [56]) are not given full consideration.

Ankum produces a rather different type of argument in support of the view that the *veteres* were more dogmatical than the classical jurists [57]). He points out that we have thirty texts which tell us that a particular decision is accepted, or proposed or so on, on account of its usefulness (*utilitatis causa* and similar expressions). Now he observes that the *utilitas*-reasoning is most frequent in the works of the three late classical jurists, Papinian, Ulpian and Paul. He continues [58]): 'Even if we take into account the relatively small number of texts of pre-classical lawyers transmitted to us, it does not seem too hazardous to state that the old republican lawyers did not use openly the *utilitas* as an element in developing the law against strict rules of logic. This goes very well with the impression of many modern scholars — which looks right to me — that the *veteres* were more dogmatical than the classical lawyers'. The argument, it must be admitted, does not seem to me to be sound. The *utilitas*-reasoning is not normally used as an argument for a totally new legal proposition. Rather, it is used to explain why a legal proposition has in fact been accepted or why an opinion already expressed by another should be accepted [59]). But to say '— was accepted on the ground of utility by jurists X and Y' is very weak. It is much better to have '— was accepted on the ground of utility' or 'the view of X and Y should be accepted on the ground of utility'. The nearest we come to the first formulation is D.41,4,2,9 (Paul 54 *ad ed.*) with *plerique putant utilitatis causa pro emptore usucapturum:* and D.46,3,95,7 (Papinian 28 *quaest.*) which has *Labeo et Pegasus putaverunt utilitatis causa recipiendum.* So it would be unreasonable to expect to find in a text by a classical author the statement

---

56) Supra, pp. 11 ff.

57) *Utilitatis causa receptum*, Symbolae David I (Leiden 1968), pp. 1ff.

58) *Op. cit.*, p. 6.

59) See the texts listed by Ankum, *op. cit.*, p. 5.

that something was accepted *utilitatis causa* by a Republican jurist. And so very few — relatively very, very few — texts in the Digest have come down to us directly from the Republican authors — less than one per cent of the whole — that it cannot surprise that not one of thirty texts is actually by one of the *veteres*.

Incidentally, another difficulty for this view must be mentioned. If, as Ankum correctly holds [60]), *utilitas* is used rather often as a reason to explain the acceptance of a dogmatically indefensible solution or as an argument for such, then it is possible that the more rigidly dogmatical the system the greater the need to justify exceptions, for instance, by *utilitatis causa*. Hence, if it were the case that the *veteres* did not use *utilitas*-reasoning, this might indicate they did not need to because the system was not so rigidly dogmatical.

60) *Op. cit.*, p. 28.

5

Private Law in the Rescripts of Carus, Carinus and Numerianus

"With the political disorders, which after the death of the Emperor Alexander Severus (235) led the Roman Empire to the edge of the abyss and choked all true creative intellectual life, died likewise classical jurisprudence. When Diocletian (284–305) restores order a half-century later, he certainly succeeds in preserving the legal classicism in its vital elements; but he can no longer renew its productive force". This statement of Kaser[1] on the end of classical law and the law of Diocletian represents clearly the view of most modern scholars[2]. But it raises an immediate question. If classical jurisprudence and all creative intellectual life came to such an abrupt end with the death of Alexander Severus[3], how was Diocletian able to preserve legal classicism? Where did he, after 50 years of chaos, find properly trained lawyers who could issue classicising rescripts in his name? The problem is not much diminished when one observes that, so far as our sources go, the years 293 and 294 were the most productive for his rescripts, since quite a number date from earlier years—48 are expressly attributed to 286 and 95 to 290[4]. Not enough time elapses for the education of professors of law to train Diocletian's jurists.

This paper is an attempt to establish the quality of legal expertise which existed on the eve of Diocletian's accession, in the reign(s) of Carus, Carinus and Numerianus. All the surviving rescripts of these Emperors which deal with private law will be examined to establish the law in them, their sophistication (or lack of it) and the precision of their legal terminology. The rescripts will also be related to those of earlier Emperors and of Diocletian.

Introduction

In 282 A.D. in the seventh year of the reign of the Emperor Probus, the army in Raetia proclaimed as Emperor the praetorian prefect M. Aurelius Carus who was an Illyrian by birth. When the news reached Sirmium where Probus then was he was murdered by soldiers. Carus, on receiving this information (in October?), sent a dispatch to the Senate informing it of his elevation by the troops and nominated his elder son, M. Aurelius Carinus, and soon after the younger, M. Aurelius Numerianus, as co-rulers with the rank

1. *Das Römische Privatrecht* II (Munich 1960), p. 3.
2. Cf., e.g., Jolowicz and Nicholas, *Historical Introduction to the Study of Roman Law*, 3rd edit., (Cambridge 1972), p. 7; Levy, *West Roman Vulgar Law, The Law of Property* (Philadelphia 1951), p. 1 (ends the classical period about 240 A.D.). Taubenschlag, *Das Rômische Privatrecht zur Zeit Diokletians*, now in *Opera Minora* I (Warsaw 1959), pp. 9 f.

This article was ready for publication before the appearance of the splendid study by Wieacker, *Le droit romain de la mort d'Alexandre Sévère à l'avènement de Dioclétien* (235–284 après J.-C.), RHD 49 (1971), pp. 201ff. The major conclusions of both studies accord, and I have thought it best to leave the present article unmodified.

3. Thus, A. H. M. Jones, describes the period between Alexander Severus and Diocletian simply as "The Anarchy": *The Later Roman Empire* I (Oxford 1964), pp. 21ff.
4. See the lists given by Krueger in the stereotype edition of the *Corpus Iuris Civilis* II, 11th edit. (Berlin 1954), pp. 494f.

of *Caesares*. Not much later both Carinus and Numerianus were created *Augusti*, and then Carus, leaving Carinus in charge of the West, set out with Numerianus for Mesopotamia where he met with considerable success in battle before he was killed (around the 29th August 284) by a stroke of lightning or his soldiers. Numerianus was killed by his father-in-law, Arrius Aper, on the return journey. On the discovery of the murder, the officers elected Diocletian Emperor on 17th November, 284. Carinus moved East with his army and lost his life by treachery in a battle—which he seemed to be winning—in the valley of the Margus in the summer of 285.

From this short span of troubled time we have 26 surviving rescripts[5,6], 8 of which cannot be precisely dated but of the others the earliest is from 13th January, 283[7], and the latest 8th December 284[8]. This number compares favourably with the surviving 4 issued under the sole name of Gallienus (260–268), the one or two of Claudius Gothicus (268–270), the 5 or 6 of Aurelian[9] (270–275) and the 4 of Probus (276–282). 16 of the rescripts of Carus and his sons involve matters of private law.

The rescripts present nothing startling at first sight. Mostly they are quite short, as was usual, the shortest of all having only 7 words, but one, C. 5, 52, 2, is quite long. The sole reference to juristic opinion is in C. 6, 42, 16: *Cum virum prudentissimum Papinianum respondisse non ignoramus*. Again there is nothing surprising in this; in the rescripts from the death of Alexander Severus to this time there are very few references to the jurists; two others to Papinian[10], one to Modestinus[11], and two or three general citations[12]. Similarly, references to and reliance on other sources of law are about what we might expect; C. 8, 14(15), 4 tells us that a rule was *notum* and *constitutum*; C. 10, 11, 4 refers to the diversity of statutes; C. 6, 49, 3 refers to the *senatusconsultum Trebellianum*; and C. 5, 71, 7 to an unnamed *senatusconsultum*[13].

The Individual Rescripts[14]

The law of persons is more prominent in the rescripts than any other major division of the law. Though there are no rescripts which tell us anything about the form of marriage or divorce, two concern aspects of dowry.

1. C. 3, 32, 9:

> Doce ancillam, de qua supplicas, dotalem fuisse in notione praesidis: quo patefacto indubium non erit vindicari ab uxore tua nequivisse.

5. 25 according to Krueger, *Corpus Juris Civilis* II, p. 494, who seemingly passes over C. 4, 20, 4.

6. For the purpose of this article no distinction need be or will be drawn between the three Emperors.

7. C. 7, 64, 5.

8. C. 4, 20, 4.

9. C. 1, 23, 2 of 270 A.D. is wrongly ascribed to Alexander, and may be of either Claudius or Aurelian.

10. C. 6, 37, 12 [Gordian, 240 A.D.]; 7, 32, 3 [Decius, 250 A.D.].

11. C. 3, 42, 5 [Gordian, 239 A.D.]. In this case Modestinus had given a *responsum* to the soldier who later wrote to the Emperor.

12. C. 6, 20, 4 [Gordian, 239 A.D.]; 7, 4, 10 (9) [Valerianus and Gallienus, 260] and (?) 8, 10, 4 [Philippus A. and Philippus C., 245].

13. In the period from 235 to the accession of Carus there are in the *Codex* 12 references to a named or unnamed *senatusconsultum:* 2, 11 (12), 15; 2, 22 (23), 1 (2); 4, 13, 1; 4, 28, 6; 4, 29, 7; 4, 29, 8; 4, 29,9; 4, 29, 10; 4, 29, 12; 6, 49, 2; 9, 9, 16; 10, 46 (45), 1.

14. To avoid any possible misunderstanding it is emphasised that we are concerned with the rescripts only, not with the state of law in general in 283–4.

There is an obvious scribal error in the text. *Indubium non erit* is impossible and should be something like *in dubium non venit* or *dubium non erit.*

The rescript is addressed to a man named Antonius, obviously in one of the imperial provinces[15]. The main legal rule in the text is plain, and unexceptionable even in classical law, namely that objects brought to a husband by a wife as dowry cease to belong to the woman[16]. Further aspects of the situation require clarification. It seems there is a dispute between the husband and wife over the ownership of a slave girl. (If the husband and wife were living in amity and the woman's successful *vindicatio* had been brought against a third party, the husband would never have applied to the Emperors for a ruling, and they could not have begun the rescript, *Doce*). The situation claimed by the husband would then seem to be this. The *praeses*, governor of the province, had looked into the matter and declared the slave girl had been given to the husband as dowry, the wife then somehow brought a successful *vindicatio* for the slave. The Emperors tell the husband to show the ruling of the *praeses*, and it will then not be doubted that the wife could not have vindicated. It is no new thing for a *praeses* to act as judge in the *cognitio* procedure and the practice is evidenced as early as Severus and Antoninus at the beginning of the 3rd century[17]. We cannot tell why the wife's *vindicatio* was successful. Nor is there any indication why the decision of the *praeses* is to be preferred to that reached in the *vindicatio.*

2. C. 8, 14(15), 4:

Satis notum est et idem constitutum bona earum in dotem data, quae nuptae sunt his qui primipili sarcinam subeunt, obnoxia necessitati ei teneri: verum certo ordine, ut scilicet tunc demum ad hoc mulieris patrimonium periculum respiciat, si universis viri ac nominatorum facultatibus exhaustis nihil residuum inveniatur. [283]

Wolff[18] regards the rescript as interpolated from *verum.* That part of the text, he claims, is in the style of late imperial legislation whereas the first part does look as if it comes from a rescript. But his particular arguments are not persuasive. He objects[19] to *facultates,* but the plural with a meaning such as 'property, wealth, resources' is common both in legal [20] and non-legal Latin[21] even from an earlier period. *Scilicet,* as often, is regarded as a sign of interpolation[22], but to someone who raised the question to which the Emperors are replying it is only proper that the rescript explain the order of liability. It would have been unsatisfactory to end the rescript at *teneri.* Lastly, Wolff objects to *ad periculum respiciat.* But this objection appears to involve a misunderstanding of the text. *Periculum* is the subject, not the object, of *respiciat: periculum respiciat ad hoc mulieris patrimonium.*

The rescript tells us that the dowry of a woman married to a *primipilus*[23] can be taken to pay her husband's duty debts, but only after all the resources of the husband and of his

15. Appears from the governor being designated *praeses.*
16. Cf., e.g., Corbett, *The Roman Law of Marriage* (Oxford 1930), pp. 177ff.; Bonfante, *Corso di diritto romano* I: *diritto di famiglia* (Milan 1963), p. 445.
17. Cf., C. 3, 8, 1 [203 A.D.]; 7, 62, 1 [209]; for other relevant rescripts see Kaser, *Das Römische Zivilprozessrecht* (Munich 1966), p. 345, n. 37.
18. *Zur Stellung der Frau im klassischen Römischen Dotalrecht,* ZSS 53 (1933), pp. 297ff at p. 360.
19. Following Bonfante, now *Corso* I, p. 456.
20. Cf. the Digest texts listed in *Vocabularium Iurisprudentiae Romanae* II (Berlin 1933), 791f.
21. Cf., e.g., Lewis and Short, *A Latin Dictionary* (Oxford, reprinted 1951), p. 719.
22. And often it is, though usually it is a mark only that the text has been condensed.
23. For the meaning of *primipilus* see infra, p. 48.

nominatores have been exhausted. The wording of the text—*qui primipili sarcinam subeunt* and *obnoxia necessitati ei teneri*—shows that what is under consideration is debts incurred by the *primipilus* through his service, that is, to the fisc. Presumably, the *nominatores* would not be liable for any civil debts incurred by the *primipilus*. There is nothing surprising in the *nominatores* being called upon to pay the official debts of the *primipilus* since from at least the time of Gordian *nominatores* were liable to the fisc if a magistrate became insolvent when he was holding office[24]. What is possibly strange is that the claim on the wife's dowry—which does belong to the *primipilus*— is postponed until the property of the *nominatores* is exhausted, but we cannot properly estimate the novelty here since in fact the order in which tacit hypothec claims were preferred or exacted can scarcely be discovered[25]. It was, of course, well established in classical law that the dowry was a privileged debt in favour of the wife but it could be called upon to satisfy some other debts, apparently at least the cost of burial and, more significantly for us, debts owed to the fisc[26].

There is a looseness in juristic language in that although the dowry belongs to the husband it is referred to as *mulieris patrimonium*. But the usage is very natural and not new since even for classical law we have texts which talk of the dowry as if it were the wife's[27].

Once *primipilus* had been the term for the leading centurion of a legion but now it was really a retirement rank from the civil service. There was an obscure tax known as *pastus primipili*. When the *princeps* of a provincial *officium* retired and was promoted to *primipilus* he had the duty of conveying the goods collected by way of tax from his province to the army which was to receive them, and moreover he was apparently expected to tip the *dux* of the receiving area[28]. The development of this system is not clear[29] but the position of *primipilus* obviously imposed a great financial burden as early as Caracalla[30]. We have five rescripts of Diocletian concerning legal problems arising from such debts[31], and one, C. 12, 62(63), 3, shows that the dowry is a privileged debt but is postponed to the debts owed to the fisc.

It might, at this point, be appropriate to deal with the one text on gifts before marriage:

3. C. 5, 3, 7:

Si, cum ante nuptias munera darentur, ita conventum est atque huiusmodi conscripta pactio est, ut, si qua fors extitisset contra voluntatem eius et matrimonium distraxisset, tunc quae data erant apud eum qui dedisset heredemve eius remanerent, potest, qui eius hereditatem accepit, cui pacta puella munera supra dicta lege susceperat, eadem iure postulare[32].

24. C. 11, 34 (33), 1 [Gordian]; 11, 34 (33), 2 [*Idem*]; 11, 36 (35), 2 [*Idem*] (liability for persons appointed to a *munus*): cf., C. 10, 2, 3 [Diocletian et Maximianus] (liability for *exactores*).

25. Cf., e.g., Buckland, *Textbook of Roman Law*, 3rd edit. revised by Stein (Cambridge 1963), p. 480.

26. Cf., e.g., Corbett, *Marriage*, pp. 190f.; Lenel, *Edictum*, pp. 429f.

27. That all are interpolated is most unlikely: cf., e.g., Bonfante, *Corso* I, pp. 44ff.; Wolff, *Stellung*, pp. 357ff.

28. For this and more detail see Jones, *The Later Roman Empire* I, p. 459.

29. Cf. Jones, *The Later Roman Empire* II, pp. 1194f., n. 117.

30. C. 7, 73, 1. This tells us that when the property of a *primipilus* is seized by the fisc, the goods which the wife can clearly prove to be hers are to be separated and returned to her.

31. C. 4, 9, 1 [294]; 4, 31, 11; 12, 62 (63), 2; 12, 62 (63), 3; 12, 62 (63), 4 [refers to Aurelian].

32. Donatuti appears to think that the text is not in proper form, and objects specifically to *apud—remanerent: Le cause delle condictiones*, Studi Parmensi I (1950), pp. 35ff. at p. 101 and n. 302.

The addressee is a woman named Iunciana, probably the widow. Before the marriage the future husband gave gifts to the bride, and it was agreed and a written document to that effect was drawn up that if, against the husband's wishes, the marriage was ended, then the gifts would remain with the donor or his heir. Apparently the husband subsequently died, and the Emperors declare that the person who accepted his inheritance can demand the return of the gifts from the woman under the agreement. The rescript contains nothing strange. The gifts were made under a resolutive condition and on the occurrence of the condition they should be restored[33], presumably the action available being a *condictio*. There is no sign of a *stipulatio* but also there was not the slightest need for one[34]. Again, there is nothing surprising in the *pactio* declaring that the gifts should also be returnable to the donor's heir. This is not creating an obligation *post mortem*—even without the clause the heir would be able to recover with the *condictio*[35]—but simply avoiding a possible difficulty of interpretation: that is, the donor is making it plain that he wants his heir's right to the gifts to be superior to that of his wife, unless he (the donor) deliberately ends the marriage. As a corollary, of course, the *pactio* means that the gifts are returnable even when the marriage ends by death. The phrase *matrimonium distraxisset* is appropriately used of death[36]. And *munus*, though it has other meanings too, commonly signifies 'gift'[37]. Indeed, in so far as a distinction can be drawn between *donum* and *munus*, the latter is here more appropriate, since according to Labeo *munus* is a *donum cum causa, ut puta natalicium nuptalicium*[38].

We have no rescripts of Carus, Carinus and Numerianus on any aspect of *patria potestas*, but two involve emancipated sons. If these two texts alone were available for our consideration no statistical argument could be drawn from them, but we do have the rescripts of earlier post-classical Emperors and of Diocletian. These show that *emancipatio* had become extremely common. Thus from the accession of Maximinus to the accession of Carus we have 51 rescripts in the Code which refer in any way at all to parent and child, and 12 of these show that there has been an *emancipatio*[39]. Since there may have been an *emancipatio* in some of the others which was not mentioned because it was not relevant, and since some of these other rescripts concern infants, adoption, the *ius liberorum* etc., it emerges that *emancipatio* of grown-up children must have been very common. For the reign of Diocletian the corresponding figures are 112 and 36[40].

33. Cf., e.g., D. 39, 5, 2, 7 (Julian 60 *dig.*); *h.t.* 3 (Ulpian 76 *ad ed.*).
34. Cf., e.g., D. 39, 5, 2, 5 (Julian 7 *dig.*).
35. And there is no *stipulatio*.
36. Cf., D. 24, 3, 33 (Africanus 7 *quaest.*).
37. E.g., D. 50, 16, 18 (Paul 9 *ad ed.*); C. 5, 3, 2 [Alexander].
38. D. 50, 16, 194 (Ulpian 43 *ad ed.*).
39. The 12 are: C. 1, 18, 3; 2, 26 (27), 2; 3, 29, 2; 4, 12, 1; 4, 29, 8; 5, 6, 3; 5, 14, 4; 5, 71, 3; 6, 20, 6; 7, 71, 3; 8, 53 (54), 2; 9, 34, 2. The others are: C. 2, 22 (23), 1 (2); 2, 22 (23), 2 (1); 4, 28, 6; 4, 35, 8; 5, 4, 6; 5, 4, 7; 5, 4, 9; 5, 6, 4; 5, 6, 6; 5, 12, 6; 5, 12, 7; 5, 14, 3; 5, 17, 2; 5, 28, 5; 5, 46, 2; 6, 20, 4; 6, 21, 9; 6, 25, 5; 6, 30, 3; 6, 30, 4; 6, 42, 14; 6, 42, 15; 6, 58, 2; 7, 2, 7; 7, 9, 2; 7, 73, 6; 8, 7, 1; 8, 46 (47), 4; 8, 47 (48), 1; 9, 1, 9; 9, 51, 6; 10, 39 (38), 3; 10, 41 (40), 1; 10, 52 (51), 2; 10, 52 (51), 3; 10, 62 (60), 2; 10, 65 (63), 1; 10, 69 (67), 1; 12, 36 (37), 4.
40. The 36 are: C. 2, 2, 3; 2, 20 (21), 5; 3, 28, 25; 3, 29, 5; 3, 29, 8; 4, 5, 5; 4, 13, 2; 4, 19, 15; 4, 21, 11; 4, 26, 8 (9); 4, 51, 5; 5, 16, 16; 5, 17, 5; 5, 62, 19; 6, 8, 4; 6, 14, 1; 6, 19, 1; 6, 20, 9; 6, 20, 11; 6, 20, 15; 6, 46, 5; 6, 57, 2; 6, 59, 1; 8, 47 (48), 2; 8, 47 (48), 9; 8, 48 (49), 1; 8, 48 (49), 2; 8, 48 (49), 3; 8, 48 (49), 4; 8, 53 (54), 11; 8, 53 (54), 17; 8, 53 (54), 22; 8, 54 (55), 5; 10, 50 (49), 2; 10, 52 (51), 4; 10, 62 (60), 3. The others are: C. 2, 3, 23; 2, 4, 26; 2, 42 (43), 4; 2, 50 (51), 7; 2, 53 (54), 5; 2, 55 (56), 3; 3, 28, 22; 3, 28, 24; 3, 29, 4; 3, 31, 10; 3, 36, 13; 4, 1, 7; 4, 12, 4; 4, 13, 3; 4, 13, 4; 4, 13, 5; 4, 19, 14; 4, 20, 6; 4, 26, 9 (8); 4, 43, 1; 4, 44, 8; 5, 4, 11; 5, 4, 12; 5, 4, 15; 5, 4, 16; 5, 18, 7; 5, 18, 10; 5, 24, 1; 5, 49, 2; 5, 70, 4; 5, 72, 3; 6, 19, 2; 6, 20, 12; 6, 20, 13; 6, 20, 14; 6, 20, 16; 6, 22, 3; 6, 24, 7; 6, 26, 8; 6, 30, 11; 6, 55, 5; 6, 55, 6; 6, 55, 7; 6, 56, 2;

4. C. 5, 71, 7:

> Si ad resolvendam donationem, quam in emancipatum te pater contulerit, minor annis cautionem emisisti, cum huiusmodi scriptura contra senatus consulti auctoritatem data sit, non oberit iuri tuo.

A *pater* made a gift to a son who had been emancipated, and the son while still a minor issued a document to have the gift set aside. Later the son enquired about the legal position and was told by the Emperors that since writing of that sort was contrary to the precept of the *senatus consultum* it did not adversely affect his legal rights.

The *senatus consultum* in question must be that *ad orationem Severi* of 13th June, 195 A.D.[41] and hence, though it is not stated, the gift must have been of land[42]. As reported in D. 27, 9, 1, 2 (Ulpian *35 ad ed.*) the relevant part of the *oratio* ran:

> Praeterea, patres conscripti, interdicam tutoribus et curatoribus, ne praedia rustica vel suburbana distrahant, nisi ut id fieret, parentes testamento vel codicillis caverint. quod si forte aes alienum tantum erit, ut ex rebus ceteris non possit exsolvi, tunc praetor urbanus vir clarissimus adeatur, qui pro sua religione aestimet, quae possunt[43] alienari obligarive debeant, manente pupillo actione, si postea potuerit probari obreptum esse praetori. si communis res erit et socius ad divisionem provocet, aut si creditor, qui pignori agrum a parente pupilli acceperit, ius exsequetur, nihil novandum censeo.

There have in the past been suspicions as to whether the *oratio* originally spoke of *curatores* as well as *tutores*[44], but even if this view is correct there seems little doubt that long before the time of Carus, the *senatus consultum* was applying to transactions by both *pupilli* and *minores*[45].

The Emperors' decision itself seems perfectly straightforward and reasonable. Just possibly we might have expected elaboration on one aspect of the problem. The *oratio* exceptionally permitted the land to be sold when the father had allowed for the contingency by will. In this case the gift by the father to the son was *inter vivos* and the father obviously was willing that the son be allowed to transfer the land, since the transfer was to be to the father himself. It might have been arguable for the father that by a wide interpretation the *oratio* would have no adverse effect on the *cautio*. But the point is not mentioned.

There are two curiosities in the text. First, nothing is said about the *cautio* being issued with the approval of the minor's *curator*. It is reasonable to assume that if this minor emancipated son had a *curator* he would be the father, so there would be an additional reason for the *cautio*—whether with or without the *curator's* approval—being ineffective.

7, 10, 6; 7. 33, 8; 7, 64, 8; 8, 8, 2; 8, 16 (17), 6; 8, 38 (39), 3; 8, 38 (39), 6; 8, 46 (47), 5; 8, 46 (47), 6; 8, 46 (47), 7; 8, 46 (47), 8; 8, 46 (47), 9; 8, 47 (48), 3; 8, 47 (48), 4; 8, 47 (48), 5; 8, 47 (48), 6; 8, 47 (48), 7; 8, 47 (48), 8; 8, 50 (51), 17; 8, 53 (54), 14; 8, 55 (56), 6; 9, 1, 14; 9, 12, 3; 9, 22, 10; 9, 51, 9; 10, 32 (31), 4; 10. 32 (31), 5; 10, 32 (31), 9; 10, 40 (39), 7; 10, 52 (51), 5; 10, 62 (60), 4; 12, 36 (37), 5.

41. There is no other appropriate, and besides, that *senatus consultum* is the object of C. 5, 71. On the *senatus consultum* see Volterra, *Senatus consulta*, Novissimo Digesto Italiano (Turin), pp. 103f. of offprint.

42. Constantine extended the rule also to country slaves, *mancipium rusticum: C.Th.* 3, 32, 1.

43. Lenel emends to *possessiones: Palingenesia Iuris Civilis* II (reprinted Graz 1960), 659, n. 4.

44. Cf. Solazzi, *La minore età nel diritto romano* (Rome 1913), pp. 116f.; Albertario, *L'oratio Severi riferita in* D. 27, 9 *e la cura dei minori*, Studi di diritto romano I (Milan 1933), pp. 475ff. at p. 492. Riccobono, *Stipulatio ed instrumentum nel diritto giustinianeo*, ZSS 43 (1922), pp. 262ff. at 318f. The last two regard our text as interpolated.

45. Cf. Lenel, *Die cura minorum der klassischen Zeit*, ZSS 35 (1914), pp. 129ff. at p. 168, n. 2.

Secondly, to set aside the gift one would have expected—for classical law at least—either a *mancipatio* of the land back to the father or at least a *stipulatio*[46]. Neither seems to have occurred. This fact, too, strengthens the case for holding that the minor's property rights were not diminished. Since both the difficulty over the father's interest if he were the *curator* and the absence of any *mancipatio* or *stipulatio* would only strengthen the case for the Emperors' clear decision it was probably felt there was no need to discuss them specifically.

But for us there is the significant fact that the parties themselves had resorted only to the written *cautio* and that the father had not demanded a *mancipatio* or even a *stipulatio.*

5. C. 8, 55(56), 3:

Possessionem, quam in vos emancipatos per donationem mater contulit, ex paenitentia sola alienare non potuit. [284]

The Emperors declare that when a mother had transferred property by way of gift to her two emancipated sons, she could not later transfer the property to another person simply because she changed her mind. The same decision would have been given in classical law, and there is in it nothing untoward.

Biondi claims that the point in time had been reached when givers maintained that a gift was revocable in all cases; and that Diocletian reacted vigorously against such a claim, re-affirming that a *donatio perfecta* was irrevocable[47]. But this present rescript of Carus, Carinus and Numerianus, as well as C. 5, 71, 7 which we have just discussed, shows that the attitude of Diocletian was not a new one. Indeed, even earlier post-classical rescripts show that other Emperors, too, did not take the view that a gift could be revoked just because the donor changed his mind: C. 9, 34, 2 [Gordian, 239] and 8, 55, 2 [Probus, 277].

Contrary to the usage of the classical jurists, the word *possessio* appears in the rescript with the meaning of "property", "thing" or even perhaps "ownership" and not with the technical sense of "possession". *Pace* Levy[48] and Kaser[49] who both think that the relaxation of the technical usage of *possessio* began with Constantine, the word *possessio* in the post-classical period before Carus already usually meant "property", "thing" and probably sometimes "ownership". Thus, if we leave aside the texts which talk of *bonorum possessio* and *in possessionem mitti* we have 32 rescripts from 235 A.D. to the accession of Carus which contain the word *possessio.* In 23 it seems to mean something like "property"[50]. Only in 9 does it appear to have the technical sense of "possession"[51]. But even before this, right at the end of the classical period, *possessio* in the sense of

46. A *stipulatio* if for instance the father's gift had been promised by *stipulatio* but there was no actual *mancipatio* to the son.

47. *Successione testamentaria e donazioni*, 2nd edit. (Milan 1955), p. 698.

48. *West Roman Vulgar Law, The Law of Property*, (Philadelphia 1951), pp. 19ff.

49. *Das Römische Privatrecht* II (Munich 1960), pp. 177ff.

50. C. 2, 4, 9 [Gordian, 241]; 2, 19 (20), 5 [*Idem*, 239]; 2, 50 (51), 6 [Valerianus and Gallienus, 254]; 3, 32, 6 [Gordian, 239]; 4, 31, 8 [*Idem*]; 4, 32, 17 [Philipp and Philipp]; 4, 38, 1 [Valerianus and Gallienus]; 4, 50, 4 [*Idem*]; 4, 64, 1 [Gordian, 238]; 4, 65, 12 [Philipp and Philipp, 245]; 5, 70, 2 [Gordian, 238]; 5, 71, 2 [*Idem*, 239]; 5, 73, 1 [*Idem*, 238]; 5, 73, 2 [*Idem*, 241]; 7, 26, 5 [*Idem*, 238]; 7, 73, 6 [*Idem*, 240]; 8, 13 (14), 9 [*Idem*, 239]; 8, 23 (24), 1 [*Idem*, 238]; 8, 27 (28), 8 [*Idem*, 239]; 8, 29 (30), 4 [*Idem*, 240]; 8, 44 (45), 14 [*Idem*, 239]; 10, 16, 2 [Valerianus and Gallienus, 260]; 10, 16, 3 [Decius, 249].

51. C. 2, 19 (20), 3 [Gordian, 238]; 3, 32, 4 [*Idem*, 238]; 7, 32, 3 [Decius, 250]; 7, 36, 1 [Gordian]; 8, 26 (27), 1 [*Idem*, 239]; 8, 55 (56), 1 = V.F. 272 [Philipp, 249]; V.F. 19 [Gallienus, 260]; V.F. 30 [Aurelian, 271]; V.F. 288 [Probus, 280].

"property" occurs 4 times in the rescripts of Caracalla[52] and twice in those of Alexander Severus[53], but significantly not in the rescripts of earlier Emperors[54].

Interestingly in the rescripts of Diocletian, *possessio* with its technical sense is much more common: 61 apparent instances[55] as opposed to only 14 which seem to have the relaxed meaning[56].

6. C. 5, 71, 6:

Minorum possessionis venditio, per procuratorem delato ad praetorem vel praesidem provinciae libello, fieri non potuit, cum ea res confici recte aliter non potest, nisi apud acta causis probatis, quae venditioni necessitatem inferant, decretum solemniter interponatur[57]. [283]

With this rescript we are back to the *senatus consultum ad orationem Severi* of 13th June, 195[58], and this time specifically to the provision "*quod si forte aes alienum tantum erit, ut ex rebus ceteris non possit exsolvi, tunc praetor urbanus vir clarissimus adeatur, qui pro sua religione aestimet, quae possunt alienari obligarive debeant*".

The rescript tells us that a minor's property—*possessio* is again the word used—cannot be sold when a written statement is delivered to the *praetor* or *praeses provinciae* by a *procurator*. Such a matter demands, the respondent is told, the official's decree solemnly recorded in the public acts when the reasons which make the sale necessary have been approved. That is, the Emperors seem to require that the official enquire fully into the necessity of the sale and give a formal decision. It is not enough simply for the magistrate to be notified.

The decision—active consideration of the facts being required from the official—is exactly what one would expect in classical law. It is in accord with the *qui pro sua religione aestimet* of the *senatus consultum* and it is in harmony with D. 27, 9, 5, 9–14 (Ulpian 35 *ad ed.*). The force of the official's *decretum* is emphasised also in D. 27, 9, 7, 4 (*Idem*), *h.t.* 8, 2 (Ulpian *2 de omn. trib.*) and *h.t.* 9 (Ulpian *5 opin.*).

The *senatus consultum*, true to the classical tradition, was concerned only with affairs in Rome and hence the only official mentioned is the *praetor urbanus*. The interest of the post-classical Emperors in the provinces is, in this rescript, evident from the mention of the *praeses provinciae* as well as the *praetor*[59].

52. C. 3, 34, 2 [215]; 3, 44, 2 [216]; 4, 19, 2 [215]; 8, 13 (14), 6 [213].
53. C. 5, 56, 3 [228]; 8, 44 (45), 9 [222].
54. This fact, properly suggestive of a historical linguistic development, is fatal to any idea that *possessio* meaning "property" is generally interpolated in pre-Constantine rescripts. Levy rightly calls attention to D. 50, 16, 78 (Paul 3 *ad Plautium*) which shows that the looser usage was in vogue but not among the jurists; *Vulgar Law*, p. 20.
55. C. 2, 54 (55), 1; 3, 32, 13; 3, 32, 15; 3, 32, 26; 3, 36, 15; 3, 38, 8; 4, 19, 12; 4, 19, 20; 4, 21, 12; 4, 26, 10; 4, 27, 1; 4, 38, 3; 4, 38, 9; 4, 49, 5; 4, 49, 8; 4, 50, 6; 4, 50, 8; 4, 65, 23; 4, 65, 25; 5, 3, 8; 5, 16, 16; 5, 16, 23; 5, 18, 9; 6, 2, 10; 7, 14, 10; 7, 14, 11; 7, 26, 7; 7, 26, 8; 7, 32, 4; 7, 32, 5; 7, 32, 6; 7, 32, 7; 7, 32, 8; 7, 32, 9; 7, 33, 4; 7, 33, 5; 7, 33, 7; 7, 33, 8; 7, 33, 9; 7, 33, 10; 7, 35, 4; 7, 35, 6; 7, 36, 2; 7, 45, 9; 7, 48, 3; 8, 1, 3; 8, 4, 1; 8, 4, 3; 8, 4, 4; 8, 6, 1; 8, 27 (28), 13; 8, 35 (36), 5; 8, 53 (54), 6 = V.F. 282; C. 9, 22, 18; V.F. 293; 297; 312; 313; 314; 315; 316. The picture would not be substantially changed if texts were also counted which used only *possessor* or *possidere*. Three texts talk of *possessio libertatis:* C. 7, 16, 14; 7, 22, 1; 7, 22, 2.
56. C. 3, 32, 15; 3, 36, 14 (?); 4, 12, 3; 4, 21, 8; 4, 50, 5; 5, 16, 13; 5, 16, 15; 5, 51, 6; 5, 74, 1; 8, 23 (24), 2; 10, 40 (39), 4; V.F. 24 (?); V.F. 41; V.F. 285.
57. Lenel expressly declares the rescript to be not interpolated: *Cura minorum*, p. 168, n. 2. Albertario would again excise the reference to the *minor: L'oratio Severi*, p. 494.
58. Cf. *supra*, pp. [6] f.
59. Whither the rescript was addressed cannot be determined.

7. C. 5, 52, 2:

Si divisio administrationis inter tutores sive curatores in eodem loco seu provincia constitutos necdum fuit, licentiam habet adulescens et unum eorum eligere et totum debitum exigere, cessione videlicet ab eo adversus ceteros tutores seu curatores actionum ei competentium facienda. 1. In divisionem autem administratione deducta sive a praeside sive a testatoris voluntate unumquemque pro sua administratione convenire potest, periculum invicem tutoribus seu curatoribus non sustinentibus, nisi per dolum aut culpam suspectum non removerunt vel tarde suspicionis rationem moverunt, cum alter eorum non solvendo effectus sit, vel suspicionis causam agendo sua sponte iura pupilli prodiderunt. 2. Nec prodest eis dicentibus contutorem suum non administrasse pupillares res. 3. Sin vero ipsi inter se res administrationis diviserunt, non prohibetur adulescens et unum ex his in solidum convenire, ita ut actiones, quas adversus alios habet, ad electum transferat[60]. [284]

Here, too, the use of *provincia* and *praeses* betrays the interest in the provinces.

The rescript tells us in the *principium* and §3 that if there was no division of administration among *contutores* or if the division was made by the *contutores* themselves the *adulescens* could sue one of them *in solidum* and recover the whole sum due to him, but he had to cede to the *tutor* who was sued his own right of action against the others. There is nothing new in the youth's action *in solidum* against one *tutor*, but it does not appear that the plaintiff was required in classical law to cede his actions to the sole defendant, though such cession was certainly competent[61,62]. Any such innovation here[63], though, cannot be regarded as showing a marked decline in legal standards.

The rescript also tells us that if the administration of the *tutela* was divided either by the *praeses* or in accordance with the wishes of the testator, each *tutor* can be summoned for his own administration and that the *tutores* are not at risk for the behaviour of their colleagues unless, through their own fraud or negligence, they did not have a colleague removed by the *crimen suspecti tutoris*, or else they moved the *suspicionis ratio* late when one of them had become insolvent, or else betrayed the pupil's rights by bringing of their own volition the *suspicionis causa*. All this is in accord with classical law[64], except, of course, that the classical texts talk not of the *praeses* but of the *praetor* who is acting in terms of his Edict[65].

In some places in the rescript, but not systematically throughout[66], the position of *curatores* is assimilated to that of *tutores*. This is a process which began considerably

60. Despite earlier doubts it now seems to be generally accepted that the rescript is not interpolated: cf., e.g., Wesener, *Die Durchsetzung von Regressansprüchen im Römischen Recht*, Labeo 11 (1965), pp. 341ff. at p. 353.

61. And otherwise an *actio utilis* might be given to the condemned *tutor*.

62. Cf. Kaser, *Privatrecht* II, p. 330 and n. 25; Wesener, *loc. cit.* The relevant classical texts are: D. 27, 3, 1, 13, 14, 18 (Ulpian 36 *ad ed.*); 27, 3, 21 (Papinian 1 *defin.*); 26, 7, 38, 2 (Idem 12 *quaest.*); 26, 7, 42 (Idem 1 *defin.*); C. 5, 58, 2 [Caracalla, 212]. Ulpian in D. 27, 3, 1, 18 tells us that not only before but even after condemnation the *tutor* can ask for cession of actions against a *contutor*, but the point may be that cession is still possible after condemnation and the text need not indicate that the plaintiff is obliged to cede the rights. Papinian in D. 26, 7, 38, 2 vigorously denies that cession can be compelled.

63. But such a compulsory cession of actions appears—though not against a *contutor*—in C. 4, 65, 13 [Valerianus and Gallienus, 259]; cf. Levy, *Die Konkurrenz der Aktionen und Personen im klassischen Römischen Recht* I (Berlin 1918), p. 238 and n. 2.

64. Cf., e.g., D. 26, 7, 3, 2 (Ulpian 35 *ad ed.*); Buckland, *Textbook*, p. 161; Kaser, *Das Römische Privatrecht* I, 2nd edit. (Munich 1971), p. 362.

65. Cf. Lenel, *Das Edictum perpetuum*, 3rd edit. (Leipzig 1927), pp. 316f.

66. The absence of proper repetition of *seu curatores* is not necessarily to be taken as a sign of interpolation.

earlier than Carus, even though the exact steps in the development have not been traced with precision. From Cassius Dio (consul for the second time in 229) we learn, however, that a minor who has a *curator* was in much the same position as a *pupillus*[67], from rescripts of Septimius Severus and Caracalla that *administratio* properly describes the functions of a *curator*[68]; and from various sources that there might be a plurality of *curatores*[69].

8. C. 7, 2, 9:

Servo tuo defunctus, licet te heredem scripsisse proponatur, tamen directam libertatem dare non potuit: iure enim directo libertatem servis alienis dare nemo potest. [283]

The Emperors declare that a testator cannot directly give liberty to the slave of another even if this last is instituted heir; for, they say, no one can by direct operation of law give liberty to other people's slaves. A perfectly straightforward decision, in keeping with the principles of classical law.

9. C. 3, 28, 17:

Cum filium tuum te praeterita sororem heredem instituisse proponas, inofficiosi querellam apud praesidem provinciae persequi potes. [284]

Carus and his sons tell a mother who was passed over in her son's will in favour of a sister that she has a right to the *querella inofficiosi*. The decision in this case, too, would have been the same in classical law. The plaintiff in the *querella* did not have to be a *suus heres* of the testator, but only a close enough relative, and D. 5, 2, 8, 5 (Ulpian *14 ad ed.*) implies that a mother who was passed over by a son would have the *querella*[70].

Significantly, though, the mother is told she can bring the case *apud praesidem provinciae* and not before the centumviral court.

10. C. 6, 49, 3:

Si per fideicommissum hereditas rei publicae relicta est, ex Trebelliano senatus consulto, quod ab intestato quoque locum habet, quartae partis et fructus eius vobis restitutio competit.

In classical law the decision, would have been the same, namely that, if an inheritance was left by means of a *fideicommissum* to the State, the heir would be able to recover one fourth of the inheritance and its fruits. The rescript is also very clearly and competently expressed.

So far as I am aware the rescript has not been held interpolated but it is likely that such is, in fact, the case. The *senatus consultum Trebellianum* of 56 A.D. was supplemented by the *senatus consultum Pegasianum* of about 73 A.D. and it was this latter which provided the heir could retain one quarter[71]. The Emperor Justinian abolished the

67. 52, 20; cf. Partsch, *Studien zur Negotiorum Gestio* I (Heidelberg, 1913), pp. 87f. and p. 88, n. 1: see also C. 2, 21, 3 [Diocletian, 293].
68. C. 5, 37, 1 [206]; 5, 37, 2 [207].
69. E.g., C. 5, 37, 2; 5, 37, 12 [Gordian, 241]; 5, 43, 2 [Caracalla, 215]; D. 26, 7, 3 *pr* (Ulpian 35 *ad ed.*).
70. Further to the *querella* see above all the texts in D. 5, 2; and cf. now Watson, *The Law of Succession in the Later Roman Republic* (Oxford 1971), pp. 62ff. and the authorities cited.
71. Cf. above all G. 2, 253–259.

senatus consultum Pegasianum, adding *inter alia* its provision about one quarter on to the *senatus consultum Trebellianum*[72]. Hence it might be reasonable to suppose that Carus, Carinus and Numerianus had written of the *senatus consultum Pegasianum* and that this was altered to *Trebellianum* by the compilers.

Finally on the rescript it should be noted that in classical law too, the *senatus consultum* also applied to cases of intestate succession[73].

11. C. 6, 42, 16:

Cum virum prudentissimum Papinianum respondisse non ignoramus etiam legata huiusmodi fideicommisso contineri, id est ubi heres rogatus fuerat, quidquid ex hereditate pervenerit, post mortem restituere, animadvertis etiam praeceptionis compendium testatoris verbis comprehensum esse. 1. Sane quoniam in fideicommissis voluntas magis quam verba plerumque intuenda sunt, si quas pro rei veritate praeterea probationes habes ad commendandam hanc patris voluntatem, quam fuisse adseveras, apud praesidem experiri non vetaris. [283]

A testator appointed his daughter, Isidora, heir—presumably there was at least one other heir—and also left her a *legatum per praeceptionem*, but the daughter was asked to make over *post mortem*, "*quidquid ex hereditate pervenerit*". The daughter is told by the Emperors that also the benefit of the *praeceptio* is included within that clause, and the decision is justified by the reply of Papinian that in such a *fideicommissum* even legacies were included. The decision is straightforward, and there is nothing strange in the heir's being asked to make over the property she received to another *post mortem*[74].

The rescript continues in §1 to observe that, since in *fideicommissa* intention is regarded more than words, the heir is not forbidden to bring an action before the *praeses* if she really has proof of what she declared was her father's intention. Again, nothing here is juridically strange.

But there is an aspect of the rescript that is of considerable interest. The reply is basically unhelpful to the respondent but it is couched in what appear to be tactful terms. Thus the decision that the respondent has to hand over even the *legatum per praeceptionem* is supported by a reference to Papinian; and not only is this put in the most prominent place but the jurist is described as *vir prudentissimus*. Almost, one might feel, the Emperors are taking refuge behind the authority of the jurist. Again in §1 it is noticeable that the Emperors are politely discouraging. Isidora is not told that she is free to bring the action, but that she is not forbidden to bring the action[75].

In this text too, *praeses* show the rescript was directed to a province.

12. C. 8, 53(54), 5:

Si donatio per epistulam facta non paret, verba tamen testamenti, quibus liberalitas testatricis confirmata est, fideicommissum continere non ambigitur. [284]

72. J. 2, 23, 7.
73. Cf., e.g., D. 36, 1, 1, 5 (Ulpian 3 *fid.*).
74. For an extreme instance (impossible after Hadrian) see the will of Dasumius of 108 A.D.; Bruns, *Fontes Iuris Romani*, 7th edit. (Tübingen 1919), pp. 304ff.
75. Just possibly, though, this phrasing reflects the wording of Isidora's letter.

This rescript has often been held interpolated[76]. The approach of Riccobono[77] seems to be extreme. He reconstructs the rescript as follows:

> Donatio per epistulam facta non valet, si mater tua possessionem rerum singularum tibi non tradidit. verba tamen testamenti, quibus liberalitas defunctae matris confirmata est, fideicommissum continere non ambigitur.

He argues (a) a clause was certainly cut out which contained the requirement of *traditio* or *manicipatio* and this is proved by similar texts in the *Fragmenta Vaticana.* (b) The phrase "*non paret*" is new in this context. *Donatio per epistulam* which is not followed by delivery just has no existence. (c) The mention of *testatricis* is irregular especially because the rescript now appears to be composed impersonally. Also it is not exact to say "The *testatrix*'s liberality is confirmed by the will" but "the *testatrix* confirmed in the will the act of donation made in an *inter vivos* transaction". Hence, says Riccobono, the relationship between the respondent, Falconilla and the *testatrix*, probably her mother, would have been given.

But such wide ranging revision of the rescript is unnecessary. The fact which emerges from the rescript and which is most legally relevant is that a *fideicommissum* in the will confirmed a gift of doubtful validity. That is what is stressed in the text, and it is really all that matters. There was no need to say anything about the existence or non-existence of a *traditio* or to declare that the *donatio* was not valid. Again, any argument that a reference to *testatrix* is too impersonal has force only if one assumes—as one has no right to do—that she was a close relative of Falconilla and that this was stated in the letter to the Emperors. Of course, whether the *testatrix* was Falconilla's mother or not is legally irrelevant[78]. Also whether it is strictly logical or not to say "The *testatrix*'s liberality is confirmed by the will", it is a very natural and reasonable way to express the point.

The rescript, in fact, shows that here, too, no change had occurred in the law since the classical period. A *donatio* per *epistulam* was not effective unless it was followed by delivery[79]. *Fideicommissa* were, of course enforceable.

13. C. 9, 22, 9:

> Si docueris apud praesidem provinciae ab intestato te heredem eius extitisse, qui codicillos scripserat, ordinarium est, ut in hereditatis possessione constitutus fideicommissa praebeas, quae iure relicta sunt, nisi consilium est codicillos falsos arguere. 1. Quod si criminaliter coeptum interventu indulgentiae sopitum est, habes tamen residuam indagationem, potest de fide scripturae civiliter quaeri. [284]

In the *principium* an heir on intestacy is told that it is the normal thing, once he has been given possession of the inheritance, to perform the *fideicommissa* which the deceased had written as codicils unless it is his (the heir's) intention to maintain that the codicils are false. There is nothing unclassical or unusual about this. As early as the time of Gaius it was

76. Cf. *Index Itp. Cod.*

77. *Traditio ficta*, ZSS 33 (1912), pp. 259ff. at pp. 288f.; cf. *Mélanges Girard* II (Paris 1912), p. 463.

78. I do not understand the position of Biondi who without explanation seems to regard the text as concerning *donatio* (followed by *fideicommissum*) by a *pater* to a person in his *potestas; Successione testamentaria e donazioni*, 2nd edit. (Milan 1955), p. 717.

79. Cf., e.g., *F.V.* 263 (Papinian 12 *resp.*).

established both that valid *fideicommissa* could be left by someone who was intestate and that the *fideicommissum* could be in an unconfirmed codicil[80].

§1 presents us with greater problems. It tells us that if a criminal action had been begun (against the beneficiary under the codicils) and was stopped by *indulgentia*, the heir on intestacy has another investigation available to him and he can *civiliter quaeri* about the genuineness of the writing. We are, of course, not concerned here with the criminal action but only with the private law.

The problem is to know what private law action is involved. The *principium* made it clear that the heir had not performed the *fideicommissum*, yet he apparently has an action against the beneficiary. As '*habes tamen residuam indagationem*' and '*potest ... civiliter quaeri*' show, what is envisaged is not just the heir's right to an *exceptio* if he is sued by the beneficiary[81]. H. Krüger[82] seems to think of a *querella falsi testamenti*, but such a remedy is nowhere named, though the term *querella falsi* does appear in C. 9, 22, 12 [Diocletian, 293]. Krüger also thinks this *iudicium privatum* appears in ten rescripts, including two earlier than that which concerns us. But these two earlier rescripts are concerned with essentially different situations. C. 9, 22, 2 [Alexander Severus, 223] relates to a debtor's defence that the claim[83] is based on a forgery, and that is also basically the point of C. 9. 22, 5 [Alexander Severus, 230][84]. Neither involves a private law action in which the plaintiff asserts a forgery.

Some of the later rescripts cited by Krüger[85] certainly show that it was possible to bring a private action to impugn the veracity of a will or other document. But these, when they involve the bringing of an action on account of a forgery, with the possible, uncertain exception of C. 9, 22, 24 [Valentinian, Theodosius and Arcadius, 389], all relate to the very different case where the plaintiff argues that something ought to be given to him. In our rescript the action allowed to the respondent is one where he is alleging that there is a forgery, and hence he is not obliged to give something.

The action, indeed, seems to be unnecessary. We would have expected the advice to the respondent to be that if he thought the codicils were forged then he should defend any action the beneficiary brought against him for performance of the *fideicommissum*; or if he paid he should then seek to recover, perhaps by a *condictio* or by an action alleging forgery[86]. The rescript should be regarded, I suggest, as exhibiting post-classical tendencies.

In this text, too, the reference to *praeses provinciae* reveals that the rescript is addressed to someone in a province.

14. C. 4, 54, 6:

Cum te fundum tuum certae rei contemplatione inter vos habita exiguo pretio in alium transtulisse commemoras, poterit ea res tibi non esse fraudi, quando non impleta promissi fide dominii tui ius in suam causam reverti conveniat. et ideo aditus competens iudex fundum cuius

80. Cf., e.g., G. 2, 270, 270a.
81. Though this is one opinion put forward in the Gloss.
82. *Querela non numeratae pecuniae*, ZSS 58 (1938), pp. 1ff. at p. 13.
83. Whether the claim relates to succession or not is not stated.
84. Though the action this time is certainly based on a *fideicommissum*.
85. They are: C. 9, 22, 11 [Diocletian, 287]; 9, 22, 12 [*Idem*, 293]; 9, 22, 16 [*Idem*, 294]; 9, 22, 17, 1 [*Idem*, 294]; 9, 22, 23 [Valens, Gratianus and Valentinian, 376]; 9, 22, 24; *C.Th.* 9, 19, 2 [Constantine, 326].
86. Since there were, apparently, criminal proceedings against the beneficiary, the heir would not even require to vindicate his honour if he did not perform.

mentionem facis restitui tibi cum fructibus suis sine ulla ludificatione sua auctoritate perficiet, praecipue cum diversa pars receptis nummis suis nullam passa videri possit iniuriam.

In consideration of a specific thing an estate was sold at a very low price and the estate was transferred and the price paid. The remainder of the bargain was not performed by the buyer, though it was contained in a pact to the effect that if there was no performance the *ius dominii* would revert to the seller[87]. The seller is now told that the facts do not disclose fraud on his part, and the judge can have the estate and its fruits restored to him, especially because the other party does not seem to have suffered any injury since his money was returned to him[88]. The decision is perfectly in harmony with classical standards[89].

15. C. 2, 55(56), 2:

Si contra compromissum adversarius tuus apud electum arbitrum praesentiam sui facere detrectavit, placitae poenae videtur obnoxius. [283]

Two persons with a dispute made a *compromissum* to have the matter settled by an *arbiter* whom they chose. Contrary to the *compromissum* one did not appear before the *arbiter* and the Emperors declare he is liable to the penalty agreed upon.

There is nothing unclassical in this[90]. The provision of an agreed penalty for non-appearance also existed in classical law. A stipulation for its exaction would have been necessary until Justinian but the taking of a stipulation here is assumed as happens also in classical law. The person chosen to settle the dispute is not the technical *arbiter* of classical procedure, but the term *arbiter* is used of the arbitrator under a *compromissum* also in classical times. For all these points it is enough to point to the texts collected in Digest 4, 8, and even simply to the famous D. 4, 8, 21, 10, 11 (Ulpian *13 ad ed.*).

16. C. 2, 11(12), 19:

Interlocutio praesidis, quae indicta est, infamem eum de quo quaeris fecisse non videtur, cum non specialiter ob iniuriam vel admissam vim condemnatus, sed ita praesidis verbis gravatus est et admonitus, ut ad melioris vitae frugem se reformet. [284]

All that concerns us here is that as in classical times so in 284 A.D. condemnation (*suo nomine*) in an *actio iniuriarum* or an *actio vi bonorum raptorum* automatically resulted in a defendant being rendered *infamis*[91]. It is not surprising that an *interlocutio praesidis* which is *indicta* does not bring *infamia*[92].

Again the rescript was directed to a province.

87. It does not emerge from the rescript whether the pact had a suspensive or resolutive effect; nor probably was this a question put before the Emperors.

88. Felgentraeger, *Antikes Lösungsrecht* (Berlin–Leipzig 1933), p. 109, n. 35 regards *Praecipue —iniuriam* as interpolated, and claims that in Justinian's Code, *praecipue cum* is interpolated; but the usage is frequent in classical Latin: Horace, *Ep.* 2, 1, 261; Pliny, *Ep.* 3, 10, 4; Quintilian, *Inst. Orat.* 9, 2, 85.

89. For pacts in general see De Zulueta, *The Roman Law of Sale* (Oxford 1945), pp. 55ff.

90. Cf. Buckland, *Textbook*, p. 532.

91. Cf., e.g., D. 3, 2, 1 (Julian 1 *ad ed.*); G. 4, 182; *lex Iulia municipalis*, 108ff.

92. Even though a pact does.

The remaining 10 rescripts—C. 4, 20, 4 [284]; 7, 45, 6 [283]; 7, 64, 5 [283]; 7, 64, 6; 9, 46, 4 [283]; 10, 11, 4 [284]; 10, 42(41), 5; 10, 43(42), 1; 10, 48(47), 1; 11, 36(35), 3—do not appear to concern private law and will not be discussed. But 4 of them are certainly directed towards a province[93].

Conclusions

The first and most important conclusion must be that on the eve of Diocletian's accession the legal standard of the jurists of the Imperial chancellery was certainly not contemptible. Admittedly not one of the rescripts portrays great subtlety or admirable creativity, but the quality of decision is reasonably high. Only one rescript, C. 9, 22, 9[94], displays what can be regarded as a derogation from the high standards of classical law, and part of that ruling may perhaps indeed be due to a blunder. One other rescript, C. 5, 52, 2[95], shows, so far as our sources go, an innovation but one which may well be considered an improvement on classical law[96].

Likewise there is apparent no general loosening of the precision of the technical language of the classical jurists with the exception of the one word, *possessio*. And the shift of meaning here had occurred long before Carus, Carinus and Numerianus and even before the end of the classical period.

Secondly, the world of the rescripts is very different from that represented in the books of the classical jurists. Whereas the jurists fix their gaze steadfastly on Rome, 11 of the 26 rescripts of the three Emperors refer directly to the provinces. In respect of social behaviour it is clear that it was common for a *paterfamilias* to emancipate his grown-up sons[97]. And legal formalities were not always observed [98]. Moreover, three rescripts—not examined here—concern public *munera*[99], and two involve *nominatores*[100].

Postscript

Unfortunately a weakness in my cross-indexing system caused me to miss a rescript of 283 A.D. which is to be found in *Cons.* 1.10. The rescript runs:

> Cum fraudis studio transactionem interpositam esse dicas, quod inter vos gestum esi, infirmat iuris auctoritas.

The Emperors declare that a *transactio* which had been made with fraudulent intent has no effect. The decision seems perfectly in keeping with classical law and also with that of the time of Diocletian.

Transactiones were treated as *pacta* and were therefore covered by the edict *de pactis et conventionibus* which ran, *Pacta conventa, quae neque dolo malo neque adversus leges plebis scita senatus consulta decreta principum neque quo fraus cui eorum fiat facta erunt, servabo*[101]. Informal *pacta* which were not covered by the civil law had no legal force

93. C. 7, 45, 6; 7, 64, 5; 7, 64, 6; 10,43 (42), 1.
94. *Supra*, pp. 57 f.
95. *Supra*, pp. 54 f.
96. Possibly there is another novelty in C. 8, 14(15), 4; *supra*, pp. 46 f.
97. Cf., C. 5, 71, 7; 8, 55(56), 3; *supra*, pp. 50 f.
98. Cf., C. 5, 71, 7.
99. C. 10, 42 (41), 5; 10,43 (42), 1; 10, 48 (47), 1.
100. C. 8, 14 (15), 4; 11,36 (35), 3.
101. Cf. Lenel, *Das Edictum perpetuum*, 3rd edit. (Leipzig 1927), p. 65.

except in so far as they were protected by the praetor. Hence since the praetor would not preserve or keep unharmed a fraudulently made *pactum* or *transactio* it would have no legal validity and should be of no effect[102]. This is stated in other texts[103].

Schulz claims that a *pactum* made *dolo malo* was valid[104], hence to the defendant's *exceptio pacti* must be opposed the plaintiff's *replicatio doli*. Whether this opinion is correct or not need not be discussed here since the wording of the rescript of Carus and his sons in *Cons*. 1.10 is vague enough to admit of the interpretation that though the *transactio* is valid it is not eforceable on account of the *dolus*. What matters to us is that in this rescript Carus, Carinus and Numerianus cannot be regarded as giving different law from that of the classical period[105].

This rescript, therefore, is in line with the others of these three Emperors[106].

102. Though, if I have understood him correctly, Schindler claims that the wording of this edict and of that *quod metus causa* says nothing about the nullity or contestability of pacts made *dolo* or *metu*; *Consultatio veteris cuiusdam iurisconsulti*, Labeo 8 (1962), pp. 16 ff. at p. 28.

103. Cf. e.g. *Cons*. 1.6 [196 A.D.], 7 [213 A.D.] (= C. 2.3.6, with an alteration), 8 [222 A.D.]; C. 2.4.13 [290 A.D.]; 2.19.7 [293 A.D.]. Some of these concern *metus*, not *dolus*, but that should not affect the point at issue.

104. *Die Lehre vom erzwungenen Rechtsgeschäft im antiken römischen Recht*, ZSS 43 (1922), pp. 17 ff. at p. 194; on this view see now Schindler, *Consultatio*, pp. 27 ff., and the authors he cites.

105. Though it was not stated, the rescript assumes that the *transactio* was formless and was not made by *stipulatio*. The questioner may have made that plain.

106. It should be observed that it may be suspected though not proved that this rescript too was destined for a province: the addressee was a certain Aurelius, the name taken by those who gained citizenship as a result of the *constitutio Antoniniana*.

6

The Rescripts of the Emperior Probus (276-282 AD)

Scholars tend to date the onset of the "post-classical period" of Roman law to 235 A.D., the year when the Emperor Alexander Severus was murdered by his troops. The line of great jurists had just about come to an end—Ulpian had been murdered by the mutinous Praetorians in 223—and for the next fifty years, until the accession of Diocletian, the Empire was in a state of chaos.

The post-classical period itself divides neatly into eras: early post-classical (or epiclassic as F. Wieacker suggests[1]), Diocletianic, Constantinian, and so on, right up to the time of Justinian. One thing these eras have in common is relative neglect by modern legal historians. Yet, they have a charm and fascination of their own. The charm is that, for the first time in Roman law, we have primarily to study texts that we know concerned real people and real situations; the sources, almost entirely imperial rescripts,[2] reflect the immediate practical concerns of the addressees, not the interests of the jurists. The fascination lies not only in observing the changes in legal institutions as people react to new social, political, economic, and religious pressures, but, above all, in tracing the growth of state interference with personal relations and dealings. A change takes place that has suggestive parallels with Britain and elsewhere in the 19th and 20th centuries.

In an earlier study,[3] I examined the private law in the rescripts of Carus and his two sons, the Emperors who ruled from 282 to 284, immediately before the accession of Diocletian, and found as the main conclusion that, despite everything, the quality of legal decision had remained reasonably high. This paper considers the four rescripts that survive from the troubled reign of the preceding Emperor, Probus. Probus was pushed to the fore by Syria and Egypt in 276 after the murder by his troops (or death induced by threats) of the Emperor Tacitus, and he outmanoeuvered Florianus, who was favoured by the rest of the Empire. Probus was accepted as Emperor when Florianus was put to death by his own soldiers

---

* Professor of Civil Law, University of Edinburgh. M.A. 1954, LL.B. 1957, University of Glasgow; M.A. 1958, D. Phil. 1960, D.C.L. 1973, University of Oxford.

[1] Wieacker, *Le Droit romain de la Mort d'Alexandre Sévère à l' Avènement de Dioclétien (235-284 apr. J.-C.)*, 49 Revue Historique de Droit français et étranger 201, 223 (1971). That article is mainly devoted to an examination of the rescripts of Gordian (238-244).

[2] For Egypt one must add the papyri.

[3] Watson, *Private Law in the Rescripts of Carus, Carinus and Numerianus*, 41 Tijdschrift voor Rechtsgeschiedenis 19 (1973).

in the autumn of that year. After a reign marked by much fighting against internal and external enemies, Probus was—inevitably it seems—killed by his own men in 282.

Surprisingly, through all the chaos in the half century after 235, the imperial chancellery continued its work.

The first rescript of Probus, addressed to a man named Fortunatus, has survived without a date.

> C. 5.4.9. Si vicinis vel aliis scientibus uxorem liberorum procreandorum causa domi habuisti et ex eo matrimonio filia suscepta est, quamvis neque nuptiales tabulae neque ad natam filiam pertinentes factae sunt, non ideo minus veritas matrimonii aut susceptae filiae suam habet potestatem.
>
> If, with the knowledge of neighbours or other persons, you had at home a wife for the sake of procreating children, and from that marriage a daughter was recognised by you, then although no relevant documents were drawn up for the marriage or for the birth of your daughter, none the less the truth about your marriage or the daughter you recognised has its full validity.

This is one of numerous post-classical rescripts on marriage, and is primarily concerned with the very existence of and evidence for the marriage of Fortunatus. The text tells us that no written document was drawn up attesting the marriage, and while we are left in no doubt that such a document was legally unnecessary, it is evident that such documents were common. Fortunatus' worries as to the validity of his marriage and the status of his daughter are obviously caused by the non-existence of documents. It also emerges that at this time, as in classical law, no religious or civil ceremony was needed to mark the wedding; from the silence of the text we might even deduce—with only slight hesitation—that there had been no ceremony since otherwise it would have provided valuable evidence of the parties' intentions. What was important[4] in classical law and later for the beginning of marriage was that the woman be taken to the man's home,[5] and there is some indication of this in the word *domi*, "at home." Yet, though this taking home was of great significance, it was not sufficient to distinguish marriage from concubinage. The former also required *affectus maritalis*, the intention to be married. The chancellery emphasises this requirement by declaring that if Fortunatus had a wife with the intention of procreating children, then the union was marriage.

[4] At least where the wedding was *inter absentes*, the *deductio in domum* was essential. Another early post-classical rescript, from the reign of Aurelian, C. 5.3.6, shows that where, as usual, the wedding was *inter praesentes*, marriage was considered to begin when the bride was in the bridegroom's house.

[5] *Cf., e.g.*, P. Corbett, The Roman Law of Marriage 95 (1930).

This phrasing is reasonable and in no way unfavourable since Fortunatus wishes the union—from which he has a daughter—to be recognised as marriage.[6]

More interesting is the question of evidence. Something more than the unsupported statement of the man is wanted, yet there is no document and apparently no ceremony. Knowledge of neighbours or other people of how the parties regarded themselves is sufficient for the purpose. It is the mental attitude behind decisions of this kind that opens the way to the much later (and non-Roman) constitution of marriage "by habit and repute."

Fortunatus is also concerned about the status of the daughter whom he had accepted as his. Again, her status had not been recorded in a document,[7] but he is given reassurance.[8]

To judge from the tense *habuisti*, "you *had* a wife at home," Fortunatus' wife is dead. In this case it is most likely that Fortunatus will have wanted the marriage to be established to avoid some of the disabilities that were imposed on the unmarried and childless.[9]

There is nothing surprising in the legal decision—no derogation from classical standards, no post-classical innovation. Most striking is the rescript's banality. Why should anyone need an imperial rescript on this point? Indeed, how could anyone at that period enter a marriage with no ceremony or celebration, no formalities or writing? If the bride had brought the bridegroom a dowry, the amount, terms, and conditions must also have been unrecorded in writing. The answer can only be that Fortunatus, although a Roman citizen, was of the lowlier classes. Legal advice at the highest level was not restricted to the rich and powerful.

A second rescript dates from 280 and is addressed to a woman Massicia.

---

[6] Interestingly, in the Republic the censors took an oath from certain citizens at least that they would have a wife for the sake of procreating children. Aulus Gellius, Noctes Atticae 4.3.2., 17.21.44.

[7] For a discussion of these documents see F. Lanfranchi, Ricerche sul valore giuridico delle dichiarazioni di nascita in diritto romano (1951).

[8] S. Solazzi considers there are interpolations in the rescript, and above all that there was no reference to a daughter or to other people, apart from neighbours, being aware of the existence of the marriage. Solazzi, *Pater est quem nuptiae demonstrant,* 7 IURA 131, 136 (1956). But he seems overcritical. He feels that the chancellery would not have written "*aut susceptae filiae*" but "*et susceptae filiae*" if her status had been in question. But the use of "*aut*" seems perfectly natural. And he seems to take "*vel aliis*" as referring to malicious persons, gossips and such like. But if *alii* are called upon, it is people who know the situation and who can testify to the *existence* of the marriage.

[9] *See, e.g.,* W. Buckland, A Text-Book of Roman Law from Augustus to Justinian 292 *et seq.* (3d ed. P. Stein 1963).

> C. 8.53.4. Si functiones per eum, cui donata res non erat, vel ab actoribus ipsius nomine celebratae sunt, tibi obesse non potest.
>
> If the taxes on a thing were paid by a person to whom the thing had not been given, or by agents acting in his name, this fact can not cause you harm.

The rescript also appears in the *Fragmenta Vaticana* 288, which reveals that originally it was considerably longer. Sadly, *Fr. Vat.* 288 itself is in a very fragmentary state and cannot be reconstructed with any degree of certainty,[10] but it does fill in the background. It appears that Massicia had intended to make a gift—quite possibly there was even a document relating the gift[11]—but the gift was never completed, and she remained owner of the thing in question. The "donee" either personally or through his agents paid the taxes (*functiones*) on the thing in his own name and Probus reassures Massicia that this act is not prejudicial to her.[12]

In this instance too, there is little to be said about the law in the case. As in classical law, so in this rescript, there was no complete gift until the donor transferred the thing by physical delivery.[13] Until the gift was complete, he or she had a perfect legal right to change his mind. Likewise, a non-owner did not become owner (or affect the real owner's title) by acting as if he were the owner.

But the text falls neatly into the post-classical social scene in two ways. First, the rescript is one of several—the third rescript of Probus is another—that concern a gift where the donor changed his mind, either before the gift was complete or, too late, after the gift had been made.[14] The whole topic of gift, in fact, has an unexpected prominence in the post-classical sources. Indeed, in what is in effect the preamble to his famous constitution of 316 A.D.

---

[10] For very different reconstructions see 2 J. Baviera, Fontes Iuris Romani Antejustiniani 526 (2d ed. 1964); P. Girard & F. Senn, Textes de droit romain 533 (7th ed. 1967); E. Huschke, Iurisprudentiae Auteiustinianae quae supersunt 798 (5th ed. 1886). In the sixth edition of Huschke, most of the gaps in the text are left unreconstructed. 2 E. Huschke, Iurisprudentiae Auteiustinianae quae supersunt 304 (6th ed. E. Seckel & B. Kübler 1927).

[11] The text is too fragmentary for us to establish the rôle of this document. C. 8.53.1, which is dated 210 A.D., allows transfer of ownership by delivery of a document without a corresponding delivery of the thing, but the almost universal opinion of modern scholars is that this rescript, as it stands, cannot give the law of that period (or even of Justinian). *Cf., e.g.*, 2 M. Kaser, Das römische Privatrecht 203, n.68 (1959); E. Levy, West Roman Vulgar Law 146-48 (1951).

[12] S. Riccobono regards the rescript in C. 8.53.(54).4 as interpolated by Justinian and would delete the "*non.*" Riccobono, *Traditio ficta*, 33 Zeitschrift der Savigny Stiftung 259, 290-92 (1912).

[13] Or bound himself by a contract such as *stipulatio*.

[14] There seem to be six further instances of "repentance" before Diocletian: C. 5.16.11, 8.55(56).1, 8.55(56).2, 8.55(56).3, 9.34.2; Fr. Vat. 272.

reforming the law of gift, the Emperor Constantine declares he has investigated many actions arising from gifts, and he enumerates as one of the causes of the disputes, incomplete gifts being taken as perfected, *"inchoata pro perfectis . . . controversiam faciant."*[15] Secondly, as is the case with many rescripts, the addressee is a woman. It would appear that they had as much right as men to approach the Emperor for a legal opinion, and that many were fully active in looking after their interests.

The third rescript, from the year 277, is addressed to one Felix.

> C. 8.55(56).2. Si apud provinciae praesidem aviam filiae tuae quasi paenitentia ductam subtracta instrumenta donationum igni exussisse constiterit, vereri te non oportet, ne id, quod iure vires acceperat, ex post facto possit in dubium revocari.

> If it was established in front of the provincial governor that the grandmother of your daughter, guided by a change of heart as it were, took back the documents of gifts and burned them, you need not fear that what had achieved legal efficacy can be rendered doubtful by subsequent conduct.

The basic point of the rescript is plain: a validly made gift cannot be revoked by subsequent behaviour of a donor who has changed his mind. In all probability the rescript has been shortened: a gift of a physical thing to be complete required that there be delivery of the thing. Nothing is said about delivery in the rescript as it stands, and it is reasonable to think that some reference to delivery has been cut out for the sake of brevity. The point, however, is not very material.

What is important, though, is what the rescript reveals about the mistaken views of non-lawyers on the state of the law. A gift required no writing and, indeed, writing had no role to play in the substantive law. (In practice, however, a written document might serve as some evidence that a gift had been made, though the sources stress that a document, even one filed with a public office, did not mean there was a gift unless delivery had occurred.[16] Certainly, however, the document would reveal the donor's intention to make a gift.) Yet, here we have a grandmother who had made gifts tearing up the relevant documents obviously with the intention to revoke. Presumably, she was under the impression that the documents were important for the efficacy of the gifts.

---

[15] Fr. Vat. 249. The constitution is repeated (with alterations) in C. Th. 8.12.1 and C. 8.53.25, but in these versions the preamble has been excised.

[16] *Cf., e.g.,* Fr. Vat. 263, 266a, 268, 285, 297; D. 41.2.48 (Papinian *10 resp.*), 6.1.77 (Ulpian *17 ad ed.*).

The fourth rescript is addressed to Octavianus in 278.

> C. 2.16(17).1. Saepe rescriptum est ante sententiam signa rebus, quas aliquis [*alius*—Mommsen] tenebat, imprimi non oportere. et ideo ea rebus aut fructibus apud te constitutis illicite imposita poteris ipse licite detrahere, ut amotis his causa, quae ex officio tibi infertur, terminetur.
>
> It has often been laid down by rescript that, before a legal decision, it is not proper to set seals on things which another person was holding. Hence when seals were illegally placed on things or their fruits which had been placed in your keeping, you can lawfully remove the seals, so that when they have been removed, the action which is brought against you by public officials may come to an end.

This is one of only two rescripts in the title of the Code, 2.16(17), concerned with the proposition that no one, without the authority of a judge, should place seals on things that another person has under his control. The other rescript is rather later, from the reign of Diocletian. The opening clause of our rescript, however, shows that it was by no means the first on the subject.[17]

The precise situation confronting Octavianus cannot be wholly reconstructed. It is possibly safe to assume that the rescript in its present guise has been rather generalised to give it wider applicability. However that may be, the general situation is plain. Octavianus had been given custody of property of which he was not owner.[18] Another person—probably the owner or someone who claimed real rights over the property—set his seal upon the objects in question, although Octavianus claims that he had no judicial decision to support this behaviour. Exactly what real right was being claimed by this party cannot be established since the act of sealing did not amount to a claim of any particular title.[19] In any event, the effect of the presence of the seals on the property was to make it appear that Octavianus had no right to physical custody, and public officials then brought an action against Octavianus, presumably to make him give up control. Octavianus asked the Emperor for a ruling and was, of course, told that since the seals had been affixed unlawfully he could simply remove them, and this would bring the official action against him to an end.

---

[17] It was common for a rescript to claim support from the fact that the same proposition had also been laid down in earlier rescripts.

[18] This appears from the use of the word "*constitutis*," which would be oddly used if Octavianus had control of property which he owned.

[19] Thus, in C. 2.16(17).2 it is envisaged that the person who sets his seal improperly on property held by another might be the owner or the pledge creditor. For other instances of sealing see the texts referred to in the entries *signo* and *signum* in 5 Vocabularium Iurisprudentiae Romanae 543 *et seq.* (1939).

The purpose behind the legal rule is to avoid self-help: a person who believes he has a legal right to a thing must not take steps to assert his control until he has a judgement in his favour. Rulings of such kind are prominent at all periods of Roman law. Of great interest is the reason Octavianus wishes the rescript, namely to bring to a close a certain mode of conduct by state officials. Examination of post-classical rescripts shows this to be a very common purpose, whether or not it is alleged that the conduct of the officials is improper.

These, then, are the surviving rescripts of the Emperor Probus. None contains a great legal innovation; none shows a drastic lowering of legal standards. Their importance lies in what they reveal about general matters. Despite the enormous military and economic problems of the age, the imperial chancellery functioned; rescripts were issued to the most ordinary individuals, men and women alike. There was no need for a rescript to be concerned with an important principle or difficult point of law. Whereas the classical jurists write as if they were concerned only with law at Rome itself, the rescripts show the practical realities: one of them, C. 8.55(56).2, with its mention of the *provinciae praeses* was obviously addressed to a person in a province, and it is probable that others, even all of them, were too. What is possibly most revealing of all is that every one of them is saying in effect that "lawyers' formalities" are not conclusive or are not effective in law, that truth is to prevail over writing or acts.[20]

---

[20] I am grateful to Professor A.M. Honoré for his comments on a draft of this paper. Honoré's own paper on the making and authorship of early post-classical rescripts, which will appear in 3 Aufstieg und Niedergang der römischen Welt (H. Temporini ed.), will be fundamental for all future research.

7

Legal Change: Sources of Law and Legal Culture

I. Introduction

The most important general legal questions, it seems to me, both in theory and practice, concern, first, the nature of the relationship between a society and the legal rules that operate within it, and, second, the forces that cause law to change. The questions are obviously intimately connected. Yet so little serious scholarship—scholarship based on legal and other materials rather than on an ideologically predetermined position that dictates the conclusions—has been devoted to these questions that even deciding where to start an investigation or which lines of research to pursue presents formidable problems. My researches into the growth of the law, including the vagaries of legal development,[1] have resulted in four related books; and none of the last three was foreseen by me when the previous one was published.

I wish in this paper to reconsider my main conclusions, especially in the light of criticism, and attempt a new synthesis. My approach was dictated by disappointment with the results of traditional comparative

---

[1] *See, e.g.*, Watson, *The Definition of Furtum and the Trichotomy*, 28 Revue d'Histoire du Droit 197 (1960) (The threefold division of theft, into theft of a thing, theft of use, and theft of possession, which appeared in civil law countries did not exist in Roman law. It was derived by later scholars from a poorly constructed definition of theft in Justinian's *Institutes* which led professors deliberately to alter the wording of the definition in the *Digest.*); Watson, *The Development of Marital Justifications for Malitiosa Desertio in Roman-Dutch Law*, below, chapter 19, pp. 213ff. (For a time the South African courts recognized neither constructive desertion nor justifications for desertion, following the views of Dutch jurists, notably Hendrik Brouwer (1625-1683) who may have misunderstood the German, Henning Arnisaeus (died 1636?). But as a result of misunderstanding Brouwer, the courts reverted to the position of Arnisaeus, and accepted both constructive desertion and marital justifications for desertion.); Watson, *Some Cases of Distortion by the Past in Classical Roman Law*, 31 Revue d'Histoire du Droit 69 (1963); Watson, *The Notion of Equivalence of Contractual Obligation and Classical Roman Partnership*, 97 Law Q. Rev. 275 (1981) (Of all Roman contracts, only partnership involves the notion that the contracting parties benefit or suffer loss in the ratio of their contribution, and this resulted from the fact that partnership originated in the law of succession.).

law, legal history, and sociology of law.

Traditional comparative law does not seek systematically to explain differences and similarities between legal rules and approaches to law in various systems. Usually explanation is merely incidental to a primarily descriptive work. Examples can be chosen from two books by noted authors. J.P. Dawson in *Oracles of the Law* seems to be content to consider different systems of law at different times.[2] He draws no conclusions embracing the various systems from his investigations. Barry Nicholas in *French Law of Contract,* limits his efforts to an attempt to set out the elements of a branch of one legal system as they appear to someone familiar with another system.[3] However excellent these two books (and others like them) may be, they reveal very little about the general features of legal change or about the direction of change, even when they deal expressly with sources of law and even though they contain much legal history.

Legal history seemed to offer better prospects for an understanding of legal change. Any theory of the relationship between law and society must rest, I believe, on detailed knowledge of the history of individual legal systems. Indeed, an investigation into several systems is necessary if one is to discover general causes of legal change. The tendency to focus on only one system explains the three weaknesses commonly found in works of traditional legal history. The first derives from the fact that it is always possible to find immediate local causes that impel any legal change. Concentration on one system may cause one to overlook similar changes in other systems, all of which may be partially explained in terms of transnational factors. For instance, to understand codification in French law and the sharp distinction it draws between public law and private law, it is not enough to look simply at conditions in France: one must also take into account the fact that codification and a sharp distinction between public and private law are both much more frequently found in civil law systems than they are in common law systems. One must always ask why a particular change occurred and not another. Second, concentration on one legal system means that it is easy to overlook the extent to which that system is indebted to another. English legal historians, for example, frequently have underestimated the impact of Roman law on English law.[4]

The third common weakness is that legal historians tend to con-

---

[2] J. P. Dawson, The Oracles of the Law (1968).

[3] B. Nicholas, French Law of Contract v (1982).

[4] This does not apply to all English legal historians, particularly not to J. Barton, Roman Law in Medieval England (*Ius Romanum Medii Aevi*) part V, at 13a (1971).

centrate on change and innovation. They wish to explain why an innovation occurred when it did. But to understand law and society one must also explain why a legal change did not occur when society changed, or when perceptions about the quality of the law changed. Why, one must always ask, did the legal change not occur before? One example may suffice. England has permitted divorce (other than through an act of the legislature) since 1857. A.H. Manchester explains the timing of the change in the law in terms of the demise of Utilitarianism (whose proponents, such as Bentham, valued stability of marriage) as the dominant philosophy, and its replacement by individualism.[5] The similar change in America, led by Pennsylvania in 1785, is explained rather differently by L. Friedman. He finds that only then did the modern concept of the family reach fruition, and marriage (perceived as a life-long arrangement when the family was the center of social organization, and when domestic intimacy was greater) was unable to bear the strain.[6] At the very best, however, these explanations can only be partial. Among European countries that became Protestant at the time of the Reformation, England was exceptional in not permitting divorce. The dominant view among Protestant theologians of the time, including those in England, was that marriage was not a sacrament: it could be dissolved by humans and should not be a matter for the ecclesiastical courts. For instance, among the "High" school of theology, both J. Cosin and H. Hammond expressed the view that divorce and remarriage were both possible. The highly revered Martin Bucer in a book dedicated to King Edward VI favored divorce. The *Reformatio Legum Ecclesiasticarum* which was drafted by Thomas Cranmer, submitted in 1552, and published in 1571, and which is regarded as a true index of contemporary Protestant opinion, also favored divorce. The *Reformatio* was never enacted. Moreover, it seems that from 1548 to 1602 (apart from the reign of Mary) divorce operated in practice.[7] In these circumstances, an explanation of a change in the law to permit divorce in England in the nineteenth century (and rather earlier in North America to which English law had been transplanted) cannot satisfactorily be restricted to happenings and attitudes at the time of the appropriate legislation. A convincing explanation must also explain why England was an exception to the general rule that Protestant countries introduced divorce, why the ecclesiastical courts there retained

---

[5] A. H. MANCHESTER, A MODERN LEGAL HISTORY OF ENGLAND AND WALES 360 (1980). Bentham himself had favored the possibility of divorce.

[6] L. FRIEDMAN, A HISTORY OF AMERICAN LAW 183 (1973).

[7] *See* G. E. HOWARD, 2 A HISTORY OF MATRIMONIAL INSTITUTIONS 73-80 (1904).

jurisdiction, and why (if particular historical factors prevailing around 1530 account for the failure to introduce divorce) in the conditions prevailing after the reign of Henry VIII, it took so long for England to permit divorce.

Sociology of law, as it is usually practiced, provides the least help in understanding legal change and the relationship between legal rules and the society in which they operate. The lack of a historical dimension means there is no way to measure the speed—or absence thereof—of a response to changed circumstances. Equally important, the emphasis on law-in-action blurs appreciation of the extent to which law may be dysfunctional. In all legal conflicts there will be winners and losers, but this by no means necessarily indicates that the legal rules are the best that could be devised and imposed upon society for the benefit of the winners. The legal rules may be unduly cumbrous, complex, or ambiguous. Transactional costs may be unnecessarily high. To notice that in court actions an advantage always rests with those able to pay for the best legal services or those most accustomed to using legal services—important though that is—does not indicate that the relevant rules are the most advantageous that could be achieved for these people. That a society or its ruling elite will not tolerate law that is destructive of the society or its elite does not imply that the operating rules are the most suitable for the society or for its elite. That law generally operates to protect the *status quo,* and hence to protect those having power, does not in itself mean that the rules are the best that could be achieved by the power elite.[8] A close scrutiny of the effect of law-in-action often results in a failure to consider the options that are available to, and knowable by, those able to effect changes in the law.

There are, of course, numerous works of legal history written from a sociological perspective, and they provide many insights. Certainly, the sociological perspective is necessary for any understanding of legal development. I am not arguing that the way law operates in practice is to be discounted. On the contrary, it is very relevant. But a focus on law-in-action leads to a discounting of the importance of legal rules and to a lack of awareness of their imperfections and their impact.

It would appear that the issues that are the concern of traditional comparative law, legal history, and sociology of law, and the methodology appropriate to these disciplines, will not lead scholars to satisfying answers to the two questions I posed at the outset of this Article. To understand the nature of legal change and the relationship between le-

---

[8] In a time of revolution, a new power elite may use law to change the *status quo* to its own advantage. The principle is the same.

gal rules and society, I believe it is necessary to look at a number of legal systems and at the changes in them over a long period of time. What is needed is an approach based on a combination of traditional comparative law, legal history, and sociology of law.

A first step, the realization of the enormous extent of legal transplants, resulted in *Legal Transplants.*[9] Borrowing from another system is the most common form of legal change. For proof of this, one need only consider the reception of Roman law in later Europe; the spread of English law through the countries of the common law, even into parts of the United States never under British rule; the impact of the French *Code civil* on the other civil law systems, and the extent to which the law of one state in the United States is affected by that of the others.

The power of law to survive through centuries is equally apparent. As a consequence a great deal, if not most, of law operates in a territory for which it was not originally designed, or in a society which is radically different from that which created the law. These phenomena highlight the impact of authority for legal change, whether the authority is that of a particular legal system such as that of ancient Rome or of individual lawyers such as Blackstone.

A second book, *Society and Legal Change,*[10] has essentially negative conclusions. It appeared to me that rules of Western private law were (and are) out of step with the needs and desires both of the society in which they operated (and operate) and of its ruling elite to an extent that renders existing theories of legal development and of the relationship between law and society implausible. Not only were and are legal rules often dysfunctional, but awareness of this by those in a position to effect change frequently did not (and does not) lead to improvement of the law.

In a third book, *The Making of the Civil Law,*[11] this time restricted to those Western systems usually called "civil law systems," I attempted to show that the legal tradition itself played an enormous role in the development of legal rules and approaches to law.

The fourth and most recent book, *Sources of Law; Legal Change and Ambiguity,*[12] is devoted to the proposition that for very long

---

[9] A. WATSON, LEGAL TRANSPLANTS, AN APPROACH TO COMPARATIVE LAW (1974) [hereinafter cited as LEGAL TRANSPLANTS].

[10] A. WATSON, SOCIETY AND LEGAL CHANGE (1977) [hereinafter cited as LEGAL CHANGE].

[11] A. WATSON, THE MAKING OF THE CIVIL LAW (1981) [hereinafter cited as CIVIL LAW].

[12] A. WATSON, SOURCES OF LAW; LEGAL CHANGE AND AMBIGUITY (forthcoming, University of Pennsylvania Press, 1984) [hereinafter cited as SOURCES].

stretches of time Western systems make do with sources of law that are inadequate for the development of satisfactory or unambiguous law. Once again, awareness of these deficiencies in the sources of law by those in a position to make improvements frequently does not lead to reform.

I now wish to put these four books together, but in a different order, in the hope of achieving a synthesis.

II. The Making of the Civil Law

Let me start with the third book in the sequence, which has met with considerable criticism from J.P. Dawson.[13] That criticism, I think, illustrates the strength of my case. My central theme was that the legal elements that have gone into the makeup of modern Western legal systems are everywhere the same. Modern scholars, however, divide most of these systems into either civil law systems or common law systems. The difference is the consequence of civil law systems' adoption, in whole or in part, of Justinian's *Corpus Juris Civilis* of the sixth century A.D. as law of the land or at least as direct and highly persuasive authority.[14] Modern common law systems also borrowed much of their substantive law from Rome. The distinguishing factor between the two types of systems is that modern civil law also adopted the *Corpus Juris Civilis* as the organizing instrument. The parts of the *Corpus Juris* that concern us most are the *Code,* a collection of legal pronouncements by the Emperors; the *Digest,* a collection of fragments from the writings of jurists of the late Roman Republic and, more especially, of the classical period; and the *Institutes,* an elementary textbook for first-year law students, which also had the force of law. Together these works contain a huge mass of legal learning.

Dawson rightly points out that the *Digest* is "the most admired . . . part of the *Corpus Juris,*" but he thinks I take from the Roman jurists who are recorded in the *Digest* their predominant position and instead elevate the elementary textbook for first-year law students, Justinian's *Institutes* to this position (at least for the years 1500 to 1800).[15] He rightly says that I argue that inevitably any society that accepts the *Corpus Juris* as being in force "gives a place of particular honor to Justinian's *Institutes,*"[16] and he also quotes (as an example of "simi-

---

[13] Dawson, Book Review, 49 U. Chi. L. Rev. 595 (1982).

[14] Civil Law, *supra* note 11, at 4. I also accept as civil law systems those that derive from such systems.

[15] Dawson, *supra* note 13, at 596.

[16] Civil Law, *supra* note 11, at 62.

larly extreme statements")[17] my assertion that "particular prominence falls on Justinian's *Institutes,* because it is both the fundamental book for beginners and is the authoritative attempt to give a systematic structure to law."[18] Dawson has not quite taken my point, especially when he says that I make the students' handbook "appear as the most important surviving monument of Roman Law."[19] To say, as I do, that the *Institutes* will be given "a place of particular honor" is not to say that in every regard they will be viewed as the predominant part of the *Corpus Juris.* I merely argued that their particular and inevitable role was to provide the basic *structure* of modern civil law systems. From any perspective, the *Digest* and, to a lesser extent, the *Code* would provide more of the substance of law, and especially more of the detailed rules.

Nor is the reason for this role of the *Institutes* hard to find: they were the only part of the *Corpus Juris Civilis* in which the law was set forth in a reasonably satisfactory, systematic way. To my knowledge, no one has ever regarded the arrangement of the *Digest* as systematic—not even in 533, the year of its promulgation—and criticism of its structure has been loud and prolonged. Given the emphasis in teaching from the *Corpus Juris* and the correlative neglect of other law, the relative coherence of the structure of the *Institutes,* and the unsystematic structure of the rest of the *Corpus Juris* and other works on local law, it was only reasonable and natural to use the *Institutes* as the model.

Dawson notes that I describe "at length writings of the sixteenth through the nineteenth centuries that, appropriating the title of *Institutes,* gave short and elementary summaries of rules of strictly local origin and application,"[20] and he says that "these later *Institutes* varied greatly in style, arrangement and quality."[21] But these later *Institutes* did not only appropriate the name *Institutes,* they also appropriated many of the characteristics of Justinian's handbook. Above all, they are short systematic summaries of local law, and the great majority of them have unmistakably the general (even detailed) arrangement of Justinian's *Institutes.*[22]

---

[17] Dawson, *supra* note 13, at 596 n.3.

[18] Civil Law, *supra* note 11, at 103. I come much closer to the truth, he suggests, when elsewhere I describe the *Institutes* as an "elementary textbook [that] never stood in first place as a statement of the law. The *Digest* and the *Code* were both treated much more seriously." *Id.* at 136.

[19] Dawson, *supra* note 13, at 596.

[20] *Id.* at 596-97.

[21] *Id.* at 597.

[22] Let me give just one additional early example that I did not discuss in my book because, although it was written by a civilian and under civilian pressures, it was not produced in a civil law country: John Cowell's *Institutiones Juris Anglicani* (1608).

Even the standard variations from Justinian in those later *Institutes*—the frequent omission of procedure and of criminal law—are explicable only on the basis of the civilian tradition: the former, because the heroes of the civil law systems were professors uninterested in what happened in court; both, because Roman procedure and criminal law were neglected by the professors teaching the *Corpus Juris.*[23]

Dawson correctly observes that some of these local *Institutes* "had the evident purpose of interposing barriers to the spread of Roman law by preserving local idiosyncracies or advancing new and original points of view."[24] But it then becomes even more significant that works of this type, such as Georg Beyer's, *Delineatio Juris Germanici* (1718), adopted the overall structure of Justinian's *Institutes.* The structure had become endemic, and even works intended to inhibit the spread of Roman rules popularized the structure of the Roman handbook.

Actually, the appeal of Justinian's *Institutes* for those trying to systematise the local law was so powerful that the *Institutes* sometimes served as the principal model for legal works on subjects even when it was inappropriate. For example, it was used as a model for feudal law in Sam Stryk's (1640-1710) *Examen juris feudalis* and Alexander Bruce's (died 1729) *Principia juris feudalis;* for German public law in J.F. Rhetius's (1630-1707) *Institutiones juris publici Germanici Romani;* for German town law in the seventeenth century, in *Lübeck, Statuta, Stadt-Recht und Ordnungen;* and even for a commentary on Justinian's *Novellae* in P. Gudelinus's (1550-1619) *Commentarii de iure novissimo.*

Dawson rightly proceeds to emphasize "the strenuous and concerted effort of medieval minds to comprehend and adapt to their own needs the massive legacy in law from antiquity."[25] And he emphasizes the intellectual demands on those who made use of the enormous volume of complex literature. He says, but does not further explain: "It was a formidable compilation of book learning whose transmission and elaboration were almost necessarily functions of learned men, most of

---

This short account of English law is divided into books and chapters, all of which correspond precisely in their placing and even in their titles, to the books and chapters of Justinian's *Institutes.* Cowell does not even add a single new chapter.

[23] Dawson rightly says that I see these *Institutes* of local law as "the direct descendants of Justinian's *Institutes,*" but does not say that he disagrees. Dawson, *supra* note 13, at 597 n.4 (quoting CIVIL LAW, *supra* note 11, at 65). If he does disagree, I should like to know what model he thinks inspired so many *Institutes* from different jurisdictions, having striking similarities with one another and, incidentally, with Justinian's handbook.

[24] Dawson, *supra* note 13, at 597.

[25] *Id.*

them sponsored by universities."[26] But why, in contrast to early common law, was there so much book learning, whose elaboration was almost necessarily the function of learned men, most of whom were predominantly professors (even if they also practiced)? For me, there is only one satisfactory answer to these questions: Justinian's *Corpus Juris Civilis* was treated as authoritative. When a complex, ancient, written work is treated as important for the law, the obvious way to learn it is from the books themselves, not from observing practitioners at work. The old books with all their (and with subsequent related) complexities will have to be expounded by learned men; the learned men will generate further elaboration, and they will teach and study in something akin to universities rather than Inns of Court.[27]

It must be stressed that regarding the *Corpus Juris* as authoritative in the conditions of medieval Europe, resulted in the neglect of the remainder of local law (apart from canon law) in university-style education. There are two main reasons for this. First, most local law was unwritten, to be discovered as custom by the courts; and authoritative treatment of it was not open to professors. Second, local law was very local: professors who were ambitious for money or fame would want to be known outside of their immediate territory, and would opt for the international discipline.[28] Other local law would be and was downgraded, and the law in the *Corpus Juris* became still more stressed.

It was also precisely because the tasks of understanding the *Corpus Juris Civilis,* of explicating it, and even of reinterpreting it to fit modern local conditions, were so mammoth that, in my opinion, it took centuries before scholars were able to produce new syntheses, as Dawson says, "to sketch designs for a more harmonious and durable edifice of ideas of a kind that Roman law had never had."[29] What Dawson omits to mention is that these designs in France as well as in Italy, Holland, and Germany were, for the most part, primarily based on the structure of Justinian's *Institutes.* These designs, in turn, became the model for the most distinctive feature of modern civil law systems, their civil codes. Although scholars may disagree as to which of the two elementary handbooks, F. Bourjon's *Le Droit commun de la France et la coutume de Paris reduits en principes, etc.* or G. Argou's *Institution au droit François,* was the main influence on the structure of the French *Code civil,* no one (I believe) will deny that their design was derived from Justinian's *Institutes* and from similar later *Institutes*

---

[26] *Id.*
[27] *See* Civil Law, *supra* note 11, at 24-38.
[28] *Id.* at 27-29.
[29] Dawson, *supra* note 13, at 599.

of local law. The end result of this enormous, sustained intellectual effort was a legal system, vastly different from anything the classical Roman jurists (who did not have the benefit of Justinian's *Institutes*) even knew, and which displays Max Weber's logically formal rationality.[30]

Dawson then turns to my claim that "modern civilian law reports retain many elements from their precodification ancestors."[31] My claim, I believe, rests on observable fact, and my intention was to show the durability of the legal tradition even after fundamental legal change. Dawson says, "French opinions can hardly follow models derived from olden times because French courts under the old regime were strictly forbidden to publish the reasons for their opinion."[32] Although it is true that the French courts were then forbidden to publish their reasons, Dawson himself has provided, for the years 1600-1789, accounts of various unofficial reports, by judges and attorneys alike, which *do* give the court's or their own reasons.[33] Other examples can be found in *The Making of the Civil Law.*[34]

Dawson next turns to a characteristic that I ascribe to civil law systems, namely, that they are more open to philosophy than are common law systems.[35] This, he says, I attribute to two factors: "first, the influence of Justinian's *Institutes,* whose account of Roman law was so simple that philosophers could understand it (!!)."[36] Here Dawson is

---

[30] For an exceptionally clear account of Weber's meaning, *see* Trubek, *Max Weber on Law and the Rise of Capitalism,* 1972 WIS. L. REV. 730.

[31] CIVIL LAW, *supra* note 11, at 52.

[32] Dawson, *supra* note 13, at 600. *See also* J. DAWSON, *supra* note 2, at 286-305.

[33] J. DAWSON, *supra* note 2, at 314-38.

[34] CIVIL LAW, *supra* note 11, at 44. These seem to be excluded from consideration by a preceding footnote of Dawson's: "Those dating from before the year 1800 do not prove much, for they were prepared independently by private reporters." Dawson, *supra* note 13, at 599 n.13. I do not think that my argument that modern civil law reports retain many elements from precodification ancestors is affected by the observation that modern reports are official, and that earlier reports were unofficial. Dawson correctly says: "German opinions are filled with citations (not of course to Roman law but to modern German court decisions and the writings of modern German jurists) and also with pages of explanatory and argumentative discourse." *Id.* at 600. This is certainly true and corresponds precisely, *mutatis mutandis,* to the old German reports where the citations were to the *Corpus Juris,* the writings of jurists, statutes, and court decisions. I do not recognize my own position in the suggestion attributed to me that modern German High Court opinions are "extremely formal and meager." *Id.* at 600 n.15. What I said was that in comparison with Italian and French reports, the German reports are "written in an even more abstract form." CIVIL LAW, *supra* note 11, at 178. Perhaps Dawson was misled in that I said the reports do not give juristic opinions. This was said, however, to contrast German law with French law, in which a jurist's note is appended to the report.

[35] Dawson, *supra* note 13, at 600.

[36] *Id.*

obviously provoked, but I do not see why. What I said was that the *Institutes* and local *Institutes* "provide a simple account of the law and enable philosophers to feel that they know the law and what it is about, and that they can discuss it comfortably."[37] I wonder if Dawson would deny that, as a matter of fact, European philosophers, great and small, did write comfortably about law relying largely on Justinian's *Institutes* and also on local *Institutes?* My second factor was the leadership in civil law systems of academics who were more willing and able than practitioners to build up the systematic, philosophical, and structural side of the law.[38] Although England played a full part in eighteenth century rationalism, rationalism's effect on English law was minimal in contrast to its effect in the rest of Europe. In my view, one should expect this from a small, self-sufficient group of practitioners intensely focusing on litigation.[39] Dawson then says that this calls for an explanation and that I provide one, namely that civil law systems are open to philosophy and common law systems are not. This, he says, "will satisfy those willing to endow 'systems' with human attributes—with minds that open or close, as the case may be."[40]

Dawson's own explanation is revealing. Throughout most of the history of English common law, he finds "an almost total lack of human resources, that is, of expositors who were trained and were believed to be needed to explain, to organize, and also to criticize the legal system."[41] But does not this dearth of such expositors in England, in sharp contrast to continental territories where the Reception was most marked, itself demand explanation? The explanation, I believe, we have already seen. When an old, complex, written work like the *Corpus Juris Civilis* is accepted as authoritative, the obvious way to

---

[37] CIVIL LAW, *supra* note 11, at 83.

[38] *Id.* at 84.

[39] Dawson actually says that during the period of reappraisal in law in some continental countries "England produced only Blackstone." Dawson, *supra* note 13, at 601. The logic of that paragraph (and of the following one) demands that this opinion is mine. I would deny strongly that such a limited view of English legal writing was ever mine. *See* Watson, *Justinian's Institutes and Some English Counterparts,* in STUDIES IN MEMORY OF J.A.C. THOMAS 181-86 (P. Stein & A. Lewis eds. 1983).

[40] Dawson, *supra* note 13, at 601. This surely is a debating point. My position would rather be that legal systems develop through the operation of human intellects. These intellects work on the basis of their own knowledge, experience, and originality. The first two qualities depend on the existing, known elements of the legal system and legal education; and in part so does the third. But in addition, progress within a legal system will occur only when views propounded are found acceptable to others in the legal community. Views whose originality stands outside of the legal tradition will find acceptance less easily. I do not think there is anything in this, or in my book, to justify Dawson's opinion that I make "it appear that in a 'system' a deficiency such as a mind that is closed is congenital and therefore incurable." *Id.*

[41] *Id.*

learn it is from books, which in turn provoke systematic inquiry into the law.[42] The basic differences between civil law and common law systems flow naturally from the acceptance in the former of the *Corpus Juris* as authoritative.

Dawson also contests my explanation for the fact that in modern times, codification is a typical attribute of civil law systems and is very much rarer in common law systems. There is, I argued, a propensity towards codification in civil law systems.[43] Dawson thinks I have trouble showing this propensity because the reasons I give for successful modern codification have little to do with the civil law tradition.[44] These reasons are: first, the *Institutes*, both the local *Institutes*, those various short systematic treatments of local law which show that the law can be simply stated, and Justinian's *Institutes* which show that the short treatment can be enacted as law; and second, "the conviction generated by eighteenth century rationalism that law ought to be the embodiment of reason and in being written down could be improved."[45] Now it seems to me that these two reasons have a great deal to do with the civil law tradition. The first because the local *Institutes* were the direct descendants of Justinian's *Institutes,* the second because the Enlightenment had a much greater impact on law in civil law systems precisely because they were more open to philosophy. Dawson says, "Some earlier advocates of codification had urged that codification could make law more intelligible by reducing its volume and complexity, but Watson rejects this explanation, reasoning that although English law in the eighteenth century was wholly unintelligible to the general population, codification was not even thought of in England."[46] Now I never would claim, and never have, that a desire for intelligibility and simplicity was not a powerful incentive towards codification.[47] Nor would I claim, nor have I, that codification was not even thought of in England. There were, in fact, numerous advocates of codification in England. For example, there is Jeremy Bentham in the eighteenth century, Francis Bacon and the Levellers in the seventeenth century, and Reginald Pole in the sixteenth century.[48] My concern in *The Making of the Civil Law* was with two questions: first, why successful codification is typical of civil law systems but not of common law systems;

---

[42] *See supra* text accompanying notes 23-28.

[43] Civil Law, *supra* note 11, at 99-130.

[44] Dawson, *supra* note 13, at 601-02.

[45] *Id.* at 602.

[46] *Id.*

[47] Civil Law, *supra* note 11, at 101.

[48] See the quotation given by F.W. Maitland, English Law and the Renaissance 41-44 (1901).

and second, why successful codification emerged relatively late in civil law countries. For these questions the simple explanation of a desire to simplify the law cannot be enough.

One point made by Dawson may incidentally be very instructive for understanding codification in lands that accepted the *Corpus Juris* as authoritative. He points to the labor and time involved in preparing a new code instead of borrowing much from one already in force elsewhere. It took, he observes, eighty-seven years for a code to be produced in Prussia, and thirty-seven in Germany.[49] But the earliest modern civil code of all, that of Bavaria, the *Codex Maximilianeus Bavaricus civilis,*[50] which owes its impetus to Prussian initiatives, took only six years. Work was begun in 1750, and the code was complete in 1756. In the intervening years, codes on criminal law and procedure had also appeared. The swiftly produced *Codex Maximilianeus Bavaricus civilis* is very heavily inspired by Justinian's *Institutes;*[51] the *Allgemeines Landrecht für die Preussischen Staaten* is not.[52] Are we to see in this only a coincidence? Or are we to believe that codification was relatively easier in territories where Justinian's *Institutes* had been treated as law, and where these *Institutes* (or local versions of them) were regarded as providing a suitable model for a civil code?

Dawson has his own explanation of civil law codification: "For the countries that led the way in codifying, I would ascribe the impulse not to a kind of unity produced by the borrowings from Roman law but to just the opposite: a legal inheritance that was too diversified and abundant to be managed otherwise."[53] For at least six reasons relating to civil codes or to the general structure of modern civil law systems, I believe this explanation is insufficient, even though a desire to simplify the law was one immediate important cause of codification. First, it does not explain why codification occurred at the time it did. Second, it does not account for the powerful role of Justinian's *Institutes* in generally systematizing the civil law even before codification. Third, it fails to explain the obviously large dependence of most modern codes, both in arrangement and in the extent of treatment of rules, on Justinian's and later *Institutes.* It also cannot account for omissions, notably of commercial law, from most civil codes. (My explanation is that what counts as commercial law in civil law countries was not included in Justinian's *Institutes.*) Fourth, it does not account for the very marked

---

[49] Dawson, *supra* note 13, at 602.
[50] *See* Civil Law, *supra* note 11, at 102.
[51] *Id.* at 104-05.
[52] *Id.* at 106-08.
[53] Dawson, *supra* note 13, at 603.

division between public law and private law in civil law systems. (The former was of little interest to the Roman legal writers, and was not treated in Justinian's *Institutes.*) Fifth, it cannot explain why the distinction between substance and procedure is so sharp in civil law systems. Sixth, Dawson's view cannot explain why the approach to law is much more theoretical in civil law than in common law systems.

For each of the points on which Dawson's explanation of modern codification is unilluminating, a satisfactory account of modern civil law systems must, I believe, provide answers. Answers are all to be found in the acceptance of the *Corpus Juris Civilis* as authoritative.

Although *The Making of the Civil Law* was concerned only with civil law systems, it is possible to draw several conclusions relating to general study of legal change. The contrast between civil law and common law systems is due to the acceptance of Justinian's *Corpus Juris Civilis* as authoritative by the former and not by the latter. The acceptance of this common organizing instrument allows the force of the legal tradition to emerge clearly in different states. It does not mean that the legal tradition will have less of an impact on legal change when there is no organizing instrument.

III. Society and Legal Change

If the legal tradition itself largely determines the pattern of change, then it would appear that legal systems are not always sensitive to wider local political, social, and economic issues. Legal rules may not be the best that could be devised, with the knowledge available at the time, for the society at large or for the ruling elite. The theme of *Society and Legal Change*[54] was that many important rules of private law in the West were, and are, dysfunctional. This thesis, which is in flat opposition to the views of most sociologists of law and of most theorists of law,[55] is perhaps most easily understood when we look at a quotation which is almost its contrary. In the concluding paragraph of his book, *A History of American Law,* L.M. Friedman writes:

> If by law one means an organized system of social control, any society of any size and complexity has law. As long as the country endures, so will its system of law, coextensive with society, reflecting its wishes and needs, in all their irrationality, ambiguity, and inconsistency. It will follow every twist and turn of development. The law is a mirror held up

[54] Legal Change, *supra* note 10.

[55] Friedman, Book Review, 6 Brit. J.L. Soc'y 127 (1979).

> against life. It is order; it is justice; it is also fear, insecurity, and emptiness; it is whatever results from the scheming, plotting, and striving of people and groups, with and against each other. All these things law will continue to be. A full history of American law would be nothing more or less than a full history of American life.[56]

Of course, all this is mere assertion, and rhetorical assertion at that. Friedman has certainly not attempted to demonstrate in any systematic way that his history of American law is a history of American life, following every twist and turn of development. The theory is based on a common notion of the relationship between law and society, but the theory is one for which systematic proof is not offered. It is not proof of such a theory that an immediate cause can be found in a society for most legal changes.

In *Society and Legal Change* I was not seeking to put forward a positive view regarding the precise relationship between society and the legal rules that operate within it. Rather I was primarily putting forward the negative proposition that the relationship is not as close as existing theories of legal change and of law and society suggest.[57] The elements of my argument may be easily summarized. All legal rules are created by a cause; and this cause of creation is commonly, but not always, rooted in social, economic, or political factors important to the life of the society or its leaders.[58] I would now add that a great part of the cause may be rooted in transnational aspects of the legal tradition, which otherwise have little or nothing to do with social, economic, or political conditions. Once created, legal rules tend to live on; for reasons of course, but often for reasons which have no direct importance for the life of the society or its leaders. Often the legal rules are in obvious conflict with the best interests and desires of the ordinary citizens and the ruling elite, but nonetheless continue in existence. I used the term 'divergence of law and society' to indicate not just that the rule was not the best fitted to meet the needs and desires of a given society, but also that the dysfunction was known to the people concerned, and especially

---

[56] L. FRIEDMAN, *supra* note 6, at 595. For a review that adequately demonstrates Friedman's failure to take account of the relative autonomy of law, *see* Tushnet, *Perspective on the Development of American Law: A Critical Review of Friedman's "A History of American Law,"* 1977 WIS. L. REV. 81.

[57] At best, there are so many exceptions to, or anomalies for, the main theories that the theories themselves become cumbersome, vague, and equivocal; and lose their capacity to explain. One might compare the "awareness of anomaly" described by T.S. Kuhn to the role it plays in scientific revolutions. *See* T.S. KUHN, THE STRUCTURE OF SCIENTIFIC REVOLUTIONS 62-63, 67-68, 78 (2d ed. 1970).

[58] LEGAL CHANGE, *supra* note 10, at 7.

to those able to effect change.[59] It must be stressed that I am not concerned with the phenomenon of time lag where it simply takes time for law to catch up with broader societal change: when scores of years or even centuries intervene between the divergence and the reform, lack of phase cannot solely be due to the pace of societal change.[60] I suggest that the dynamic causal relationship between law and society which is often thought to keep the former in close harmony with the latter simply does not exist. Of course, I am not claiming that there is no connection between law and society. Rules that would be destructive of, or otherwise intolerable to, society or its ruling elite will be replaced, but it is a *non sequitur* to argue from that to the conclusion that law reflects the needs and desires of society or its ruling elite.

To demonstrate my thesis I concentrated on legal growth and the absence thereof in what are, I believe, the two most famous systems of Western private law: Roman law and English law. If numerous cases of divergence, enduring for centuries, could be found there, then, I claimed, my thesis could be accepted.

As I expected, my views have met with much opposition. This criticism resolves itself into six main objections. I think it correct to state that in general my historical accuracy has not been challenged. The weight of the objections rests elsewhere.

A first objection, levelled most strongly by R.L. Abel, is that although I purported to offer a social theory of law, I did not do so; and that in fact, my assertions "simultaneously deny the possibility of any theory and contradict both our daily experience and virtually all scholarly research on law in society."[61] I did not intend, and do not think I claimed, to set forth a social theory of law in *Society and Legal Change*. My main aims were to show that existing theories postulate too close a relationship between the needs and desires of a society or its ruling elite on the one hand, and of its legal rules on the other; and to suggest some explanations for the divergence. Likewise, my assertions, referred to by Abel, that society tolerates a great deal of inappropriate law; that inertia is a serious cause of divergence; that the most important element in legal development has been the transplanting of rules, principles, and systematics; and that there is no close, inherent, necessary relationship between legal rules and the society in which they operate,[62] do not, I believe, rule out the possibility of any theory of law in

---

[59] *Id.* at 5.

[60] *Id.* at 7.

[61] Abel, *Law as Lag: Inertia as a Social Theory of Law* (Book Review), 80 MICH. L. REV. 785, 793 (1982) (reviewing LEGAL CHANGE, *supra* note 10).

[62] *See* Abel, *supra* note 61, at 793 (quoting LEGAL CHANGE, *supra* note 10, at ix,

society. Rather, they indicate that any theory will have to be complex and take into account, for instance, inertia and transplanting—all the causes of divergence in fact—as well as issues of power and will. The theory must not assume a simple mechanical and automatic relationship between law and society with a few admitted but unimportant exceptions.

This view admittedly contradicts virtually all scholarly research on law in society. But that may be, I suggest, because the focus of that research is inappropriate, inexact, or insufficient.[63] In the nature of things, traditional sociologists of law and legal anthropologists cannot admit that important legal rules may be largely dysfunctional; that would be to deny the possibility of any theory of legal development based on sociological or anthropological observations. No wonder Abel is ill at ease.

A ground for deep misconception already mentioned must again be emphasized to clear it out of the way. Legal sociologists have shown beyond doubt that persons able to hire the best lawyers will, on average, fare better in legal dealings, in law-in-action, than will those who have to make do with less competent attorneys; and that those who have frequent dealings with attorneys or with particular types of legal transaction will on average fare better than those who do not. There is thus a built-in bias in favor of certain groups, who usually will be the members of the ruling elite or the wealthy: those having political, social, or economic power, as against those who do not possess such power. All this is easy to show. But that should not then lead to an assumption, made all too often, that the legal rules themselves necessarily benefit some recognizable and powerful group, or that they are the best that could be devised for that group and still be tolerated by others. Often the question of the fitness of an actual rule for its purposes is not raised by sociologists. If it is, and if the deficiences of the rule are observed, then it will be suggested that the deficiences were not known to those concerned, or were only recently known and law had not yet caught up, or that the powerful group was not powerful enough, or was too prudent, to push through a more advantageous rule.

What is missing from the sociologists' approach is the historical element: a precise study through centuries of the possibility of persistence of defects in legal rules, principles, and systematics, when curable defects were known and not remedied. Of course, if such defects exist, as I claim is the case, then a theory explaining them would have to take

---

79, 130).

[63] *See supra* text accompanying notes 1-8.

account of the characteristics of other legal systems. In the growth of human institutions, a pattern of harmony always seems more easily accounted for than dissonance. Sociologists of law usually do not have the linguistic skills or the knowledge of the history of various legal systems to begin to construct a theory that acknowledges the possibility of serious long-term divergences.

Legal anthropologists are worse off. The primary material necessary to allow them to trace the history of individual systems of "primitive law" is simply unavailable. It is of primary significance that Abel claims my views deny the possibility of any theory. From the standpoint of a sociologist of law or of a legal anthropologist that seems correct: they are irretrievably condemned—if they want a general theory—to claim that law is always functional (with insignificant exceptions).[64]

Comparative legal history offers the choice of a different possibility. The choice, I believe, deserves exploration. The significance of the extent of the dilemma facing those such as Abel becomes even more apparent when one takes account of remarks such as his: "Since I possess no expertise in the historical data themselves, the object of this Essay will be to clairfy that theory and criticise it from the perspective of contemporary scholarship in law and social science,"[65] and "Although I know nothing of the actual facts, it seems plausible to me that . . . ."[66] For Abel, the perspective of modern sociology of law so obviously leads one to the correct result that an examination of the data is not needed. He cannot conceive that the data of comparative legal history may suggest possibilities beyond the effective scope of traditional sociology of law or legal anthropology.

A second objection as stated by Abel is that I do not make plain whether I am dealing with law in books—juristic writings, judicial decisions, and the authoritative pronouncements of legislatures—or with law-in-action, namely the actual behavior of lesser legal officials or lay persons, which, it is said, may differ.[67] He concludes I meant the former. The law I dealt with, says Friedman, is scarely "living law."[68] I

---

[64] The word "functional" is used here broadly, to include the notions of symbolic and legitimizing functions. But the notion is often grossly abused, since every time a legal rule or attitude seems to contradict a theory, the rule or attitude can be claimed to be symbolic or legitimizing. This notion cannot be tested. *See* Langbein, *Albion's Fatal Flaws,* 98 PAST & PRESENT 96, 114-15 (1983).

[65] Abel, *supra* note 61, at 785.

[66] *Id.* at 801. Actually, what seems plausible to Abel is just downright wrong, as someone more familiar with the relevant data could tell him.

[67] *Id.* at 785.

[68] Friedman, *supra* note 55, at 127. Friedman's point may be slightly different. *See infra* text accompanying notes 70-79.

was, as I repeatedly stated and must now emphasize, primarily concerned with positive rules of law. What I wanted to show was that the rules as set down, were not the most satisfactory available to the society. I do recognize that there can be a big difference between the rules as they are authoritatively set down, and as they are actually enforced by lesser officials or used and understood by individuals. But I cannot accept Abel's classification as exhaustive, or his distinction as basically meaningful. To a very considerable extent the behavior of lesser officials is hemmed in and restricted by rules of positive law, and the behavior of individuals is also affected by legal rules. If this were not so there would be no point to having legal rules at all. Without rules of positive law, it is difficult even to imagine a discipline of sociology of law. The contrast between rules of positive law and law-in-action is by no means absolute. Of course, if what was under consideration was law that was only in books, law that was not living and had no practical impact, then, as I expressly said, the observation that the law was out of step with society would have little impact.[69] But I sought to choose examples of divergences where the impact of rules of positive law either could not be avoided or could be avoided only by taking pains and usually by incurring large transactional costs.

The third objection to my thesis is that the examples of survival of dysfunctional law that I gave are "little bits and pieces, left over from other periods. Very often, these fragments survive precisely because they are so minor that it is hardly worth the trouble to wipe them off the face of the earth."[70] So my examples, it is said, relate to rules that have either no practical impact or one so trivial that it is scarcely noticed. But let us look at some of these examples. Would an observer of English law seriously maintain that, despite criticism for centuries, there was no practical impact of the vagaries of land tenure as the system existed until 1925? And that before the legislation of that year, the absence of compulsory registration of title of land—a weakness in the law that Henry VIII sought to remedy in 1535—was of no consequence except to academics in their ivory towers?[71] If the oddities of the law of libel, especially for unintended libel before 1952, are accepted, would the same observer deny the claim of the Newspapers Mutual Insurance Society Ltd. that "Libel costs a lot of money"?[72] For

---

[69] LEGAL CHANGE, *supra* note 10, at 126. Often a legal rule is deliberately framed to allow officials discretion. But that situation is not the most relevant here.

[70] Friedman, *supra* note 55, at 127.

[71] For these examples, see LEGAL CHANGE, *supra* note 10, at 47-60.

[72] *See id.* at 61-75. The Society also observed that for every claim that reaches court, dozens are settled. *Id.* at 68.

For Abel, however, defamation will have rapidly declined in importance with a criminal law, are all the apparent absurdities and injustices flowing from the retention and deformation of benefit of clergy[73] to be assigned to the inflamed imagination of scholars spending their lives "embroidering and decorating some little swatch of material"?[74] The delusion of practical reality must have infected authoritative legislatures in view of the numerous, but sadly not comprehensive, statutes that they passed.[75] In Rome, did it really make no practical difference in commerce that the contract of sale—an object of pride because it could be contracted at a distance by letter or by messenger—could not contain a guarantee against eviction or against latent defects unless the parties (or persons subjected to their power) were face to face?[76] Or that the Romans never developed direct agency though the notion was well known to them?[77] Was it really without commercial significance that barter was long not recognized as a contract and that law in this area always remained underdeveloped?[78]

To the foregoing questions I, for one, would not be satisfied with an answer that simply said, without an investigation into the facts, that there could have been no important practical consequences since otherwise the law would have been changed. Examples of divergences can easily be expanded beyond those given in the book. One further instance from England may suffice. Frederic Maitland wrote: "The law of Husband and Wife is in an awful mess (I don't think that a layman would readily believe how bad it is) . . . ."[79] The problems arising from that well-known awful mess, many of which were wanted by no recognizable group, some of which in practice could not be avoided, some of which cost money and trouble, were based on positive rules of law but made their impact—surely not trivial—felt in law-in-action.

In this general connection there seems to be for those who disagree with me an irresistible temptation to overstate their case and exaggerate my position. Illuminating examples occur in both Friedman and Abel.

---

mass, urban, industrialized society; for those involved "the precise content of the rules is irrelevant. The more complex and arbitrary they are, the better." Abel, *supra* note 61, at 799.

[73] *See* LEGAL CHANGE, *supra* note 10, at 92-94.

[74] Friedman, *supra* note 55, at 129.

[75] *See* LEGAL CHANGE, *supra* note 10, at 92-94.

[76] *Id.* at 14-22.

[77] *Id.* at 20.

[78] As an illustration of the last point it may be mentioned that an agreement to barter only became a contract and (in the absence of fraud) only had legal consequences when one party delivered; it could not be made by letter. Imagine the problems for merchants in different cities.

[79] C. FIFOOT, FREDERIC WILLIAM MAITLAND 53 (1971) (quoting F.W. Maitland). For an account that illustrates the mess, see A. MANCHESTER, A MODERN LEGAL HISTORY OF ENGLAND AND WALES 361-88 (1980).

The former observes that while parts of Roman law survive, whole chunks have gone.[80] The interesting question, he suggests, is the *principle* of survival, and this he finds in continued usefulness to society. "This is what kept the mortgage and the trust alive, while other parts of medieval law went to their graves."[81] But on this I should like to make three points. First, it is very easy to overestimate the extent to which ancient law has not survived. Thus, legal institution and legal rule (at least as law-in-action) do not exist in a vacuum. They are attached to social institutions. A legal institution, in fact, is a social institution backed by legal rules and looked at from the legal point of view. If the social institution disappears then so do, or at least so should, the legal institution and the legal rules. Thus, ancient Rome had a law of slavery and legal rules about slavery precisely because it had the social institution of slavery. It would make no sense in estimating the extent of disappearance of Roman legal rules in the contemporary West to point out that none of the rules of the law of slavery survive. In the West the social institution of slavery has gone. Rather one should look to a place and time in the recent past where the social institution survived, such as 19th century Spanish America, and consider the impact there of the Roman law of slavery. It is worth observing, however, that even when the vital social institution has gone, related legal rules may survive with important practical dysfunctional qualities. An obvious example would be the survival in England of dysfunctional land tenures long after the social institution of feudalism had otherwise disappeared. Second, the test for my thesis is not whether dysfunctional Roman or medieval legal rules still exist, but whether they continued in operation for a long time after they ceased to be functional. Third, I have never denied—could anyone?—that utility is part of the principle of survival of legal rules. Legal rules that work well obviously have a greater chance of survival than have those that work badly. The question that I find needs an answer and one that should not be given only on *a priori* reasoning is whether the principle of survival involves more than continuing usefulness.

Abel has his own exaggeration: that my constant refrain in the book is "that most laws are useless."[82] My refrain is very different and far less extreme, namely that much of law is out of step with the needs and desires of society "to an extent which renders implausible the existing theories of legal development and of the relationship between law

---

[80] Friedman, *supra* note 55, at 128.
[81] *Id.*
[82] Abel, *supra* note 61, at 797.

and society."[83]

The fourth objection to my thesis involves a complex of issues that can, I think, be reduced to one: the approach, it is claimed, is too atheoretical. Thus, for Friedman, "[t]hroughout the book Watson tells us that this or that rule of law is absolutely fundamental, or basic, or terribly important: but we are not told what it means to be basic, fundamental or important or what is so basic about these particular rules."[84] J.N. Adams is troubled by my avoidance of concepts like class, elite, and status groups, and he objects that I do not distinguish between major and minor instances of divergence.[85] Abel objects that most of the time I treat "society as an undifferentiated, personified whole," or that I view "society as either an organic whole or as a series of interest groups utterly dominated by a monolithic ruling class."[86]

On one level this complex objection is accurate, and I accept it cheerfully and without remorse. I did try to be as atheoretical as was consistent with the subject. The study of legal change and of law and society from a comparative historical standpoint is in its infancy. The data have to be collected carefully then analyzed accurately before one should attempt to construct a theory. The data come first, and the theory should emerge from the data. Theoretical distinctions, when they would not be helpful, should be avoided.[87] It was on this basis that I did not try to draw a line between major and minor instances of divergence. The line drawn would have been arbitrary and would have given rise to unnecessary and harmful controversy. I also thought that it would have been obvious to everyone that many of the divergences I discussed were major. For instance, the first divergence studied related to much of the structure of the Roman system of contracts, which has been the most admired part of Roman law. The second concerned the Roman *patria potestas*. The power at private law of the oldest living male ancestor over his descendants of whatever age or rank was enormous; for example, for a very long time only he could own property. This system cannot have been economically efficient. Nor can one claim the system satisfied some deep psychological need, since the Romans

---

[83] LEGAL CHANGE, *supra* note 10, at ix.

[84] Friedman, *supra* note 55, at 127.

[85] Adams, Book Review, 42 MOD. L. REV. 121, 123 (1979).

[86] Abel, *supra* note 61, at 787.

[87] Naturally, no approach, even in the collecting of data, will ever be entirely value-free. My own approach in the collecting of data was based on what seemed to me to be both apparent and often overlooked, namely that, in Western legal systems, many legal rules and whole branches of the law could be regarded as fundamentally unsatisfactory by those in a position to influence or effect legal change, without the change occurring.

sought assiduously to circumvent it. The failures in English law until recently to develop compulsory land registration or to deal adequately with the tenure system must, on any reckoning, be regarded as cases of major divergences. The English law of defamation was the subject of a report of a Select Committee of the House of Lords in 1843 and of two Commissions, the Porter Committee which reported in 1948 and the Faulks Committee which reported in 1975. Surely, *pace* Friedman and Abel, this indicates the subject is important; and all three Committees reported that the law was seriously defective.

I do not accept that I view society as an undifferentiated whole or as a series of interest groups utterly dominated by a monolithic ruling class. On the contrary, I agree that, in a well-rounded theory that intended to quantify the extent and causes of divergence, it would be appropriate to explain concepts like class, elite, and status groups, but for the limited purposes of *Society and Legal Change*, such explanation could be and was avoided for a very good reason. One difficulty in quantifying divergences is precisely the fact that in any society there are many recognizable groups, and their interests with regard to what the law should be may often be very different. It may then be suggested that rules that are unsatisfactory for the majority suit some powerful group and are therefore maintained; and that the rules, all taken together, form a pattern "in which the various interests of groups and individuals are represented according to their strength in the society."[88] Precisely to circumvent that difficulty I expressly[89] chose instances where there was no recognizable group or class—apart possibly from lawyers[90]—which had any interest, economic or social, in resisting change. With regard to the defects in the Roman contract of sale which would obstruct commerce, there is no social class of buyers and a different one of sellers.[91] The absence of registration of title of land in England and the pecularities of tenure could benefit no observable class or group and were harmful to landowners, precisely the people most able to effect change in the law. Substantial damages for unintentional libel were harmful to newspaper owners, etc., but there is no recognizable group who would be likely to be unintentionally libeled and so benefit: there is no class of people named Artemus Jones or who own restaurants called "The Spider's Web".[92] It might be suggested that Roman

[88] LEGAL CHANGE, *supra* note 10, at 9.
[89] *Id.*
[90] *See infra* text accompanying notes 126-35.
[91] Actually, the rules would not benefit buyers or sellers. LEGAL CHANGE, *supra* note 10, at 15.
[92] *See id.* at 65-66.

fathers formed a group or class, but they were not a cohesive social, economic, or political group. In public life no distinction was made between males who were not subject to paternal power and those who were. Sons could, and often did, occupy the highest offices of state and were in a good or even the best possible position to change the law. The approach I adopted in this regard does not dismiss the theoretical framework of sociology of laws; rather it sidesteps it for the time being.

A fifth objection I must regard as perverse. Abel writes: "He [Watson] examines a legal rule, asks whether *he* would want such a rule if he were a member of that society, decides that he would not, and concludes that the law serves *no* purpose."[93] Continually I sought to show that those involved with the law at the time and in a position to effect change were aware of the defects, without a change resulting for some time.

Thus, for example, from its creation, probably in the later third century B.C., until around 200 A.D. (or later) the Roman contract of sale did not usually contain inherent warranties against eviction or against latent defects. But the Romans did want warranties against eviction and against latent defects. We know this because there are literally hundreds of texts in the Roman sources on the subject of these warranties. But in the effort to take express warranties the great advantage of consensuality was lost because the only way to obtain the guarantees was by the contract of stipulation which required the parties to be face to face. Also, as is made clear, leaving the taking of the warranties to buyers resulted in awkward drafting problems. Lest it be suggested that for long the Romans were unaware of the possibility of inherent warranties, let me mention that from at least the fifth century B.C. the ceremony of *mancipatio,* the common mode of transfer of certain important types of property, did precisely contain an inherent warranty against eviction.[94]

Again, it was mentioned above that barter as a legal institution was long underdeveloped in Rome and never became a commercially efficient contract. That the Romans knew that barter had legally unsatisfactory remedies and that the matter was one of importance is easily demonstrated. The Sabinian school of jurists claimed that barter was a form of the contract of sale and, to prove this, argued from a mistranslation of a quotation from Homer, who was scarcely a legal authority for the Romans. They would not have relied on such a poor argument for a weak case if they had not thought the matter significant. The

---

[93] Abel, *supra* note 61, at 791.
[94] *See* LEGAL CHANGE, *supra* note 10, at 14-15.

converse argument, which prevailed, of the rival Proculian school was based purely on considerations of legal logic and not on economic, social, or political consequences: the price had to be in money, they said, otherwise one could not determine what was the thing sold and what was the price.[95]

Roman law did not recognize the principle of direct agency, even in the sixth century A.D., but that the Romans were aware of its commercial usefulness is shown by the use they made of it from the second century A.D. in their province of Egypt where Roman law was less strictly applied.[96]

That those with the power to effect changes in English law knew even before 1925 that the absence of compulsory land registration was dysfunctional is obvious from the stated intentions of those who sought to introduce it: Henry VIII in the sixteenth century, Oliver Cromwell in the seventeenth century, the registers for Middlesex and Yorkshire in the eighteenth century, the 1829 report of the Real Property Commissioners, and various acts of the nineteenth century.[97]

The arbitrary nature of the distinction between libel and slander and the injustices caused by it were known to and disapproved of by Sir James Mansfield, Lord Chief Justice, in 1812; the Select Committee of the House of Lords in 1843; F. Carr in 1902; famous scholars such as Sir William Holdsworth, Spencer Bower, Sir Frederick Pollock, Professor E.C.S. Wade, and Professor Winfield; and the Faulks Committee. Probably no English academic has supported the distinction in this century, but it still exists.[98] Examples showing that I am not imposing my views of dysfunction, but that those involved were aware of the defects, can be multiplied.[99]

To return for a moment to implied warranties against eviction and

---

[95] *See id.* at 19.

[96] *See id.* at 20; LEGAL TRANSPLANTS, *supra* note 9, at 33.

[97] LEGAL CHANGE, *supra* note 10, at 56-57.

[98] *Id.* at 63-65.

[99] The instance Abel selects to illustrate my imposition of value judgments is revealing. I had observed, *id.* at 34-37, that it was a weakness of Roman law that the nature of the unavoidable and important (as to consequences) distinction between manifest and non-manifest theft was never clarified; and that it is surprising that, to the best of our knowledge, the Romans never discussed the basis of the distinction. I then incidentally mentioned modern explanations of the basis of the distinction and argued that one of them was illogical. Abel seized on this claim of illogic as an illustration of my imposition of my own standards on the Romans. Abel says that I "offer[ed] no evidence that the Romans shared [my] feelings." Abel, *supra* note 61, at 791. This is quite true. My point was, and is, that the law was deficient in not deciding what counted as manifest or as non-manifest theft, and that though the Romans knew of the problem, and exposed it, they never asked why the distinction was made. My treatment of modern scholarly accounts was simply intended to show that a basis for the distinction is hard to find. The Romans offered none.

against latent defects in the Roman contract of sale, there is an insoluble problem here for those who, like Friedman, believe that "law is a mirror held up against life."[100] The problem is that the Roman jurists eventually did regard such warranties as inherent in the contract.[101] Friedman and I would both hold that those able to effect change regarded inherent warranties as desirable. But Friedman must hold either that inherent warranties were not previously desirable, or at least not previously desirable to those able to make the change. But no one who knows Roman law would think that the class of people who effected the change, the jurists, had undergone alteration.[102] And there is nothing in Roman economic history to suggest either a change in the kinds of sale that were being made, or in the relative bargaining power of buyer and seller.[103] The difficulty for Friedman is all the greater in that the evolution of inherent warranties was gradual. The insoluble problem for Friedman, of course, is a general one, and applies in many contexts.

A sixth and very different objection, that I am apolitical or antipolitical or conservative, is best left until later in this paper.

IV. Legal Transplants

Very little need now be said about the subject of the first book, *Legal Transplants.*[104] I think it is now generally accepted that in the West most of the law of most jurisdictions is the result of borrowing from elsewhere. More interesting though, and perhaps not so widely accepted, is the common existence of a "transplant bias."[105] Although a totally inappropriate rule is very unlikely to be voluntarily borrowed, it often happens, and at least in the past usually did, that the borrowing system does not systematically search for the best rule from else-

---

[100] Friedman, *supra* note 6, at 595.

[101] *See, e.g.*, J.A.C. Thomas, A Textbook of Roman Law 284 (1976).

[102] *See* W. Kunkel, Herkunft und soziale Stellung der römischen Juristen 114 (2d ed. 1967).

[103] *See, e.g.*, M. Rostovtsev, The Social and Economic History of the Roman Empire (P.M. Fraser ed., 2d ed. 1957).

[104] For critical reviews, see, e.g., Kahn-Freund, Book Review, 91 L.Q. Rev. 292 (1975); Seidman, Book Review, 55 B.U.L. Rev. 682 (1975).

[105] Friedman, for example, does not appear to agree with me. I am not sure that I fully understand Friedman's position. He says, "there is a good deal more *choice* in borrowing than Watson suggests. Borrowing is done systematically." Friedman, *supra* note 55, at 128 (emphasis in original). If he means that one foreign system is continually chosen as the donor, then the borrowing from that system may be done systematically, but the judges or jurists who do the taking often do not choose the best solution to their legal problem. If he means that before borrowing takes place the judges or jurists systematically look for the most appropriate solution in a number of societies, he is historically wrong.

where, but rather looks consistently to one system, which at times will not have the most appropriate rules. The well-known dependence of other societies (which were politically free) on Roman, English, and French law are cases in point. Often the foreign rules are borrowed without investigation into whether the rules are the best possible or even appropriate. The main causes of this transplant bias are, I think obvious: the general high standing of the donor system; the general high prestige, apart from its law, of the donor state; a shared legal tradition of the donor and borrower; and the accessibility—for instance, in writing or in a code—of the law to be borrowed.

Two examples, not discussed in *Legal Transplants,* from medieval Germany may be chosen as further illustrations.[106] In the thirteenth century, law in Germany was almost entirely customary, and the custom was very local at that. At the beginning of the century there existed nowhere a written official or unofficial account of customary law. But before 1235, probably between 1221 and 1222 or betwen 1221 and 1224, Eike von Repgow produced his *Sachsenspiegel,* 'Saxon Mirror', an unofficial account of what happened in practice in the bishoprics of Magdeburg and Halberstadt. As a written account of legal customs in one corner of Germany it had no rival. Of its two parts, one has survived in over 150 manuscripts, the other in over 200, and it was translated into a number of German dialects, back into Latin (its original language) at least three times, into Dutch and, it is said though personally I can find no trace, into Polish. Its influence was enormous; it was the only account (at the time) of law that was accessible and Germanic, and it was also of high quality. Thus, even custom transplants. A second example can be found in the transplanting of law among German towns which took place extensively during the fourteenth century, although some did take place even before that. Towns would adopt the town law of another town, and the "daughter" towns might in their turn be accepted as "mothers" for law by other towns. The "mother" town would be selected not just for the quality of its law, but because of its general high standing and also because its law was in the tradition wanted by the "daughter." But the law of the most famous "mother," Magdeburg, was adopted widely even in Poland. Strangely, in that instance the law of the "mother" town was often unwritten and relatively inaccessible.

---

[106] For these two examples, see SOURCES, *supra* note 12, at 25-50.

V. Sources of Law

Sources of Law; Legal Change and Ambiguity has not yet had the benefit of criticism. The main theme is that at various times within the Western legal tradition there has been profound indifference among those capable of making law about the quality of the sources of law and about their fitness for developing the law and for clarifying ambiguities. A few examples will suffice. Opinions of jurists were among the most fruitful sources of legal growth in Rome. The jurists often disagreed on important issues and when they did there was, with very minor exceptions, no way of ranking their opinions. Many of the disputes that we know raged in the second century A.D. existed until they were settled by the Emperor Justinian in the sixth century. For instance, the Proculian school of jurists held that a male reached puberty when he completed his fourteenth year, the Sabinians required actual physical development, and Justinian in 529 settled the dispute in favor of the Proculians. But attainment of puberty had important consequences which resulted from the operation of law and which could not be altered by the behavior of interested parties.[107] Problems must have arisen in practice; fatherless youths in their early teens are not, I suspect, free from the perils of mortality. On this and other issues, however, no definite solution was forthcoming for centuries. What does seem to me to be significant is that though many of the most distinguished jurists were also high ranking public officials and bureaucrats, not one of them ever, so far as we know, arranged for the resolution of such a juristic dispute by legislation. They seem to have preferred the ambiguity. The other sources of Roman law also contained serious defects.[108]

Similarly, after the Reception of Roman law in Western Europe a major source of law was the writings of jurists, professors, and attorneys, from the eleventh century onwards. But no system ever developed for determining the ranking of individual jurists. There was even no agreement on the relative weight to be attributed to the different types of juristic writings, whether glosses, commentaries, treatises, collections of opinions, collections of legal advice, or even attorneys' briefs. With a

---

[107] When a male was not in the power of his father (i.e., usually when the father was dead), he would have a guardian until he reached puberty. He could enter a transaction that might (even in theory) injure his patrimony only if he had his guardian's permission. He could not make a will at all, and if he had been appointed heir by his father's will and a substitute heir was also appointed (in case the boy died before puberty), then if he did so die, the estate went to the named substitute heir, not to the boy's own heirs on intestacy.

[108] *See* Sources, *supra* note 12, at 1-24.

few exceptions such as Giovanni Battista de Luca (1614-83), very little attention was even paid to this issue. When, as was very frequently the case, there was no local statute on point—statutes in private law were rare—or custom or precedent from the highest court of the jurisdiction, there was not even agreement regarding whether one should resort first to the authority of the jurists or to the law of a neighboring state. De Luca favored the latter alternative. What was to count as a "neighboring state" or how the law of competing neighboring states was to be ranked was also not established, apart from the principle that neighboring did not mean "territorially adjacent" but "similar in law." For example, De Luca considered Spanish fueros as neighboring law, presumably from a perspective in Naples.[109]

In modern England the most important sources of law are statutes and precedents. It is notoriously difficult to find the appropriate or correct statutory law for a number of reasons. The same subject may be dealt with in many Acts. In the case of building operations there were, in 1970, 179 national Acts and 220 local Acts.[110] In 1949, the law relating to the validity of a marriage was contained in as many as 40 statutes.[111] This problem has been recognized since at least the time of Sir Nicholas Bacon, the Lord Keeper (1509-79), and has been the object of the (unsuccessful) attention of Kings Edward VI (1537-53) and James I (1566-1625), and Sir Francis Bacon (1561-1626).

Likewise, the drafting of individual Acts is notoriously poor, and the standards of discussion very inadequate. Parliament also has difficulty in finding time to pass much needed legislation. In fact, it has long been known that the Parliament, as presently constituted, is just not an appropriate body for making satisfactorily intelligible legislation, especially of a comprehensive type. "It would be as impossible to get in Parliament a really satisfactory discussion of a Bill codifying the Law of Evidence as to get a committee of the whole House to paint a picture," said Sir James Fitzjames Stephens who wanted the law of evidence set out in one Act.[112] "It is [a] matter of amazement that Englishmen should be content to have the laws by which they are governed in

---

[109] Pompeo Neri Badia, who in 1745 was appointed by the Grand Duke of Tuscany to prepare a code (which was never completed), proposed that there should be no recourse to the law of another place because of the confusion this system had created in Tuscany. The *Leggi e constituzioni* of 1770 of Sardinia and Piedmont, bk. 3, tit. 22, ¶ 9, did ban recourse to the law of a neighboring place, and such a ban had earlier been read, by implication, into a provision of 1729. The confusion resulting from the practice was well-known long before anything was done about it anywhere; even later it continued elsewhere. *See* SOURCES, *supra* note 12, at 51-67.

[110] G.W. PATON, A TEXTBOOK OF JURISPRUDENCE 246 (4th ed. 1972).

[111] *See* A. MANCHESTER, *supra* note 79, at 361.

[112] G. CHASE, A DIGEST OF THE LAW OF EVIDENCE xxii (1898).

such an inaccessible shape as they are; but, no doubt, one explanation of this state of things is the hopelessness of passing through Parliament, without mutilation, any carefully considered exposition of any great branch of law," wrote Sir Nathaniel Lindley in the context of the Partnership Act, in 1890.[113] Richard Crossman wrote in his *Diaries of a Cabinet Minister* that when he was a Cabinet Minister he never bothered to read any of the Bills he got through Parliament and that he did not bother to understand the individual clauses, nor did many Members of Parliament, not even the spokesman for the Opposition. He also wrote that the Opposition used up their questions on the early clauses.[114] In 1981, Lord Hailsham of St. Marylebone, Lord High Chancellor of Great Britain, claimed: "Parliament in general and the House of Commons in particular has long since ceased to believe that its main business is to act as an efficient legislature."[115] But Members of Parliament are not concerned. A committee of the unofficial *Statute Law Society* in 1970 issued a questionnaire on quality of statute law to users of statutes, and received responses from only 7% of those to whom it was sent; from barristers and solicitors they received a 10% response. By far the lowest response, 2%, was from the Members of both Houses of Parliament.[116]

It is in this context that Abel's objections that I am "not really an admirer of liberal democracy"[117] and am setting up a "fundamentally apolitical" theory of legislation should be set.[118] I was suggesting a law-making body intermediate between the courts and the legislature.[119] This body would be subordinate to the legislature which would remain supreme, and its main work would be the preparation of bills which would become law if not objected to by the legislature. Its desirability stems from the lack of interest in legislation, especially for private and commercial law, shown by the present legislatures.[120]

---

[113] N. Lindley, A Treatise on the Law of Partnership 2 (W. Lindley 6th ed. 1893).

[114] 1 R. Crossman, The Diaries of a Cabinet Minister 629 (1975).

[115] Hailsham, *Obstacles to Law Reform,* 34 Current Legal Probs. 279, 286-87 (1981).

[116] *See* Sources, *supra* note 12, at 76-92. For a history that reveals the defects in English lawmaking by legislation, see A. Manchester, *supra* note 79, at 32-49.

[117] Abel, *supra* note 61, at 806.

[118] *Id.* at 807.

[119] But not with autocratic powers as stated by Abel. *Id.* at 807; Legal Change, *supra* note 10, at 133. The idea is developed in Watson, *Two-Tier Law—A New Approach to Law-Making,* 27 Int'l & Comp. L.Q. 552 (1978).

[120] One might think of non-legislative lawmaking procedures in the United States, such as court rulemaking or the pronouncements of administrative agencies. See also the suggestion of Justice Stevens, and Justice Brennan's response. Brennan, *Some Thoughts on the Supreme Court's Workload,* 66 Judicature 232 (1983). There is also

English law also has a system of binding precedent. The element in a decision that is binding is the *ratio decidendi,* that is, the propositions of law that the court appeared to consider necessary for its judgment. Usually the court will not declare what was the *ratio decidendi,* and judges in subsequent cases are therefore forced to find it themselves. This task may often prove to be quite difficult especially because there is no theoretical method for uncovering the *ratio.* This reliance on precedent may create persistent ambiguity. Obviously, it does not necessarily result in improved quality in the law, because the subsequent court may, as the first could also have done, give an unfortunate *ratio.* The conclusion I reached was that where, as often, the sources of law are inadequate for keeping the law up to date and for removing ambiguity, and the inadequacy is apparent to those involved in the system, then those with the capacity to change the law must have in fact a positive disinclination against reform of the sources. The reason for this, I suggested, is to be found in group psychology. The Roman jurists *qua* jurists owed their prestige and power to their skill in handling abstract legal problems. To win prestige, they had to impress their fellow jurists with skillful, complex arguments. Solving difficult legal problems through legislation would not win jurists the approval of their fellows. Similarly, Members of Parliament are more interested in party politics and economic issues than in law reform. Yet much of their prestige comes from their role as legislators, and they are unwilling to concede any of their power in this regard.

English judges, too, are a group with a strong *esprit de corps.* Much of their high prestige depends on the fact that their decisions are binding in future cases. Yet their *esprit de corps* would be endangered if a judge stated too directly the *ratio decidendi* of a particular case when fellow judges might feel compelled to voice their disagreement. Members of such legal elites attach much weight to the opinion of their fellows. They are unwilling to suggest a course of action that could diminish the prestige, power, or earning capacity of the group.

VI. An Attempted Synthesis

It should still be maintained, I would claim, that legal rules—including many that have a great impact on practical life—frequently are and have been dysfunctional, that is, out of step with the needs and desires both of society at large and of its ruling elite,

---

a growing awareness in the United States that something is amiss with the legislative process. *See, e.g.,* G. Calabresi, A Common Law for the Age of Statutes (1982).

and that this is not and has not been unknown to those who can reform the law. To a considerable, but as yet unmeasured, and possibly unmeasurable, extent this is because the sources of law themselves are often inadequate to the task of keeping law up to date and of removing its ambiguities. When this situation persists for a long time it suggests that those who can influence legal change have a positive disinclination against radical reform. In addition, the legal tradition itself plays an important role in shaping legal change in a number of ways. For example, borrowing from other systems, the form taken by most legal change, is by no means always the result of a systematic search for the best solution. A bias tends to favor some particular system, and this bias is rooted to some extent in the legal tradition. Moreover, even in times of revolutionary change, the legal tradition is the product of history, particularly of legal history. A remark of Karl Marx is very *a propos:*

> Men make their own history, but they do not make it just as they please; they do not make it under circumstances chosen by themselves, but under circumstances directly encountered, given and transmitted from the past. The tradition of all the dead generations weighs like a nightmare on the brain of the living.[121]

From the foregoing, it should be obvious that law exists and flourishes at the level of idea, and is part of culture. As culture it operates in at least three spheres of differing sizes, one within another. As these spheres decrease in size law becomes a more pervasive and dominant element in the culture of that sphere. The spheres are: the population at large, lawyers, and the lawmakers. By "lawmakers," I mean the members of that elite group who in a particular society have their hands on the levers of legal change, whether as legislators, judges, or jurists.

For present purposes, we may accept as a definition of culture in general the summary formulation of A.L. Kroeber and Clyde Kluckhohn:

> Culture consists of patterns, explicit and implicit, of and for behavior acquired and transmitted by symbols, constituting the distinctive achievements of a human group, including their embodiments in artifacts; the essential core of culture consists of traditional (i.e. historically derived and selected)

---

[121] Marx, *The Eighteenth Brumaire of Louis Bonaparte* in K. Marx & F. Engels, Selected Works 96 (1968).

> ideas and especially their attached values; culture systems may, on the one hand, be considered as products of action, on the other as conditioning elements of further action.[122]

Law, of course, is functional and practical. To some extent, it facilitates social and economic life. At a minimum, it exists to institutionalize dispute situations and to validate decisions given in the appropriate process which itself has the specific object of inhibiting unregulated conflict. It may do this without having the rules best adapted for society as a whole or for leading groups. It is important, too, that not all groups in a society are affected by legal rules to the same extent. One group, though, is always affected: the lawyers. They earn their living by the law. A change that made the law simpler or less ambiguous or reduced the volume of disputes, actual or possible, could have an adverse effect on their income. In addition, the stock-in-trade of a practicing attorney is his or her knowledge of the *existing* law. A drastic change could reduce the most experienced practitioner almost to the level of a beginner.

For a rule to become law it must be institutionalized. It must go through the stages required for achieving the status of law. A new formulation expressed by a jurist might become accepted by other jurists; or a court may utter a judgment which the system recognizes as binding precedent and makes part of general law; or social ideas might be put in the acceptable form, pass through the stages in the legislature that are regarded as necessary and become a statute. Because lawyers and lawmakers are involved in all of these processes a rule cannot become law without being subjected to legal culture. Equally important, a legal change may result from legal culture alone. For example, a jurist may develop a new rule based on his or her studies that may find favor with his or her fellows because its logical elegance appeals to them. This does not mean, however, that a rule developed in this manner will necessarily have no practical effects.[123]

But when practical economic or social reasons suggest that the law should be changed, the pressure for such a change must also operate on the culture.[124] If such practical pressure starts with the lawmakers, it is only their culture that is involved; if it starts with the lawyers, their

---

[122] A.L. Kroeber & C. Kluckhohn, Culture: A Critical Review of Concepts and Definitions 181 (1952).

[123] The Proculians denied the advantages of the contract of sale to barter-like transactions, because it would not be possible to determine who was buyer and who was seller.

[124] For the importance of "pressure forces" for legal change, see Watson, *Comparative Law and Legal Change,* 37 Cambridge L.J. 313, 324-26, 332-33 (1978).

own culture is involved and the pressure must be directed against the culture of the lawmakers; if it starts with the population at large (or some segment of it, other than lawyers) then its legal culture is involved, but the pressure must, once again, be directed against the culture of the lawmakers, usually through the medium of lawyers. Thus, even when practical needs and the social pressures arising from them determine that a legal change must occur, both the timing and the nature of the change will be mediated through the legal culture, particularly through that of the lawmakers. As Marshal Sahlins says in a different context: "The general determinations of praxis are subject to the specific formulations of culture; that is, of an order that enjoys, by its own properties as a symbolic system, a fundamental autonomy."[125]

In an earlier work I sought to set out the factors that govern the legal changes that are made, and those include, naturally enough, the needs that are felt by a group that acts as a pressure force.[126] But what has emerged from these four books is my appreciation of the enormous power of the legal culture in determining the timing, the extent, and the nature of legal change. Social, economic, and political conditions that affect other groups within society are important, of course, but their impact on the legal rules must not be exaggerated. For example, such conditions may lead to the existence of barter as a social institution in a particular society at a particular time, but the legal rules surrounding barter may be only a very approximate fit of those desired by traders and may instead derive largely from the influence of the legal culture. Legal issues, such as whether barter should be given the status of contract; whether a contract of barter comes into being simply on agreement; or whether writing is required for the formation of the contract; whether delivery alone creates the obligation; and whether the remedy for breach is specific performance, money damages, the return of goods already delivered, or the money value of delivered goods may all be determined, not out of concern for present mercantile practice or merchants, but rather by the tenets of the existing legal culture. These tenets, in turn, may have been created in the distant past. Mercantile practice may itself come to be influenced by the rules established on the basis of legal culture.

Failure to appreciate the power and the autonomy of legal culture may lead scholars into interesting and illuminating errors. For instance, the avowedly Marxist Mark Tushnet, in discussing the American law of slavery, says: "The insertion of slave law into a bourgeois framework

[125] M. Sahlins, Culture and Practical Reason 57 (1976).

[126] Watson, *supra* note 124. *See also,* Civil Law, *supra* note 11, at 182-84; Watson, *Society's Choice and Legal Change,* 9 Hofstra L. Rev. 1473 (1981).

therefore causes new problems, as bourgeois principles must accommodate the incompatible principles of slave law."[127] He feels that the principal problem thus identified is that in a bourgeois society labor power is considered fungible with money, but in slave law "we should find a reluctance to treat all forms of property, and especially slaves, as reducible to a common measure in money."[128] If law were determined by the social relations of production, we would expect to find the reluctance Tushnet posits. But, in fact, in ancient Rome, a quintessential slave society, all private law actions without exception, even those brought claiming ownership of a slave, were for money damages or penalty. And in nineteenth and twentieth century Germany, a quintessential bourgeois society, actions for compensation in money are limited to a few express exceptional cases. For instance, even for damage to property, the *Bürgerliches Gesetzbuch (BGB)* section 249 gives an action for compensation in kind as the primary remedy, though the creditor can choose compensation in money as an alternative.[129] Section 241 says that the effect of an obligation is that the creditor is entitled to claim *performance* from the debtor.[130]

The claim that culture is fundamentally autonomous would be challenged, I think, by some Marxists. But I am convinced by Sahlins: "The first problem, how to account for the kinds of goods a society will produce, their precise form and content, is a question without answer in Marx's theory. . . . The 'system of needs' must always be relative, not accountable as such by physical necessity, hence symbolic by definition."[131] No theory of economic materialism will explain why dog is not eaten in the United States; why the flesh of steers is highly favored when the eating of soya beans could produce the same material results; why men wear or wore ties around their necks; or why women wear or wore ribbons in their hair. If it be suggested in reply to the last point that in view of their economic dependence women had to appear "feminine" the particular choice of hair ribbons as opposed to neckties would still be without explanation.

The formulation of a culture is a process of rendering experience

---

[127] M. TUSHNET, THE AMERICAN LAW OF SLAVERY 1810-1860 at 158 (1981) [hereinafter cited as M. TUSHNET, SLAVERY]. But elsewhere, Tushnet has demonstrated a keen awareness of the relative autonomy of law, although apparently only within a classical Marxist framework. Tushnet, *Perspectives on the Development of American Law: A Critical Review of Friedman's "A History of American Law"*, 1977 WIS. L. REV. 81.

[128] M. TUSHNET, SLAVERY, *supra* note 127, at 157-58.

[129] BÜRGERLICHES GESETZBUCH [BGB] § 249 (W. Ger.).

[130] BGB § 241.

[131] M. SAHLINS, *supra* note 125, at 148, 150.

meaningful and, as Franz Boas argued,[132] "necessarily proceeds on a theory—of nature, of man, of man's being in nature. This theory, however, remains unformulated by the human group that lives it."[133] This unformulated theory is, of course, shared by the members of the group. The more basic an element of the culture, the more diffident a member of the group will be in modifying it and the more violent will be the attack by the group on anyone who suggests change.

This view of the legal culture begins to explain three of the striking features of legal growth. First, even in a time of conscious legal reform, the sources of the law are often not considered candidates for reform. The formal mechanism for making legal rules is more basic in the culture than are individual legal rules. Second, it provides one explanation for the well-known phenomenon that often fundamental law reform, especially reform of the sources, proceeds from, or is suggested by, someone outside of the two inner circles of legal culture. The best illustration for this is the fact that the impetus towards codification of the law in the interest of clarity or simplicity often does not come from lawyers or legislatures and traditional lawmakers but from dictators or other powerful leaders who have made their reputation in other activities: for example, Lipit-Ishtar, Hammurabi, Moses, Julius Caesar, Pompey the Great, Justinian, Frederick the Great, Napoleon, or Ataturk. That their dominating position could get their laws passed more easily is not the issue: what matters is that they proposed and pushed strongly for radical reform of the sources. To the extent that they were outside of the culture, they were less influenced by it. They were more aware of the defects and confusions of the law, and less sensitive to the susceptibilities and pressures of the members of the inner ring of the legal subculture. Similarly, for Sir William Blackstone, English law was near-perfection; for Jeremy Bentham, it was anathema. Creative judges, too, are often outsiders in some sense, or set apart in some way from their colleagues: an outstanding example is Mansfield, a Scot in England. Another Scot in England who, impatient with the complexities of English law, was responsible for much reform is Henry Brougham.[134] In fact, much of the struggle in England in the nineteenth and early twentieth centuries for procedural reform was led by the public, not by the bar.[135]

---

[132] *See generally,* F. Boas, Race, Language and Culture (1966).

[133] M. Sahlins, *supra* note 125, at 70 (discussing Boas's theories and works).

[134] *See* J. Baker, An Introduction to English Legal History 186-87 (2d ed. 1979).

[135] *See* Sunderland, *The English Struggle for Procedural Reform,* 39 Harv. L. Rev. 725 (1926). For the opinion that in the United States the reform of the law of evidence would not come from the bar, see E.M. Morgan, The Law of Evidence

Third, the concept of a legal culure I have described allows for a better understanding of the transnational character of legal change. To a considerable degree, the lawmakers of one society share the same legal culture with the lawmakers of other societies. This is particularly clear when a complex, ancient, written work like Justinian's *Corpus Juris Civilis* is accepted as authoritative in a number of states. Thus, to the extent that law is determined by economic forms and is not autonomous, and to the extent that the legal culture is based on local traditions, the law of two neighboring territories need not converge; but to the degree that the culture is shared by the two sets of lawmakers, it will.

One final point should be stressed. If the arguments put forward here are sound, then law is often dysfunctional with regard to society as a whole or groups within it. When this is so, the cause is frequently to be found in the legal tradition. In other words, law operates as culture not only where the practical effects of the rules are economically, socially, or politically indifferent to society as a whole, to powerful groups, or to the ruling elite, but even where they are positively detrimental.

---

66 (1927). It is a commonplace in science that

> [a]lmost always the men who achieve these fundamental inventions of a new paradigm have been either very young or very new to the field whose paradigm they change. . . . [O]bviously these are the men who, being little committed by prior practice to the traditional rules of normal science, are particularly likely to see that those rules no longer define a playable game and to conceive another set that can replace them.

T. Kuhn, The Structure of Scientific Revolutions 90 (2d ed. 1970) (footnote omitted).

II

Archaic Law at Rome

8

Roman Private Law and the Leges Regiae

According to tradition Rome was founded by Romulus in 753 B.C. and was ruled by seven kings until the expulsion of Tarquin the Proud in 509.[1] Later writers, particularly Dionysius of Halicarnassus and Plutarch, attribute a considerable volume of legislation to these kings, especially to Romulus, Numa Pompilius and Servius Tullius.

The story of this legislation is doubted by modern scholars [2] in two ways. First it is maintained that at such an early time law would not be created by legislation. Secondly it is claimed that law such as is described for the period could not then have existed, but is either an invention of the history writers or is the law of a later period which has been pushed back in time.[3] The doubts are so profound that it has been said we know as good as nothing about law before the *decemviri*.[4]

In this article I should like to argue that the rules for private law recorded by the tradition actually do give us, in general, the substance of Roman law as it was in the regal period. Secondly I wish to suggest that the idea of legislation in the time of the kings is perfectly plausible, though legislation then cannot strictly be proved. Rejection of this second proposition by scholars need not, of course, involve rejection of the first.

I

To test the strength of the ancient tradition and the objections to it we will look for a pattern in the reported provisions. The pattern, if one is found, can then be examined to see if it bears the signs of historical invention or if it relates to a later period of Roman development or to a foreign state. A large proportion of the rules concern sacral law, but two branches of private law are prominent in the sources, the law of patron and client and the power of the head of a family, and we will consider these in turn.

Romulus separated the more powerful from the lower classes and legislated on the duties of each. The patricians were to be priests and magistrates and decide legal cases. The plebeians were to cultivate the fields, rear animals and engage in commerce. The plebeians were entrusted to the care of the patricians, and each plebeian was permitted to choose a patron for himself.[5] The law of patronage was then established. The patricians were to interpret the law for their clients, to bring law suits for them if they suffered injury, and to assist them if they sued. The clients were to assist their patrons in marrying off their daughters if the parents lacked funds (i.e. help in providing a dowry), to ransom their patrons or their patron's children from the enemy if they were captured, and to pay the damages awarded against their patrons in private suits and fines imposed in public actions. It was unlawful both for patron and client to bring an action against the other, to bear witness against the other or cast a vote against the other. If anyone was convicted of such a crime he was liable under the law of treason established by Romulus, and anyone could kill such a condemned person as one dedicated to the god of the underworld.

These provisions give a picture of a relationship of lord and dependant much more extreme than any known at Rome for a later period. What, however, is remarkable is their similarity with the feudal law of medieval England, and especially with the extraordinary burdens known as ' aids '. Thus, under this heading Pollock and Maitland declare: [6]

> ' The duties implied in the relation between man and lord are but slowly developed and made legal duties. There long remains a fringe of vague obligations. The man

[1] The precision of the dating need not concern us.

[2] Cf. e.g. Wenger, *Die Quellen des römischen Rechts* (1953), 353 ff.; Gioffredi, *Diritto e processo nelle antiche forme giuridiche romane* (1955), 33 f.; Guarino, *L'ordinamento giuridico romano*, 3rd ed. (1959), 82 ff.; Gaudemet, *Institutions de l'Antiquité*, (1967), 381 f.; Kaser, *Das römische Privatrecht* i, 2nd ed., (1971), 30; and the authors cited.

[3] It is at times conceded that some of the provisions (especially those of sacral law) may go back to the regal period.

[4] Wieacker, ' Die XII Tafeln in ihrem Jahrhundert ', *Entretiens sur l'Antiquité classique XIII, Les Origines de la république romaine* (Fondation Hardt, 1967), 293 ff. at p. 300.

[5] Dionysius of Halicarnassus 2, 9, 1–2.

[6] *The History of English Law* i, 2nd ed. (reprinted 1968), 349 f.

> should come to the aid of the lord in all his necessities; the man's purse as well as his body should be at his lord's disposal if the lord is in a strait. Gradually the occasions on which an aid of money may be demanded are determined. Glanvill [7] mentions the aid which helps a lord to pay the relief due to his overlord, the aid for knighting the lord's eldest son and marrying his eldest daughter; also he raises the question whether the lord may not demand an aid for the maintenance of a war in which he is concerned; such a demand, he thinks, can not be pressed. From the Normandy of Glanvill's time we hear of the aid for the lord's relief, for marrying his daughter and knighting his eldest son. The charter of 1215 mentioned as the three aids, which the king might take without the common counsel of the realm, that for redeeming his body, that for marrying his daughter and that for knighting his son; and such aids were to be reasonable. As is well known, the clause which dealt with this matter appeared in no later edition of the charter. During John's reign the prior of St. Swithin's took an aid from his freeholders, farmers and villeins for the payment of his debts; the bishop of Winchester took an aid for the expenses to which he had been put in the maintenance of the king's honour and the dignity of the church; the abbot of Peterborough took an aid to enable him to pay a fine to the king; the earl of Salisbury to enable him to stock his land.'

Elsewhere the same authors discuss the sanctity of homage : [8]

> ' That a lord should make an attack on his man, or a man on his lord, even under the forms of law, is scarcely to be tolerated. If the man will bring an appeal, a criminal charge, against his lord, he must first " waive the tenement ". When a king is going to declare war upon his barons he first defies them, for there should be no attack while there is affiance. Henry III in 1233 defied the Marshal, who then was no longer his man, but " outside his homage " ; before the battle of Lewes he defied the earls of Leicester and Gloucester, who thereupon renounced homage and fealty. We can hardly say that all this lies outside the sphere of law, for rebellions and wars are conducted on quasi-legal principles: that is a characteristic of the time.'

To plot against the life of one's lord was petty treason, and petty treason was only gradually marked off from high treason.[9]

These similarities between the purported *leges regiae* and English feudal law cannot be the result of borrowing, however indirect. The characteristics of English feudal law can owe nothing to Dionysius. Nor can we reasonably believe that Dionysius' imagination was so fertile that he could from nothing invent laws so perfect for a feudal society that at a much later date in a very different country very similar rules [10] did come to exist. For the same reason we can dismiss the possibility that Dionysius' source was a political pamphlet—which had no origin in an actual legal system—designed to glorify monarchy for the benefit of some such personage as Sulla, Julius Caesar or Augustus.[11]

Two possible approaches remain for those who think these rules of law could not exist in the Rome of the kings. The first is to claim that Dionysius (or his source) transferred them (with whatever motive) from some other state. But what state ? It seems impossible to find the model. Dionysius [12] tells us that under the laws of Romulus the position of the plebeians was better than that of the *thetes* and *penestae*. In fact the position of the plebs was very different from that of the *thetes* in Athens or of the *penestae* in Thessaly; and that Dionysius should refer to them suggests that in his experience there was no closer parallel to the position of the plebs. Also against this approach is the evidence for the sanctity of the bond between patron and client in later Roman law. The XII Tables [13] enacted, ' Patronus

[7] Glanvill's book seems to have been completed between November, 1187 and 6th July, 1189.

[8] *History* cit. i, 303.

[9] Cf. Pollock and Maitland, *History* ii, 503 f.

[10] The rules of English law which interest us derive from the relationship resulting from land tenure. But they are not rules which seem to be immediately consequent upon land-holding, and similar rules can readily be envisaged for a lord-dependant relationship which was not based on land-holding.

[11] For different and convincing arguments against the source being such a *Tendenzschrift*, see Balsdon, ' Dionysius on Romulus: a Political Pamphlet ? ' *JRS* lxi (1971), 18 ff.

[12] 2, 9, 2–3.

[13] VIII, 21.

si clienti fraudem fecerit, sacer esto ': so a patron who defrauded a client was still dedicated to the gods of the underworld and could be killed. Cato claimed that the old Romans thought it more holy (*sanctius*) to defend *pupilli* than not to defraud a client,[14] that one gave evidence against *cognati* (blood-relatives connected through males) on behalf of a client but that no one gave evidence against a client.[15] Massurius Sabinus wrote at the beginning of the Empire that earlier generations ranked duties, first to a pupil under one's guardianship, then to a guest, next to a client, then to a *cognatus*, finally to a relative through marriage.[16] From the comic writers of the Republic we see that it was a solemn duty to act in court for friends and dependants.[17]

The second approach for the sceptics is to claim that the rules attributed to Romulus did exist at Rome but only at a later date. Against that argument it should be emphasized that we do have evidence for later times including the early Republic,[18] that this evidence shows the importance of the patron-client relationship but in a much weaker form than that attributed to Romulus. The evidence, in fact, is consistent with the hypothesis of a gradual move away from an almost feudal relationship as Rome grew in size.

The implausibility of these last two approaches of the sceptics becomes more obvious when we look at the texts on the power of the *paterfamilias*.

According to the sources, Romulus compelled the Romans to bring up all their male children and the first-born daughter: no offspring younger than three could be killed unless it were born a monster or was badly injured at birth; in which case it could be exposed by the parents provided they showed it to five near neighbours who testified to the fact. For those who disobeyed the laws Romulus established penalties which included forfeiture of half their property.[19] Romulus introduced by statute marriage by *confarreatio* by which the wife came into the *manus* of her husband.[20] The wife's relatives, together with her husband, could sit in judgement on her if she was accused of adultery or wine drinking, and Romulus allowed them to put her to death.[21] Romulus gave the father complete power over a son for the whole of his life; he could imprison him, beat him, put him bound to field work, and kill him. The father could even sell the son, and would acquire through the son until the third sale, but after a third sale the son was free from his father.[22] Plutarch tells us that Romulus enacted a harsh law that a wife could not divorce her husband but a husband could divorce a wife for poisoning of offspring,[23] for substitution of keys,[24] for adultery; if he sent her away for a different reason, half of his property was to go to the wife, half was to be consecrated to Ceres. Anyone who sold his wife was to be dedicated to the gods of the underworld.[25] Numa is said to have enacted that if a father permitted his son to marry *cum manu* he no longer had the right to sell his son.[26] Servius Tullius enacted that if a son struck his father who called out, the son was to be dedicated to the parental gods. And a similar law where a daughter-in-law struck the *paterfamilias* is apparently ascribed to Romulus and Tatius.[27]

The similarities between these reported provisions and later *patria potestas* are obvious. In the Republic the father's power over his children existed for life and was all-embracing, and a wife *in manu* was very much subject to his control. But strangely, in the Republic the powers of the father were far more absolute. As early as the XII Tables there was no check on his power to expose infants. The father had power of life and death even over grown up children and although the rule relating to three sales remained there is no sign of Numa's

[14] ' quam clientem non fallere '. The negative formulation, which seems rather strange, is used so that Cato can speak in terms of defrauding a client, a direct reference to the provision of the XII Tables.

[15] Aulus Gellius, *NA* 5, 13, 4; cf. Watson, *The Law of Persons in the Later Roman Republic* (1967), 104.

[16] Aulus Gellius, *NA* 5, 13, 5; cf. Watson, *Persons* 104 f.

[17] e.g. Plautus, *Cas.* 563 ff.; Terence, *Eun.* 335 ff.

[18] Cf. above all, Wieacker, art. cit. (n. 4).

[19] Dionysius of Halicarnassus 2, 15, 2.

[20] Dionysius of Halicarnassus 2, 25, 1.

[21] Dionysius of Halicarnassus 2, 25, 6.

[22] Dionysius of Halicarnassus 2, 26, 4–6; 2, 27, 1–2.

[23] Abortion ?

[24] Attempted adultery ? Illicit drinking or tampering with the food store ? The exact function of this provision is not clear but need not detain us. Locks with keys were widely diffused over the eastern Mediterranean in the period contemporary with regal Rome, and among people in close contact with Italy, e.g. Greeks and Phoenicians. The so-called *balanos* lock was known in Egypt as early as the time of Rameses II (1292–1225): cf. Diels, *Antike Technik* 2nd ed. (1920), 52. In Cyprus, tombs of about 700 B.C. have false doors with imitation locks, all in stone.

[25] Plutarch, *Romulus* 22, 3–4.

[26] Dionysius of Halicarnassus 2, 27, 4.

[27] Festus, s.v. *plorare*.

restriction where the *pater* permitted his son to marry.[28] By the later Republic there were no restrictions on the husband's right to divorce, and the sole penalties for unjustified divorce related to his right of retaining his wife's dowry.[29] By then, too, his right to kill a wife *in manu* for adultery was unfettered, and the wife's relatives had no say in the matter.[30]

This development—increase in extent and force of *patria potestas*—is the reverse of what would be expected by persons unskilled in comparative anthropology. Hence the provisions cannot be the invention of historians of a later age. Likewise, because of their relationship with the known rules of Republican Rome, they cannot have been transferred to the Rome of the kings from either a different state or a later time.

Moreover, the two areas of private law for which we have adequate sources apparently developed very differently in subsequent centuries. The bonds of *patronatus* loosened, *patria potestas* increased in strength. This divergence is further evidence that the rules attributed to the kings are not the work of a later political or moral theorist inventing patterns. The development which is apparent between the regal period and the time of Dionysius does not seem to accord with any ancient idea of progress.

Thus the general picture of the private substantive law in the time of the kings, as represented by later tradition, is worthy of belief even though there may be doubts on the accuracy of detail. The emphasis on sacral law (which will not be examined here) in the sources is also what one might expect from that early period.

We should note, however, that sacral law is prominent even in the substantive rules on *patronatus* and the family. Breaches of the rules of *patronatus* resulted in the wrongdoer becoming *sacer*. The same fate awaited a son or daughter-in-law who struck the *paterfamilias*. Marriage by *confarreatio* was a religious ceremony and involved sacrifices and the presence of the *pontifex maximus* and *flamen dialis*. Half of the property of a husband who divorced (or sent away) his wife for a reason other than that permitted was dedicated to Ceres. There is little information in the sources on other aspects of what we would tend to consider private law. Numa ordered landowners to mark their boundaries with stones consecrated to Juppiter Terminus: if anyone took away or moved such a stone he was to be consecrated to the god.[31] The same monarch gave various rights to the Vestal Virgins, including that of making a will during the lifetime of their father, and of acting without a *tutor*.[32] He also fixed periods of mourning for children and (at least) husbands. A widow was not to remarry during this period: if she did, she had to sacrifice a pregnant cow.[33] A pregnant woman who died was not to be buried before the unborn child was cut from her.[34] If anyone negligently killed another he could offer the deceased's relatives a ram *pro capite occisi*. Tullius Hostilius enacted that the father of triplet sons should be given support until they reached puberty.[35] Servius Tullius passed almost fifty laws on contracts and delicts;[36] and declared that manumitted slaves should receive citizenship.[37] Many of these provisions obviously also concern sacral law, some of the others may equally have done so.[38] Hence when ancient writers talk of sacral law in the time of the kings they may be including those provisions which we might regard as predominantly concerning private law.

How was knowledge of the laws of the kings transmitted to later generations? Dionysius of Halicarnassus claims[39] that of the laws of Romulus most were unwritten but some were reduced to writing. Pomponius relates that both Romulus and subsequent kings were responsible for *leges curiatae*.[40] Dionysius says that king Ancus Marcius received from the pontiffs the commentaries on religious rites which were composed by Numa and he transcribed these sacred laws on tablets which were set up in the forum.[41] The tablets did

[28] See Tab. IV, 1–2.
[29] Cf. Watson, *Persons* 48 ff. and the texts cited.
[30] Aulus Gellius, *NA* 10, 23, 4–5.
[31] Dionysius of Halicarnassus 2, 74, 2.
[32] Plutarch, *Numa* 10, 3.
[33] Plutarch, *Numa* 12, 2.
[34] *D.* 11, 8, 2 (Marcellus *28 dig.*).
[35] Dionysius of Halicarnassus 3, 22, 10.
[36] Dionysius of Halicarnassus 4, 13, 1. The number seems highly unlikely, and we have no further information on these laws.
[37] Dionysius of Halicarnassus 4, 22.
[38] Thus the obligation to cut out the *fetus* from the dead pregnant woman may have involved *fas* rather than *ius*: cf. Fraenkel, *Hermes* lx (1925), 426. The information on the XII Tables' provision on accidental killing suggests that the ram was a substitute for the killer (Cicero, *top.* 17, 64; *pro Tullio* 21, 51; *de orat.* 3, 39, 158), and perhaps originally he was religiously killed.
[39] 2, 24, 1; cf. 2, 27, 3.
[40] *D.* 1, 2, 2, 2 (*sing. enchirid.*).
[41] 3, 36, 4. This is reported also by Livy, 1, 32, 2. Cicero relates that sacral laws of Numa were still extant: *de re pub.* 2, 14, 26; 5, 2, 3.

not survive, but after the expulsion of the kings they were again copied for the public's use by Gaius Papirius, the *pontifex maximus*.[42] Elsewhere Dionysius names him as Manius Papirius.[43] For Pomponius all the laws of the kings were extant in the book of Sextus Papirius, which was called the *ius civile Papirianum* not because Papirius added anything of his own but because he collected together the laws which had been passed in no arranged sequence. This Papirius whom Pomponius calls also Publius Papirius [44] is said to have lived at the time of Tarquin the Proud. About two centuries after Pomponius, Macrobius writes as if the *ius Papirianum* was still in existence.[45] The source of knowledge of the *ius Papirianum* would seem to be the book of Granius Flaccus [46] who was probably a contemporary of Julius Caesar,[47] though the book itself must be later than October, 46 B.C.[48] Schulz very reasonably points out that Granius Flaccus cannot have invented the rules he reported—the pontifical college, says Schulz, would have denounced such an imposture—but must have made use of existing pontifical records.[49] A further, though negative, argument for holding that the tradition of the regal laws was preserved in the pontifical records is the insignificance of references to the laws in Livy which means, of course, that the tradition was not preserved in the *annales maximi*.

These accounts of the *ius Papirianum* are not unequivocal. The confusion over Papirius' praenomen is, of itself, of little significance since it not infrequently happens that a praenomen is misreported.[50] Nor does it seem particularly significant that Pomponius makes Papirius a contemporary of Tarquinius Superbus while Dionysius records him as *pontifex maximus* in the early Republic.[51] But whereas Pomponius says the *ius Papirianum* contained all the laws of Romulus and his successors, Dionysius relates that the *ius Papirianum* recorded only the sacral laws of Numa. Any resolution of this conflict will be arbitrary, but it may be observed that Dionysius himself shows a greater knowledge of all the laws of the kings than does any other writer in antiquity,[52] and no collective source of this information other than the *ius Papirianum* is known to us.[53,54] Also, as has been already mentioned, many of the laws on private law might be considered sacral laws.

42 3, 36, 4.

43 If we can assume that the early *pontifex maximus* is the same person as the first *rex sacrorum* of the Republic: 5, 1, 4.

44 *D.* 1, 2, 2, 2, cf. 36.

45 *Sat.* 3, 11, 5: 'Ego [Praetextatus] autem quod mihi magistra lectione compertum est publicabo. In Papiriano enim iure evidenter relatum est arae vicem praestare posse mensam dicatam.'

46 *D.* 50, 16, 144 (Paul *10 ad legem Iuliam et Papiam*) . . . 'Granius Flaccus in libro de iure Papiriano scribit. . . .'

47 At least a Granius Flaccus wrote a book *de indigitamentis* which was dedicated to Caesar: Censorinus, *de die natali* 3, 2. *Pace* e.g. Steinwenter, *RE* x, 1285, the identification of this Granius Flaccus with that mentioned in *D.* 50, 16, 144 does not rest solely upon the name being the same. There is also the similarity of interest. An antiquarian who published the laws of the kings which were above all sacred laws is also likely to have been interested in *indigitamenta*, that is, the list of Roman gods and their titles, and the proper mode of addressing each god.

48 Argued from Cicero, *ad fam.* 9, 21 which was written in that month to Papirius Paetus. Cicero assures the recipient that there have been Papirii who were not plebeians and he discusses those known to him, and our Papirius is not mentioned: cf. e.g. Steinwenter, loc. cit.: Schulz, *Roman Legal Science* (1946), 89, n. 4. Contra, Paoli, 'Le *ius Papirianum* et la loi Papiria', *RHD*, xxiv–xxv (1946–47), 157 ff.; but see infra, n. 53.

49 *Legal Science* 89.

50 e.g. the tribune of the plebs who proposed the *lex Falcidia* is named as C. Falcidius in Jerome's continuation of Eusebius, *Chron.* 11, 139 (in Schöne's edition), Publius Falcidius in Dio 48, 33, 5. The C. Octavius of Cicero, *ad Quintum fratrem* 1, 1, 21, is probably Cn. Octavius, consul of 76, but may even be L. Octavius, consul of 75.

51 And if we identify this Papirius with the Manius Papirius of Dionysius 5, 1, 4, he was the first *rex sacrorum* on the expulsion of the kings.

52 It should be mentioned that Livy 6, 1, 10, relates that in 389 B.C., after the capture and burning of Rome by the Gauls, a decree was passed for the searching out of treaties and laws including the XII Tables and certain *leges regiae*. Some of these were then published but those concerned with the *sacra* were kept private by the pontiffs.

53 Despite the contradiction the main tradition of the *ius Papirianum* is strong enough, I think, to exclude the identification proposed by Paoli, o.c. (n. 48), of the *ius Papirianum* with the *lex Papiria* which was the work of the tribune Q. Papirius: Cicero, *de domo* 127–129. See already against the identification, Di Paola, 'Dalla *lex Papiria* al *ius Papirianum*', *Studi Solazzi* (1948), 631 ff. (Paoli also argues that Cicero does not mention this Papirius in *ad fam.* 9, 21, because he was a plebeian.) Di Paola thinks that the *lex Papiria* is to be dated after 287 B.C. (640 ff.) and that the *lex* was the fulcrum around which in course of time were collected a group of rules, the *ius Papirianum*, largely attributed to the Roman kings (646 ff.). This view also, I suggest, is too much at variance with the tradition to be acceptable. Moreover, if the arguments in the first part of this article for the general accuracy of the substance of law in the regal period are correct, then the history of the *ius Papirianum* given by Di Paola can be excluded. Most recently, S. Tondo defends the tradition of the *ius Papirianum* in 'Introduzione alle *leges regiae*', *SDHI* xxxii (1971), 1 ff. This article, which is much more concerned with social law than private law, appeared too late for full consideration.

54 Servius *in Verg. Aen.* 12, 836 concerns the *lex Papiria*, not the *ius Papirianum*.

II

It would be asking too much to demand proof that the *leges regiae* were actual legislation. But if it is correct to maintain that the substantive rules recorded do correspond to law in existence during the regal period, and if the tradition of the transmission seems to be reasonably trustworthy, then I submit that the fundamental question becomes whether the idea of legislation is so implausible that it can rightly be excluded. And I would suggest that the idea of legislation for that period is perfectly plausible.[55]

According to Pomponius [56] the legislation passed through the *comitia curiata*. This seems reasonable enough. It is generally accepted that the *comitia curiata* then existed,[57] and though in historic times it did not legislate [58] apart from the *lex curiata de imperio*, we can be sure from the example of the *comitia calata* that it once did. The *comitia calata* was in fact nothing other than the *comitia curiata* when summoned by the *pontifex maximus* and even in much later times its resolutions on wills and *adrogatio* were true legislation though of a rather debased kind.[59] The form of the proceedings is even eminently suitable for an early assembly. A *rogatio* was put to the people: *Velitis iubeatis uti L. Valerius L. Titio tam iure legeque filius siet, quam si ex eo patre matreque familias eius natus esset, utique ei vitae necisque in eum potestas siet, uti patri endo filio est. Haec ita, uti dixi, ita vos Quirites rogo.*[60] The people then signified their approval or disapproval. The possibility of such a mode of proceeding in gatherings of early society—proposal put orally by a leader, approval or disapproval made obvious by assembled people—is confirmed by evidence of not too dissimilar behaviour on the part of the archaic Greeks,[61] the Germans [62] and the Gauls.[63] Writing would not be required for any such legislation in the *comitia curiata* and was apparently never needed for legislation in the *comitia calata*. Hence on that ground we need not dispute Dionysius' statement that most of Romulus' laws were unwritten but some were put into writing.[64] The historicity of some kings, especially Romulus himself, is doubtful at best. But true legislation by an actual king could easily be fathered on a fictitious hero.[65]

[55] Contrary to the dominant opinion, Wenger thinks legislation then not at all impossible: *Quellen* 353. I am not persuaded by Kaser's view, based above all on the *lex curiata de imperio*, *adrogatio* and *testamentum comitiis calatis*, that a *lex publica* originally was always based on a particular decision and did not contain a general rule; hence that the early *leges regiae* cannot be laws: *Das altrömische Ius* (1949), 64 ff. The idea that in the time of the kings or very early in Rome's history, *leges* were always casuistic, only becomes plausible if one can first assume that the *leges regiae* were not *leges*.

[56] *D.* 1, 2, 2, 2.

[57] Cf. e.g. Momigliano, *Oxford Classical Dictionary*, 2nd ed. (1970), s.v. *Comitia*; Palmer, *The Archaic Community of the Romans* (1970), 189 ff.

[58] According to Dionysius of Halicarnassus, by ancient statutes the people sanctioned and repealed laws by *curiae*, and Servius Tullius transferred this function (and others) to the centuries, i.e. the *comitia centuriata*: 4, 20, 2–3.

[59] We know most about *adrogatio* since the will *calatis comitiis* disappeared early. For *adrogatio* see, e.g., Watson, *Roman Private Law around 200 B.C.* (1971), 30 ff.

[60] Aulus Gellius, *NA* 5, 19, 9. For the more obscure procedure in the *comitia curiata* see Cicero, *de re pub.* 2, 13, 25; 2, 17, 21; 2, 18, 33.

[61] e.g. Homer, *Iliad* 1, 17 ff.

[62] Tacitus, *Germ.* 11; *Hist.* 5, 17; Ammianus Marcellinus 16, 12, 13.

[63] Caesar, *de bell. gall.* 7, 21. I should not be taken as suggesting that the archaic Greeks, Germans and Gauls legislated.

[64] 2, 24, 1; cf. 2, 27, 3. Gaudemet categorically denies the existence of written rules in the regal period, first because writing was then exceptional, and secondly because at the beginning of the Republic the plebeians demanded that the law be put into writing: *Institutions* 382. But one should not exaggerate the infrequency of writing in early Rome; the Latin inscription on the fibula from Praeneste is to be dated around 600 B.C.: cf. e.g. Ernout, *Recueil de Textes Latins archaïques* 2nd ed. (1966), p. 3: and the well-attested presence of Etruscans in Regal Rome in itself means that writing would there be well-known. Moreover the famous *Cippus Romanus* (reprinted in e.g. *FIRA* i, p. 30) may well date from the regal period. In general, the demand of the plebeians in the early Republic was that the law be made known to them, which does not necessarily imply that laws in writing did not exist in the hands of the pontiffs. The demand of the tribune, C. Terentilius Harsa, in 462 for law to be put into writing refers specifically to the *leges de imperio consulari*: Livy 3, 9, 5. According to Dionysius, at that time legal decisions generally conformed to the character of the consuls, but a very few of them were kept in sacred books and had the force of laws: 10, 1, 4.

[65] If the main propositions of this article, and especially of the first part, were found to be acceptable, it would be possible to take a further look at the nature of early Roman society.

I am grateful for help in various ways in the preparation of this article to Mr. Francis Cairns, Professor Reuven Yaron, Dr. Anthony Snodgrass, Mr. Robin Seager and Dr. Bernard Jackson.

9

The Death of Horatia

Central to any understanding of archaic Roman criminal law is the trial, as recorded by Livy, of Horatius for killing his sister. It is not just that the case raises so many legal issues; the jurisdiction of the father (*paterfamilias*) and of the king, the institution of a separate state procedure with two judges (the *duoviri*), the right of appeal to the people, the scope of the crime of *perduellio* (usually roughly translated as 'treason') and of *parricidium*, murder, and the use of sacral punishment. But also, on the ability to determine how accurate for the period of King Tullus Hostilius is this account of law and legal procedure will depend our wider appreciation of the reliability of the sources. It must be admitted that almost all modern scholars regard Livy's account as quite untrustworthy.

There are, as we shall see, three apparent oddities which must be explained in Livy's tale. First, why is the charge against Horatius for killing his sister, *perduellio*? Secondly, why is he not accused of *parricidium*? Thirdly, why do the *duoviri* perversely decide that the law under which the process is established compels them to convict the accused whether he is guilty or innocent. If these three peculiarities make no sense for the archaic period and a sensible explanation can be produced of how they came to be inserted later into the tradition, then we would be entitled to claim that the episode, in Livy's account, is so corrupt that little can be deduced from it for the state of early law. But if, on the other hand, sense can be made for the archaic period of these apparent peculiarities and if no satisfactory explanation can be given of why they would all have been inserted later into the tradition, then it is plausible to claim that the episode in Livey does reflect conditions in the regal period and that we should treat the legal details of the story as prima facie accurate unless the contrary can be shown.

Livy certainly will not have invented the details but must have found them in his sources, whose pedigree will not be considered in this paper.[1] At the moment it is enough to notice that the peculiarities do not appear in the other ancient writers who refer to the episode. According to Festus,

[1] But see, e.g., P. G. Walsh, *Livy, his Historical Aims and Methods* (Cambridge, 1961), pp. 110 ff.

s.v. *Sororium tigillum*, Horatius was charged with *parricidium*, and nothing is said to indicate that the *duoviri* considered they would have to convict even an innocent man. For Dionysius of Halicarnassus, 3.22 the charge was again *parricidium*, and the *duoviri* are not brought into the story at all. For Florus, 1.1.3.6, the crime committed by Horatius was *parricidium*.[2] Their testimony rather favours Livy's historical accuracy. What seem peculiarities to us in the tradition recorded by Livy were also apparently incomprehensible to these classical writers (or their sources), hence they were excised. We can understand that details that were accurate but came subsequently to seem peculiar were cut out by some later writers. But we cannot so easily assert that later writers invented absurd details which were inserted into the tale and accepted. A principle akin to *difficilior lectio* creates a presumption supporting the Livian tradition. A further strong argument in favour of the Livian version is that the trial of Rabirius in 63 B.C. for *perduellio* was patterned on a view of the law akin to that given in Livy's account of the trial of Horatius.[3]

But it is high time to recount Livy's tale. In the reign of the third king of Rome, Tullus Hostilius (762-640 B.C.), a state of war existed between the Romans and the inhabitants of Alba Longa. In view of the common threat from the Etruscans, a plan was devised to avoid the destruction of the Roman or Alban power while determining which city should have dominion over the other. Each army contained triplet brothers, the Horatii on the Roman side, the Curiatii on the Alban, and it was decided that each should fight for his city. The three Curiatii were killed and one of the Horatii survived, thus giving victory to the Romans. The armies marched home. Livy continues:[4]

[2] See also *Auctor de viris illustribus* 4.9; Valerius Maximus, 6.3.6; 8.1. *absol.* 1; *Schol. Bob. Cic. Mil.* 7; Zonaras, 7.6.4.

[3] See below, p. 127. This rejection of the version of Festus is a powerful argument against the recent claim by R. A. Bauman, *The Duumviri in the Roman Criminal Law and in the Horatius Legend* (Historia Einzelschrift 12, Wiesbaden, 1969), that the jurisdiction of the *duoviri* was not confined to cases of *perduellio*.

[4] 'Abi hine cum immaturo amore ad sponsum,' inquit, 'oblita fratrum mortuorum vivique, oblita patriae. Sic eat quaecumque Romam lugebit hostem'. 5. Atrox visum id facinus patribus plebique, sed recens meritum facto obstabat. Tamen raptus in ius ad regem. Rex ne ipse tam tristis ingratique ad volgus iudicii ac secundum iudicium supplicii auctor esset, concilio populi aducato 'Duumuiros' inquit, 'qui Horatio perduellionem iudicent, secundum legem facio.' 6. Lex horrendi carminis erat: 'Duumuiri perduellionem iudicent; si a duumuiris provocarit, provocatione certato; si vincent, caput obnubito; infelici arbori reste suspendito; verberato vel intra pomerium vel extra pomerium.' 7. Hac lege duumuiri creati, qui se absolvere non rebantur ea lege ne innoxium quidem posse, cum condemnassent, tum alter ex iis 'Publi Horati, tibi perduellionem iudico' inquit. 'I, lictor, colliga manus.' 8. Accesserat lictor iniciebatque laqueum. Tum Horatius auctore Tullo, clemente legis interprete, 'Prouoco' inquit. Itaque provocatione certatum ad populum est. 9. Moti homines sunt in eo iudicio maxime P. Horatio patre proclamante se filiam iure caesam iudicare; ni ita esset, patrio iure in filium animadversurum fuisse. Orabat deinde ne se quem paulo ante cum egregia stirpe conspexissent orbum liberis

In the van of the Romans came Horatius, displaying his triple spoils. As he drew near the Porta Capena he was met by his unwedded sister, who had been promised in marriage to one of the Curiatii. When she recognized on her brother's shoulders the military cloak of her betrothed, which she herself had woven, she loosed her hair and, weeping, called on her dead lover's name. It enraged the fiery youth to hear his sister's lamentations in the hour of his own victory and the nation's great rejoicing. And so, drawing his sword and at the same time angrily upbraiding her, he ran her through the body. 'Begone', he cried, 'to your betrothed, with your ill-timed love, since you have forgot your brothers, both the dead and the living, and forgot your country! So perish every Roman woman who mourns a foe!'

Horrid as this deed seemed to the Fathers and the people, his recent service was an off-set to it; nevertheless he was seized and brought before the king for trial. The king, that he might not take upon himself the responsibility for so stern and unpopular a judgement, and for the punishment which must follow sentence, called together the council of the people and said: 'In accordance with the law I appoint duumvirs to pass judgement upon Horatius for treason.' The dread formula of the law ran thus: 'Let the duumvirs pronounce him guilty of treason; if he shall appeal from the duumvirs, let the appeal be tried; if the duumvirs win, let the lictor veil his head; let him bind him with a rope to a barren tree; let him scourge him either within or without the pomerium.' By the terms of this law duumvirs were appointed. They considered that they might not acquit, under that act, even one who was innocent, and having given a verdict of guilty, one of them pronounced the words, 'Publius Horatius, I adjudge you a traitor; go, lictor, bind his hands.' The lictor had approached and was about to fit the noose. Then Horatius, at the prompting of Tullus, who put a merciful construction upon the law, cried, 'I appeal!' And so the appeal was tried before the people. What influenced men most of all in that trial was the assertion of Publius Horatius, the father, that his daughter had been justly slain; otherwise he should have used a father's authority and have punished his son, himself. He then implored them not to make him childless whom they had beheld a little while before surrounded by a goodly offspring. So saying, the old man embraced the youth, and pointing to the spoils of the Curiatii set up in the place which is now called 'the Horatian

facerent. 10. Inter haec senex iuvenem amplexus, spolia Curiatiorum fixa eo loco qui nunc Pila Horatia appellatur ostentans, 'Huncine' aiebat, 'quem modo decoratum ovantemque victoria incedentem vidistis, Quirites, eum sub furca vinctum inter verbera et cruciatus videre potestis? quod vix Albanorum oculi tam deforme spectaculum ferre possent. I, lictor, colliga manus, quae paulo ante armatae imperium populo Romano pepererunt. 11. I, caput obnube liberatoris urbis huius; arbore infelici suspende; verbera vel intra pomerium, modo inter illa pila et spolia hostium, vel extra pomerium, modo inter sepulcra Curiatiorum; quo enim ducere hunc iuvenem potestis ubi non sua decora eum a tanta foeditate supplicii uindicent? 12. Non tulit populus nec patris lacrimas nec ipsius parem in omni periculo animum, absolveruntque admiratione magis virtutis quam iure causae. Itaque ut caedes manifesta aliquo tamen piaculo lueretur, imperatum patri ut filium expiaret pecunia publica. 13. Is quibusdam piacularibus sacrificiis factis quae deinde genti Horatiae tradita sunt, transmisso per viam tigillo, capite adoperto velut sub iugum misit iuuenem. 14. Id hodie quoque publice semper refectum manet; sororium tigillum vocant. Horatiae sepulcrum, quo loco corruerat icta, constructum est saxa quadrato.

Spears', he exclaimed, 'This man you saw but lately advancing decked with spoils and triumphing in his victory; can you bear, Quirites, to see him bound beneath a fork and scourged and tortured? Hardly could Alban eyes endure so hideous a sight. Go, lictor, bind the hands which but now, with sword and shield, brought imperial power to the Roman People! Go, veil the head of the liberator of this city! Bind him to a barren tree! Scourge him within the pomerium, if you will – so it be amidst yonder spears and trophies of our enemies – or outside the pomerium – so it be amongst the graves of the Curiatii! For whither can you lead this youth where his own honours will not vindicate him from so foul a punishment?' The people could not withstand the father's tears, or the courage of Horatius himself, steadfast in every peril; and they acquitted him, more in admiration of his valour than from the justice of his cause. And so, that the flagrant murder might yet be cleansed away, by some kind of expiatory rite, the father was commanded to make atonement for his son at the public cost. He therefore offered certain piacular sacrifices, which were thenceforward handed down in the Horatian family, and, erecting a beam across the street, to typify a yoke, he made his son pass under it, with covered head. It remains to this day, being restored from time to time at the state's expense, and is known as 'the Sister's Beam'. Horatia's tomb, of hewn stone, was built on the place where she had been struck down.[5]

The precise meaning of the word *perduellio* and the scope of the crime are both subjects of doubt. We need not, however, at the present, examine all aspects of *perduellio*: it will be enough to show that Horatius' conduct can reasonably be explained, for early law, as a form of that offence.

It seems to be accepted that the word derives from *duellum*, an old form of *bellum*, war, warfare, with the prefix *per-*. The exact force of *per-* is not so certain, but it is either simply intensive or else intensive with the implication of wickedness. Thus, *perduellio*, etymologically, should indicate either particularly fierce war or particularly wicked war.[6] Greater etymological precision is probably not possible, nor would it for us necessarily be helpful.

The scope of the crime of *perduellio* is a matter of much dispute particularly because there are very few recorded instances. The trial of Rabirius in 63 B.C. was a revival of the procedure.[7] A sensible approach to the problem is taken by Brecht who argues very properly that we ought not to assume as cases of *perduellio* instances of wrongful behaviour which are not so termed. He divides treason into instances where the wrongdoer joins with external enemies of the state to its disadvantage, and instances where the wrongdoer attacks the condition of the state without joining external enemies. The first he calls 'Landesverrat', the second 'Hochverrat', and only the second does he regard as *perduellio*. He

[5] Translation by B.O. Foster, *Livy* 1 (Loeb Classical Library, London, Heinemann, 1919), pp. 91 ff.

[6] See e.g. C.H. Brecht, *Perduellio* (Munich, 1938), pp. 120 ff.

[7] See e.g. R.M. Ogilvie, *Commentary on Livy, Books 1-5* (Oxford, 1965), p. 114; A.H.M.

maintains that in the Roman criminal law of the time of the XII Tables there was not only *parricidium* and *perduellio* but also the further crime of treason, *proditio*. Among other differences from *perduellio*, *proditio* did not give right to an appeal to the people, and the punishment was secular not sacral.[8]

Whether or not Brecht's distinction is plausible in general,[9] it does not really fit the further text which interests us most, Dionysius of Halicarnassus, 2.10.3.

> For both patrons and clients alike it was impious and unlawful to accuse each other in law-suits to bear witness or to give their votes against each other or to be found in the number of each other's enemies; and whoever was convicted of doing any of these things was guilty of treason by virtue of the law sanctioned by Romulus, and might lawfully be put to death by any man who so wished as a victim devoted to the Jupiter of the infernal regions.[10]

I have already argued elsewhere for the broad accuracy of the ancient tradition on the laws of the kings.[11] Part of the argument – which directly concerns this text – is the existence of an unexpected pattern of similarity between the Roman provisions on patron and client and those of English mediaeval feudal law. Our present text declares that particular wrongful acts between patron and client were *προδοσία*, treason; in medieval law to plot against the life of one's lord was petty treason, and only gradually was petty treason marked off from high treason.

Although the treason in the text is against private individuals it obviously has much in common with *perduellio*, even in Brecht's restricted view of that crime; the penalty of death is sacral, not secular.[12] On the other hand, the type of offences listed do rather look like adhering to the enemy and so bring the wrong close to Brecht's concept of *proditio*. The exact nature of the client's (or patron's) offence and the available process is very much open to doubt,[13] but need not here be determined: it is

Jones, *Criminal Courts of the Roman Republic and Principate* (Oxford, 1972), p. 35; W.B. Tyrrell, *Legal and Historical Commentary to Cicero's Oratio pro C. Rabirio perduellionis reo* (Amsterdam, 1978), pp. 35 ff.

[8] *Perduellio*.

[9] For the expression of serious doubt see D. Daube, *JRS* 31 (1941), 180 ff.

[10] Translation by E. Cary, *Dionysius of Halicarnassus, Roman Antiquities* 1 (Loeb Classical Library, London, 1968), pp. 343 f. *κοινῇ δ' ἀμφοτέροις οὔτε ὅσιον οὔτε θέμις ἦν κατηγορεῖν ἀλλήλων ἐπὶ δίκαις ἢ καταμαρτυρεῖν ἢ ψῆφον ἐναντίαν ἐπιφέρειν ἢ μετὰ τῶν ἐχθρῶν ἐξετάζεσθαι. εἰ δέ τις ἐξελεγχθείη τούτων τι διαπραττόμενος ἔνοχος ἦν τῷ νόμῳ τῆς προδοσίας, ὅν ἐκύρωσεν ὁ Ῥωμύλος, τὸν δὲ ἁλόντα τῷ βουλομένῳ κτείνειν ὅσιον ἦν ὡς θῦμα τοῦ καταχθονίου Διός.*

[11] 'Roman private law and the *leges regiae*', *JRS* 62 (1972), 100 ff.

[12] Dionysius' use of Greek makes it impossible to determine whether terminologically he was thinking of *perduellio* or proditio. Προδοσία is etymologically connected with the latter, but that fact is not helpful since it is also a natural translation of *perduellio*.

[13] For views expressed see Brecht, *Perduellio*, pp. 31 ff.

enough for us that in a situation where a particular duty of obligation existed between one private citizen and another and where a vital part of the relationship was the subordination of one to the other a serious offence against the duty could be named treason. This text of Dionysius is the sole one where a name of any kind is ascribed to the wrong.

I should now like to conjecture that just as the idea of treason could apply to a serious breach of obligation by a citizen to the state (or king) or by a *cliens* to a *patronus*, so likewise it could apply in another situation where there was a particular duty of obligation between one private citizen and another, where a vital part of the relationship was the subordination of one to the other, and where serious breach, never given a name in the sources, gave rise to a sacral penalty of death. What I have in mind is, of course, a serious offence by a member of the household against the *paterfamilias*.

That a sacral death penalty was established in early law for striking the *paterfamilias* appears from Festus, s.v. *Plorare* who gives as the wording of a law of Romulus and Tatius 'Si nurus . . . sacra divis parentum estod.'; and of a law of Servius Tullius, 'Si parentem puer verberit ast olle plorassit parens, puer divis parentum sacer esto.' That, at least according to tradition, laws were passed indicates that what is in issue is not simply the father's domestic jurisdiction and right of punishment.[14] Further precision of the procedure envisaged is not necessary here. The striking of the *pater* cannot have been the only domestic offence punishable by an external process. Indeed, Plutarch[15] records that a husband who sold his wife was to be sacrificed to the gods of the underworld. It is very reasonable to suppose that killing a person subject to one's own *patermailias* was in the same category of a domestic offence punishable by an external process. It may be worth observing that in the English statute of treasons of 1350 (25 Edw. 3, s. 5 c. 2) it is treason for a wife to slay her husband.

Horatius' slaying of Horatia could have been treated, it is generally agreed,[16] as the public crime of murder, *parricidium*. It could have been punished, as Livy in his account makes plain, by the *paterfamilias* acting domestically. It could also – I think we can accept – be punished by a public process as a wrong against the father. And it seems a reasonable conjecture – on the direct analogy of a wrong by a client against a patron – that the wrong could be treated as treason. In so far as one might, following Brecht, attempt to distinguish here between *perduellio* and

[14] See already T. Mommsen, *Römisches Strafrecht* (Leipzig, 1899), pp. 567 f. For the father's domestic jurisdiction see now, A. Watson, *Rome of the XII Tables* (Princeton, 1974), pp. 42 ff.

[15] *Romulus* 22.

[16] But not by Ogilvie, *Commentary*, pp. 114 f: cf. below, pp. 442 f.

proditio, Publius Horatius' conduct would amount to the former: he did not adhere to his father's enemies.

Whatever the external procedure normally was for such a domestic offence, Tullus Hostilius used the state procedure for treason, *perduellio*, and for this he had a particular reason: the procedure gave the accused the right of appeal to the people.

Indeed, if it can be accepted that Horatius' conduct can be regarded as treason *vis-à-vis* his *paterfamilias*, then the whole episode in Livy makes sense, and all the problems can be resolved, on the well-known principle of 'passing the buck'.

Horatius slays his sister. Time elapses during which Horatius *pater* could have exercised his domestic jurisdiction but does not.[17] (Hence the claim of the *pater* later that he would have used his father's authority if his daughter had not been justly killed.) The people bring Horatius before the king for trial. The obvious charge is *parricidium*, but this the king would probably have to hear and decide for himself. There was no provision here for the appointment of *duoviri* and, above all, none for an appeal to the people. So the king 'passes the buck' and has Horatius accused – plausibly I have argued – of *perduellio* and brings into action the state procedure for that crime. Livy stresses the king's reluctance to accept responsibility for the verdict and the punishment: 'Rex ne ipse tam tristis ingratique ad volgus iudicii ac secundum iudicium supplicii auctor esset . . .' The *duoviri* in turn 'pass the buck' as best they can. They cannot find that Horatius has not slain his sister – it is only too well known that he has. So they hold, quite perversely, that the wording of the statute means that they cannot acquit even an innocent man. Hence their verdict which they intend to be understood as indicating nothing of their own view of the case or of the procedure. The 'buck' stops with the people.

On this view the episode has to be seen not as illustrating the most appropriate law and process available for sororicide, but as reflecting political reality and expediency. Horatius is a hero, and no one wishes to take responsibility for having him put to death. But he has also behaved abominably in killing his sister; and the publicity of his act and the horror it aroused demands his trial and punishment. The tension between the treatment merited by the hero Horatius and that deserved by the savage Horatius results in curious dance-like steps just within the limits of the juridically possible. The whole people has to be implicated in any judgement.

This version of the events has in its favour, I suggest, psychological veri-similitude. But it is also supported by the absence from the Roman tradition of evidence of a right of appeal in the regal period for

[17] For Festus, s.v. *Sororium tigillum*, Horatius *pater* absolved his son.

parricidium.[18] Modern scholars, in fact, are adamant that no right of appeal for *parricidium* existed so early.[19] Indeed, one might conjecture that part of the reluctance to accept the historicity of the law and procedure outlined in the story of Horatius is precisely the belief that since no appeal existed for *parricidium* none could have existed for *perduellio* There seems actually to be no evidence for the procedure available for a trial for *parricidium* in the time of the kings. Occasional texts – apart from those relating to Horatius – indicate that *quaestores* existed as early as the kings.[20] But they need not refer to *quaestores parricidii* since it can be disputed whether such *quaestores* were the original.[21] Even if *quaestores parricidii* did then exist, it by no means follows that they acted as judges rather than investigators of a murder. This, indeed, following an etymology from *quaesitores*, is usually seen as the original rôle of *quaestores parricidii.*[22] In the absence of other known machinery of justice, the king himself – as the text of Livy suggests – would have to take responsibility for the trial.[23] If Tullus Hostilius wished to give Horatius the right of appeal, and also, probably, if he wished to avoid responsibility for the trial and the punishment, the charge had to be *perduellio*, not *parricidium*. A trial for *parricidium*, though legally appropriate, was not in the political interests of the king.

(For the king's attitude another sentence of Livy is instructive, though it is not directly related to our main theme: 'Tum Horatius auctore Tullo, clemente legis interprete, "Provoco" inquit.' The translation I have adopted from Foster seems too weak: 'Then Horatius, at the prompting of Tullus, who put a merciful construction upon the law, cried, "I appeal!"' Why, if Tullus simply suggested the appeal, is he described as a mild interpreter of the law? 'Auctore Tullo', it seems to me, is reminiscent of a legal phrase like *auctore tutore*. The king is giving the appeal his *auctoritas*, he

18 The Roman tradition that *provocatio* existed under the kings may derive from that right for *perduellio*. Cicero, *pro Milone*, 3.7; Livy 1.26.6; Festus, s.v. *Sororium tigillum* all refer to the case of Horatius. Cicero, *de re publica*, 2.31.54, though couched in general terms, could derive from sources concerned only with one offence.

19 One strand of scholarly opinion in fact holds that even later when it did exist *provocatio* was directed against the *coercitio* of magistrates, not against the decisions of judges: see e.g. W. Kunkel, *Untersuchungen zur Entwicklung des römischen Kriminalverfahrens in vorsullanischer Zeit* (Munich, 1962), pp. 24 ff. Against the view that *provocatio* was not known in the duumviral process see R.A. Bauman, *Duumviri*, pp. 1, 13 ff.

20 D.1.13.1 (Ulpian, *sing. de off. quaest.*); Tacitus, *ann.* 11.22. But see e.g. T. Mommsen, *Römisches Staatsrecht* 2, 3rd edn. (Leipzig, 1887), 523 ff.

21 See, e.g. K. Latte, 'The Origin of the Roman Quaestorship', *Transactions of American Philological Association* 67 (1936), 24 ff., who, however, accepts a date in the mid-fifth century for the introduction of the quaestorship.

22 See e.g. M. Kaser, *Das altrömische Ius* (Göttingen, 1949), pp. 53 f.

23 In a primitive monarchy it would seem natural, as Jones says, for the king to act as judge. Indeed, Jones who believes that Horatius was tried for *parricidium* suggests that the trial was by the king: *Criminal Courts*, p. 43. Valerius Maximum, 8.1. absol. 1, who does not record the charge against Horatius does name Tullus the judge.

is backing the appeal. In this sense he is the *clemens legis interpres*, making it apparent that he favours the granting of the appeal. Tullus is playing a very canny political game.)

A different explanation that is very ingenious but not in the end persuasive is produced by Ogilvie for the failure to bring a charge of *parricidium*.[24] Horatia, he asserts, was herself a criminal, guilty of *proditio* because she had mourned an enemy. Hence, he says, she was *accusanda* and *damnanda*, and so Horatius' offence was that of forestalling the due processes of the law by executing a criminal who had not yet been sentenced to death, and therefore the crime fell within the scope of *perduellio*. Ogilvie produces three texts – D.3.2.11.3; 11.7.35; Suetonius, *Tiberius* 61 – to support his proposition that ancient law forbade the mourning of an enemy. But the passage from Suetonius is hardly relevant – it relates to a prohibition by the Emperor Tiberius made to meet a particular political need and which does not concern an enemy, but specifically *capite damnati*. The two Digest passages[25] say 'non solent lugeri . . . hostes', 'it is not the custom to mourn the enemy' and 'minime maiores lugendum putaverunt eum . . .', 'our ancestors did not think a person should be mourned . . .', and may mean only that the requisites demanded for mourning are not and should not be observed where the deceased is an enemy. They do not indicate that any such mourning was actually a crime, even less that it was the crime of *proditio* or was punishable by death. Likewise, I think it correct to state that there is no evidence for any period that to kill someone who is not dangerous but who might be charged with a capital offence was not considered murder. Nor does such a suggestion seem to me personally to be plausible. Again I have found no evidence that to take the law into one's own hands was ever considered to be treason. One would expect that if killing a person who had committed a capital offence was not to be murder, then the behaviour would either not be criminal or would give rise only to a relatively minor charge.

The *duoviri* had to give their verdict. But they wriggled out of any responsibility for it by claiming that a verdict for condemnation was necessary under the statute and that they could not absolve even an innocent accused.[26] Now, whatever the wording of the statute, the opinion of the *duoviri* must be considered as contrary to the meaning of the law; and must be regarded as deliberate misrepresentation. The accuracy of Livy's wording will be considered in a moment, but first we must look at the trial

[24] *Commentary*, pp. 114 f. see also A. Magdelain, 'Remarques sur la Perduellio', *Historia* 22 (1973), 405 ff. at p. 409, and the authors he cites, n. 13.

[25] I would accept that the passages are indicative of an old practice.

[26] Livy's words here cannot square with the view most recently propounded by Tyrrell, *Commentary*, pp. 19 ff. that the *duoviri* were not judges and were appointed when the culprit's guilt was self-evident.

for *perduellio* of Gaius Rabirius in 63 B.C. Labienus, responsible for the prosecution, urges that Cicero is attempting to abolish the ancient procedure for *perduellio*.[27] Cicero, in turn, claims that Labienus is cruelly attempting to restore a frightful ancient procedure and punishment and declares 'Is this the man who dares to style himself a friend of the people and me an enemy of your interests, though he has hunted out all these cruel punishments, this cruel language, not from what you and your fathers can remember but from the records of the Annals, of the archives of the Kings.'[28] Rabirius, like Horatius, might rather have been charged with murder, but for political reasons Julius Caesar preferred the trial should be for *perduellio*. The precedent in the annals, the archives of the kings, can only be that of Horatius[29] and, to paraphrase A. H. M. Jones,[30] Cicero's argument implies that others besides himself believed that the trial of Horatius was for *perduellio*; and that that trial had at least some of the features, e.g. *provocatio*, mentioned by Livy. To our immediate purpose Cicero claims 'this friend of the people has brought it about without your consent [i.e. the people's] not that a Roman citizen should be put on trial, but that a Roman citizen should be condemned to death without his case being heard': 'hic popularis a IIviris iniussu vestro non iudicari de cive romano sed indicta causa civem Romanum capitis condemnari coegit.'[31] From the reports of the trials of Horatius and Rabirius it appears that the verdict of the *duoviri* in trials for *perduellio* is automatically that of 'guilty'. The most plausible explanation is that for the latter case the former, in this regard too, has come to serve as a precedent. Hence, the failure of the *duoviri* to reach a verdict on the actual merits of the case seems to have been an integral part of the story of Horatius.

Cicero provides considerable support for Livy's accurate recording of the tradition of the wording of the *lex* and the surrounding procedure: 'I, lictor, conliga manus' 'Caput obnubito, arbori infelici suspendito' in *pro Rabirio* 4.13. Naturally the wording has been modernized.[32] It has, however, been claimed that the *lex horrendi carminis* is a relatively late product of the annalists' fantasy or of contamination.[33] But the arguments for this do not seem convincing. For K. Latte the formulation must be relatively late because 'verberato vel intra pomerium vel extra

[27] Cicero, *pro Rabirio perduellionis* at e.g. 3.10.

[28] 5.15. 'Hic se popularem dicere audet, me alienum a commodis vestris, cum iste omnis et suppliciorum et verborum acerbitates non ex memoria vestra ac patrum vestrorum sed annalium monumentis atque ex regum commentariis conquisierit . . .'

[29] We should not be misled by Cicero's ascription of the law to Tarquinius Superbus; 4.13. He wishes to portray Labienus as wicked as possible hence the claim that the statute on which Labienus builds his case is the work of the worst of the kings.

[30] *Criminal Courts*, p. 10.

[31] 4.12.

[32] See e.g. Brecht, *Perduellio*, pp. 157 f.

[33] See e.g. Kunkel, *Untersuchungen*, p. 22 n. 50, following Latte and Bleicken.

pomerium', the drawing of a distinction between beating inside or outside of the *pomerium*, makes sense only when the right of a magistrate to punish inside the *pomerium* was already limited; thus, he says, it presupposes the *lex Valeria* or something similar.[34] But the clause need have nothing to do with any aspect of a magistrate's powers. The emphasis on *intra pomerium* or *extra pomerium* is rhetorical, based on the disgrace that will accrue in either case.[35] I am not sure that I understand the objections of J. Bleicken[36] as to the accuracy of the tradition of the wording. The *lex* says 'duumviri perduellionem iudicent'; and Bleicken insists that the main proponent of the veracity of the wording, Brecht, had shown that 'iudicare aliquid alicui' was the prosecution formulation of a magistrate *sine imperio*. But that fact by itself, I feel, cannot exclude the use of 'iudicare aliquid alicui' in a different context. Again, Bleicken says that in the apparent *lex*, *certare* (which indicates a conflict, necessarily here between the appellant and the *duoviri*) can only be used in the sense that the people decide between the judgement of the magistrate and the justification of the appeal, and he asks rhetorically whether an old statute can use such language? One might rhetorically ask 'Why not?' Bleicken followed by Magdelain,[37] also stresses that the legislator could not have omitted from the *carmen* the mode of nomination of the *duoviri* and other procedural matters, and that the omission cannot have been due to excision by Livy. But I am not persuaded that an early legislator laying down the duties of judicial offficers would necessarily set out the mode of appointing these officers: we may be expecting a degree of completeness foreign to archaic legislators. (It should not be forgotten that in fact we have exceedingly little information on the structure of early Roman laws. What we have suggests a different approach from our own as to what ought to go into a law.)[38] If he did, such a clause might well not be included in Livy's sources, direct or ultimate, which would be primarily concerned only with matters affecting the Horatian episode. Livy, too, to heighten the speed of the drama could well excise what was not immediately relevant.[39]

It has not been my intention in this paper to attempt the elucidation of all aspects of law and procedure in the case of Horatius. Rather I have

34 *RE supp*. 7, s.v. Todesstrafe, 1599 ff. at 1614.

35 Though it does not affect the argument of this paper I accept the view of W.A. Oldfather that the penalty envisaged was death by beating and then suspension of the corpse, and not crucifixion: 'Livy 1.26 and the Supplicium de More Maiorum', *Transactions of American Philological Society* 39 (1908), 49 ff.

36 'Ursprung und Bedeutung der Provocation' *ZSS* 76 (1959), 324 ff. at p. 335.

37 'Remarques', p. 412.

38 Thus, the XII Tables regulate aspects of the legal process, but have nothing on the forms of action; legislate on both *mancipatio* and *stipulatio* but set out the forms of neither; etc.

39 Also against Bleicken on this point see Bauman, *Duumviri*, pp. 13 ff.; Tyrrell, *Commentary*, p. 16.

wanted to explain how the apparent oddities in the story could make sense and could fit into a setting during the period of the kings. There is otherwise no evidence which must lead us to a later date for the law and procedure in the episode. What, however, is the greater purpose of the story? Ogilvie sees it as the paradigm case of *perduellio*.[40] He may be correct, but it is not a typical case of *perduellio* and the difficulties that modern scholars have in accepting the episode as involving *perduellio* must count against his explanation. I would propose something rather different. The episode is the paradigm not just of one major criminal offence and the appropriate procedure, but of criminal jurisdiction and procedure in general, and especially of the overlap of competing jurisdictions. Thus, the father could have judged Horatius for treason against him, but he did not do so. The king could himself have tried Horatius for murder. Instead he opts for the charge of treason and invokes the procedure appropriate for *perduellio* against the state rather than that – more particularly in point – against the *pater*. The *duoviri* use their jurisdiction abusively, leaving the field which is quite unoccupied to the jurisdiction of the people.

So far as possible I have avoided discussing scholarly views on the later insertion of the Horatian legend. Partly I wished to give as simple as possible an exposition of how the case could fit into the early framework. This exposition should stand alone. Partly, since no one could easily discuss all the views propounded, I wished to avoid the charge of selectivity. What does seem to be the case, though, is that authors who reject the story as a later invention do not feel called upon to account for all the details of the story. Two examples, one of a Roman lawyer, the other of a Roman historian, may suffice as illustrations.

For V. Arangio-Ruiz,[41] the falsification of the annals was to satisfy the pride of the family of the Horatii who competed with the gens Valeria for the honour of being responsible for the *provocatio ad populum*. The true source of *provocatio*, he suggests, was the *lex Valeria* of 300 B.C. But in the interest of the gens Horatia was invented the *lex Valeria Horatia de provocatione* of 449 B.C., and the supporters of the Valerii in turn envisaged a statute of P. Valerius Publicola in the first year of the Republic, 509 B.C. Further back, for a law voted in the public assembly, one could not go. But, says Arangio-Ruiz, a final return to the offensive was made by the Horatii who pretended that under King Tullus Hostilius our Horatius exercised the *provocatio ad populum*. But, I submit, Horatian family pride would not seem to be boosted by the claim that a Horatius, slayer of his sister, was even the first – not stated in any surviving version of the story – to make use of a right of appeal invented by another. A further difficulty is

[40] *Commentary*, p. 115.

[41] *Storia del diritto romano* 7th edn. (Naples, 1957), pp. 2 ff.; cf. Brecht, *Perduellio*, p. 131.

the lack of distinction or power of the Horatii – hence their inability to affect the tradition of the annalists – after 300 B.C. which, on Arangio-Ruiz's view (as the date of the *lex Valeria*) must be the *terminus post quem* for any tampering with the relevant parts of the annals. The last serious Horatius was the military tribune of 378 B.C.,[42] and for the first century B.C. the political distinction of the *gens* rested on a *legatus* in Africa in 43 B.C.[43] Nor does this theory of Arangio-Ruiz explain why the trial was for *perduellio*, and was not for *parricidium*, or why the *duoviri* blatantly misinterpreted the law.

According to A. H. M. Jones,[44] in 63 B.C. Julius Caesar wished for various political reasons to have Rabirius charged with *perduellio*, not *parricidium*. Hence the precedents had to be tampered with, and Horatius' trial, actually for murder, had to be converted into one for *perduellio*. But Jones does not attempt to explain how Caesar's watchful contemporaries could accept the falsification. Cicero, consul in that year, who defended Rabirius seems not to have questioned the accuracy of the annals. Nor do the Horatii appear to have expressed surprise at this modification of their family tradition. Moreover, why in the falsification do the *duoviri* claim they would have to condemn even an innocent man? If it be suggested that this had been part of the original story and referred to *parricidium* we are left with an even bigger puzzle. The judges' behaviour was never part of a precedent for *parricidium*, but was for *perduellio* once Horatius' trial was made to be for the latter crime. But why then did the judges of Rabirius feel they had to follow this precedent which, since it had only just been invented could never have been used in other previous trials for *perduellio*? The difficulty becomes insurmountable when we realize that Caesar himself was one of the *duoviri*, and, according to Suetonius,[45] Caesar's bitter hostility to Rabirius when he passed sentence was much in Rabirius' favour in the eyes of the populace.[46]

A further view, that of A. Magdelain, also requires mention because he claims that it is precisely the inability of the *duoviri* to absolve under the law that shows the law is a later fabrication, just because it is legally

[42] Livy, 6.31.1,5.

[43] Cicero, *ad fam.* 12.30.7.

[44] *Criminal Courts*, pp. 43 f.

[45] *Divus Iulius*, 12.

[46] I am indebted to a letter from my friend Mr Robin Seager for this further argument: 'But what is also important is surely this: it was never on the cards that proceedings would have been allowed to reach a conclusion, and it's highly unlikely that even those who initiated them ever meant that they should be pushed through to the bitter end. Therefore the details just weren't important enough to have been invented ad hoc: they already existed and could be taken over, since they were convenient enough: *if* Caesar cared (which I doubt), he could condemn without incurring odium since he could say he had no choice and without anything drastic following from it, since appeal was inevitable.'

inept.[47] The *duoviri*, he thinks, were an expedient for having the choice of condemnation or absolution depend upon the people; and the beauty of the story would have been spoiled if one of the *duoviri* had absolved Horatius. So far this might seem plausible, but I cannot follow him when he says 'On the other hand it would have been inelegant to let the *duoviri* spontaneously pronounce a condemnation. For the affair to be necessarily brought before the people, it was proper that the law obliged the magistrate to condemn.' A successful appeal to the people from a spontaneous and unfettered condemnation by the *duoviri* would, it seems to me, illustrate even more fittingly that the ultimate decision rested with the people. Moreover the wording of the *lex horrendi carminis* as we have it in Livy does not seem to compel a condemnation. 'Duumviri perduellionem iudicent' does not necessarily imply that there must be a finding of guilty: 'Let the *duoviri* hear a case of *perduellio*.[48] The taking of that clause, presumably in conjunction with the next, by the *duoviri* as meaning they had no choice but to condemn is arbitrary. What we need from any explanation of the behaviour of the *duoviri* is why they voluntarily and unnecessarily interpreted the statute as not giving them power to absolve.[49]

[47] See the entry *iudico* in *Oxford Latin Dictionary* 4 (Oxford, 1973), 979.

[48] 'Remarques', p. 413.

[49] I am grateful to Professors Neil MacCormick and R.M. Ogilvie and Mr Robin Seager for their helpful criticisms.

10

The Original Meaning of Pauperies

The very name, *actio de pauperie,* presents us squarely with the problem (1). Why should this action — dealing with damage caused by animals — and this action alone come to be called 'the action on poverty' ? For the word *pauperies* in the later Republic and the Empire does have the primary meaning of 'poverty'. This problem does not stand by itself. The *actio de pauperie* is old, and goes back at least to the XII Tables. Why does it — apparently at least — give a remedy for damage of all kinds, whereas the later *lex Aquilia* of 287 B.C. (2) (which deals with injury by human beings including slaves) provides an action in Chapter 1 only for the killing of slaves and *pecudes* (animals which go in herds), and originally in Chapter 3 only for the killing of other animals and the wounding of all kinds of animals and slaves (3) ? Again, why does the Twelve Tables' provision seem to begin 'If a fourfooted animal caused *pauperies,* poverty' and not 'If a fourfooted animal caused *damnum,* financial loss' ? The term *damnum* seems prima facie much more

(1) The name does not appear in the relevant Digest title, 9.1, but seems to be in D. 9.2.37.1 (Iavolenus *14 ex Cassio*) and J. 4.9.1. *De pauperie agere* occurs in D. 19.5.14.3 (Ulpian *41 ad Sab.*). Whether the name was used technically before Justinian need not concern us here. Müller denies that the expression *actio de pauperie* occurs in the sources : *RE* supp. X, 521 *s.v. pauperies.*

(2) The date of promulgation of the statute in its 3 Chapters. Earlier Chapters 1 and 2 at least had existed in some form : cf. above all, Daube, "On the Third Chapter of the *Lex Aquilia*" *LQR* lii (1936), pp. 253 ff. at pp. 266 ff.

(3) This is to accept the arguments of Daube on the original scope of Chapter 3. Of course there are other actions for injuries caused by humans, but these are referable to the special talents of men.

reasonable, it existed at the time of the XII Tables (4) and it is, naturally enough, used in the *lex Aquilia* (5). And incidentally perhaps, why does the *actio de pauperie* lie for injury caused by any fourfooted animal whereas Chapter 1 of the *lex Aquilia* gives an action for the killing of slaves and *pecudes*, but certainly not for the killing of other fourfooted animals ? These problems form a group and will be together the primary subject of this paper.

Let us start our investigation with a look at the word *pauperies*. The word in the Latin of the Republic and Empire appears in legal and non-legal contexts (6). It seems to occur in the surviving sources first in the XII Tables' provision : Ulpian says '*Si quadrupes pauperiem fecisse dicetur, actio ex lege XII Tabularum descendit*' (7). Ulpian, of course, is not quoting the words of the provision of 451 B.C. and it has been doubted whether the word *pauperies* actually occurred in it. There is, in fact, little reason for doubt, but the doubt itself is significant and will be looked at in due course (8). At the moment it is enough to notice that in the legal Latin sources of any period *pauperies* is used only of this injury by an animal, and is never applied to any other kind of wrong (9) ; and that for this injury it is clearly a technical expression.

In the surviving non-legal Latin sources *pauperies* appears first in Ennius (239-169 B.C.).

Senex sum : utinam mortem oppetam, prius quam evenat
Quod in pauperie mea senex graviter gemam (10).

And it then occurs 4 times in Plautus (11). The usual under-

(4) 12.3.

(5) D. 9.2.27.5 (Ulpian *18 ad ed.*) ; cf. now WATSON, *Roman Private Law around 200 B.C.* (Edinburgh, 1970), p. 153.

(6) MÜLLER says the word in scarcely to be found in non-juristic Latin texts : *loc. cit.* This is just not so.

(7) D. 9.1.1 pr. (*18 ad ed.*).

(8) *Infra*, p. 134.

(9) Cf. *Vocabularium Iurisprudentiae Romanae* IV, 572.

(10) From the *Hecuba* in Nonius 494, *pauperies, pro paupertate*.

(11) *Au.* 190 ; 722 ; *Tru.* 573 ; *St.* 175. In the last text the reading is not found in all manuscripts. Some editors also accept *pauperiem* as the

standing of the meaning and usage of the word can be illuminated by a glance at a typical dictionary entry. Thus, Lewis and Short have '*poverty* (poet. and in post-Aug. prose for the class. paupertas). I Lit. [then come examples which we need not repeat] II Transf. in jurid. Lat., *injury, damage, loss,* which one suffers from an animal (perh. mentioned in the Twelve Tables) : etc.' (12). This account at once seems questionable in at least two respects. First, how could there be such an extreme transfer of meaning, and at such an early date ? Remember that if we accept the presence of the word in the XII Tables, *pauperies* in this so-called transferred sense is evidenced almost two and a half centuries before we have it with its ordinary meaning (13). Secondly, should we really see the early non-legal usage of *pauperies* as poetic even though it clearly was so in the 1st century B.C., and though *paupertas* survives in Ennius (14) and is more common in Plautus than *pauperies* (15) ? Ennius certainly uses archaic words (16) at times and to that extent his vocabulary is poetic, but he also employs words which were perfectly ordinary in his day but later fell out of use except — partly, indeed, because they appear in his work — among the poets (17). Into which category *pauperies* fits could not be determined from looking at the works of Ennius alone. This is true even though the particular fragment under discussion certainly derives from Euripides, *Hekuba,* 497 f. But Plautus is a different case. His vocabulary tends to be colloquial except when he has a specific end in view. And it is not easy to see that a specific literary function is served by *pauperies* in the *Aulularia* :

reading in *Tri.* 109 : cf. LODGE, *Lexicon Plautinum,* ii (reprinted, Hildesheim, 1962), p. 298.

(12) *A Latin Dictionary* (Oxford, 1879), p. 1318.

(13) Though too much stress should not be placed on this, in view of the nature of the surviving Latin sources.

(14) From his *Alexander* in Varro, *de ling. lat.* 7.82.

(15) *Au.* 206 ; *Ep.* 530 ; 556 ; *Per.* 347 ; 348 ; *Ru.* 918 ; *St.* 134 ; 177 ; *Tri.* 109 ; *Vi.* 95. Also in some mss in *St.* 175.

(16) E.g. *induperator, quaesentibus, poste* (for *post*), *noenu(m)*. It is easier to spot morphological archaisms.

(17) E.g. *textrinum, volup, propagmen, momen, subices, repagula.*

190 meam pauperiem conqueror.
virginem habeo grandem, dote cassam atque inlocabilem.

721b tantum gemiti et mali maiestitiaeque
hic dies mi optulit, famem et pauperiem.

Nor indeed in the *Truculentus* unless it could be argued — though I think not — that the word is chosen to give a slightly comic pomposity :

572-3 velut haec meretrix meum erum miserum sua blanditia intulit in pauperiem :
privabit bonis, luce, honore atque amicis.

And it is still more difficult to see the word as poetic in the *Stichus* :

174 Gelasimo nomen mi indidit parvo pater,
(propter pauperiem hoc adeo nomen repperi)
quia ind'iam a pusillo puero ridiculus forem ;

All in all it seems as if *pauperies* was a word in ordinary use in the time of Plautus, and hence of Ennius.

A rather different history of the word *pauperies* seems to me much more likely than that inherent in the entry in Lewis and Short. Originally the usage was neither technical nor poetic. But it was used in the XII Tables — and perhaps earlier — in connection with injury by animals and eventually acquired a technical transferred connotation. Consequentially in non-legal Latin, the common usage gave way to the equivalent form *paupertas* and before the end of the Republic *pauperies* survived only in poetic diction ([18]).

Pauperies is a noun which corresponds to the adjective *pauper*. It is the state of being *pauper*. The ending *-ies* is common, especially for abstract nouns ([19]), and has no other particular significance in point of meaning. Hence, incidentally, we can dismiss a view such as that of Kaser, " Auch ' pauperies ' ist der a n g e -

(18) Hence for Nonius it was worthy of note that Ennius in his *Hecuba* used *pauperies*. " *Pauperies, pro paupertate* ", he says : 494.

(19) Cf. KÜHNER-HOLZWEISSIG, *Ausfüfrliche Grammatik der lateinischen Sprache* i, 2nd edit. (reprinted Darmstadt, 1966), pp. 401 ff.

r i c h t e t e Schaden, der ärmer macht " [20]. There is in the word *pauperies* no hint of the comparative, *pauperior,* ' ärmer ', poorer. The XII Tables gave an action if an animal caused the state of being *pauper.* Obviously here *pauper* cannot simply be translated as 'poor'. Apart from any other consideration whether the victim became poor or not would depend on his total wealth. If my ox killed your ox and you had no other you might become poor, but not if you had 100 more. We can surely exclude the possibility that in the former case the *actio de pauperie* would lie though it would not in the latter.

Hence we are forced to look for an earlier meaning of *pauper* and *pauperies.* Walde-Hofmann derive *pauper* from *pau̯o-pars* ' wening erwerbend, wenig sich schaffend ' [21] or from *pauc(o)-pars* possibly from *pau̯e[ro-]-pars*; and Ernout and Meillet from *pau-per-os,* ' qui produit peu ' [22]. Some such derivation is now regarded by etymologists as certain [23]. In so far as a distinction is to be drawn between ' wenig erwerbend ' and ' qui produit peu ' the latter is perferable since the second element of the word is that which appears in *pario.* Ernout and Meillet, indeed, conjecture — reasonably enough in the circumstances — that *pauper* was first used of land and of animals [24].

If then the word *pauperies* itself is old and was created at a time when *pauper* still meant ' producing little ' [25], its original sense is likely to have been something like ' the state of producing little or of being unproductive '. The XII Tables' provision would then mean ' If a fourfooted animal caused the state

(20) *Das altrömische Ius* (Göttingen, 1949), p. 224.

(21) *Lateinisches Etymologisches Wörterbuch* ii, 3rd edit. (Heidelberg, 1954), p. 268.

(22) *Dictionnaire étymologique de la langue latine* ii, 4th edit. (Paris, 1960), p. 490.

(23) I confess I do not quite understand the position of KASER, *Ius,* p. 224 n. 37, who begins " Zu ' pauper, opi-parus, der wenig Erwerbende ' Walde 8c ". *Opi-parus* surely means something like, ' w e a l t h-producing '. Nor is MÜLLER satisfactory : *loc. cit.*

(24) For Walde-Hofmann the sense of *pauper* as ' unproductive ' is a secondary development.

(25) Cf. *infra.*

of being unproductive' ([26]). The clause would thus originally cover only injuries to the instruments of production, primarily slaves and *pecudes*; and only such injuries as would seriously affect the slave's or animal's productivity. Not only does the name *actio de pauperie* now make sense, but we can clearly see a close relationship between this action and Chapter 1 of the *lex Aquilia* ([27-28]). We can also see why the XII Tables did not say this action would lie for *damnum,* financial loss — not all loss was being brought within the scope of the action.

But now, the sufficient antiquity of the word *pauperies* must be established. It almost certainly appeared in the XII Tables despite all the doubts which have been expressed ([29]). Thus, the *formula* issued by the praetor unquestionably contained the word *pauperies* and began : *Si paret quadrupedem pauperiem fecisse* ([30]). Though the formula cannot be precisely dated it can scarcely be earlier than 200 B.C. and on the general view it must be considerably later ([31]). But even before 200 B.C. the word *pauperies* in non-legal Latin had the ordinary sense of 'poverty'. Since the word cannot have been put into the *formula* with that sense, it must have had an earlier legal history which

(26) This could be so even if by the time of the XII Tables the sense of 'poverty' was already common since the word *pauperies* could already have been usual in the legal context.

(27) Which is, of course, earlier than Chapter 3.

(28) Cf. *infra*, pp. 138.

(29) E.g. by MOMMSEN, *Römisches Strafrecht* (reprinted Graz, 1955), p. 834 n. 4; LISOWSKI, *RE. supp. VII*, 657 *s.v. noxalis actio*; KASER, *loc. cit.*; MÜLLER, *loc. cit.*

(30) Cf. D. 9.1.1 pr., 1, 2, 3 ; LENEL, *Edictum perpetuum*, 3rd edit. (Leipzig, 1927), p. 195.

(31) There must have been a *legis actio* and despite all the many divergences of opinion it would be almost unanimously held that *formulae* were introduced in spheres where there was a *legis actio* only after the *lex Aebutia* of around the middle of the 2nd century B.C. My own divergent opinion is that there is evidence for the formulary *condictio* in Plautus, *Ru* 1376 ff. [cf. now *Roman Private Law around 200 B.C.* (Edinburgh, 1970), p. 127 n. 3] and the possibility cannot be excluded that in other areas too, a *formula* had come into existence side-by-side with a *legis actio*. But such *formulae* could scarcely be much earlier than 200 B.C.

was definite enough to give the word a technical meaning in the very restricted sphere of damage by animals. It is difficult to see how this could have occurred unless the word *pauperies* had appeared in some source, which can only be the XII Tables. Moreover, most modern scholars who doubt the presence of the word in the XII Tables give neither specific reasons nor suggest alternative wording. Those who are more precise suggest that the more indefinite concept of *noxa* might have been used (32). Presumably this idea comes to them from the beginning of D. 9.1.1.

> Si quadrupes pauperiem fecisse dicetur, actio ex lege duodecim tabularum descendit : quae lex voluit aut dari id quod nocuit, id est id animal quod noxiam commisit, aut aestimationem noxiae offerre.
>
> 1. Noxia autem est ipsum delictum.

This emphasis on *noxia* and its meaning certainly implies that the word *noxia* or *noxa* did appear, but is no indication that *pauperies* did not. The use of the word *noxia* in the XII Tables might have been only in connection with the obligations of the animal's owner, and so be similar to the word's rôle in the *formula* : *Si paret quadrupedem pauperiem fecisse, qua de re agitur, quam ob rem Numerium Negidium Aulo Agerio aut noxiam sarcire aut in noxam dedere oportet, quanti ea res est, tantam pecuniam aut in noxam dedere iudex Numerium Negidium Aulo Agerio condemna, si non paret absolve* (33). Thus, there seems no specific reason to doubt the presence of the word *pauperies* in the XII Tables. One might, indeed, suspect that behind the doubts lurks an unspecific unease with the general strangeness of the word.

One can, moreover, go further and show both the antiquity of the word *pauperies* and its original meaning, 'lack of produc-

(32) E.g. MOMMSEN, *loc. cit.*; MÜLLER, *loc. cit.*

(33) For this reconstruction of the *formula* see LENEL, *loc. cit.* The point is not affected if KERR WYLIE's reconstruction of the *intentio* — with *aut quadrupedem dare oportet* in place of *aut in noxam dedere oportet* — is accepted : '*Actio de pauperie, Dig. lib. ix, tit. 1*' *Studi Riccobono* iv (Palermo, 1936), pp. 462 ff. at p. 466; followed by MÜLLER, *RE* supp. x, 526.

tivity '. Thus, it is a noun of the fifth declension. Such nouns have various morphological origins but fall into three main groups.

(i) Those with probably original s-stems : *spes, fides.*

(ii) Those with dipthongal stems : *res, dies.*

(iii) Those in *-ies*; a very large class.

(i) and (ii) need not be regarded further. (iii) can be subdivided :

(a) verb roots + *-ies*; *acies, facies, rabies, species, congeries, progenies, effigies,* etc.

(b) noun stems + *-ies*; *luxuries, materies, intemperies,* etc.

(c) adjective stems + *-ies*; *maceries, fallacies, barbaries,* etc.

(d) nouns ending in *-ities,* almost all of which are formed from adjectives (*avarus* > *avarities, segnis* > *segnities*) or from nouns which could be used as adjectives (*amicus* > *amicities, puer* > *puerities*).

Of these, almost all the nouns in (b), (c) and (d), have doublets in *-ia* or *itia* — though *intemperies* only in the plural *intemperiae* — which exist alongside the forms in *-ies* and are more common than they are. It is not always possible to prove exactly which of these alternative forms is the older, though in many nouns *-ies* is certainly a later and analogical formation on the basis of an existing form in *ia.* There is, moreover, no doubt that the *-ia* suffix is the older; it is common in Indo-European whereas *-ie* is not. It can, in fact, be regarded as very probable that for all the nouns in (b), (c) and (d) the original form was that in *-ia* or *-itia,* with the form in *-ies* or *-ities* a later analogical substitution. The only noun in classes (b), (c) and (d) which does not seem to have a known alternative form in *-ia* is *caesaries* which possibly belongs under (b), but since its exact formation is not clear it should perhaps not be given too much weight, especially since a form in *-ia* must be the basis for *caesariatus.*

The nouns in class (a), however, do not have alternative forms in *-ia* with the exception of *effigia* which is found in Plautus. It therefore seems very likely that the forms in *-ies* are original for these verbal formations, showing the suffix *-ie* added directly to the verbal roots, *ac-, spec-, gen-,* etc.

There is no trace of a word *pauperia*. If this is not a mere historical accident — and there is no particular reason to think it is — then *pauperies* cannot be an analogical formation of the type of (b), (c), (d), but must belong to (a); that is to the class of verbal formations which have no doublets in *-ia*. Consequently it is highly probable that at the time of the formation of the word *pauperies, pauper* was still regarded as a verbal compound with the meaning 'producing little'; and that therefore *pauperies* bore the original meaning of 'lack of productivity'.

In course of time the meaning of *pauperies* changed both in legal and non-legal usage. It seems reasonable to think — but there is no direct evidence — that while the legal and non-legal usage was still unitary the more general sense of 'poverty' developed. This would not be a useful meaning in the context in which the word occurred in the XII Tables and so a separate legal meaning eventually emerged. The history of the change cannot be traced in any detail, but the new meaning is best seen in D. 9.1.1.3.

> Ait praetor 'pauperiem fecisse'. pauperies est damnum sine iniuria facientis datum : nec enim potest animal iniuria fecisse, quod sensu caret (34-35).

Pauperies now means 'loss caused without wrong on the part of the doer' and its use is restricted to loss caused by animals (36). Thus, by this stage injuries of all kinds at least to animate objects (37) are covered by the statute including those of minor consequence. Significently, it appears from D. 9.1.3 (Gaius 7 *ad ed. prov.*) that it had not always been agreed that injuries to free men were within the action's scope : *Ex hac lege iam non*

(34) Suspicions of interpolation seem to be restricted to the very beginning of the text : LENEL, *Edictum*, p. 195 n. 5; *Palingenesia Iuris Civilis* ii, (reprinted, Graz, 1960), 607 n. 1; KERR WYLIE, '*Actio de pauperie*', p. 481.

(35) The corresponding passage in J. 4.9. pr reads : ... *nec enim potest animal iniuriam fecisse dici, quod sensu caret. haec quod ad noxalem actionem pertinet.*

(36) Cf. Paul *ex Festo, s.v. pauperies* : *Pauperies damnum dicitur, quod quadrupes facit.*

(37) Cf. *infra*, p. 138.

dubitatur etiam liberarum personarum nomine agi posse, forte si patrem familias aut filium familias vulneraverit quadrupes :... (38).

When this changeover to an action for any kind of *damnum* caused by an animal occurred cannot be determined since there is no sign of the earlier position in the legal sources. But it would seem plausible to suggest that it is early, say before 200 B.C.

Finally, a few more words about the original scope of the *actio de pauperie.* It would be foolish to attempt too great precision. We cannot tell whether serious injury to land causing a lack of productivity (39) would be covered, though the similarity with Chapter 1 of the *lex Aquilia* might suggest not. Again, too much must not be argued from this similiarity; especially, it should not be claimed that the *actio de pauperie* lay only for the k i l l i n g of a slave or animal of the class of *pecudes.* There is a great gulf even in time between the two statutes. It could properly be suggested, though, that at the unknown time when

(38) This text has been much discussed and interpolations have been claimed both in the part printed and in the remainder of the text. It has even been suggested, with hesitation, that *ex hac lege iam non dubitatur* might be a Tribonianism : KERR WYLIE, '*Actio de pauperie*', p. 510; BELOW, *Die Haftung für lucrum cessans im römischen Recht*, pp. 43 f. But none of this affects us since there seems to be agreement that originally the action did not extend to injuries to free men. See also on the text, SANFILIPPO. 'Il risarcimento del danno per l'uccisione di un uomo libero nel diritto romano', *Annali Catania* v (1951), pp. 118 ff. at p. 122; PRINGSHEIM, 'Die Verletzung Freier und die *lex Aquilia*', *SDHI* xxviii (1962), pp. 1 ff. at p. 5; IMPALLOMENI, review of Below, *IURA* xvi (1965), pp. 226 f.

(39) A different situation from that covered by the *actio de pastu,* hence we need not embark on the question whether an *actio de pastu* was provided by the XII Tables : see e.g. MÜLLER, *RE.* supp. X, 523.

No text tells us that the *actio de pauperie* would not lie for damage to land, but equally no text indicates that it would : *quidve depasta sit* in *P.S.* 1.15.1 is best taken as referring to the *actio de pastu.* D. 9.1.2 pr. (Paul *22 ad ed.*) shows that the action was available for damage to inanimate moveables.

Chapter 1 was first promulgated (40) the *actio de pauperie* had not yet been extended to cover all injuries (41).

(40) Cf. *supra*, p. 129 n. 2.

(41) A number of friends have improved this study by their criticism and I wish to express my thanks to all, especially to Mr R.M. Pinkerton for his extremely generous help on philological matters and to Dr Alan Rodger.

11

Tignum iunctum, the XII Tables and a Lost Word

A text of the scholar Festus, which is famous among Latinists and lawyers alike, reads:

> *Tignum non solum in aedificiis, quo utuntur, appellatur, sed etiam in vineis, ut est in XII: " Tignum iunctum aedibus vineave et concapit ne solvito ".*

For the quotation from the XII Tables, the manuscripts show some variation for *vineave*: *victum* in *W*, *vineaque* in *V* and *minerve* in *X*. But these we can happily leave aside and come to the crux of the text, *concapit,* which appears in all the manuscripts. " *Concapit,* a corrupt word, and difficult of explanation " say Lewis and Short [1] ! And the emendations proposed are numerous and lacking in general approval [2]. J.J. Scaliger suggested *e concapi*, Cuiacius *et concapit<um>*, Mommsen *e compage*, Götz *e concapidine*, Müller *e concape*, but Schoell reverts to *e concapi* and Huschke has *sei concapit.* Riccobono excises the words altogether [3]. To show that the age of invention is not over I wish to propose and defend yet another emendation which will have its own particular virtues, legal and linguistic.

(1) *A Latin Dictionary* (Oxford, 1951), p. 396.

(2) Cf. G. Melillo, *Tignum iunctum* (Naples, 1964), pp. 13ff.

(3) For references to these scholars and appropriate editions see Melillo, *loc. cit.*; C.G. Bruns, *Fontes Iuris Romani Antiqui*, 7th edit. by O. Gradenwitz (Tübingen, 1909), p. 26; and S. Riccobono, *Fontes Iuris Romani Antejustiniani* i, 2nd edit. (Florence, 1941), p. 46.

The clause of the XII Tables read, I suggest, " *Tignum iunctum aedibus vineave concaput ne solvito* ".

What it may well be asked is *concaput,* and what does it mean? Answer: It is a noun, compounded from *cum* and *caput,* exactly like *compes* is compounded from *cum* and *pes.* And as *compes* means 'something attached to the feet, fetters' so *concaput* has the sense 'something attached to the head or top, support'. The clause in question then originally meant 'Do not take away a beam built into a house or a support from a vine'.

To justify this reconstruction one must first explain *concaput,* then show that substantial benefits accrue from the reconstruction, and finally indicate how the present state of the text in Festus could be reached from the suggested original wording of the XII Tables.

The word *concaput* does not appear anywhere in Latin. Proof that there ever was such a word cannot be directly provided, no more than proof exists in any other instance where it is alleged that a word must have occurred though it is otherwise unknown. The best that can be done is to show that if the word did exist, then (a) its formation would be regular, (b) that it would reasonably bear the meaning ascribed to it, and (c) that difficulties for the text — which otherwise have no solution — disappear entirely.

The formation of *concaput* from *cum* and *caput* is perfectly regular: before c, d, f, g, j, s, t and v *con* is the form adopted from *cum* [4]. This, of course, is in itself no justification for holding that the word *concaput* actually existed. But the suggestion gains in plausibility when it is recalled that compound formations with the preposition *cum* are common in early Latin, and that several are known from Plautus to have existed but are not evidenced thereafter: thus for instance, the nouns, *commers, consuetio*; adjectives, *confusicius, consucidus*; and verbs, *collabasco, collutulento, concaleo, conscreor.* Moreover more than one word which we know appeared in the XII Tables was not in use

(4) R. Kühner - F. Holzweissig, *Ausführliche Grammatik der lateinischen Sprache* i, 2nd edit. (reprinted Darmstadt, 1966), p. 927.

in more historical times: *ricinium, adsiduus* (as a noun), *lessus, heredium, obvagulare, rupitia.*

No difficulty arises for the meaning which has been suggested for *concaput.* We have evidence from early times that *caput* was used to mean not only 'head' in a literal sense applying to humans and animals, but also the 'top' of other things (5). And vines would be attached, or would attach themselves at their tops to the supports: *Quam altissimam viniam facito,* says Cato the Censor (6).

The first major advantage to accrue from the emendation to *concaput* is that a reasonable meaning can now be ascribed to *tignum.* On any other reconstruction of *e concapit,* — or indeed even if the words are excised altogether — *Tignum iunctum aedibus vineave* must be taken together as one phrase. The meaning of *tignum* then has to be wide enough to refer to supports for vines. But *tignum,* as has been emphasised by scholars, normally means in other contexts 'a beam' (7). Only with regard to this clause of the XII Tables does it ever appear that *tignum* was even used to mean 'building materials' (8). It might reasonably be suggested that the word was used in the XII Tables to signify building material of all kinds yet even so, of course, a word with a narrow meaning like 'beam' would here have especial importance; removal of a beam could adversely affect the existence of the whole structure, removal of a roof tile would not. But the idea that the XII Tables used the word *tignum* with a still wider meaning including supports for vines seems very difficult to accept. The Romans of the Empire betray their puzzlement. Festus himself in the text which opened this article quotes the provision of the XII Tables really to show that *tignum* was a word which was even used in connection with vines as well as houses. Obviously such a use needed to be noted. Very

(5) See the entries in *Thesaurus Linguae Latinae iii* (Leipzig, 1907), 408ff.

(6) *De agri cult.* 33.2.

(7) Cf. A. Ernout & A. Meillet, *Dictionnaire étymologique de la langue latine* ii, 4th edit. (Paris, 1960), p. 691.

(8) Cf. Ernout & Meillet, *loc. cit.*

few juristic texts on the subject of *tignum iunctum* have survived, but a surprisingly large proportion of these is devoted to explaining the meaning of *tignum*. Thus around the middle of the 2nd century A.D. Gaius took *tignum* in the XII Tables as meaning all kinds of material which make up buildings:

> D. 50.16.62 (*26 ad ed. prov.*). *Tigni appellatione in lege duodecim tabularum omne genus materiae, ex qua aedificia constant, significatur.*

Half a century later Ulpian spelled out the details, and explicitly made *tignum* apply also to everything necessary for vines:

> D. 47.3.1.1 (*37 ad ed.*). *Tigni autem appellatione continetur omnis materia, ex qua aedificium constet, vineaeque necessaria. unde quidam aiunt tegulam quoque et lapidem et testam ceteraque, si qua aedificiis sunt utilia* (*tigna enim a tegendo dicta sunt*), *hoc amplius et calcem et harenam tignorum appellatione contineri. sed et in vineis tigni appellatione omnia vineis necessaria continentur, ut puta perticae pedamenta.*

In several ways this is a most revealing text. To begin with, Ulpian explains that *tignum* has a broad meaning. He continues that some say that a roof tile, a stone, a brick etc. are included. Though he does not say so directly it appears that he shares this view of *tignum*. Next he defends this very wide usage by a false etymology: *tigna* derives from *tegendum*. From Ulpian's treatment it seems to emerge that there are problems in attributing to *tignum* the meaning of 'materials of all kinds for a building'. But then Ulpian comes to the vines, and has *sed et in vineis*. *Sed et*, 'but even', introduces a more extreme case. A further text of Ulpian confirms one's impression.

> D. 10.4.7.pr (*24 ad ed.*). *Tigni appellatione omnem materiam in lege duodecim tabularum accipimus, ut quibusdam recte videtur.*

From this also it is apparent that *tignum* in the XII Tables was invested with a meaning much wider than was usual, that such a meaning was not accepted by all jurists without protest, and that Ulpian favoured the wide meaning. The more one looks at these four texts of Festus, Gaius and Ulpian, the more difficult it becomes to believe the XII Tables could ever have used *tignum* to include the meaning of 'support for vines'. The reconstruction *concaput* would enable us to restore a natural meaning to *tignum* for the first time.

If the arguments to this point are correct, then it follows that the loss of the word *concaput* (and its meaning) from the XII Tables' clause had occurred before Festus who apparently lived in the later second century A.D. The probability, indeed, is that the loss was earlier since it is likely that the corruption *et concapit* occurred in two stages ([9]).

The second major advantage which accrues from the reconstruction *concaput*, is that one avoids the further problems raised by all other emendations. It is not proposed here to have a full discussion of these reconstructions; the failure of any to win wide support makes that unnecessary. It is enough to stress that they fall into two types each of which has its own difficulties. One type makes *et concapit* refer to a joining together, a unification, of the material with the building or vine. Mommsen's *e compage* is a good example ([10]). The real problem here is to understand why any reference to the joining was necessary or desirable since it already appears clearly from *iunctum*. The difficulty is not diminished if one takes *e compage ne solvito* as a single phrase. The other approach is to deduce from *et concapit* a reference somehow or another to theft, an approach based largely on the similarity in appearance between *concapit* and *furtum conceptum* ([11]). But there is simply no room for a reference to theft in this clause. If one were to suggest that the clause concerned only stolen material then it seems absurd that stolen material and only stolen material could not be removed when incorporated into a building. If the suggestion were that the

(9) Cf. infra, p. 342. One cannot conclude from D. 50.16.62 that the version known to Gaius was corrupt.

(10) T. Mommsen, 'Festi codicis quaternionem decimum sextum', *Abhandlungen der Berliner Akademie der Wissenschaften* (Philol.-Hist. Kl., 1864), pp. 57ff at p. 76.

(11) Cf. e.g. M. Voigt, *Die XII Tafeln* ii (Leipzig, 1883), pp. 574ff.

clause referred specially to theft in order to show that no material, whether stolen or incorporated innocently, could be removed, then one must concede that a reference to innocently taken material has apparently been lost. The text would need far greater emendation.

There was, of course, an *actio de tigno iuncto* available to the owner of the material for double its value and this action was established by the XII Tables ([12]), and necessarily by a different clause. It has long been a matter of dispute whether the action was available only when the builder was in bad faith, or was given even against an innocent builder ([13]). We need not enter into this dispute: the prohibition against the removal has its motivation — the avoidance of disproportionate economic loss — which is distinct from any penalisation of the builder. The prohibition could exist even where a builder was not penalised.

Finally we must consider the history of the corruption of the clause *Tignum iunctum aedibus vineave concaput ne solvito.* Once the word *concaput* had gone out of use any scribe might be forgiven for misreading an '*i*' for a '*u*'. When that had happened it would not seem that *vineave* could be taken with *concapit* and *Tignum iunctum aedibus vineave* would be understood together. *Concapit* would just not fit at all, but the rest of the text would be perfectly sensible; hence it would be a natural step to distance *concapit* — which now looked like a verb — from the remainder of the provision by the insertion of an *et*, so that *et concapit* looked like a separate clause, and the rest of the text could be interpreted and understood without it ([14]).

(12) D. 47.3.1pr ; 10.4.6 (Paul *14 ad Sab.*) ; 24.1.63 (Paul *3 ad Nerat.*).

(13) Cf. e.g. MELILLO, *Tignum iunctum*, pp. 42ff ; M. KASER, *Das römische Privatrecht* ii, 2nd edit. (Munich, 1971), pp. 138f and the authors they cite.

(14) I am grateful to Mr. Roy PINKERTON for very generous advice.

Emptio: 'Taking'

According to Festus, "*Emere, quod nunc est mercari, antiqui accipiebant pro sumere*" and modern philologists do accept some such meaning as the original in Latin.[1]

The *Thesaurus Linguae Latinae*[2] however, thinks there is no certain example of this sense of *emere* and considers the instances adduced by Skutsch[3] to be scarcely convincing. I should like to produce for consideration a different instance drawn from the derivative *emptio* or *emptor*. The instance in question may not take us as far back as *emere* = *sumere* but will at least to *emere* = *accipere*.

Roman legal tradition[4] tells us that the codification of the mid-fifth century B.C.,[5] the XII Tables, contained a provision on the *statuliber*, that is, a slave ordered to be free under his master's will when a condition was fulfilled. The clause in question seems to have been along the lines that if the slave was to be free when he made a certain payment to the heir then, even if he were transferred by the heir, he obtained his freedom by giving the sum to his purchaser It appears that in this clause either the recipient from the heir was designated as *emptor* or the transaction was called *emptio* or perhaps both these nouns occurred. Thus *Epit. Ulp.* 2.4 has:

> Sub hac condicione liber esse iussus: SI DECEM MILIA HEREDI DEDERIT, etsi ab herede abalienatus sit, emptori dando pecuniam ad libertatem perveniet; idque lex duodecim tabularum iubet.

And more significantly, it is in this context that we find in D.40. 1.29.1, "*quoniam lex duodecim tabularum emtionis verbo omnem*

---

[1]) Thus, e.g. Ernout & Meillet, *Dictionnaire étymologigue de la langue latine*, i 4th edt. (Paris, 1959), p. 195; and Benveniste, *Le Vocabulaire des institutions indo-européennes* i (Paris, 1969), p. 137, who says it means 'prendre' but in the particular sense, 'tirer à soi'.

[2]) V. 511.

[3]) *Kleine Schriften* (Leipzig, 1914), pp. 145ff., 206.

[4]) *Epit. Ulp.* 2.4; D. 40.1.25 (Modestinus 9 *diff.*); *h.t.* 29.1 (Pomponius 18 *ad Quintum Mucium*).

[5]) Grave doubts have been expressed in the past as to the accuracy of the traditional dating of the XII Tables but see now, above all Wieacker, 'Die XII Tafeln in ihrem Jahrhundert', *Entretiens sur l'Antiquité classique xiii, Les Origines de la République romaine* (Fondation Hardt, Vandœuvres-Genève, 1967), pp. 293ff.

alienationem complexa videretur".[6]) It cannot reasonably be doubted that in the wording of this provision as it came down to later ages[7]) either *emptio* or *emptor* was to be found; and there is no particular reason to consider that in this respect the wording had undergone alteration.[8])

Thus, we should accept as a working hypothesis that the word *emptio/emptor* existed by the mid-fifth century B.C. and was used in the XII Tables. Yet beyond doubt, the Roman contract of sale, *emptio venditio*, was not then in being[9]) and further, an essential element of the very idea of sale, coined money, was also lacking.[10],[11]) If we wish to give to *emptio* here a meaning akin to that which it had in later times we would have to say that the provision of the XII Tables applied and was intended to apply only when the slave was transferred for a prestation in bronze or silver (if we suppose that these metals had become the standard measures of exchange[12]). On this view the *statuliber* could not get his freedom if he fulfilled the condition after he had been transferred in exchange for other property such as oxen or goats, or had been delivered as a gift, or as dowry on behalf of the heir's daughter, or consequent upon the death of the heir. Yet why should these cases (which would make up a fair proportion of all alienations) have been exluded from the scope of the Code's provision? And if they were at first excluded, what changed circumstances persuaded later jurists that the scope should be wider, that *emptio* should be treated—exceptionally and

[6]) Though the point is not of importance in the present context this view of Pomponius inverts the situation. *Emptio*, whatever it may mean, is used of a transaction viewed (in its property aspect) from the standpoint of the recipient; *alienatio* from that of the transferor.

[7]) Primarily through the *tripertita* of Sextus Aelius Paetus Catus, consul of 198 B.C.

[8]) See infra, p. 149.

[9]) Sometime in the 3rd century B.C. would seem to be the earliest date which any modern legal scholar would allow for the creation of the contract.

[10]) The introduction of coinage is put very much later than the mid fifth century B.C.: cf. e.g. Sydenham, *The Roman Republican Coinage* (London, 1952), pp. 1ff.; Mattingly, *Roman Coins*, 2nd edit. (London, 1960), pp. 3ff.; Crawford, *The Roman Republican Coinage* (Cambridge, 1974), pp. 3ff., 589f.

[11]) *Emptio venditio* requires that the counter-prestation (or at least part of it) be in coined money, though the Proculians argued that *permutatio* was also *emptio venditio*; e.g. G. 3.141.

[12]) As might be permissible from the reports of the *lex Aternia Tarpeia* and the *lex Menenia Sestia* reputedly of 454 and 452 B.C.: for the sources for these see Rotondi, *Leges publicae populi romani* (Milan, 1912), pp. 200f.

as a deliberate misinterpretation—as including all these other situations? In the absence of a convincing answer to either of these questions we should accept that we have in the XII Tables' provision on the *statuliber* an instance where *emptio/emptor* means "taking/taker" or at least "receiving/recipient". On this view, of course, problems and questions of interpretation would arise only when *emptio* acquired a more restricted meaning.[13])

To return for a moment to the accuracy of the tradition of the wording. If one believes that *emptio/emptor* did not appear in the original but is later, then one must wonder how, when and why the change came about. If the alteration occurred at a time when *emere* meant 'to take' or 'to receive', the basic situation (for us) is unchanged; but if when *emere* meant 'to buy' then how could any verbal change so restricting the scope of the provision prove acceptable? And why ever was it made? There seems to be no answer.[14]) In fact, one might even go so far as to state that the use of *emptio/emptor* with a sense wider than any involved in the context of sale is the strongest evidence of the accuracy of the tradition on the clause's wording.[15],[16])

---

[13]) Ironically, the presence of *emptio/emptor* in the tradition has been one factor leading some modern scholars of Roman law to doubt the accuracy of the reports on the provision: Riccobono in *Fontes Iuris Romani Antejustiniani* i (Florence, 1941), p. 51; Voci, *Diritto ereditario romano* i, 2nd edit. (Milan, 1967), p. 75; Impallomeni, *Le Manomissioni mortis causa* (Padua, 1963), p. 19. The best answer to these doubts is, of course, the evidence provided by philologists that *emere* originally meant 'to take'. See also Kaser, *Das römische Privatrecht* i, 2nd edit. (Munich, 1971), p. 114.

[14]) The same difficulty would exist if one were to suppose that the whole provision is a later invention.

[15]) It has been suggested that in the wording for *mancipatio*, "mihi emptus esto hoc aere aeneaque libra" refers not to 'purchasing' but to 'taking' [Kaser, *Eigentum und Besitz im älteren römischen Recht*, 2nd edit. (Cologne, Graz, 1956) pp. 108, 117, 135, 141] or to 'receiving' [Prichard, 'Terminology of *mancipatio*', *Law Quarterly Review* lxxvi (1960), pp. 412ff.; cf. Jolowicz and Nicholas, *Historical Introduction to Roman Law* 3rd edit. (Cambridge, 1972), p. 149]. Such a view may well be correct but it cannot help us here, since any such meaning attributed to "emptus esto" in the *mancipatio* derives from external factors. In the context the meaning could easily be "let him have been bought": "hoc aere aeneaque libra" points to a purchase.

[16]) I am grateful to Mr. R. M. Pinkerton for his generous help with this note.

III

Legal Origins

13

Ius Aelianum and Tripertita

D. 1.2.2.7 (Pomp. *sing. ench.*). *Postea cum Appius Claudius proposuisset et ad formam redegisset has actiones, Gnaeus Flavius scriba eius libertini filius subreptum librum populo tradidit, et adeo gratum fuit id munus populo, ut tribunus plebis fieret et senator et aedilis curulis. hic liber, qui actiones continet, appellatur ius civile Flavianum, sicut ille ius civile Papirianum: nam nec Gnaeus Flavius de suo quicquam adiecit libro. augescente civitate quia deerant quaedam genera agendi, non post multum temporis spatium Sextus Aelius alias actiones composuit et librum populo dedit, qui appellatur ius Aelianum.*

D. 1.2.2.38: *...deinde Sextus Aelius et frater eius Publius Aelius et Publius Atilius maximam scientiam in profitendo habuerunt, ut duo Aelii etiam consules fuerint, Atilius autem primus a populo Sapiens appellatus est. Sextum Aelium etiam Ennius laudavit et exstat illius liber qui inscribitur 'tripertita', qui liber veluti cunabula iuris continet: tripertita autem dicitur, quoniam lege duodecim tabularum praeposita iungitur interpretatio, deinde subtexitur legis actio. eiusdem esse tres alii libri referuntur, quos tamen quidam negant eiusdem esse: hos sectatus ad aliquid est Cato...*

These two texts from Pomponius' *liber singularis enchiridii* are the sole sources which mention the *ius Aelianum* and the *tripertita* and they seem to present us with an insoluble problem. What is the relationship between the books with these names? On the one hand the *ius Aelianum* and the *tripertita* cannot, it seems, be the same work[1]. Thus in § 7 Pomponius tells us that the *ius Aelianum* was a collection of the forms of *legis actiones*, in § 38 that the *tripertita* contained the clause of the XIII Tables, to which was joined the jurist's *interpretatio*, and then the *legis actio* was given. But on the other hand, how can the

---

[1] Though no argument should be drawn from the existence of two distinct names. The titles of books in classical antiquity are notoriously variable. [2] To

ius Aelianum and the *tripertita* be different works? In § 7 Pomponius accepts without question the genuineness of the *ius Aelianum*. He does the same for the *tripertita* in § 38 but adds " three other books are said to be of the same jurist, but some writers deny they are his ". There seems no place here for a fully authenticated *ius Aelianum* distinct from the *tripertita*. Not surprisingly, modern scholarly opinion is divided as to whether the *ius Aelianum* and the *tripertita* are names for the same work, or different works of the same jurist [2]. The extent of the conflict is strikingly shown by the two entries in *Pauly-Wissowa*. In the entry on *" Sextus Ailius Q.f.P.n. Paitus Catus "* (by Klebs) we are told that doubt on the identification of the two titles is unfounded [3]; in that on *Ius Aelianum* (by Danneberg) that the identification is not justified [4].

But a way out of this impasse can be found, I suggest, if we take a wider look ot the *liber singularis enchiridii*.

In D. 1.2.2.4 Pomponius gives his version of the introduction of the XII Tables. On the pasing of these *leges*, he tells us in § 5, juristic interpretation became necessary, and this part of law he calls *ius civile*. In § 6 he reports that actions were formed from the XII Tables, that these were *certae* and *sollemnes* so that the people could not sue just as they wished, and that this part of law is called *legis actiones*, that is *legitimae actiones*. The text continues: *" et ita eodem paene tempore tria haec iura nata sunt: lege* [5] *duodecim tabularum ex his fluere coepit ius civile, ex isdem legis actiones compositae sunt "*. The *interpretandi scientia* and the *actiones* were the preserve of the College of Pontiffs one of whom was chosen each year to be in charge of private action. The people availed themselves of this practice, we are told, for about 100 years. § 7, as we have seen, explains how the *legis actiones* became known to the people at large. Then comes § 8:

Deinde cum esset in civitate lex duodecim tabularum et ius civile, essent et legis actiones, evenit, ut plebs in discordiam cum patribus perveniret et secederet sibique iura constitueret, quae iura plebi scita vo-

---

Casavola and the references he gives in *NNDI*. 9 (1963) 376 f, sv. " *Ius Aelianum* ", add d'Ippolito, *Sextus Aelius Catus*, *Labeo* 17 (1971) 271 ff. especially from p. 279. [3] *PWRE*. 1 (1894) 527. [4] *PWRE*. 10 (1919) 1202 ff. at 1203. Even, says the author, if one accepts with Jörs three independent parts in the *tripertita*. [5] Probably there is some scribal corruption in the text here, but *cantur. mox cum revocata est plebs, quia multae discordiae nascebantur de his plebis scitis, pro legibus placuit et ea observari lege Hortensia: et ita factum est, ut inter plebis scita et legem species constituendi interesset, potestas autem eadem esset.*

These texts § 4 to § 8 (we need proceed no further) purport to show the historical progression of law in the Republic. Thus, § 8 begins, "*Deinde*", "Thereupon". There can be little doubt that in this text the secession of the plebs and the *lex Hortensia* are those of 287 B. C., and not earlier secessions and *leges,* real or imaginary [6]. So if we can attribute any weight — as I think we must — to Pomponius' historical plan and he is accurate, the *ius Aelianum* should be earlier than 287. If this is correct then the *ius Aelianum* cannot be the work of Sextus Aelius Pactus Catus, consul of 198, censor in 194 [7], author of the *tripertita.*

Other indications of an early date are not lacking. Pomponius in § 7 says that Sextus Aelius composed the *ius Aelianum* a short time after the *ius Flavianum* ("*non post multum temporis spatium*"). Gnaeus Flavius who was responsible for that work was the scribe of Appius Claudius, censor of 312, consul in 307 and 296, who died after 280 [8]. According to Pomponius, Gnaeus Flavius was made tribune of the plebs, senator and curule aedile as a result of the publication of the *ius Flavianum.* Livy [9] claims that it was while he was curule aedile that he published the "*civile ius, repositum in penetralibus pontificum*". Cicero [10] and Pliny the Elder [11] both state that it was while he was a scribe that Gnaeus Flavius published the legal calendar; and elsewhere Cicero also attributes the publication of the forms of action to him [12]. Flavius was curule aedile in 304 B.C. [13] so that year gives us a *terminus ad quem* for the *ius Flavianum.* It seems unlikely that Pomponius could say 'a short time later' of a work produced presumably about a century afterwards by the consul of 198. But "*non post multum temporis spatium*" is very appropriate for a book published before 287. Again,

---

the sense is clear and the question need not detain us. [6] It was the *lex Hortensia* of that year which gave *plebiscita* the force of statute: cf. KASER, *RPR.* 1² (1971) 199; SCULLARD, *A History of the Roman World, 753 to 146 B.C.*³ (1961) 100. [7] KUNKEL, *Herkunft und soziale Stellung der römischen Juristen*² (1967) 8. [8] Cf. KUNKEL, *Herkunft* 6. [9] Liv. 10.46.5. [10] Cic. *pro Mur.* 11.25. [11] Plin. *N. h.* 33.6.17. [12] Cic. *ad Att.* 6.1.8; *de or.* 1.41.186. [13] Cf. BROUGHTON, *The Magistrates of the Roman Republic* 1 (1951) 168.

though the purpose of the *ius Aelianum* was to make public the *genera agendi* which were not included in the *ius Flavianum,* it apparently gave *legis actiones* alone [14]. This is best explained on the hypothesis that *formulae* were not yet in existence when the *ius Aelianum* was published. Yet around 200 B.C. there were *formulae* at least for the *condictio* [15], the *actio tutelae* [16], and the actions on the consensual contract of sale, hire and partnership [17]. So the *ius Aelianum* should be placed some time before that date; and hence it appears to be considerably earlier than the *tripertita.*

The suggestion is, therefore, that the Sextus Aelius who compiled the *ius Aelianum* is not the same personnage as the Sextus Aelius who wrote the *tripertita.* The problem of reconciling Pomponius' § 7 and 38 then disappears. On the one hand, the *ius Aelianum* and the *tripertita* are not the same work. On the other, Pomponius can accept the authenticity of the *ius Aelianum* without question in § 7 while mentioning doubts in § 38 as to whether the three books, other than the *tripertita,* attributed to the consul of 198 were really by him.

It is no objection to this hypothesis that the Sextus Aelius of the *ius Aelianum* would then disappear from the remainder of the *liber singularis enchiridii* and be not mentioned in the list of jurists from § 36 on, whereas Sextus Aelius consul of 198 is discussed in § 38. The explanation would be simply that the first Sextus Aelius was not considered to be a jurist but only a compiler. Gnaeus Flavius who issued the *ius Flavianum* is also not mentioned in the list of jurists [18].

The Sextus Aelius of the *ius Aelianum* cannot be more nearly identified but there is nothing surprising or suspicious in that. Aelius was a very common *nomen* [19], and though we have no earlier recorded instance of a Sextus Aelius, Sextus as a *praenomen* for an Aelius is not in itself odd [20].

---

[14] Appears from § 8. [15] Cf. now WATSON, *Roman Private Law around 200 B.C.* (1971) 127. [16] Cf. WATSON, *Private Law* 39. The *actio tutelae* is the oldest *bonae fidei formula* and was intended from the start for actions between citizens: cf. my forthcoming *Law Making in the Later Roman Republic,* Chapter 5. [17] Cf. the references in WATSON, *Private Law* 129 nt. 2. The *tripertita* likewise did not contain *formulae* but this is the result of its nature as a work on the XII Tables. [18] Whereas Appius Claudius is mentioned in § 7, and — because he was considered to be a jurist — reappears at § 36. [19] See the individuals listed in *PWRE.* 1. 489 ff. [20] The possibility cannot be excluded, though nothing should be made of it, that the Aelius of the *ius Aelianum* did not have

This hypothesis is, of course, based on Pomponius, and it might be suggested that Pomponius on this matter was rather confused. That possibility cannot be rejected. But it should then be stressed that we have no other evidence for the existence or substance of the *ius Aelianum*. What I hope has at least firmly emerged from the present study is that for Pomponius — our sole source — the *ius Aelianum* was composed shortly before 287 B.C., that it therefore could not have been thought to be the work of Sextus Aelius Paetus Catus, consul of 198 B.C., and that hence, in the eyes of Pomponius the *ius Aelianum* and the *tripertita* were totally distinct works by different authors.

Finally, to return to § 7 for a moment. We have seen that 304 B.C. is a *terminus ad quem* for the *ius Flavianum*. In explaining the publication for the *ius Aelianum* a few years later, Pomponius says, "*augescente civitate, quia deerant quaedam genera agendi*". So he attributes the need for the *ius Aelianum* to a growth in the size of the state [21]. Whether it is correct or not that new actions were needed because the *civitas* was larger [22], it is certain that within a few years of the publication of the *ius Flavianum* the *civitas* was enlarged. For instance about 304 itself, *civitas sine suffragio* was given to Arpinum and Trebula and a powerful colony was established et Sora. Territory of the *Aequi* was annexed and on this was placed a colony at Alba Fucens in 303 or 300 with six thousand colonists, and at Carsioli in 302 or 298 with four thousand colonists [23] [24].

---

the *praenomen* Sextus. It could easily happen that this *praenomen* was attributed from the better known author of the *tripertita*. Names, and especially *praenomina*, are notoriously subject to error. Thus in § 38 itself, Pomponius' Publius Atilius should probably be Lucius Acilius; cf. KUNKEL, *Herkunft* 10; WIEACKER, *Die römischen Juristen in der politischen Gesellschaft des zweiten vorchristlichen Jahrhunderts, Sein und Werden im Recht. Fgbe von Lübtow* (1970) 183 ff. at p. 194. KUNKEL, *Herkunft* 22 stresses that in Pomponius, D. 1.2.2, many of the names are due to mistakes. Or, if the composer of the *ius Aelianum* was not otherwise known, this work itself might come to be put into the corpus of writings of the consul of 198, and actually be one of the doubtful books Pomponius had in mind in § 38.

21 "*Augescente civitate*" canot refer simply to the development of institutions within the state.

22 Pomponius' "*augescente civitate*" may even be purely conventional and not intended to be taken too seriously.

23 On all this see, e.g. ADCOCK, in *Cambridge Ancient History* 7 (1968) 608; SCULLARD, *Roman World* 114.

24 I am grateful for the comments of Mr. John Barton, Mr. Francis Cairns and Mr. Robin Seager who read a draft of this paper.

14

The Origins of fiducia

The date of the appearance of *fiducia* cannot be ascertained with any precision, but there can be little doubt that it was actionable in the time of Plautus. Kaser, although he believes that the *actio fiduciae* arose first in the 3rd century B.C.,[1] states that while *fiducia* was known to Plautus one cannot deduce from that anything as to the age of the action. This view, I submit, is incorrect. Plautus' comedies not only enable us to say that, at that time, *fiducia* could be the subject of an action, but also indicates how it developed.

> Epidicus 697-9:
> PERIPHANES. qua fiducia ausu's primum quae emptast nudiustertius filiam meam dicere esse? EPIDICUS. lubuit: ea fiducia.
> PERIPHANES. ain tu? lubuit? EPIDICUS. aio. vel da pignus, ni ea sit filia.

This text in itself gives no sign of *fiducia* being actionable but it is worth quoting since it shows Plautus punning on *fiducia* and *pignus* which must, therefore, have been familiar to his audience. *Qua fiducia etc?* means here „On what reliance etc?", and *pignus* means "wager" and the joke in the text consists in bringing together *fiducia* and *pignus* with these non-legal meanings while they must be, at the same time, the forms of real security. If these securities did not exist there is no pun and the passage is merely boring.

An equally clear reference to *fiducia* as a form of real security is in Mostellaria 37. Tranio, the town slave, asks Grumio, the country slave, what it has to do with him if he (Tranio) likes to drink and go whoring:

> mei tergi facio haec, non tui fiducia. (My back, that is, not yours, will have to pay for it.)

But the main texts for us are the following:

> Trinummus 116-8:
> MEGARONIDES. quid tu, adulescentem, quem esse corruptum vides, qui

[1] ZRG 61 (1941) p. 182.

tuae mandatus est fide et fiduciae,
quin eum restituis, quin ad frugem corrigis?

Ibid. 140-5:
CALLICLES. subigis maledictis me tuis, Megaronides,
novo modo adeo, ut quod meae concreditumst
taciturnitati clam, fide et fiduciae,
ne enuntiarem quoiquam neu facere palam, ut mihi necesse sit iam id tibi concredere.
MEGARONIDES. mihi quod credideris sumes ubi posiueris.

Aulularia 584-6:
EUCLIO. Fides, novisti me et ego te: cave sis tibi
ne tu immutassis nomen, si hoc concreduo.
ibo ad te fretus tua, Fides, fiducia.

These must be compared with the opening lines of the Formula Baetica.

> Dama L. Titi ser(vus) fundum Baianum, qui est in agro, qui Veneriensis vocatur, pago Olbensi, uti optumus maxumusq(ue) esset, HS n(ummo) I et hominem Midam HS n(ummo) I fidi fiduciae causa mancipio accepit ab L. Baianio, libripend*e* –, antest(ato) –. Adfines *f*undo dixit L. Baianius L. Titium et C. Seium et populum et si quos dicere oportet.

From these texts I should like to argue that from the beginning there was in the *mancipatio fiduciae causa* a clause *fide et fiduciae* or something very similar, and that the existence of this clause is all important for the development of *fiducia*.

To begin with, in the Formula Baetica the correct reading is *fidi fiduciae*. As Mommsen says,[2] duplication is common in legal forms, e.g. *in diem tertium sive perindinum*; *quanti aequius melius erit*; *quam rem sive litem dicere oportet*. But where we have duplication there is always a strong suggestion of formality, such as is to be found in the words of a *stipulatio* or of a *formula*. Moreover, we cannot say that *fidi fiduciae causa* is inserted in the Formula Baetica with no other purpose than to show the nature of the *mancipatio*. If that had been so, we would have expected simply *fiduciae causa* just as we find *donationis causa*.[3]

Secondly, we must not ignore the meaning of the three Plautine passages. All concern a situation where something or someone has been or will be entrusted to another- exactly the situation in legal *fiducia*. And we have no examples of a different usage.

Thirdly, in the three passages of Plautus there is a joke which is reasonably funny – but otherwise is very weak or non-existent – if we can

[2] Corpus Inscriptionum Lainarum II 5042.

[3] Cf. the *negotia* in Bruns Fontes Iuris Romani Antiqui 7th edit. (1919, Tübingen) nos 136 (p. 335); 137 (p. 336); 138 (pp. 336-7); and 140 (3 and 4) (p. 339).

say that he is using technical legal terms. This an important point in dealing with a comic writer. In the first passage of the Trinummus, one old gentleman (Megaronides) complains to another (Callicles) that a young man entrusted to the latter for safe keeping has been allowed to go completely to the bad. For emphasis, Megaronides says he was entrusted *tuae . . . fide et fiduciae*. This would suggest to the reader in rather a dry way that the *adulescens*, like a piece of property, was transferred *fiduciae causa* and that Callicles has broken a legal as well as a moral duty in not looking after him properly. *Tuae* also is unemphatic, thus laying the stress on *fide et fiduciae*. The second passge from that play is less close to the legal concept of *fiducia*, but the humour of the passage lies in the ridiculous idea of a secret being given *fide et fiduciae*. The legal joke is then taken up by Megaronides with *mihi quod credideris sumes ubi posiueris*. The fun here consists in taking up the idea of the secret as corporeal property which is to be entrusted by one to the other. In both of the above passages, if one does not concede that *fide et fiduciae* is a technical phrase, there is no joke.[4] The third text is perhaps even more illuminating. Euclio is going to hide treasure in the temple of *Fides* relying on, he says, *tua, Fides, fiducia*. If the sole joke here is the pun on the faith (*fiducia*) of the goddess Faith (*Fides*), then it is not a very good one, especially with which to end a scene. It is very much improved if *fide et fiduciae* was a technical phrase. The use of the vocative and ablative would be a neat variation on the two datives.

Fourthly, in all these four texts, *fides* comes first and *fiducia* last. This is unlikely to be purely coincidental and suggests a standard formulation.

Fifthly, we have the curious fact that this juxtaposition is nowhere else found (so far as I can discover) in Latin during the time when *fiducia* was in existence. Yet if we were to ascribe *fide et fiduciae* to Plautine fulness, it must be admitted that other writers were equally verbose. The absence of the phrase elsewhere can only be explained as follows. Non-legal writers would not juxtapose *fides* and *fiducia* in order to give emphasis because the juxtaposition would inevitably call to mind the legal concept of *fiducia* and give rise to an unwanted pun; only comedians would normally desire this effect. Also, we do not find it in legal writers mainly as a result of the disappearance of *fiducia* and the destruction of the texts. After *mancipatio* (and with it *fiducia*) became obsolete,[5] we do find the juxtaposition in St Augustine De civitate Dei 10.9.1:

> Fiebant autem simplici fide atque fiducia pietatis, non incantatoribus et carminibus . . .

Now there need be no fear of making an unwanted pun. But it is

4 There is nothing like this in Terence who is notoriously less Roman than Plautus and of lesser value to jurists.

5 Cf. Levy West Roman Vulgar Law: The Law of Property (1951, Philadelphia) p. 128.

interesting that the use is quite different from that of Plautus and the Formula Baetica where *fide et fiduciae* were unqualified, whereas here these words are qualified by an adjective (*simplici*) and a noun in the genitive (*pietatis*).

If then we can deduce from Plautus and the Formula Baetica that *fide et fiduciae* (or something similar) was a standard formulation[6] then we must hold that it was a clause in a reasonably formal institution. Generally speaking, one does not find standard formulations appearing, for instance, in *emptio venditio*, but rather in the stipulations attaching to such or in the parts of the *formulae*. In this case, the formal clause must have been inserted in either the *mancipatio* or an accompanying stipulation. Mommsen has suggested[7] that some similar clause was in the latter. This, however, is extremely unlikely, since it would then be hard to see any reason for a separate *actio fiduciae* to develop. Since the parties to the transaction had to be face to face for the *mancipatio* there could never be any difficulty in taking a stipulation. Accordingly, it is most probable that the clause was in the *mancipatio* as is indeed suggested by the Formula Baetica. And then, of course, it would be actionable as a result of the well known clause of the XII Tables (6.1):

> Cum nexum faciet mancipiumque, uti lingua nuncupassit, ita ius esto.

Although undoubtedly the purpose of this clause was originally very different, little difficulty would be found in interpreting the *lex* to cover our case.[8] And so a formal *legis actio* would arise which, however, would have to decide the case according to the words *fide et fiduciae*, that is, on the basis of good faith.[9] Eventually, the *legis actio* would give way to a *formula* (or *formulae*) and the *bonae fidei* element would be more and more stressed.

Three arguments could be raised against this view.

First, Lenel once maintained[10] that there were two *formulae* for *fiducia*, one of which contained the clause *ut inter bonos bene agier oportet et sine fraudatione*, while the other was of the standard type for *bonae fidei* obligations *quidquid ob earm rem Nm Nm Ao Ao dare facere oportet ex fide bona.*

[6] Beseler says that without doubt the conjunction of *fides* and *fiducia* is formal and very old: ZRG 45 (1925) p. 426.

[7] ZRG 6 (1885) p. 274.

[8] For an equally wide interpretation (or deliberate misinterpretation) cf. G. 1.132.

[9] Similarly, sometimes the action arising on a stipulation would have to be decided in accordance with *bona fides*. Df. Daube Novation of Obligations giving a Bonae Fidei Iudicium ZRG 66 (1948) p. 91 ff.: Arangio-Ruiz La Compravendita in diritto romano (2nd edit., Naples, 1956) p. 64 FF.

[10] Edictum Perpetuum 2nd edit. (Leipzig, 1907) p. 284.

There is little evidence for the latter[11] and indeed later Lenel became non-committal,[12] but neverthless it must have existed. Gaius in his Institutes 4.33 tells us:

> Nulla autem formula ad condictionis fictionem exprimitur. sive enim pecunia*m* sive rem aliquam certam debitam nobis petamus, eam ipsam DARI NOBIS OPORTERE intendimus, nec ullam adiungimus condictionis fictionem. itaque simul intellegimus eas formulas, quibus pecuniam aut rem aliquam nobis dar*i* oportere intendimus, sua vi ac potestate valere. eiusdem naturae sunt actiones commodati, fiduciae, negotiorum gestorum et aliae innumerabiles.

Accordingly, *dari* (or *dare*) *oportere* must have appeared in a formula for *fiducia* and this does not seem possible in the one containing *ut inter bonos & c* for the existence of which we have complete proof.[13] So there must have been another *formula* with an *intentio ex fide bona*. Lenel then suggests that the former must have been an *actio in factum* and although this is denied by Rotondi[14] and Arangio-Ruiz[15] it would be very difficult to account for the existence of two *formulae in ius*. Accepting then, the existence of an *actio fiduciae in factum* it might be argued that this is very much contrary to the suggested development of *fiducia* through a *legis actio* based on the XII Tables. But a simple explanation can be given for the existence of an *actio in factum*. The *legis actio*, needless to say, would only give protection when the words *fide et fiduciae* were in the *mancipatio* but inevitably there would be cases where *mancipatio* was made *fiduciae causa* and these words were omitted. Because of the stress on *bona fides* in this particular *legis actio* it would be felt that practorian protection should be given where the clause was omitted and a *legis actio in factum* or a *formula in factum* would be accordingly introduced.[16] And when the *legis actio fiduciae* was abolished a

[11] The usual argument (cf. Lenel op. cit. 3rd edit. Leipzig, 1927 p. 292 f.) runs as follows((1) G. 4. 62 includes the *actio fiduciae* in the list of *bonae fidei iudicia*; but so also does it include the *actio rei uxoriae* where the *intentio* was different and probably ran *quod eius melius aequius erit*: (2) Cicero de off. 3. 70 has *fidei bonae nomen manare latissime idque versari in tutelis societatibus, fiduciis mandatis, rebus emptis venditis, conductis locatis*; but *bonae fidei nomen* may simply mean 'the concept of good faith'.

[12] Loc. cit. (3rd edit.).

[13] Cicero Ad fam. 7.12.2; de off. 3.61; 3.70 (cited in note 11).

[14] Scritti giuridici II (Milan, 1922) p. 3 f.

[15] „Le formole con *demonstratio* e la loro origine", Rariora (Rome 1946) p. 56 n. 1.

[16] C. Longo's argument (La fiducia Milan 1946 p. 9) that an *actio in factum* was impossible during the period of the *legis actiones* is very weak. G. 4.11. at the most can mean only that at the time of the introduction of *legis actiones* the *edicta praetoris* did not exist. For the view that *formulae* were introduced early in cases *inter cives* see Kunkel, „Fides als schöpferisches Element im römischen Schuldrecht", Festschrift Koschaker II p. 1 ff; Kaser, „Das altrömische Ius" Göttingen 1949 p. 290 ff; and Watson "Consensual Societas between Romans and the Introduction of the Formulae" 1962 RIDA p. 431 ff.

formula in ius was established in its place, side by side with the *formula in factum*.

The second objection would be that in fact the tablets from Pompeii make it probable that it was not necessary to inset a clause *fide et fiduciae* in a *mancipatio fiduciae causa*.[17] But this has already been dealt with en passant. With the disappearance of the *legis actio*, *bona fides* would alone decide whether the *mancipatio* was or was not *fiduciae cause* and the clause *fide et fiduciae* would become optional and no doubt eventually not very common. The attestation of its use in the Formula Baetica is, to a great extent, the result of that common phenomenon that often forms which are outmoded in the ruling centre survive for a considerable period in provinces and colonies. The Formula Baetica is also archaic in its *optumus maxumusque* and the form *fidi* for the genitive.[18]

The third objection is that levelled by C. Longo against the theory of Oertmann[19] and Pernice that the *legis actio* was available because of the insertion of a clause *fidi fiduciae causa*, namely that *fiducia* was operated both by *mancipatio* and *in iure cessio* and that the clause of the XII Tables could refer only to *mancipatio* and so the constitution of *fiducia* by *in iure cessio* is left unexplained. Two answers can be given to this. First, there is no evidence that *fiducia* could be constituted by *in iure cessio* during the period of the *legis actiones*. All our evidence is for the formulary period. And it is not *a priori* unlikely that, at an early period, there could be such a difference in the scope of *mancipatio* and *in iure cessio*. After all, it seems that it was never possible to testate by *in iure cessio* although a will *per aes et libram* was common. Secondly, it may well have been the case that one could have had an *in iure cessio* with a stipulation on the side in which the recipient promised to transfer the *res* to its former owner on the fulfilment of certain conditions.[20]

The above interpretation of the development of *fiducia* would also explain why the sources talk of *pactum fiduciae*. *Pactum* here means, as often[21] a term of clause which is part of a larger whole.

[17] Bruns Fontes cit. Negotium 134 pp. 332-4.

[18] Cf. Aulus Gellius 9.14; Mommsen loc. cit.

[19] Die Fiducia im römischen Privatrecht (Berlin 1890). This was not available to me, but I am kindly informed by Miss Ann Kettle that he also (p. 97) makes some use of the texts of the Trinummus cited above.

[20] It is very difficult to see what form the *addictio* could take even in classical law.

[21] E.g. *pactum protimeseos, pactum displicentiae*.

15

The Origins of Consensual Sale: A Hypothesis

The invention of the consensual contracts, of which *emptio venditio* is perhaps the earliest [1]), was such a great advance in legal thinking that scholars tend to pay little attention to the defects in these institutions. But the defects in early consensual sale are substantial and probably significant. An examination and attempt at explanation of these defects may well result in giving us a better picture of how consensual sale originated.

There are three clear defects in early sale.

First, the seller was under no obligation to make the buyer owner of the object sold. This, however, is probably not significant. Even in the case of *mancipatio*, the transferor seems to have been under no legal duty to make the transferee owner. The *actio auctoritatis* was available only if the transferee were evicted. Arangio-Ruiz [2]) has tried to explain this rule in sale by saying that *emptio venditio* began in the relations between Romans and peregrines and that valuable *res mancipi* could therefore be transferred only by *traditio* which came to be looked upon as the method of performance. But not only is an explanation of this kind unnecessary, it is, as we shall see later, unconvincing.

Secondly, the seller had only to deliver possession and if the buyer were then evicted the seller was not liable unless he had given a stipulation against eviction. This continued to be the position even into classical law. This defect in consensual sale is, I submit, extremely significant. One cannot explain it by saying

---

1) One cannot argue, as sometimes seems to be done, that because sale was commercially the most important of the four consensual contracts it was therefore the first to emerge. Law does not necessarily develop so logically as that.

2) E. g., in *La compravendita in diritto romano* 2nd edit. (Naples, reprinted 1956) p. 176 ff.

that the Romans did not think of the possibility of having an inherent warranty against eviction. Such an inherent warranty had already existed for a long time in the case of *mancipatio*. Nor can one say that the things sold by consensual sale and not then delivered by *mancipatio* would be of so little value that the buyer would not want a remedy if he were evicted. This is self-evidently not true. Nonetheless, one must say that for some reason the Romans did not think it necessary or desirable that there should be an inherent warranty against eviction in *emptio venditio*.

Thirdly, the seller was not liable for latent defects (provided, of course, he was unaware of them). At first sight this may not seem significant. After all, a legal system might well work on the principle that the buyer must take the goods as he finds them. But this lack of significance of the rule cannot be reasonably maintained when we turn our attention to the Aedilician Edict. This Edict was issued no doubt — the point will emerge later — after the introduction of consensual sale and Daube, very plausibly, conjectures 199 B. C. [3]). Its purpose was to compel the seller of slaves and animals in the market-place to disclose most kinds of hidden defects and to make him liable if he did not. This provision was not extended to sales outside the market and of other things until late classical law and possibly not even until Justinian. Yet one would have thought all buyers would have benefitted equally from such protection. Certainly, the policy of the law is not necessarily the same in all sale situations, but it would appear almost as though there was a prejudice against the *actio empti*. The evidence which we have from Varro shows that in the Republic it was usual for the buyer to exact stipulations against latent defects from the seller [4]) and there is not the slightest indication that he was thinking primarily or at all of sales in the market-place [5]).

---

3) *Forms of Roman Legislation* (Oxford, 1956) p. 91 ff; *cf* Honoré in Studies in the Roman Law of Sale dedicated to De Zulueta, edited by Daube (Oxford 1959) p. 134.

4) *De re. rust.* 2.2.6; 2.3.5; 2.4.5.; 2.5.10,11; 2.10.5.

5) The same applies to the documents from the Empire which have survived:

A number of deductions can be drawn from the above discussion of the defects in early consensual sale.

First, it shows that Arangio-Ruiz' hypothesis to explain why the seller need not transfer ownership is unconvincing. That hypothesis amounts to saying that if it had been reasonably possible to make the transfer of ownership the primary duty of the seller this would have been done. But if that had been so and it had not been possible to establish that under *emptio venditio* the seller must transfer ownership to the buyer, we would have expected that the seller be compelled to give the best title possible considering the nature of the object sold and the nationalities of the parties, or at least that he be liable if the buyer were evicted. But the seller was not made liable if the buyer were evicted and, therefore, there can have been no pressing desire that the seller be made to give ownership.

Secondly, it suggests that too much emphasis ought not be placed on the part played by *bona fides* in the emergence of sale. No doubt, good faith was important, but nonetheless the two main continuing obligations of the seller were not within the scope of the *bonae fidei* action.

Thirdly, it means that commercially *emptio venditio* was less helpful than one might have expected. In any contract for an object of value — and it is reasonable to imagine that the introduction of *emptio venditio* was inspired by a need felt in connexion with objects of value — the buyer would want to be protected against eviction and against latent defects. To obtain such protection he would need to take stipulations from the seller. Hence, in practice, it would be just as necessary for the parties (or persons subject to them [6])) to an *emptio venditio* to be face to face

F. I. R. A. III nos. 87; 88; 89; 132; 133 (these last two mention the Edict, as does document no. 60 from Herculaneum published by Arangio-Ruiz and Pugliese Carratelli, ix La parola del passato (1954) p. 55 — but this does not prove that the sales were under the jurisdiction of the Aediles which was restricted to the city of Rome); 135; 136; document no. 61 from Herculaneum published *op. cit.* p. 55 f at p. 56.

[6]) The *actio mandati* which would, in a rather clumsy way, have allowed some kind of representation was probably not then in existence: *cf infra* n. 18 and Watson *Contract of Mandate in Roman Law* (Oxford 1961) p. 21 ff.

as for parties to a stipulation. Contracts made *per epistulam* or *per nuntium* would be sorely deficient.

Fourthly, it means that, even if one believes *emptio venditio* to be the work of the *praetor peregrinus*, one cannot say that the consensual contract was introduced for the benefit of peregrine merchants who were unskilled in the strict *ius civile* and who could therefore be taken advantage of by the wily Romans. If a peregrine did not know enough Roman law to take a stipulation he might find himself in as bad a position after the introduction of the consensual contract as before. A stipulation still had to be taken to give a buyer reasonable protection.

If we turn now to the specific problem of the origins of consensual sale, I submit we ought to look for an answer to circumstances in which the deficiencies of the consensual contract can be reasonably explained. Above all, that is, we must ask why did the Romans not find it important to have warranties against eviction and latent defects inherent in *emptio venditio*, and why did they not realise the mercantile advantages which would accrue if an important sale could be satisfactorily arranged by a letter or through a messenger?

It seems to me that there is an answer to this question and only one. *Emptio venditio* arose to fill the interstices left by taking stipulations. Before sale arose, let us assume, it was customary to create the obligations arising from the desire to transfer a thing for money by stipulations. In the simplest case, sale of ready goods for present cash and where there was to be no *mancipatio*, stipulations would be wanted only by the buyer for protection against eviction and against latent defects. In more complex situations, others would also be wanted and taken, for instance, by the seller for payment of the price [7]), or by the buyer for delivery by a fixed date. But however simple or complex, the constants would always be the stipulation or stipulations against eviction and latent defects. And the more complex the factual situation, the greater the risk that the obligations arising from the stipulations would not be fully reciprocal or would not

---

7) *Cf* Varro *De re. rust.* 2.2.5; D.18.1.40.2; 44.1.14.

cover all the contingencies. In such a situation the *bonae fidei* action was introduced to fill gaps left by the stipulations. The action was kept separate from the actions on the stipulations but for the *bonae fidei* action to be available, there had to be a stipulation or stipulations and an agreement to transfer a thing for money. In course of time it would be felt less necessary to attempt to cover all contingencies by *stipulatio* and it would be enough that any relevant stipulation be taken. The *actio empti* or *venditi* would then cover all other terms inherent in the agreement of the parties. The stipulations which in fact always would be taken would be those giving the buyer a guarantee aginst eviction and against latent defects because they, and they alone, would be appropriate in even the simplest transaction. Eventually, it would be recognised that the *actiones empti* and *venditi* could be given even where there had been no stipulation, but by the time this had happened their dependence upon the stipulations against eviction and latent defects would be so marked that they were not allowed to encroach upon their field. Hence, it was not until classical law at the earliest that it was recognised that warranties against eviction and latent defects were inherent in *emptio venditio*. Thus, one must not say that, at the beginning, stipulations against eviction and latent defects had to be taken because the *actio empti* did not cover these obligations. Rather, the *actio empti* did not cover these obligations because that action was dependent upon the presence of these stipulations. A development such as this would explain not only why the *actio empti* did not cover eviction and latent defects but also why the Romans were not conscious of the disadvantages of the parties to an *emptio venditio* having to be face to face. It may be asked why stipulations continued to be taken to cover two obligations and not just to cover one. The answer to this probably is that, as the texts of Varro show[8]), where warranties against eviction and latent defects were both wanted (*i.e.*, where there was no *mancipatio*) they were in fact covered by one single stipulation. Where there was *mancipatio*, the position would be slightly different.

---

[8]) *De re rust.* 2.2.6; 2.3.5; 2.4.5.

There would be no need to take a stipulation against eviction because of the availability of the *actio auctoritatis*. But the very existence of the *actio auctoritatis* would here also prevent the *actio empti* covering this aspect of the transaction.

It might be objected to this suggested development that if consensual sale had arisen to fill the gaps left by taking stipulations it would have been much more rational simply to imply terms into the stipulations. Against that objection one could say, firstly, that it would not have been desirable to imply terms in stipulations because stipulations were used in so many fields. What was wanted was a change in the law in one area — that of transfer of goods for money — and any change in the nature of stipulation would have had far more sweeping effects. Secondly, it would have been thoroughly un-Roman to approach the problem in that way. A consideration of the *actio de dolo* will illustrate this. The *actio de dolo*, it seems to me, was introduced not only with a narrow scope but with the main function of giving a remedy to someone defrauded under a stipulation (or perhaps other *stricti iuris* agreement) where the fraudulent person had kept to the letter of the stipulation and hence no action on the contract was available. Not only is there testual support — admittedly slight — for this view of its origin but only thus can one explain why the action which lay only for *dolus* gave nothing but simple damages. It was, in fact, a contractual remedy [9]). The *actio de dolo*, too, widened its scope and became independent of contract but traces of its origin can still be seen. In this case also a remedy was wanted for situations in which there was a *stricti iuris* contract but no action was available under the contract and here again a change was made, not by altering the nature of the contract or the scope of its action, but by introducing a new action which was nonetheless dependent upon the existence of the contract.

Until now, for ease of exposition, a rather too simple and

---

9) *Cf* Watson *Actio de dolo and actiones in factum*, lxxviii ZSS (1961) p. 392 ff; xxxi Tijd., infra, p. 199. These are perhaps expressed rather too narrowly since there is no reference to the contract *litteris*.

perhaps rather static approach has been taken. This has enabled us to avoid a difficulty which must now be faced. The *actiones empti* and *venditi* cannot have arisen in the simplest possible situation of ready cash for present goods for there the stipulations against eviction and latent defects would have covered all the outstanding obligations. We must look to the more complicated cases where either delivery of the goods or payment of the price or both was to be deferred. And in these cases, stipulations for delivery of the goods or for payment of the price would be just as much the standard practice as stipulations against eviction and latent defects. How did it happen, then, that the *actiones empti* and *venditi* came to cover the field of these stipulations, but not of those against eviction and latent defects? The answer is to be found, I suggest, in the relationship between the duty to deliver the goods and the duty to pay the price. Such duties in the consensual sale are reciprocal, not in the sense that they must be performed at the same time, but that a party to the sale cannot exact the obligation from the other unless he has performed or is ready to perform his obligation[10]). This reciprocity is very much the desire of the parties, but it is precisely this reciprocity which is extremely difficult to achieve by stipulation, especially if it were not intended to insist upon the performance of the two obligations at exactly the same time. But once it was realised that, provided there was a stipulation to establish the relationship, the parties need not attempt to cover by stipulation every possible contingency, the jurists would feel that there were certain advantages in leaving particular aspects of the transaction untouched by stipulation. And this would be especially true of the primary duties of delivery of the goods and payment of the price. Even at a fairly early stage of development it could be envisaged that reciprocity of these obligations should follow from the concept of *bona fides*. So it would come about that even where delivery and payment were not to be immediate, stipulations to cover these obligations would not always be taken. To this ex-

---

10) Each of these duties, of course, consists in a single act, not in a continuing obligation.

planation it might be objected that reciprocity in the *bonae fidei* obligations does not date far back [11]). The evidence for this view is Varro *de re. rust.* 2.2.5,6. In that text Varro tells us that the buyer can successfully sue the seller *ex empto vendito* if there has been no delivery even if he has not paid, and the seller the buyer *simili iudicio* if he has not paid. But Meylan has already pointed out [12]) that the seller took a stipulation for the price and that this would destroy the bilaterality. The seller's obligation would be on the contract of sale, that of the buyer on the stipulation [13]). The text, therefore, would not appear to be evidence that there was no reciprocity in the prime obligations of *emptio venditio.* It is no objection to this explanation of the extension of the *bonae fidei* actions to the primary duties of delivery and payment that a number of texts show that stipulations for the price were often still taken [14]). Matters of legal practice take a long time to die [15]), and one can see that at times it would be advantageous to the seller, if he were in a strong enough position, to exact a stipulation from the buyer.

Moreover, the present hypothesis avoids a major difficulty inherent in most explanations of the origins of consensual sale since it does not involve holding that legal science took an enormous leap forward. On the present view, the jurists (or praetor) did not at one move introduce the completely revolutionary concept of a contract valid simply because of the parties' agreement. Rather, we have a long development with it becoming gradually more and more realised that not every part of the transaction had to be in solemn form in order to be valid.

---

11) *Cf,* for example, Kaser *Das römische Privatrecht* I (Munich, 1955) p. 442 n. 10.

12) Scritti Ferrini IV (Milan 1949) p. 179 ff.

13) In the text *simili iudicio* is loose usage on the part of Varro. It cannot imply that the seller is using an *actio ex vendito.*

14) *E. g.,* Cato *de ag. cult.* 146; Varro *de re. rust.* 2.2.6; D. 18.1.40.2; 44.1.14.

15) Thus, at the present time, certain standard clauses in Scottish deeds of security, which do not at all express the real desire or intention of the parties, are the result of the mediaeval law against usury which was abolished in Scotland in the later 16th century.

When and by whom were the *bonae fidei* actions for sale introduced? If one accepts that *formulae* were allowed between *cives* before the *lex Aebutia* [16]), one is not restricted to saying that, at least so far as Roman citizens were concerned, consensual contracts did not exist before the middle of the second century B. C. [17]). A more realistic date can be suggested, perhaps in the middle of the third century B. C. Nor is there any particuluar reason to ascribe the introduction to the peregrine praetor. There is no indication that it was he, rather than the urban praetor, who took the initiative, and domestic as well as foreign trade would benefit from the existence of the *bonae fidei* action [18]).

---

16) *Cf*, above all, Kunkel *Fides als schöpferisches Element im römischen Schuldrecht*, Festschrift Koschaker II p. 1 ff; Kaser *Das altrömische Ius* (Göttingen 1949) p. 290 ff.

17) It is apparent that Cato *de ag. cult.* 146 is thinking of a consensual contract of sale since he recommends the taking of a stipulation from the buyer for the payment of the price by a certain date and in the circumstances this does not cover all of the buyer's obligations: *cf* Jolowicz *Historical Introduction to Roman Law*, 2nd edit. (Cambridge, reprinted 1954) p. 303; von Lübtow xlviii, 3 Eos (1957) p. 368. Moreover, it is especially significant that stipulation is mentioned here only in the case of the price since we know from other sources (referred to in n. 14) that it was common practice, even at a time when there can be no doubt that consensual *emptio venditio* existed, to take such a stipulation, whereas there is no evidence that there was a similar practice for delivery of the *res* &c.

18) *Cf supra*, 167. Elsewhere I have argued that there was no reason to credit the peregrine praetor with the introduction of *mandatum* [*Contract of Mandate cit.* p. 18 ff; *cf* reviews by Kaser xxx Tijd. (1962) p. 263; Niederländer lxxix ZSS (1962) p. 540; Yale lxxviii LQR (1962) p. 589.] and suggested that consensual *societas* between Romans existed before the *formula(e)* of the peregrine praetor was influential ['*Consensual societas between Romans and the Introduction of formulae* ix RIDA (3e sér.) (1962) p. 431 ff]. One can in the latter case perhaps go further. As soon as the *formula* of the peregrine praetor came into being it would have been important for the *formula* of the urban praetor if that *formula* were later. Since such influence is lacking, the *formula* of the urban praetor must have been earlier or just as early. In the case of *locatio conductio*, too, it is very difficult to see traces of foreign influence: *cf* Kaser *Das altrömische Ius* p. 297 f. If it be the case that the peregrine praetor is not responsible for any of the *formulae* for the consensual contracts, then the odd fact that *mandatum*, unlike the others, is never said to be *iuris gentium* [*cf* Watson *Contract of Mandate cit.* p. 18 ff] might be explained on the basis that the Romans thought that no other system gave legal validity to a contract resembling mandate.

Emptio venditio is said in D. 18.1.1.2 (Paul *35 ad ed.*) to be *iuris gentium* but there is no reason to think that this means it arose at the instigation of the peregrine praetor. It may mean, as, for instance, does the similar remark in D. 46.4.8.4 (Ulpian *48 ad Sab.*) about *acceptilatio* [19]), only that the institution was open to peregrines [20]).

---

19) *Acceptilatio* existed at the time of the *lex Aquilia* (G. 3.215) and hence before the introduction of the *praetor peregrinus*. Against the suspicion of Solazzi [*L'estinzione nel diritto romano* I 2nd edit. (Naples 1935) p. 248] that in D. 44.4.6.8. the reference to *ius gentium* is interpolated, see Watson, viii RIDA (3e sér.) (1961) p. 406 ff.

20) This study was completed before the appearance of Cancelli *L'origine del contratto consensuale di compravendita nel diritto romano*: *appunti esegetico-critici* (Milan 1963). His conception of the development is very different from mine, and since a study like the present one must stand or fall on the basis of its general plausibility, this is scarcely the place to enter upon a critique of others' views.

16

Consensual Societas between Romans and the Introduction of the Formulae

A very common view still held seems to be that until the second half of the second century B.C. and the passing of the *lex Aebutia, formulae* were not available in actions between *cives* (1). This has been very forcefully attacked, especially by Kunkel (2) and Kaser (3), and the purpose of the present note is merely to add another argument to theirs.

The general view of the development of *societas* is as follows. The original type of partnership was *ercto non cito* which occurred when a *pater* died and his *sui heredes* did not divide the estate. It was, therefore, a partnership of all the property of the partners. Next, the praetor established a *legis actio* by which other people who wished to set up a similar partnership could do so. Then with the growth of Roman trade and the introduction of the peregrine praetor (4) *peregrini* could, from the second half of the third century B.C., form a consensual contrat of partnership and *cives* could contract such with *peregrini*, but not with other *cives* alone. And finally, the *lex Aebutia* of about 140 or 120 B.C. extended the formulary system to

(1) E.g. Girard, *Manuel élémentaire de droit romain*, 8th edit. (Paris 1929), p. 1055 ff. ; De Zulueta, *The Institutes of Gaius*, 2 (Oxford 1953), p. 252 f. ; Arangio-Ruiz, *Storia del diritto romano*, 7th edit. (Naples 1957), p. 151 f.

(2) 'Fides als schöpferisches Element im römischen Schuldrecht', *Festschrift Koschaker*, 2, p. 1 ff.

(3) Above all in *Das altrömische Ius* (Göttingen 1949), p. 290 ff.

(4) But for the correct view of the jurisdiction of the *praetor peregrinus* see Daube 'The peregrine praetor', 1951, J.R.S., p. 66 ff. *Contra*, Serrao (who seemingly mistranslates Daube), *La 'Iurisdictio' del pretore peregrino* (Milan 1954), especially p. 10 ff.

actions between *cives* and so *cives* could, *inter se*, form a consensual *bonae fidei* partsnership.

But such a development of *societas* is impossible.

Partnership of all one's assets is only suitable among farmers and between very close relatives and friends. It is conceivable, but only just, that brothers would enter into such a contract although they were traders. But in almost all cases where the parties were merchants, something other, such as a partnership of one type of business or even of one transaction, would be wanted. Accordingly, the type of partnership protected on the common view by the peregrine praetor must have been a *societas unius negotii* (5) and perhaps occasionally *societas unius rei*. It cannot have been, except possibly on very rare occasions, a *societas omnium bonorum*.

But if the consensual contract of partnership *inter cives* developed a century after consensual partnership involving at least one peregrine, we would inevitably find the main influence on the former to be the existence of the latter. First, because the main reason for extending the formulary system was to extend the benefits hitherto enjoyed by peregrines and by citizens dealing with peregrines, and the most obvious way to do so is to take over appropriate *formulae* en masse. Secondly, it is easier and much more convenient to model a *formula* on an existing *formula* rather than on an existing *legis actio*, and especially to model a *formula* involving a consensual *bonae fidei* agreement on another such *formula*. Thirdly, *ercto non cito* in its two forms would give very considerable protection to those citizens who wanted a *societas omnium bonorum* ; protection in the second half of the second century B.C. would be primarily needed for those who wanted a mercantile contract and the merchant class was extremely powerful at that period.

However, it is abundantly clear that the *formula* of the *praetor urbanus* for *societas* was modelled on *ercto non cito* and not on a *formula* of the *praetor peregrinus*. Only one *formula* was given by the urban praetor and that was for *societas omnium*

(5) Cf. Arangio-Ruiz, *La Società in diritto romano* (Naples 1950), p. 29.

bonorum. This is generally accepted [6] and is rightly deduced from the facts that in the case of *beneficium competentiae* Sabinus argued from *societas omnium bonorum* to *societas unius rei* [7] and that *societas omnium bonorum* is always dealt with first in the commentaries [8]. But, pace Arangio-Ruiz [9], it cannot be argued that, in the *formula, omnium bonorum* are 'Blankettworte', *i.e.* words inserted instead of leaving a blank space. It is, to begin with, not the type of situation where one finds 'Blankettworte' — they occur where one is given *Aulus Agerius* and *Numerius Negidius* for the names of the parties, where a specific object is mentioned to represent any object which may be claimed, and where a certain sum is mentioned by way of damages where in practice the sum would be a variable. Again, one does not, in the very nature of things, have to argue from the 'Blankettworte' to the specific cases, as is done in *societas*, since the function of 'Blankettworte' is simply to show that the action is generally available. Lastly, if there were more than one type of partnership, but still a limited number, the *formula* need only have said *Quod As As cum No No societatem coiit*. 'Blankettworte' here would be, at the very least, quite superfluous. Likewise, it is not a pattern *formula* on the lines of those found in *iniuria*, where an extreme case is given as an example to show the furthest limits of the action [10] — again for the last reason given above and because in fact *omnium bonorum* in the *formula* merely caused the jurists difficulty in deciding whether specific rules also applied to other cases.

Therefore, the date of the introduction of the *formula* for consensual partnership between citizens must be pushed back to a time when a partnership of all one's property was, if not

(6) Cf. Lenel, *Edictum Perpetuum*, 3rd edit. (Leipzig 1927), p. 297 ff. ; Arangio-Ruiz, *loc. cit.*

(7) D. 17.2.63 pr. ; cf. D. 42.1.16.

(8) D. 17.2.1.1 ; h.t. 3 pr. ; h.t. 5 pr. ; G. 3.148 ; cf. Lenel, *op. cit.*, p. 297 n. 8.

(9) *Op. cit.*, p. 29 n. 4.

(10) See Daube, '*Ne quid infamandi causa fiat.* The Roman law of defamation', *3 Atti del congresso internazionale di diritto romano e di storia del diritto*, p. 413 ff.

the only type practised, at least overwhelmingly the most common, and to a time before the *formula* of the peregrine praetor would be influential. So, such a consensual partnership must have been recognised in Rome long before the passing of the *lex Aebutia* and before the time when the formulary system is thought to have been introduced. It is impossible to say with any accuracy when consensual partnership between Romans was recognised, but it was probably sometime in the third century B.C. A form of partnership less than *societas omnium bonorum* was recognised at least as early as Quintus Mucius (11).

***

The sole positive reason for placing the introduction of the formulary system between Romans as late as the second half of the second century B.C. is Gaius' Institutes 4.30.

> Sed istae omnes legis actiones paulatim in odium venerunt. namque ex nimia subtilitate veterum qui tunc iura condiderunt eo res per ducta *est*, ut vel qui minimum errasset *litem* perderet. itaque per legem Aebutiam et duas Iulias sublatae sunt istae legis actiones, effectumque est ut per concepta verba, id est per formulas, litigaremus.

From this passage it is argued that *formulae* were unknown in cases between Romans until they were introduced by the *lex Aebutia* and extended by the two *leges Iuliae* (12). But that is not what the text says. It does not say that the *lex Aebutia* and the *leges Iuliae* introduced *formulae* but that they abolished the *legis actiones* and brought it about that we sue by adapted pleadings, that is by *formulae*. That last phrase is ambiguous and need only mean that they made actions under the *formulae* very common. One might compare it with phrases like 'The

(11) D. 17.2.11.

(12) The disputes as to the relative scope of these *leges* need not concern us here. See Buckland, *A Textbook of Roman Law*, 2nd ed. (Cambridge 1932), p. 628. For a rather different account of the *lex Aebutia*, see Kaser, 'Die *lex Aebutia*', *Studi Albertario*, I (Milan 1953), p. 25 ff. It is hoped to go into this question more fully later.

Labour Government brought it about that young men go to University' or 'Thomas Cook & Son brought it about that British people visit the Continent'. Neither phrase means to imply that these two activities were unknown before the establishment of a Labour Government and Messrs Cooks. So the phrase is extremely dangerous ground on which to erect a theory which has so many objections on other scores (13). Its true meaning is, I suggest, that the formulary system which was already in existence for certain cases was extended by these statutes to cases where a *legis actio* had been optional or alone possible. The situation may have been that in some cases where the XII Tables, for instance, established a *legis actio* no relevant *formula* had hitherto been framed ; or if there were both a *legis actio* and a *formula* the type of action used may have been in the choice of one or other of the parties and an unscrupulous defendant with no real defence might insist on the *legis actio* in the hope that the plaintiff might make a mistake in the words, or a dishonest plaintiff decide on the more rigid *legis actio* to exclude a particular *exceptio* (14). That Gaius was thinking of something of this sort appears from the reason he gives for the passing of the *lex Aebutia*, namely, that *legis actiones* were unpopular because a party who made the slightest mistake lost his case. On the general view, a much more serious objection to the pre-Aebutian system would be that since one had to sue one the words of a statute, many actions which would seem very reasonable (15) would necessarily be excluded because they did not come within the scope of a statute. This surely would have been a greater reason for the unpopularity of the *legis actio*

(13) E.g. see, for the prior existence of consensual and *bonae fidei emptio venditio*, CATO, *De Agri Cultura* 146, 147, 148 ; D. 19.1.38.1 : for a real action in *pignus*, CATO, *op. cit.*, 146 (the transaction in at least this text is outside the scope of the *interdictum Salvianum*). For an example of the difficulties caused by refusing to accept the existence of *formulae* before the *lex Aebutia*, see ARANGIO-RUIZ, *Il Mandato in diritto romano* (Naples 1949), p. 7 n. 1.

(14) Gaius 4.108 tells us there were no *exceptiones* in *legis actiones*.

(15) And they would be known because they were available in cases involving *peregrini*.

system and could scarcely have been ignored by Gaius. And if the *lex Aebutia* had introduced the formulary system in cases between citizens it would have been much more important for its effect in broadening the law than for cutting away procedural handicaps, but yet that side of it is not mentioned by Gaius. Nor is that aspect of it considered by Aulus Gellius who is our only other source for the *lex*.

> Noctes Atticae 16.x.8. « Sed enim cum 'proletarii' et 'adsidui' et 'sanates' et 'vades' et 'subvades' et 'viginti quinque asses' et 'taliones' furtorumque quaestio 'cum lance et licio' evanuerint omnisque illa Duodecim Tabularum antiquitas, nisi in legis actionibus centumviralium causarum lege Aebutia lata consopita sit, studium scientiamque ego praestare debeo iuris et legum vocumque earum quibus utimur ».

Here, too, the *lex Aebutia* is mentioned only for the part it played in the downfall of the *legis actiones*. Moreover, if the *lex* had suddenly introduced *formulae* for the first time, in even a limited way, it would have been a statute of great importance and one would have expected to find many other references to it (16).

(16) Although I still hold to my opinion that *mandatum* first arose in cases between *cives* and that the *actio mandati* cannot be much earlier than 126 B.C., I now feel that some of my arguments are doubtful and that the emphasis on the *lex Aebutia* was misplaced : *Contract of Mandate in Roman Law* (Oxord 1961), pp. 1-23.

17

The Early History of fideicommissa

Augustus was the first to make *fideicommissa* legally binding.[1] Before that, it is usually held, *fideicommissa* occurred in wills and created a strong moral obligation for their fulfilment.[2] This general view of the stage before legal protection is, I submit, oversimple and in particular the force of the moral obligation is not nearly so strong as is supposed.

One question must be put at the outset. Why, if *fideicommissa* were not legally enforceable, did testators leave bequests in that form and did not appoint the intended beneficiary their heir or legataee? A first answer[3] is that the beneficiary in mind often could not take the *hereditas* or a *legatum*. Thus, Gaius' Institutes , 2.285, say: '*Ut ecce peregrini poterant fideicommissa capere; et fere haec fuit origo fideicommissorum . . .*'. Not only was the right of peregrines to take under a will restricted, so also was that for instance of a woman by the *lex Voconia* where the testator was in the first class of the census, or of an outlaw. The *fideicommissum* was therefore an attempt to circumvent or evade the law.[4] But this conclusion shows that the answer is not complete. A person who is seeking to circumvent or evade the law, even if he is not doing anything illegal, normally wishes to avoid publicity so far as reasonably possible. But a will is inevitably rather a public document. Why then does the testator write the *fideicommissum* into the will rather than drop a word to the right effect into the ear of his future heir? There seems to be only one logical reply. The testator does not trust the heir to act morally, and he wants the publicity of the will so that social pressure may be brought to bear on the heir.

[1] Inst. 2.23.1; 2.25 pr.

[2] Cf., e.g. Biondi, *Successione testamentaria e donazioni*[2] (Milan, 1955) 286 ff.; Kaser, *Das römische Privatrecht* I (Munich, 1955) 630 f.; Genzmer, *La genèse du fidéicommiss comme institution juridique*, RHD. 40 (1962) 319 ff.; Daube, *Roman Law. Linguistic, Social, and Philosophical Aspects* (Edinburgh, 1969) 96 ff.

[3] Given, e.g. by Biondi, *o.c.* 287; Kaser, *o.c.* 630; Genzmer, *o.c.* from p. 335; Daube, *o.c.* 96.

[4] Cf. Biondi's choice of language: 'Poiché da prima il fedecommesso stava fuori della legge, serviva ben spesso a frodarla, soprattutto in tema di capacità sia di ricevere che di disporre': *o.c.* 287.

The testator's distrust of the heir's moral feelings is however, even greater than has yet been suggested here. No single instance of a simple, unprotected, *fideicommissum* from the time before they were legally recognised has survived in the sources, lay or legal. The two situations from Cicero normally relied upon for the moral force of a *fideicommissum*[5] both show the testator – in vain[6] – taking other precautions.

The first case is recorded in *de finibus*.[7]

> 2.17.55. memini me adesse P. Sextilio Rufo cum is rem ad amicos ita deferret se esse heredem Q. Fadio Gallo, cuius in testamento scriptum esset se ab eo rogatum ut omnis hereditas ad filiam perveniret. id Sextilius factum negabat. poterat autem inpune; quis enim redargueret? nemo nostrum credebat, eratque veri similius hunc mentiri, cuius interesset, quam illum, qui id se rogasse scripsisset, quod debuisset rogare. addebat etiam se in legem Voconiam iuratum contra eam facere non audere, nisi aliter amicis videretur. aderamus nos quidem adolescentes, sed multi amplissimi viri, quorum nemo censuit plus Fadiae dandum, quam posset ad eam lege Voconia pervenire. tenuit permagnam Sextilius hereditatem, unde, si secutus esset eorum sententiam, qui honesta et recta emolumentis omnibus et commodis anteponerent, nummum nullum attigisset. num igitur eum postea censes anxio animo aut sollicito fuisse? nihil minus, contraque illa hereditate dives ob eamque rem laetus. magni enim aestimabat pecuniam non modo non contra leges, sed etiam legibus partam. quae quidem vel cum periculo est quaerenda vobis; est enim effectrix multarum et magnarum voluptatum.
>
> 2.18.58. si te amicus tuus moriens rogaverit, ut hereditatem reddas suae filiae, nec usquam id scripserit, ut scripsit Fadius, nec cuiquam dixerit, quid facies? tu quidem reddes; ipse Epicurus fortasse redderet, ut Sextus Peducaeus, Sex. F., is qui hunc nostrum reliquit effigiem et humanitatis et probitatis suae filium, cum doctus, tum omnium vir optimus et iustissimus, cum sciret nemo eum rogatum a Caio Plotio, equite Romano splendido, Nursino, ultro ad mulierem venit eique nihil opinanti viri mandatum exposuit hereditatemque reddidit. sed ego ex te quaero, quoniam idem tu certe fecisses, nonne intellegas eo maiorem vim esse naturae, quod ipsi vos, qui omnia ad vestrum commodum et, ut ipsi dicitis, ad voluptatem referatis, tamen ea faciatis, e quibus appareat non voluptatem vos, sed officium sequi, plusque rectam naturam quam rationem pravam valere.

Quintus Fadius Gallus instituted Publius Sextilius Rufus his heir but he really wanted the *hereditas* to go to his daughter. This, the texts make clear, was not permissible under the *lex Voconia*. Now, Fadius did not just instruct Sextilius in the will to hand over the *hereditas* to the daughter: he

[5] The situation in Valerius Maximus, 4.2.7, does not involve a *fieicommissum* or anything similar: cfr. Genzmer, *o.c.* 332 ff.

[6] The fact that in these instances the testator's precautions were unavailing should not in itself be regarded as significant. The instances would not otherwise have been recorded.

[7] For the usual interpretation of this see above all Genzmer, *o.c.* 336 ff.

claimed in the will that he had already asked Sextilius to hand over the *hereditas* (and the implication is that Sextilius had agreed). Thus, in the first place, Fadius was not satisfied that a mere *fideicommissum*, of no legal force, would be performed by Sextilius. In the second place, Fadius was equally not satisfied with his earlier request to Sextilius. He is now making it public in the hope that social pressure will make Sextilius behave properly.[8] It is noteworthy that Cicero does not even say that in the will Sextilius was asked to hand over the estate to Fadia.

No less instructive is Sextilius' behaviour. He summoned his friends and discussed his problem with them. He denied the arrangement with the testator, and added that he had sworn to preserve the *lex Voconia* and would not dare to act contrary unless his friends thought otherwise. [The psychology of the situation is interesting. None of his friends believed him but none advised him to give to Fadia more than she was entitled to under the *lex Voconia*. In all likelihood this is exactly what Sextilius expected.] The implication of his behaviour is plain. Sextilius does not expect to suffer too much moral obloquy for failure to perform a trust imposed by the will. But he is concerned to point out that he is not breaking his word to Fadius.[9]

The second case is recorded in *in Verrem* II, 1.47.123f.

> Superbia vero quae fuerit, quis ignorat? quem ad modum iste tenuissimum quemque contempserit, despexerit, liberum esse numquam duxerit? P. Trebonius viros bonos et honestos conplures fecit heredes; in iis fecit suum libertum. Is A. Trebonium fratrem habuerat proscriptum. Ei cum cautum vellet, scripsit, ut heredes iurarent se curaturos, ut ex sua cuiusque parte ne minus dimidium ad A. Trebonium illum proscriptum perveniret. Libertus iurat; ceteri heredes adeunt ad Verrem, docent non oportere se id iurare facturos esse, quod contra legem Corneliam esset, quae proscriptum iuvari vetaret; impetrant, ut ne iurent; dat his possessionem. Id ego non reprehendo; etenim erat iniquum homini proscripto egenti de fraternis bonis quicquam dari. Libertus, nisi ex testamento patroni iurasset, scelus se facturum arbitrabatur; 124 itaque ei Verres possessionem hereditatis negat se daturum, ne posset patronum suum proscriptum iuvare, simul ut esset poena, quod alterius patroni testamento optemperasset. Das possessionem ei, qui non iuravit; concedo; praetorium est. Adimis tu ei, qui iuravit; quo exemplo? Proscriptum iuvat; lex est, poena est. Quid ad eum, qui ius dicit? utrum reprehendis, quod patronum iuvabat eum, qui [tum] in miseriis erat, an quod alterius patroni mortui voluntatem conservabat, a quo summum beneficium acceperat? utrum horum reprehendis? Et hoc tum de sella vir optimus dixit:

[8] Sextilius' promise, no matter how it was made, would also not be legally binding.

[9] Sextilius, of course, as Cicero emphasises, is a rogue. Mr Robin Seager suggests to me that Cicero himself may have voted against Sextilius' scheme: in *de fin.* 2.17.55, '*sed*' before '*multi*' implies that Cicero is dissociating himself. But at the time?

'Equiti Romano tam locupleti libertinus homo sit heres?' O modestum ordinem, quod illinc vivus surrexerit.[10]

This time the testator, Publius Trebonius, wished at least half of his estate to go to his brother, Aulus. But he could not appoint Aulus heir because Aulus had been proscribed. So he instituted several persons, including one of his freedmen, but with the requirement that they each swear an oath that they will ensure that not less than half their share goes to Aulus. It is not clear whether the requirement of the *iusiurandum* was imposed by means of a condition on the institution or by a *iussum*.[11] Nor does it here matter which. What does matter is that the course of events makes it plain that the *heredes scripti* were not intended to get *bonorum possessio secundum tabulas* before they swore the *iusiurandum*. The *libertus* swore, the others did not but went before Verres and explained that they ought not to swear the oath because it would be contrary to the *lex Cornelia*. They obtained their request and Verres gave them *bonorum possessio*. But Verres refused *bonorum possessio* to the *libertus* who had sworn.

In this case, too, the testator did not attempt to achieve his aim by a simple, legally unenforceable, *fideicommissum*. He sought to impose a *iusiurandum* upon the *heredes scripti*.

The *fideicommissa* in the will of Lucius Lentulus – with which *fideicommissa* first became legally enforceable – were hedged with another device to ensure their fulfilment. The testator was proconsul in Africa, perhaps in 4 A.D., and died during his proconsular year.[12]

Inst. 2.23.1. Sciendum itaque est omnia fideicommissa primis temporibus infirma esse, quia nemo invitus cogebatur praestare id de quo rogatus erat: quibus enim non poterant hereditates vel legata relinquere, si relinquebant, fidei committebant eorum, qui capere ex testamento poterant: et ideo fideicommissa appellata sunt, quia nullo vinculo iuris, sed tantum pudore eorum qui rogabantur continebantur. postea primus divus Augustus semel iterumque gratia personarum motus, vel quia per ipsius salutem rogatus quis diceretur, aut ob insignem quorundam perfidiam iussit consulibus auctoritatem suam interponere, quod quia iustum videbatur et populare erat, paulatim conversum est in adsiduam iurisdictionem: tantusque favor eorum factus est, ut paulatim etiam praetore proprius crearetur qui fideicommissis ius diceret, quem fideicommissarium appellabant.

Inst. 2.25.pr. Ante Augusti tempora constat ius codicillorum non fuisse, sed primus Lucius Lentulus, ex cuius persona etiam fideicommissa coeperunt, codicillos introduxit. nam cum decederet in Africa, scripsit codicillos testamento confirmatos, quibus ab Augusto petit per fideicommissum, ut faceret aliquid: et cum divus Augustus voluntatem eius implesset, deinceps

[10] For the usual approach to this see above all Genzmer, *o.c.* 335 f.

[11] Cf. now Watson, *D. 28.5.45(44) (Alfenus 5 dig.)*, *The Irish Jurist* 3 (1969) p. 377 ff. at p. 388 f.

[12] Cf. Groag, in *PW*. IV (Stuttgart, 1901) 1372 f.

> reliqui auctoritatem eius secuti fideicommissa praestabant et filia Lentuli legata, quae iure non debebat, solvit, dicitur Augustus convocasse prudentes, inter quos Trebatium quoque, cuius tunc auctoritas maxima erat, et quaesisse, an possit hoc recipi nec absonans a iuris ratione codicillorum usus esset: et Trebatium suasisse Augusto, quod diceret utilissimum et necessarium hoc civibus esse propter magnas et longas peregrinationes, quae apud veteres fuissent, ubi, si quis testamentum facere non posset, tamen codicillos posset. post quae tempora cum et Labeo codicillos fecisset, iam nemini dubium erat, quin codicilli iure optimo admitterentur.[13]

The testator, in codicils which were confirmed in advance in the will, imposed a *fideicommissum* on Augustus. It is, of course, most unlikely that this *fideicommissum* was protected by a previous promise or by the requirement of a *iusiurandum*. But the device this time is the imposition of a *fideicommissum* on the Emperor himself! The testator could hope that the Emperor – in his very special position – would be gracious enough to fulfil the *fideicommissum* And where the Emperor led,[14] which of the beneficiaries under the will could fail to follow, and not carry out the *fideicommissa* imposed on them? Again the testator is not relying simply on the *fides* of the beneficiaries.

The facts, as preserved in the surviving sources are these. We have three separate instances of a fideicommissary situation in a will made before *fideicommissa* became legally binding. In each single one of these instances the testator was not content to impose a legally unenforceable *fideicommissum* on the beneficiaries. In every case he attempted to give his request some additional force and betrayed a certain lack of faith in his beneficiaries.

The conclusions to be drawn are first that simple *fideicommissa* were very uncommon before they became legally binding, and secondly that the force on the beneficiary of the moral obligation to perform the *fideicommissum* has been exaggerated by modern scholars.[15]

[13] On the texts see above all Genzmer, *o.c.* 344 ff.

[14] There is no need here to enquire into Augustus' motives in making *fideicommissa* enforceable: but see Daube, *o.c.* 98 ff.

[15] I should not be understood as arguing either that simple *fideicommissa* were then non-existent or that there was felt to be no moral obligation for their fulfilment.

IV

Shadows of the Past

18

Some Cases of Distortion by the Past in Classical Roman Law

In the search for classical Roman law scholars sometimes argue as if the Roman jurists were infallible both in logic and language. The main point of the present paper is to give a few examples of certain ways in which the Romans were as illogical as we and allowed themselves to be fogged by what had gone before. Daube has already stressed one way in which the classical jurists, like us, were bound to the past in that very often the texts reflect — unconsciously — a historical development [1]). As he says, 'When point A originally stands alone, and then, at some stage, point B is added, juristic discussion and writing is so conservative that the sequence A — B may persist for good: we may never find B — A, we may never find the two worked together' [2]). This, indeed, may be so even where the resulting order is against all logic.

I.

Let us take one example. Some of Gaius' treatment of actions in book 4 of his Institutes is very odd [3]). After dealing with *legis actiones*, he says in § 30 that these gradually became unpopular and were replaced by *formulae* except (as he adds in § 31) in two cases. Then a page of the Verona codex is missing in which Gaius presumably dealt with *formulae quae ad legis actionem exprimuntur* since these are in fact his excuse for considering

---

1) *'Implantatio' and 'satio'*, Acta Juridica 1958, p.181 ff; *'Utiliter agere'*, XI IURA (1960), p. 69 ff at p. 106. See, for the continued existence of older law, Schwind, *Der Geltungsbegriff bei den römischen Volksschlüssen*, Studi Solazzi p. 763 ff.

2) IURA *cit.*, p. 106 n. 108.

3) Reference might be made to an article by Buckland, *The Exactitude of Gaius*, XLVIII Juridical Review (1936), p. 354 ff.

legis actiones at all [4]). This he follows, perhaps not unreasonably, in §§ 34—38 with a discussion of fictions. And in § 39 he goes on:

> Partes autem formularum hae sunt: demonstratio, intentio, adiudicatio, condemnatio.

The parts of the formula take him up to § 52, and from there to § 114 he discusses things like overclaim, *compensatio* and *deductio*, noxal actions, representation in litigation, security required of the parties and so on. Then, quite unexpectedly, in § 115 he has:

> Sequitur ut de exceptionibus despiciamus.

How to explain the position of the discussion of *exceptiones?* Buckland [5]) suggests that the *partes formularum* are those parts without which the *formula* in which they are used would be meaningless. This would distinguish the *demonstratio*, *intentio*, *adiudicatio* and *condemnatio* from *fictiones*, *exceptiones* and *praescriptiones* since any *formula* in which one of the latter group appears would be meaningful without it although the effect would be very different. But with all respect, that distinction seems too artificial. There can be no real doubt that *fictiones*, *exceptiones* and *praescriptiones* are parts of the *formula* [6]). The real reason I would suggest, for *exceptiones* being dealt with where they are is that originally there were no *exceptiones* in the *formulae* and so when they did make their appearance they were dealt with right at the end of the discussion of formulary procedure in general. Considerable evidence can be found for this proposition. The *exceptio*, in fact, does not harmonise with the *formula* [7]) as is most easily seen by taking a concrete example:

---

4) G. 4.10: *cf* De Zulueta, *The Institutes of Gaius* II (Oxford, 1953), p. 230. For these actions see Biscardi, *Une catégorie d'actions négligée*, XXI Tijd. (1953), p. 310 ff.

5) *A Textbook of Roman Law*, 2nd edit. (Cambridge, 1932), p. 649; followed by De Zulueta, *op. cit.*, p. 258.

6) Levy expressly considers this question for the case of the *exceptio* and declares strongly for the affirmative: III IURA (1952) p. 158 ff.

7) This was observed early by Lenel, *Ursprung und Wirkung der Exceptionen* (1876), p. 44 (not seen); Ihering, *Geist des römischen Rechts*, 4th edit, III i (Leipzig, 1888) p. 56.

Si paret Nm Nm Ao Ao sestertium decem milia dare oportere, si in ea re nihil dolo malo Ai Ai factum sit neque fiat, iudex Nm Nm Ao Ao sestertium decem milia condemna, si non paret absolve.

As Pétrau-Gay says [8]), there is a clear discordance between the terms of the *condemnatio* and those of the *absolutio*. The *condemnatio* is subordinated to two distinct conditions, namely, to the proof that NN ought to pay AA 10,000 sesterces and to the absence of *dolus* by AA. On the other hand, the *absolutio* is subordinated only to the absence of AA's right. The older explanation, which I accept, was that the *exceptio* was a later addition to the *formula* by the praetor. The more recent, introduced by Pétrau-Gay [9]) and accepted, it would seem, by Broggini [10]), is that this illogicality is the result of the transference of the *exceptio* from the *legis actio* to the *formula.* Against that one has to put the direct testimony of Gaius in 4.108:

Alia causa fuit olim legis actionum. nam qua de re actum semel erat, de ea postea ipso iure agi non poterat; nec omnino ita ut nunc usus erat illis temporibus exceptionum.

This tells us that in the time of the *legis actiones* there were no *exceptiones, ut nunc* [11]). It is not enough to say that Gaius knew no legal history and could get mixed up [12]). He was undoubtedly interested in legal history as his Institutes and the commentary on the XII Tables show and, of course, even in his time there were still some *legis actiones* available while many, it would seem, had been abolished only as late as the *leges Iuliae* of Augustus' reign so that there would be quite recent knowledge of them. Clear evidence is required before we can hold that

---

8) *Evolution historique des Exceptiones et des Praescriptiones* (Paris, 1916), p. 48 f. For literature etc. see Palermo, *Studi sulla 'exceptio' nel diritto classico* (Milan, 1956), p. 50 ff.

9) *Op. cit.*, p. 60 ff.

10) *Iudex Arbiterve* (Köln, Graz, 1957), p. 170 n. 31 at p. 171.

11) Whether this means there were none at all or that there were but they took a different form is disputed but does not affect the present issue: for the two views, see Pétrau-Gay, *op. cit.*, p. 18 n. 2.

12) Pétrau-Gay, for instance, *op. cit.*, p. 18 ff, shows a reluctance to consider Gaius of much authority.

Gaius is wrong. Broggini says that Pétrau-Gay's best argument is from Cicero *De Oratore* 1.168.

> Quid? his paucis diebus nonne nobis in tribunali Q. Pompeii praetoris urbani familiaris nostri sedentibus homo ex numero disertorum postulabat, ut illi, unde peteretur, vetus atque usitata exceptio daretur CUIUS PECUNIAE DIES FUISSET? quod petitoris causa comparatum esse non intellegebat, ut, si ille infitiator probasset iudici ante petitam esse pecuniam, quam esset coepta deberi, petitor rursus cum peteret, ne exceptione excluderetur, QUOD EA RES IN IUDICIUM ANTEA VENISSET.

But there is not the slightest evidence in that text that the procedure was by *legis actio* and if it was by *formula* it is no evidence for Pétrau-Gay. *Vetus atque usitata exceptio* need not suggest — especially since Cicero will tend to exaggerate its age and use to emphasise the ignorance of the pleaders — that it goes back to the *legis actio*. Nor would it seem to help that the term *exceptio* in the text is used also — perhaps humourously — for what the classical jurists call *praescriptio pro reo*. Broggini's own case appears to rest mainly on his acceptance of Kaser's [13]) view of the *lex Aebutia*. Basically, Kaser believes that a statute of that period would have a relatively narrow scope and that the *lex Aebutia* abolished only the *legis actio per condictionem* and substituted *formulae* for that procedure, and that only praetorian actions had *formulae* before. If this is correct then Broggini and Pétrau-Gay are right for in Plautus' *Rudens* 1376—1382 which is by common consent earlier in date than the *lex Aebutia* there is an example of an *exceptio* — the *exceptio legis Laetoriae* — and the procedure parodied can hardly be praetorian.

> DAEMONES: Gripe, quod tu ipsum talentum poscis?
> GRIPUS: iuratust mihi dare.
> LABRAX: lubet iurare. tun meo pontifex peiiurio es?
> DAEMONES: qua pro re argentum promisit hic tibi?
> GRIPUS: si vidulum hunc redegissem in potestatem eiius, iuratust dare mihi talentum magnum argenti.
> LABRAX: cedo quicum habeam iudicem, ni dolo malo instipulatus sis nive etiamdum siem quinque et viginti annos natus.

---

13) Studi Albertario I (Milan, 1953); supra, pp. 175 ff.

But Kaser himself who does not refer to the Plautus' text seems to accept Gaius' view that there were no *exceptiones* under the *legis actio* [14]). Rather, as I have suggested elsewhere [15]), the emphasis of Gaius 4.30 suggests that the *lex Aebutia* and the *leges Iuliae* were primarily concerned with the abolition of the *legis actio*, not with the introduction of *formulae*, and that before these statutes *formulae* were in existence side by side with the *legis actio*. I submit that if, as is probable, Kaser is right in restricting the *lex Aebutia* to actions *per condictionem*, the *lex* abolished the *legis actio* and so made procedure by *formulae* compulsory, but the relevent *formula* was available even previously. There would then be no conflict between G. 4.108 and Plautus' *Rudens* 1376 ff. [16]). The fact that in the Plautus' text Labrax asks Gripus to provide a judge should not suggest that the procedure is a *legis actio per iudicis postulationem* — such behaviour is fitting no matter what the procedure envisaged is [17]).

II.

The second example is the maxim *per hereditarium servum quod est eiusdem hereditatis heredi adquiri non potest.*

This maxim which is dealt with in four texts has been curiously

---

14) *Op. cit.*, p. 54; *Das altrömische Ius* (Göttingen, 1949), p. 116 f.

15) *Consensual societas among Romans and the Introduction of formulae*, IX RIDA (1962), p. 135 ff.

16) Immediately after *exceptiones* Gaius deals with *praescriptiones* and since the latter are generally held to be the earlier (*cf* De Zulueta, *op. cit.*, p. 281 and n. 2), it might be suggested that this is against the view just put forward. But, of course, this might be a case of the more common attracting the less common. Moreover, the evidence that *praescriptiones* are earlier, namely, that they fit better into the *formula*, (*cf* De Zulueta, *loc. cit.*) is by no means conclusive — there is no reason why an addition should not fit neatly. Or perhaps one ought to distinguish between *praescriptio pro reo* which was early and *praescriptio pro actore* which developed later than the *exceptio*. Since only the *praescriptio pro actore* persisted in Gaius' time (G. 4.133) it determined the position and attracted the mention of the obsolete type. I am indebted for this suggestion to Professor Daube.

17) *Cf.* Kübler, LVI ZSS (1936), p. 257 ff., although Beseler's translation (defended in LVII ZSS (1937), p. 356) 'Give me a man in whom I have a judge' which Kübler attacks seems accurate.

neglected by modern writers. The last person so far as I can discover who discussed it at length was Buckland in 1908 [18]).

The first pair of texts is D. 41.2.1.16,17 (Paulus 54 *ad ed.*):

> Veteres putaverunt non posse nos per servum hereditarium adquirere, quod sit eiusdem hereditatis. itaque agitatur, num haec regula longius producenda sit, ut, si plures servi legati sint, per unum an possint ceteri possideri. idem tractatus est, si pariter empti vel donati sunt. sed verius est ex his causis posse me per unum reliquorum adquirere possessionem. 17. Si ex parte heredi instituto servus legatus sit, propter partem, quam ex causa legati habet, adquiret fundi hereditarii possessionem.

These texts are obviously concerned with possession and relate to its acquisition after entry by the heir. It is clear that the rule in the maxim was restricted to the case where the slave was acquired as part of the inheritance and did not apply even where the slave was left as a legacy to one of the co-heirs. Buckland says, rightly it would appear, that the rule was regarded as ancient (*veteres putaverunt*) and was treated as a technicality. But what was the rationale of the rule? Buckland says: „It appears to rest on the unity of the inheritance: a taking by one of the slaves (whether authorised or not) of a thing in the possession of the *dominus* or of another slave would have effected no change in possession during the life of the ancestor, or while the *hereditas* was *iacens*. The same act is not allowed to produce a different effect merely because the ownership of the *hereditas* has changed". This can scarcely be correct since the objects taken by the *servus hereditarius* on behalf of the heir cannot be in the possession of the *heres* [19]). No one would argue that if the owner of a slave owned something but had no possession of it, he could not acquire possession of it through that slave [20]).

Two other texts dealing with the maxim seem, at least *prima facie*, to be concerned with the acquisition of ownership before entry by the heir.

D. 29.2.43 (Iulianus 30 dig.)

---

18) *The Roman Law of Slavery* (Cambridge, 1908), p. 259 f.

19) *Aditio* did not of itself give the heir possession of the *res hereditariae: cf* D. 41.2.30.5; 41.4.6.2; 41.4.2.18; 41.2.23 *pr.*; 47.4.1.15.

20) Buckland, no doubt, was thinking of an illogical extension of the notion of unity to account for the rule, but even so his explanation is hardly convincing.

Heres per servum hereditarium eiusdem hereditatis partem vel id, quod eiusdem hereditatis sit, adquirere non potest.

D. 41.1.18 (Ulpianus 4 ad Sab.)

Per hereditarium servum quod est eiusdem hereditatis heredi adquiri non potest et maxime ipsa hereditas.

Buckland says of these [21]) that they merely seem to lay down the truism that as the *heres* is not owner till entry, the acquisition of things by *servi hereditarii* cannot be acquisition to him and that no other obvious meaning can be ascribed to them. Worse than that, however, if the texts were only stating such a truism, they would not be restricted to acquisition of *res hereditariae* — which in any event could not be regarded as acquisitions by the slave. Buckland's solution is to make these texts, like D. 41.2.1.16, apply to the acquisition of possession after entry [22]). This, however, ignores the striking fact that the original context of the Julian text was institution and substitution of heirs [23] and that it now appears in the Digest title *De adquirenda vel omittenda hereditate;* and the Ulpian text originally appeared where he was concerned with conditional institution [24] and is now in the title *De adquirendo rerum dominio*. It is difficult to see why acquisition of possession after entry should be discussed in these places.

It seems to me very probable that the maxim arose from a rule concerning conditional institution or substitution. First, because where the maxim appears in these contexts it is stated baldly, without fripperies, and without being given any purpose [25]). It is, I think, unlikely that a strange rule would be given in a

21) *Op. cit.*, p. 259.

22) This also requires us to hold that in D. 41.1.18 *et maxime ipsa hereditas* is a very stupid gloss. Commenting on these words, De Zulueta says (*D. 41.1 & 2.* (Oxford, 1950), p. 58): „This can only refer to *aditio*, and similarly *servus hereditarius* implies that the *hereditas* is still *iacens*. But this interpretation (so the Gloss) makes the passage an utter truism. If it were possible to suppose that *aditio* had taken place, it would be tempting to refer the passage to the rule preventing acquisition of possession of *res hereditariae* through a slave of the same inheritance". Thus, the explanation he suggests does not satisfy even himself.

23) Lenel, *Palingenesia* I, 394.

24) *Ibidem* II, 1029.

25) To judge from the texts as we have them.

foreign context without any attempt being made to show its relevancy or importance. On the other hand, in the texts from Paul *54 ad edictum* which was concerned with possession we are told the scope of the rule. Secondly, and this is much more important, because even the main possession text, D. 41.2.1.16, begins *Veteres putaverunt non posse nos per servum hereditarium adquirere quod eiusdem hereditatis* and so appears to be concerned with ownership. Only later do we discover that Paul is using it in connexion with possession.

But it then seems impossible to know what the point of the maxim could have been. Indeed, the remainder of my case must rest on that very difficulty. The rule within the framework of conditional institution and substitution can have a point only if at some time the law of succession in this respect was very different from the classical law. With our limited knowledge of archaic institutions it is probably not possible to suggest a convincing hypothesis as to what this earlier law was, and the classical jurists who were less interested in legal history are unlikely to have been in a better position than we are. Nonetheless, the basic picture emerges. There was a legal rule which became embodied in a maxim. There ceased to be any situation in which the rule operated, but the powers of survival of a maxim are strong and so the maxim remained alive in legal tradition. It was related by the jurists and was indeed given a function which was not its own and was certainly not of any advantage. One might almost say that the function was given by the jurists in desperation because they could not see to what else the maxim might refer.

III.

The third example is taken from *infamia*. Praetorian *infamia* is customarily divided into two kinds, immediate and mediate. The former is the direct result of an act or behaviour of a certain kind, the latter of condemnation in one of a limited number of actions. Here we are concerned only with the latter and only with private actions. The particular part of the edict with which we are concerned runs:

D. 3.2.1. (Iulianus 1 ad ed.) [26]

. . . qui furti, vi bonorum raptorum, iniuriarum, de dolo malo et fraude suo nomine damnatus pactusve erit: qui pro socio, tutelae, mandati, depositi suo nomine non contrario iudicio damnatus erit: . . .

This text is supported by G. 4.182:

Quibusdam iudiciis damnati ignominiosi fiunt, veluti furti, vi bonorum raptorum, iniuriarum; item, pro socio, fiduciae, tutelae, mandati, depositi. sed furti aut vi <*bonorum*> raptorum aut iniuriarum non solum damnati notantur ignominia, sed etiam pacti, *ut* in edicto praetoris scriptum est; et recte: plurimum enim interest utrum ex delicto aliquis an ex contractu debitor sit. n*ec ta*men ulla parte edicti id ipsum nominatim exprimitur, ut aliquis ignominiosus s*it*, s*ed* q*ui* prohibet*ur* et pro alio postulare *et* co*gn*i*tor*e*m* dare procuratoremve habere, item <*pro*>curatorio aut cogni*to*rio nomine iudicio intervenire, ignominiosus esse *dicitur*.

And further support is in the so-called *lex Iulia Municipalis* 108 ff;

Quae municipia colonia<*e*> praefectura<*e*> fora conciliabula c(ivium) R(omanorum) sunt erunt, nei quis in eorum quo municipio colonia praefectura <*foro*> conciliabulo <*in*> senatu decurionibus conscripteisque esto, neve quo*i* ibi in eo ordine senten <<tem>> tiam deicere ferre liceto, quei furtei quod i*pse* fecit fecerit condemnatus pactusve est erit; queive iudicio fiducio pro socio, tutelae, mandatei, iniuriarum deve d(olo) m(alo) condemnatus est erit; queive lege Plaetoria ob eamve rem, quod adversus eam legem fec*i*t fecerit, condemnatus est erit.

Gaius, however, has omitted the *actio de dolo*, the *lex Iulia* does not mention the *actio depositi* [27] or the *actio vi bonorum raptorum*, and the compilers of the Digest have almost certainly cut out a reference to the *actio fiduciae* which was, of course, obsolete in their time.

But there are certain difficulties in attributing unpleasant consequences to a condemnation in one of these actions in classical

---

[26] According to Lenel, the inscription is the invention of the compilers; *op. cit.* I, 484 n. 4.

[27] Perhaps because it was not in existence? But if not, the penal action granted by the XII Tables would be. In view of Gaius' omission of the *actio de dolo* it is not wise to draw any conclusions from the absence of the *actio depositi* here — especially since the *actio vi bonorum raptorum* is also missing.

law. Firstly, *infamia* [28]) should be the result of deliberate wrongful behaviour. But there seems really to be little doubt that in mandate the standard of liability varied according to the circumstances and the mandatary might at times be liable for *culpa* [29]). The *actio depositi* will lie for *culpa* if the depositee offered to look after the *res* [30]) or if the parties agree to such a standard [31]). The *actio tutelae* in developed classical law at least also lies for *culpa* [32]). Most surprising of all, the *actio pro socio* is at times brought not on account of a partner's *dolus* or *culpa* but simply to settle accounts [33]). Yet there is not the slightest indication that *infamia* was other than the automatic result of condemnation and this has led many modern jurists to hold, despite the texts, that liability — especially in mandate [34]) — was for *dolus* only. Secondly, as Schulz says [35]), the list of actions was 'not quite free from arbitrariness, since the exclusion of the *actio commodati* cannot be reasonably explained'. The same applies to the absence of the *actio metus causa* and the *actio servi corrupti.* Thirdly, in some respects it is curious that the *actio de dolo* is infaming. Ulpian in D. 4.3.1.4. says that that the *actio de dolo* is subsidiary because it is infaming, but it is absurd that it should be intended that a man's *dolus* would make him infamous if the *dolus* did not fall within the scope of some other action. It might be suggested that the *actio de dolo* was made subsidiary and infaming because it was intended to catch out particularly crafty stragems but, considering the nature of *stipulatio* and the literal

---

28) Though G. 4.182 warns us that this is not a technical term it is more convenient to use it here. For *infamia* in general, see Kaser, *Infamia und ignominia in den römischen Rechtsquellen,* LXXIII ZSS (1956), 220 ff.

29) *Cf* Watson, *Contract of Mandate in Roman Law* (Oxford, 1961), p. 195 ff. and the texts cited therein.

30) D. 16.3.1.35.

31) D. 16.3.1.6.

32) *Cf* Kaser, *Das römische Privatrecht* I (Munich, 1955), p. 310 and the texts and references he gives, n. 30.

33) D. 17.2.52.4; *h. t.* 52.12; *h. t.* 60.1; *cf* Watson *op. cit.* p. 197.

34) *Eg.* Arangio-Ruiz, *Il mandato in diritto romano* (Naples, 1949), p. 188 ff; Schulz, *Classical Roman Law* (Oxford, 1954), p. 556

35) *Op. cit.*, p. 45.

contract, one would not have had to be especially wily to escape liability at that time, so that this cannot be the whole truth. Elsewhere I have, I hope, given a partial explanation arguing that not only did the *actio de dolo* have originally a very narrow scope but was meant primarily to cover parties to a stipulation [36]). But that is not a full explanation since it still leaves the difficulties that one might not expect the *actio de dolo* in the beginning even with its narrow scope to be infaming and much more that its position in classical law as a general subsidiary action which is infaming is ridiculous.

But these difficulties would be overcome if mediate *infamia* in private actions had ceased to exist in classical law and this can be shown to be the case.

Representation in litigation although only exceptionally permitted in the *legis actio* was general in the formulary system. The clearest account of the effect which representation had on the formula is in G. 4.86,87:

> Qui autem alieno nomine agit, intentionem quidem ex persona domini sumit, condemnationem autem in suam personam convertit. nam si verbi gratia L. Titius <*pro*> P. Mevio agat, ita formula concipitur: SI PARET NUMERIUM NEGIDIUM PUBLIO MEVIO SESTERTIUM X MILIA DARE OPORTERE, IUDEX NUMERIUM NEGIDIUM LUCIO TITIO SESTERTIUM X MILIA CONDEMNA. SI NON PARET, ABSOLVE. in rem quoque si agat, intendit P. MEVII REM ESSE EX IURE QUIRITIUM, et condemnationem in suam personam convertit. 87. Ab adversarii quoque parte si interveniat aliquis cum quo actio constituitur, intenditur dominum DARE OPORTERE, condemnatio autem in eius persona*m* convertitur qui iudicium acceperit. sed cum in rem agitur, nihil <*in*> intention*e* facit eius persona cum quo agitur, sive suo nomine sive alieno aliquis iudicio interveniat; tantum enim intenditur REM ACTORIS ESSE.

For us the most important point is that where a person sued *in personam* has a representative as early as the *in iure* stage, the principal is not condemned *apud iudicem* but the representative is. Thus a person liable to a private action which will involve *infamia* can avoid this by appointing a representative. The principal will not become *infamis* because he has not been condemned, nor will the representative because he has not been condemned

[36]) LXXVIII ZSS (1961), p. 401.

suo nomine. This is clear not only from the wording of the edict itself as given in D. 3.2.1 but is also expressly stated in D. 3.2.6.2 (Ulpianus 6 *ad ed.*)

> Si quis alieno nomine condemnatus fuerit, non laborat infamia: et ideo nec procurator meus vel defensor vel tutor vel curator vel heres furti vel ex alia simili specie condemnatus infamia notabuntur, nec ego, si ab initio per procuratorem causa agitata est.

Unfortunately, *nec ego* to the end which is what we are most interested in has been held interpolated [37] but not so far as I am aware because it is thought that the principal did become *infamis* [38] — there seem to have been no such attacks on D. 3. 2.1 in this respect. Most recently, however, Bonifacio [39] has argued very convincingly for its genuineness. Moreover, the words *ab initio* are easily explicable in terms of the formulary system since we have just seen from G. 4.86,87 that there the representative, not the principal, was condemned if the representative had acted *in iure*. They could also probably be taken to refer to the so-called „divided *cognitio* procedure" which was abolished in 342 A.D. [40], but it is difficult to see what point they could have had in the time of Justinian or in the other *cognitio* procedures. This, too, argues for the genuineness of *nec ego &c* or that at least it is a very early gloss [41].

Accordingly, in classical law there was no need for a defendant ever to suffer *infamia* as the result of condemnation in a private *iudicium* and such can only have happened occasionally and, as it were, accidentally. In almost all cases the defendant would appoint a *cognitor* or *procurator*.

---

37) *Cf. Index Itp.* and *Supplementum.*

38) The following were not available to me: Schulz, Festschrift für Zitelmann (1913), p. 11; Koschaker, *Translatio iudicii, Eine Studie zum römischen Zivilprozess* (Graz, 1905), and Duquesne, *La translatio iudicii dans la procedure civile romaine* (Paris, 1910).

39) *Studi sul processo formulare romano, I, translatio iudicii* (Naples, 1956), p. 63 ff.

40) C. 2.57.1. *Cf* Jolowicz, *Historical Introduction to Roman Law*, 2nd edit. (Cambridge, 1954), p. 406 ff. and the authorities he cites, p. 408 n.l.

41) That in *nec ego etc* only the *procurator* is mentioned is not suspicious. It would have been unnecessary and tedious to repeat the whole list.

How early this developed, however, is not easy to say since there are two unknown factors. First, when did it become possible for the *condemnatio* to give the name of the *cognitor* or *procurator* while the *intentio* named the principal? The most one can say is that if, as is generally agreed [42], the praetor Publius Rutilius who according to Gaius in 4.35 introduced the *actio Rutiliana* is the consul of 105 B.C. the *actio Rutiliana* dates from the year before 118 B.C. when he was praetor. This action allows a plaintiff (the *bonorum emptor*) who is not a representative to transfer the *condemnatio* to his own name and so it is likely to be later rather than earlier than a similar situation where the party to the action is a representative. Therefore, it is probable that the *condemnatio* in actions in general (including infaming actions) was against the representative, not the principal, as early as the end of the Second century B.C. [43]) Secondly, it is likely that this edict was not always as it now appears in the Digest, but that at least the list of actions was the result of gradual development [44]) so that one cannot be certain that the words *suo nomine* or something similar were there from the start. And if they were not, fear of condemnation involving *infamia* would effectively stop representation. But it is not altogether likely that an heir would be made to suffer *infamia* on account of his predecessor's wrongdoing and we know from the *Rhetorica ad Herennium* 2.13.19 that in 115 B.C. an action was allowed against the mandatary's heir though this had been refused in 123 B.C. [45]). So it is perhaps fair to say that the requirement of *suo nomine* was likewise needed for *infamia* from at least the end of the Second century B.C.

Thus from the end of the Republic and probably also from the end of the Second century B.C. mediate *infamia* in private

---

42) *E. g.* Krüger, *Geschichte der Quellen und Literatur des römischen Rechts* 2nd edit. (Munich, 1912), p. 62 f; De Zulueta, *Institutes cit.* I, p. 247; Berger, *Encyclopedic Dictionary of Roman Law* (Philadelphia, 1953), pp. 345 and 686, *s. v. actio Rutiliana* and *Rutilius Rufus* (*Publius*).

43) Of course, it may have been (and probably was) always against him.

44) *Cf* Schulz, *Classical Roman Law cit.*, p. 45.

45) *Cf* Arangio-Ruiz, *op. cit.*, p. 140 f.

actions was in practice obsolete even although it still appears in Julian's redaction of the Edict and in the Digest. One must, indeed, say that such a state of affairs was desired since it would have been easy to prevent the wrongdoer's escape in one way or another. Why then did mediate *infamia* remain in the Edict? Two reasons may be postulated. First, a general reluctance on the part of lawyeis to go to the trouble of abolishing a rule which does not operate in practice. Secondly, the feeling that there should be a legal reminder of the social obloquy where there was some nefarious conduct. It may be doubted, though, whether the provision would have survived if there had not also been other cases of *infamia* which in classical law still did exist as realities.

At the beginning of this section it was stated that certain difficulties arose if *infamia* did follow condemnation in certain private actions. Let us now look at the effect of the present theory on these.

The first was that in certain *bonae fidei iudicia* said to involve *infamia* the defendant would, on occasion, be liable foı *culpa*. This would have been absurd if *infamia* was the automatic result of condemnation, but is not if in practice *infamia* was obsolete. It must be said that the jurists — wisely — did not allow the strict theory of *infamia* to interfere with the development of standards of contractual liability. Originally, in these liability must have been for *dolus* only. It is probable, too, that to begin with, partners who simply wished to settle accounts could not use the *actio pro socio*. This would be no hardship since the *actio communi dividundo* would be available. Perhaps most instructive of all is a text concerning the *actio tutelae*, D. 50.16.42 (Ulpianus 57 *ad ed.*).

> 'Probrum' et obprobrium idem est. probra quaedam natura turpia sunt, quaedam civiliter et quasi more civitatis. ut puta furtum, adulterium natura turpe est: enimvero tutelae damnari hoc non natura probrum est, sed more civitatis: nec enim natura probrum est, quod potest etiam in hominem idoneum incidere [46]).

---

46) Beseler thinks the whole text is probably unclassical: *Beiträge zur Kritik der römischen Rechtsquellen* V (Leipzig, 1931), p. 75. But at least the compilers would not have made up the fragment.

This shows a full realisation that a tutor who suffered condemnation in an *actio tutelae* may well be free from moral blame. It is surely certain that if such condemnations involving all the consequences of *infamia* did in practice ever occur (except perhaps extremely rarely) such a condemnation would have led to a speedy reform of the law. We must also remember that the Sabinians and Proculians were agreed that if in a *bonae fidei iudicium* the defendant satisfied the plaintiff after *litiscontestatio* the defendant would be absolved [47]). Perhaps at this point reference ought to be made to D. 47.2.64 (63) (Macer *2 pub. iud.*):

> Non poterit praeses provinciae efficere, ut furti damnatum non sequatur infamia.

This text shows (as do those quoted at the beginning of this section) that if a *fur* were condemned *suo nomine*, *infamia* automatically followed. It need not be taken as showing that such condemnation was frequent or indeed ever occurred at all.

Secondly, it was said that the list was arbitrary and the absence from it of the *actio commodati*, *actio metus causa* and *actio servi corrupti* inexplicable. The arbitrariness is now of no consequence but, in fact, it will be seen that there is good reason for every inclusion or exclusion. The actions just mentioned are not on the list almost certainly because they came into existence only after *infamia* ceased to be a practical matter. The date of introduction of neither the *formula in factum* nor the *formula in ius concepta* for *commodatum* is known but it seems to be generally accepted that *commodatum* became actionable only in the late Republic [48]). *Depositum*, on the other hand, is on the list since, although its *formulae in factum* and *in ius* are also probably rather late, it was actionable under the XII Tables by a special penal action for double the value of the object [49]). That action, one

---

47) G. 4.114.

48) *Cf* Schulz, *op. cit.*, p. 513; Kaser, *Privatrecht cit.*, I p. 445. Pastori holds it was not recognised in the Republic: *Il commodato nel diritto romano* (Milan, 1954), p. 31 ff.

49) P. S. 2.12.11; *cf* Schulz, *op. cit.*, p. 518; Kaser, *op. cit.*, p. 446. The *actio fiduciae* is also very old: see my note *The Origins of fiducia*, LXXIX ZSS (1962) p. 329 ff.; supra, pp. 159 ff.

may presume, would involve *infamia* and this consequence would descend upon the later *actio depositi*. Even in classical law, moreover, the requirement of *dolus* was stricter for the *actio depositi* than for any other *bonae fidei iudicium*. Again, the *actio metus causa* dates from about 80 B.C. [50]) and the *actio servi corrupti*, although Republican [51]), does not seem to be very early.

Thirdly, it was stated that it was absurd that the *actio de dolo* involved *infamia* in classical law because it was a subsidiary action and so only caught those people whose fraud was not actionable otherwise. This absurdity loses all its importance if in fact there would be no *infamia* resulting from condemnation. Of course, it may on occasion have been difficult for a person accused of fraud to find a representative but even then, because of the *clausula arbitraria*, he could avoid *infamia* if he paid back the amount of the plaintiff's loss. This leaves us with the question why it should ever have been made infaming since there can be no doubt that it was not introduced until sometime in the first half of the First century B.C. and probably not until 66 B.C. [52]). This was done, I submit, because in this case the heinousness of fraud had to be especially stressed. In the other delictal actions which had deliberate wrongful conduct as their basis, *e.g.*, the *actio metus causa* and *actio servi corrupti*, society's disapproval could be shown by condemnation requiring the defendant to pay a multiple of the plaintiff's loss. This was not possible in the *actio de dolo* which lay only where there had been negotiations between the parties and so had to be treated in practical matters as a contractual remedy — hence the plaintiff could recover only what he had lost. Accordingly, to show society's disapproval of fraud of this kind the *actio de dolo* was made infaming in theory. This, of course, is not very logical, but I suggest further that the action would never have been made

---

50) *Cf* Schulz, *op. cit.* p. 600; Kaser *op. cit.* p. 212 f.

51) *Cf* D. 11.3.16 (Alfenus Varus). See in general for this action, Albanese, *Actio servi corrupti*, XXVII Annali Palermo (1959), p. 5 ff: he suggests the middle of the First century B. C. for its introduction; *op. cit.*, p. 9 and n. 10.

52) Cicero, *De nat. deor.* 3.30.74.

infaming at all if any practical sense *condemnatio* did involve *infamia* — the contrast with other actions on contracts such as the *actio empti* which could be brought for *dolus* would be too great [53]). Condemnation, of course, would — whether one had a representative or not — result in considerable social disgrace, hence the restrictions on the use of the action. Nor is it difficult to account for the inclusion of the *actio vi bonorum raptorum* which also dates from the time when the relevant type of *infamia* was obsolete. That action is for nothing other than aggravated theft and if *furtum* gives rise to *infamia* even theoretically then so must *rapina.*

So far nothing has been said about the word *pactusve* in the edict. This again causes no difficulty. It must refer to a compromise made during the action [54]) and *suo nomine* seems to apply to it as well as to *condemnatus.* Again, a pact made by a representative would involve neither him nor his principal in *infamia.* Moreover, where it is permitted full payment made *iudicis arbitrio* is not the same as a pact.

IV.

Lastly, let us consider a rule which, I think, did not so much survive in theory when obsolete as never existed. This is found in Gaius' *magna quaestio* in *societas.*

G. 3.149.

> Magna autem quaestio fuit an ita coiri possit societas, ut quis maiorem partem lucretur, minorem damni praestet. quod Q. Mucius <*contra naturam societatis esse existimavit. sed Servius Sulpicius, cuius*> etiam praevaluit sententia, adeo ita coiri posse societatem existimavit, ut dixerit illo quoque m*odo* coiri posse, ut quis nihil omnino damni praestet, sed lucri partem capiat, si modo opera eius tam pretiosa videatur ut aequum sit eum cum hac

---

53) Against this, the *actio legis Aquilia* was never infaming though like the *actio empti* it might lie where there was *dolus* or *culpa.* But the *lex Aquilia* is much older and more primitive than the *actio de dolo* and above all for some considerable time liability was not based *dolus* or *culpa* but on acting outside one's rights — a very different concept.

54) *Cf* Greenidge, *Infamia in Roman Law* (Oxford, 1894), p. 130 f.

pactione in societatem admitti. n*am* et ita posse coir*i* societatem constat, ut unus pecuniam conferat, alter non conferat, et tamen lucrum inter eos commune sit; saepe enim opera alicuius pro pecunia valet [55].)

Thus, it is stated that for Servius Sulpicius an agreement that a partner should get a greater part of the gain and suffer a smaller or indeed no part of the loss is valid only if his services seem so valuable that it is fair that he should be admitted to the partnership on such terms. The same point is discussed in J. 3.25.2.

De illa sane conventione quaesitum est, si Titius et Seius inter se pacti sunt, ut ad Titium lucri duae partes pertineant, damni tertia, ad Seium duae partes damni, lucri tertia, an rata debet haberi conventio? Quintus Mucius contra naturam societatis talem pactionem esse existimavit et ob id non esse ratam habendam. Servius Sulpicius, cuius sententia praevaluit, contra sentit, quia saepe quorundam ita pretiosa est opera in societate, ut eos iustum sit meliore condicione in societatem admitti: nam et ita coiri posse societatem non dubitatur, ut alter pecuniam conferat, alter non conferat, et tamen lucrum inter eos commune sit, quia saepe opera alicuius pro pecunia valet. et adeo contra Quinti Mucii sententiam optinuit, ut illud quoque constiterit posse convenire, ut quis lucri partem ferat, damno non teneatur, quod et ipsum Servius convenienter sibi existimavit: quod tamen ita intellegi oportet, ut si in aliqua re lucrum, in aliqua damnum allatum sit, conpensatione facta solum quod superest intellegatur lucri esse.

Here the decision is very different. Such an agreement is allowed because often a person's contribution is so valuable that it is fair that he should be admitted to the partnership on better terms. It no longer seems necessary for the validity of the clause that the contribution of the partner who receïves better terms should seem in proportion. Arangio-Ruiz [56]) argues that by some mysterious transmission of the manuscripts the rule in Justinian's Institutes represents the classical law, but that in Gaius' Institutes has intervened the hand of a postclassic who wanted to limit inequality among partners as far as possible and he points out that in sale the concept of *iustum pretium* did not exist in classical law but is postclassical. He also supports his case by pointing

---

55) We need not concern ourselves with the question of whether the reconstruction is correct: *cf* Arangio-Ruiz, *La società in diritto romano* (Naples, 1950), p. 94 ff.

56) *Op. cit.*, p. 99 ff.

to the rather similar distinction between G. 3.150 and J. 3.25.1 on the hand and the suspect D. 17.2.29 *pr.* (Ulpianus 30 *ad Sab.*) on the other.

Arangio-Ruiz' view, however, attractive as it is, was not well received by the critics [57]). Wieacker thinks it improbable that on this point Cassius [58]) decided one way, Servius another, and the late classics yet another. Van Oven holds that Servius did maintain that *bona fides* permitted such an agreement provided that (*si modo*) the activity of the partner who suffered a smaller part of the loss than he received of the gain was so precious that it justified his advantageous position. This did, he goes on, involve the control of the judge but no more than such control existed in all of the *bonae fidei iudicia.* The privileged partner, sued — despite the clause favouring him — to be made to pay a full share of the loss suffered by his partner who maintained (following Quintus Mucius) that the clause did not protect the other because it was not in accordance with good faith, would declare that in this particular case it was indeed in accordance with good faith because his activity had so much value for the partnership. Of course, he concludes, the judge will have to have the last word and will decide whether the activity did justify the exemption from loss, but this is quite a different thing from the control of the judge in postclassical law over the *iustum pretium* in sale for it is a consequence of the clause of the *formula: quidquid paret dare facere ex fide bona.* But it is respectfully submitted that this is really a distinction without a difference. If the judge in this instance intervenes only as in other *bonae fidei iudicia*, then under the clause of the *formula* just given he is bound by the terms of the partnership agreement. He can only go outside them if the defendant was fraudulent or if the terms of the contract in issue masked some other type of transaction such as gift [59]). If this is the position, as I think it is, the seeming

57) See especially the reviews of Wieacker, LXIX ZSS (1952), p. 498; Van Oven, XIX Tijd. (1951), p. 455 f; and Kaden, II IURA (1951), p. 232 ff.

58) *I. e.* in D. 17.2.29.1: *cf infra* p. 208.

59) *Cf* D. 24.1.32.24; for other *bonae fidei* contracts see D. 4.4.16.4; 18.1.36, 38, 55; 19.2.22.3.

restriction of Servius Sulpicius is of no effect. If on the other hand the *iudex* did have to decide whether the clause mirrored an actual difference in the activities &c of the partners, his control is indeed very like that of a postclassical judge considering the *iustum pretium*. Such control — I would agree with Arangio-Ruiz and Van Oven — seems unlikely.

The solution to the problem, I suggest, is rather this. The view supported by Quintus Mucius is of course the older. *Prima facie* it does appear fair that a person who is entitled to a greater share of the profits should suffer a similar share of the loss. Servius Sulpicius in bringing forward his contrary opinion wanted to state his case in the way he did simply to show how just and reasonable it could in fact be. In other words, *si modo etc.* despite its appearance as a legal rule was nothing else than an argument in favour of a change in the law. The partners would never make such an agreement unless it seemed that the activity of the favoured partner was so much more valuable — unless of course the partnership was really a disguise for something else. If this is correct, then G. 3.149 correctly represents the words of Servius Sulpicius, J. 3.25.2. the law as Servius wanted it and as it was in classical, postclassical and Justinianic law. It is perfectly in keeping with this interpretation that Servius Sulpicius should not only oppose Quintus Mucius' solution but should even take a more difficult case to argue. Such a procedure stresses his conviction of the moral rightness of his case [60]).

The same problem is discussed in the Digest with the same results:

D. 17.2.29.1 (Ulpianus 30 ad Sab.)

> Ita coire societatem posse, ut nullam partem damni alter sentiat, lucrum vere commune sit, Cassius putat: quod ita demum valebit, ut et Sabinus scribit, si tanti sit opera, quanti damnum est: plerumque enim tanta est industria socii, ut plus societati conferat quam pecunia, item si solus naviget, si solus peregrinetur, pericula subeat solus.

---

60) Is it perhaps reading too much into the text to see here traces of that rhetoric which made Cicero place Servius second only to himself among the orators? *Cf* Krüger, *op. cit.*, p. 66 f and the references he gives.

This text has been held interpolated [61]) and it is by no means perfect. *Si tanta — damnum est* is odd even apart from the confusion of indicative and subjunctive. As Arangio-Ruiz says, judging *ex eventu* the judge in most cases will have to come to the conclusion that the value of the *opera* is less than nothing. *Plerumque etc.* does not follow on what precedes and *item* just does not harmonise. Nonetheless, the substance cannot be Justinianic and it is difficult to see how it can be the work of a post-classical glossator. Above all, the similarity with G. 3.149 is against that. Immediately after discussing the agreement that one partner should share in the profits but not the loss, both (though the Digest text is not too explicit) turn to a case where one provides money the other not. Rather it would seem that both G. 3.149 and D. 17.2.29.1 go back to a common ancestor, almost certainly Sabinus. Gaius reproduces Sabinus fairly closely, taking his protagonists Quintus Mucius and Servius Sulpicius from him [62].) Ulpian after giving Cassius' unqualified opinion, is content with the authority of Sabinus who agreed with Servius. The present state of D. 17.2.29.1 is the result of drastic and clumsy shortening by the compilers. On this view, Servius' argument, though it no longer has any function, survives through Sabinus, Gaius and Ulpian and even into the time of Justinian.

It may possibly be objected that it is an overstatement to argue that Quintus Mucius' position appears *prima facie* to be the most just and that it was not necessary for Servius Sulpicius to combat it as alleged. Perhaps it will be excusable, in order to avoid this possible objection, to go further and say that *prima facie* it appears fair that partners should share equally in the profit and loss and that this rather naive idea is sometimes difficult to get rid of [63]). A striking and very suggestive example is to be found in Scots Law. The most celebrated Scottish lawyer

---

61) *Cf* Arangio-Ruiz, *op. cit.*, p. 108 ff and the references he gives.

62) The work of Servius was familiar to Sabinus: cf D. 34.2.19.17.

63) Witness the fact that in default of agreement even some modern systems say that profit and loss are to be equally divided whatever the respective contributions of the partners: For the United Kingdom, *Partnership Act* 1890 s. 24 (i); for the U.S.A., *Uniform Partnership Act* s. 18 (a).

of all, Lord Stair, wrote in the 17th century [64]) 'The nature of this contract is to have in it equality of profit and loss proportionable to the value and worth of the stock and work'. This was reported and commented on by the famous Baron Hume, a great admirer of Stair, as follows [65]) 'It is true, as Lord Stair says, that 'the nature of this contract is to have in it equality of profit and loss'; and certainly, *in dubio* — in default of evidence of a specific bargain among the parties —, such equality shall probably be maintained, as more congenial to the notion of the connection; yet still, there is nothing in morals or in reason to hinder a different arrangement'. This misrepresentation of Stair's view is best explained by saying that Hume makes Stair say what he expected him to say and this could only have happened if Hume had subconsciously felt that it was fairest that partners should have equal shares.

Inevitably, some doubt must be cast on the interpretation given of G. 3.149 and D. 17.2.29.1 by D. 17.2.29 *pr.*

> Si non fuerint partes societati adiectae, aequas eas esse constat. si vero placuerit, ut quis duas partes vel tres habeat, alius unam, an valeat? placet valere, si modo aliquid plus contulit societati vel pecuniae vel operae vel cuiuscumque alterius rei causa.

This text certainly cannot represent the substance of Ulpian's views since it was settled in classical law and before that an agreement that one partner would have a bigger share of profit than another was, without qualification, valid [66]). The most attractive solution, I suggest, is Arangio-Ruiz' [67]) and the classical part

---

64) *Institutions of the Law of Scotland* I. 16.3.

65) *Baron Hume's Lectures 1786—1822* II (Edinburgh, for the Stair Society 1949), p. 171.

66) Otherwise Quintus Mucius could not have discussed the more complex question in G. 3.149.

67) *Op. cit.*, p. 104 ff. Or perhaps *si modo etc* is taken from a discussion of a further case where there was no specific agreement as to the shares of the partners but the relative extent of their respective contributions was both unequal and clear. It could then have been argued that one partner was entitled to more because he contributed more. On this view, the state of the text would be the result of amalgamation by the compilers.

of the text ends with *placet valere*. The fact that the qualification is due to a glossator need not, however, lead to similar conclusions in the case of G. 3.149 and D. 17.2.29.1. Indeed, it would be quite plausible to argue that a post-classical jurist inserted the qualification in the *principium* as the result of the apparent qualification in § 1.

Thus, from four examples we have four ways in which the past worked illogically upon the classical law. First, the order of topics in a juristic book might lack system; secondly, a maxim expounding a rule might lead to the development of new and really unwanted law when the rule became obsolete and was itself forgotten; thirdly, law which was obsolete in practice might continue to be discussed; and fourthly, arguments might be given the appearance of rules [68]).

68) A number of friends kindly read this study and improved it by their criticism but a special debt of thanks is owed to Professor David Daube of the University of Oxford and to Dr. Herbert Hausmaninger of the University of Vienna.

19

The Development of Marital Justifications for Malitiosa desertio in Roman-Dutch Law

Desertion as a ground of divorce was introduced at the Reformation in the Protestant states and for a clear understanding of its development it is well to look first at what counted as desertion for the French Huguenot theologian and lawyer Theodore de Besze (Beza) whose *Tractatus de repudiis et divortiis* was of great influence on the German and Dutch Protestant jurists. His starting point is in Paul, I Cor. vii, especially vv. 12–15:

> 12. But to the rest speak I, not the Lord: If any brother hath a wife that believeth not, and she be pleased to dwell with him, let him not put her away.
> 13. And the woman which hath an husband that believeth not, and if he be pleased to dwell with her, let her not leave him.
> 14. For the unbelieving husband is sanctified by the wife, and the unbelieving wife is sanctified by the husband: else were your children unclean; but now are they holy.
> 15. But if the unbelieving depart, let him depart. A brother or a sister is not under bondage in such cases: but God hath called us to peace.

From this he draws the following conclusions: first, if a *fidelis* (*i.e.*, a Calvinist) is deserted by his *infidelis* (*i.e.*, presumably a Catholic) spouse, he may divorce her. Secondly, a *fidelis* may not desert an *infidelis*; but to this he adds that that spouse is a *desertor, qui a fideli conditiones intolerabiles exigit, ut si fidelem ad audienda abominanda Missae sacra, denique ad facienda, vel contra omne pietatis officium patienda quaedam, cogat infidelis.* The *fidelis* can also leave in good conscience when he fears for his life, whether from his spouse or from others, for the *infidelis* is then not only a *desertor* but a *proditor*. But where the *fidelis* leaves the *infidelis* because of ill-treatment where there is no *odium religionis*, then he cannot obtain a divorce even where he cannot return to his spouse through fear for his life. Thirdly, where a *fidelis* deserts a *fidelis* there can be no divorce, but the *desertor* should be compelled to return to his spouse. But, he goes on, the Geneva Church has rightly decided that if the *desertor*, after being summoned to return in a formal way, etc., fails to do so the marriage may be pronounced to be dissolved. *Quamvis enim iste sese religionis odio non discessisse fortasse profiteatur, tamen qui Ecclesiae cognitionem subterfugiens, contra conscientiam matrimonium dirimit, manifeste infideli, simul & religionis & conjugis desertori, merito aequiparatur.*[1] Thus, for Beza, in effect desertion is a ground for divorce and there is no justification possible for desertion except the *odium religionis* of the other spouse. But he does recognise a form of constructive desertion where the party who remains in the matrimonial home is the one whom he regards as the *desertor*, provided the breach is caused by his *odium religionis*.

Beza and the other theologians, however, were not accepted in full by later jurists. And here we must examine two German jurists before we come on to Roman-Dutch law. First, Henningus Arnisaeus who cites Beza freely in his *De jure connubiorum* and, in turn, is himself cited by Brouwer.[2] Arnisaeus, with a number of references to theologians, including Luther and Melancthon, agrees with Beza that if a *fidelis* desert a *fidelis* the latter can obtain a divorce *quia, fidem non aestimamus ex verbis, sed ex factis.*[3] Next, he says,[4] that to avoid misinterpreting Paul's intention we must examine the meaning of *desertio*. The genus of *desertio* or *absentia* is twofold, and the first limb divides into four species. First, there is absence *necessaria et probabilis* as, for example, absence on state business. Secondly, absence *probabilis sed non necessaria* as, for example, for the sake of studies. Thirdly, absence *necessaria sed non probabilis* as exile. Fourthly, absence *voluntaria sed sine contumacia* as for the sake of trade. None of these, he will eventually decide, constitutes *desertio malitiosa*, and neither does absence *ex consensu mutuo*. The same applies, he goes on,[5] to desertion *quae fit ob crimen, nequitiamve uxoris. Nam si occasionem discessui dederit, aequum non est, ut in malitia sua laetetur &, ut qui sine dolo, ex justa impatientia, fortasse etiam implacabili pertinacia, domo exclusus, solum mutavit, & malitiae cessit, praeter infortunium, etiam duriter multetur, cum culpa suos tantum tenere debeat auctores.* This leads him into a discussion of adultery by a wife who has been deserted by her husband or who flees his brutality and he concludes[6]: *Non hoc dico, quod vel adulteria mulierum ex absentia maritorum, vel desertiones virorum, ob morositatem uxorum, impune dimitti, & extra vitium poni debeant, quia mala nullius causae impulsu*

[1] In the 1651 Leiden edition the reference for the foregoing is pp. 231–253.
[2] *De jure connubiorum* 2.18.12.
[3] 6.6.4.
[4] 6.7.1 *et seq.*
[5] 6.7.3.
[6] 6.7.5.

aggredienda sunt. C SIGNIFICASTI. DE DIVORT. *Sed ei, qui occasionem malo dedit probabilem, suam malitiam emolumento esse non convenit, & quae divortium ob desertionem petit, cogitur testimonium innocentiae vitae et morum Judici prius offerre.* BEUST. PART. 2. MATR. C. 27.

Thus, Arnisaeus has generalised Beza's position; *odium religionis* has lost all its importance and with it has gone the one case of constructive desertion recognised by Beza.[7] A divorce will now be granted to a deserted spouse, provided that that spouse did not give good cause for the desertion. But the form of the discussion is odd. There is a great deal of emphasis on the intention of the spouse who goes away and the factors external to the marriage which cause the absence are minutely examined. On the other hand there is no real attempt to explain what conduct on the part of the deserted spouse before the desertion will prevent her obtaining a divorce—the adultery referred to is adultery after the parties have separated. One would have thought this point deserved—and needed—much more clarification than the other. Moreover, it is difficult to see the legal significance of *Non hoc dico —aggredienda sunt.* If these desertions caused by the conduct of the deserted wives *non impune dimitti debeant* this should signify that the wives nevertheless can get a divorce. Yet this is contrary to the ultimate conclusion. There is, to say the least, a certain confusion of thought and the discussion lays itself wide open to misinterpretation.

The second German is Carpzovius who cites Arnisaeus and shows himself to be profoundly influenced by him. He, too, is cited by Brouwer. Carpzovius, in his treatment of malicious desertion, after dealing with *necessaria* or *probabilis* absence, has [8]: *Alia vero est ratio desertionis malitiosae, quando nulla coactus causa honesta, sed vel levitate, vel impatientia freni conjugalis injusta aliisve non necessariis causis impulsus conjux a conjuge discedit: Quo casu juste divortium fieri non facile quisquam negaverit.*[9] It is not clear whether or not this corresponds exactly in meaning to Arnisaeus but there is nothing to induce one to believe that it does not. In any event, for us the most important thing, as we shall see, is the wording used.

7 This does not mean that the theologians ceased to be of importance in the law of divorce for malicious desertion: *cf.* van Leeuwen *Het Rooms-Hollandsch Recht* 1.15.4; van Zurck *Codex Batavus s.v. Houwelyk* § 30 n. 6; and *Consultatien, Advysen, en Advertissementen, gegeven en geschreven by Verscheyde Treffelyke Rechts-geleerden in Holland.* V. nos. 46 and 47.

8 *Definitiones ecclesiasticae seu consistoriales* 2.11.192.4.

9 *Cf.* the same jurist's *Practica nova Imperialis Saxonica rerum criminalium* 2.58.15.

The ground has now been sufficiently prepared for us to look at the Dutch jurists. First, Brouwer, the most influential of all in this field. He[10] gives this definition: *Malitiosus desertor est, qui nulla justa aut necessaria causa coactus, ex animi quadam levitate & malitia, vel impatientia freni conjugalis, uxoris & liberorum curam abjicit, eos deserit & oberrat, sine animo redeundi.* The direct influence on this definition of Carpzovius' *Definitiones ecclesiasticae seu consistoriales* 2.11.192—which he cites a few lines further on—is obvious.

Brouwer justifies malicious desertion as a ground for divorce because it is even worse than adultery since the adulterer returns to his wife and does not throw off completely the care of his family. This leads in to a rather half-hearted discussion of the *fidelis: infidelis* business, but then, Brouwer goes on: *Non refert praesenti in negotio, ob quam causam desertio fiat; sive ob odium religionis . . .*[11] *sive taedio conjugii, quod dissolutiorem vitam amet & aerumnas matrimonii in educandis liberis, iisque comparando victu aegre ferat: sive odio conjugis, quod malos obstipae mentis, morosae, rixosae uxoris mores, ipse levis animi maritus fere non possit. . . . Ne sub immoderata morosi viri tyrranide contabescat uxor, vel continuis rixosae furiae jurgiis enecetur maritus, magistratus est providere per lectuli & mensae separationem, non mariti vel uxoris per malitiosam desertionem: cum ut sibi quis jus dicat, vel propria auctoritate rumpat vinculum conjugii, quod ligavit Dominus, nec divina, nec humana iura patiantur.* Brouwer, therefore, recognises no justification for desertion in the conduct of the other spouse. If one's wife behaves badly one ought not to desert, the proper course is to petition for a separation from bed and board. This seems to be so even where life is made intolerable *odio religionis*, though, of course, the arguments about *fidelis* and *infidelis* do not make for clarity. It follows logically from this proposition that there can be no such thing as constructive desertion, *i.e.*, conduct so intolerable as in fact to terminate the marriage relationship and drive the other spouse away. Brouwer, in another place,[12] returns to discuss what is meant by *desertio malitiosa.* This time he examines, without the same degree of pedantry and without actually naming them, the distinctions made by Arnisaeus about *necessaria* and *probabilis* absence. There is not a word about marital justifications for desertion and this is, therefore, in harmony with his earlier treatment.

To return to Brouwer's definition. There, *malitiosus desertor*

[10] *De jure connubiorum* 2.18.12.
[11] Of course, here the *infidelis* is represented as leaving the *fidelis.*
[12] 2.32.16.

means a deliberate *desertor*, and the intention permanently to end the marriage is contained in the words *sine animo redeundi. Qui nulla justa aut necessaria causa coactus, ex animi quadam levitate & malitia, vel impatientia freni conjugalis* do not mean that desertion (as opposed to absence for business, etc.) is ever justified. No *desertor* is compelled by a just or necessary cause. The words owe their existence to the attitude of earlier (and German) jurists and they are taken straight from Carpzovius. One would not be justified in concluding that Brouwer misunderstood the German jurists' position but the oddity of Arnisaeus' treatment makes this a possibility which cannot be ruled out.

The influence of Brouwer was such that justifications for desertion do not appear again, so far as I can discover, among the seventeenth-century Dutch jurists.[13] Van Leeuwen [14] writes in terms very similar to Brouwer: *nulla justa aut necessaria causa coactus; sed levitate & malitia quadam aliisque non necessariis, neque probabilibus causis impulsus, absque animo redeundi ad conjugem, oberrat.* But to illustrate his meaning he goes on: *nam si militia, aut longiores peregrinationes, quae ex necessitate fiunt, intercedant, quantisque annis protrahantur, mulier sustinere debet.* That is, he, too, is thinking of a *justa aut necessaria causa* as something external to the marriage relationship and not the behaviour of the deserted spouse. More ambiguous, though, is the *Echt-Reglement, over de Steden, ende ten platten Lande, inde Heerlijckheden, ende Dorpen, staende onder de Generaliteyt,* dated March 18, 1656. Section 91 begins: *Soo wie sijn Echt-genoot lichtveerdelijck ofte malitieuselick verlaet, ofte uyt onlijtsaemheyt van den Houwelijcx-bant af treet, door gaet, ende sijn Portuyr laet sitten, met voornemen, om tot sijn Echt-genoot niet weder te keeren, die stelt de onschuldige vry om te hertrouwen.* There is nothing in the statute to define more precisely *lichtveerdelijck* and *malitieuselick* but in view of the similarity of the style to that of Brouwer and van Leeuwen it is most reasonable to suppose that this statute like these jurists would not admit as a defence to divorce for desertion the behaviour of the deserted spouse.

Voet demands special treatment. He does not mention justifications when dealing with malicious desertion,[15] but elsewhere,[16] arguing that a wife's adultery cannot be justified because of her husband's cruelty or refusal of conjugal rights, he says: *Quamvis*

13 *Cf.*, for instance, Huber, *Positiones jures*, lib. xxiv Pand. Tit.2.9: *Heedensdaegse Rechtsgeleertheyt* 1.6.4; van Leeuwen, *Het Rooms-Hollandsch Recht* 1.15.4.
14 *Censura Forensis* 1.15.12.
15 *Commentarius ad Pandectas* 24.2.9.
16 24.2.7.

enim ex hisce probatis malis domesticis infelix merito censenda sit; non tamen propterea in flagitium ruere debuit, ac ad medendum malo tristi remedium atque solatium in turpi malo quaerere, atque ita miseriam in scelus convertere; sed potius judicis auxilium adversus saevitiam aliosque malos mariti mores per legitimos tramites implorare. arg. L. PALAM 43 §. NON EST 5. ff. DE RITU NUPT. CAP. SIGNIFICASTI 4. & 5. EXTRA, DE DIVORTIIS. *Brouwer* DE JURE CONNUB. LIBR. 2. CAP. ULT. NUM. 12. *atque etiam ipsius vinculi matrimonialis petere dissolutionem, si maritus in voluntaria ac pertinace abstinentia, seu debiti conjugalis denegatione perduret; eo quod haec malitiosae desertionis species est; dum parum interest, utrum absens an praesens maritus uxorem redigat ad viduitatem, detrectando contumaciter ea praestare, ad quae ex conjugii natura devinctus est. Avus meus Gisbertus Voetius* POLITICAE ECCLESIAST. PART. 1. LIBR. 3. TRACT. 1. SECT. 3. CAP. 4. QUAEST. 8. Thus, for him refusal of conjugal rights amounts to malicious desertion even where the spouse who does the refusing does not leave home. The passage must not be taken to mean that cruelty can amount to malicious desertion. All Voet says of this is that the wife should invoke the assistance of a judge, and the arguments for malicious desertion are all concerned with refusal of conjugal rights (*abstinentia, debiti conjugalis denegatione, uxorem redigat ad viduitatem, detractando contumaciter ea praestare, ad quae ex conjugii natura devinctus*). Probably, for cruelty Voet, like Brouwer, was thinking of judicial separation. Voet's view that refusal of conjugal rights amounts to malicious desertion was followed in the eighteenth century by van Zurck,[17] Cos,[18] and van Hasselt.[19] There is no evidence that any other conduct of a spouse who did not leave home counted as desertion.[20]

At this point we can turn to South African law.[21] For some time the South African courts seem to follow the position of the Dutch jurists. The clearest case of this is perhaps *Mostert* v. *Mostert* [22] of 1854. That was a case brought by a husband against

17 *Codex Batavus s.v. Houwelyk* § 30 n. 6 (who gives as authority a *consilium* of the Theology and Law Faculties of Utrecht sent to the Senate on March 21, 1663).

18 *Verhandeling over de oorzaken door welke Boedelmening eindigt*, § 17.

19 *Rechtsgeleerde Brieven* 272.

20 Van Apeldoorn's view of the history of this part of malicious desertion seems imprecise and much too wide: *Geschiedenis van het Nederlandsche Huwelijksrecht* (Amsterdam, 1925) p. 182.

21 Although it is not strictly relevant to the present account it is perhaps worth noting that the eighteenth-century German jurist Leyser shows a continuance —with a slight modification—of the idea that there is no justification for malicious desertion. He says that if a wife reasonably leaves her husband because of his bad treatment she must return to him if he offers a *cautio*, otherwise she is a *malitiosa desertrix*: *Meditationes ad Pandectas*, ad lib. xxiv tit. 2, s. 314: vi.

22 Searle Reports (Cape Supreme Court) II (1853–1856) 128.

his wife for the restitution of conjugal rights, and was therefore a preliminary to an action for divorce for malicious desertion. The summons was issued only six days after the wife left her husband, and the majority of the court was in favour of granting the decree. For us, however, the main interest is in the dissenting judgment of Bell J. He said [23]: "It seems to me that two questions must be decided before we can give that decree. These are—1st. What is malicious desertion? 2nd. Must malicious desertion so ascertained precede a suit for adherence? 1st. I apprehend malicious desertion, or desertion proceeding *ex malitia, i.e.*, from design, or premeditated determination, cannot, in the absence of evidence of conduct on the part of the spouse deserted, sufficient to account for such determination, be ascertained without the lapse of a certain amount of time, if indeed that can be done even where there is such evidence. If, in answer to a suit for adherence by a husband against the wife, the wife prove that the conduct of the husband, not on one occasion merely, but for a course of time, has been so cruel or brutal that no woman could be expected to submit to a repetition of it, the court may, *without so great a length of separation*, reasonably presume that the woman will never again cohabit with the man; but even in such a case the lapse of a certain amount of time would seem to be necessary." In other words, in the absence of proof of cruelty one could not presume after six days that the wife would never return to her husband, whereas it would be easier to do so if there had been continuous cruelty on the part of the husband. That is, it would be evidence of the wife's malicious desertion that she had good reason to leave her husband. And hence, cruelty could not be a justification which would prevent her being divorced.[23a] It is especially significant that "malicious" is interpreted as "from design, or premeditated determination."

The next important case is *Heathershaw* v. *Heathershaw* [24] of 1864. The husband had previously brought an action for divorce against his wife on the ground of adultery, but this had failed because the husband himself was living in adultery.[25] The husband's mistress left his home and the husband then brought the present action against his wife for the restitution of conjugal rights.

[23] p. 132.

[23a] *Cf.* Bell J. on p. 131: "It was argued from the Bar, that all that was necessary to be ascertained, in order to sustain a suit for adherence, was proof of a settled determination on the part of one of the spouses to desert the other, and so defeat the very end of marriage. From that position I see no occasion to dissent; my difficulty is as to the character and sufficiency of the proof, . . ."

[24] Roscoe Reports (Cape Supreme Court) I (1861–1867) 186.

[25] *Cf.* Voet 24.2.6.

It was admitted by the husband's attorney that the husband contemplated obtaining a divorce by means of this action and it was argued that the infidelity of the husband was not a bar. The decree was granted and the wife was ordered to return to her husband. So far as the report goes, there was no discussion of whether the husband was committing adultery before his wife left or of why the wife deserted him. It would seem that the court felt that no conduct of the husband would justify his wife's desertion.

Evidence of a changing attitude, however, begins about 1908. In *Nield* v. *Nield* [26] a wife who had committed adultery which had later been condoned sued for restitution of conjugal rights, failing which for divorce on the ground of malicious desertion. Bristowe J. said that he began with serious doubts as to whether a plaintiff guilty of adultery which had been condoned could sue for divorce on the ground of malicious desertion but that he had been convinced by the authorities quoted to him.[27] Although he was convinced in this case, it is very doubtful if he would have been if the plaintiff's adultery, as in *Heathershaw's* case, had not been condoned. A few months previously in a different court had been heard the case of *Fick* v. *Fick*.[28] That, too, was an action for divorce on the ground of malicious desertion where the plaintiff had been guilty of adultery which had been condoned. The divorce was granted but Shiel J. said [29] that he would not have been in favour of the order if the adultery had not been condoned. Another important case is *Carter* v. *Carter*.[30] A husband who had committed adultery after his wife left him sued for a decree of restitution of conjugal rights and, failing compliance, for a divorce. Laurence J. granted the order for restitution of conjugal rights but said that the plaintiff's conduct barred him from obtaining a divorce. Of course, whether the Dutch jurists would grant a divorce for malicious desertion where the plaintiff's adultery had not been condoned is itself not clear. Certainly we know that an adulterous plaintiff could not sue for divorce on the ground of the defendant's adultery because there was *compensatio criminis*.[31] But Brouwer says [32] that *malitiosa desertio* is worse than adultery so that it is not certain that *compensatio criminis* would operate.

But the really big break occurs with the case of *Walters* v. *Walters*.[33] The plaintiff wife had intercourse with a certain man

[26] [1908] T.S. 1113.
[27] *i.e.*, Voet 24.2.6; *Johnson* v. *Johnson* (3 N.L.R. 39); *Thompson* v. *Thompson and Benee* (9 N.L.R. 106).
[28] [1908] E.D.C. 132.
[29] p. 135 *et seq.*
[30] [1909] Supreme Court Reports 248.
[31] Voet 24.2.6.
[32] 2.18.12.
[33] [1911] T.P.D. 42.

six months before her marriage and became pregnant by him. Two months before the marriage she cohabited with the defendant who married her without knowing of her previous *stuprum* and resulting pregnancy. After the birth of the child the husband refused to live with her and she sued for restitution of conjugal rights or divorce. The court held that the plaintiff's conduct prior to the marriage was sufficient cause for the defendant's refusal to live with her and that therefore the desertion was not malicious. Accordingly, the plaintiff's claim was refused. Curlewis J.'s opinion was read by Wessel J., and at one point [34] said: "But in our law the desertion must be malicious, and it is not sufficient for one spouse merely to state that the other spouse has deserted him or her. It must be proved that the desertion, either from its inception or by reason of its continuance, is malicious, that is, that the deserter had no sufficient cause, so far as the complaining party was concerned, for the desertion. *Brouwer* (*de Jure Connubiorum* 2.18.12) gives the following definition: *Malitiosus desertor est, qui nulla justa aut necessaria causa coactus, ex animi quadam levitate et malitia, vel impatientia freni conjugalis, uxoris et liberorum curam abjicit, eos deserit, et oberrat sine animo redeundi.* And it follows that, if the party who complains of having been deserted has given sufficient cause for the act of desertion, such desertion cannot be said to be malicious." In complete contrast to the case of *Mostert* the word "malicious" is here understood as "that the deserter had no sufficient cause, so far as the complaining party was concerned, for the desertion." Thus, Brouwer's definition was used as authority for the proposition that if the plaintiff gives the defendant good ground for leaving, the latter is not guilty of malicious desertion and so no divorce will be granted. This, as we have seen, was not at all what Brouwer meant and was not the opinion of the other Dutch jurists. Nevertheless, the definition through its use of *nulla justa aut necessaria causa coactus, ex animi quadam levitate & malitia, vel impatientia freni conjugalis* which derives from Carpzovius' *nulla coactus causa honesta, sed vel levitate, vel impatientia freni conjugalis injusta aliisve non necessariis causis impulsus* who would, in all probability, allow justifications for desertion to bar the divorce did lay itself wide open to such misinterpretation. This case has been used in many others to justify the refusal of a divorce where there was good reason for one spouse to desert, and Brouwer's definition has been continually cited as authority for the proposition, even by textbook writers.[35] Thus, the present law of

[34] p. 45.
[35] *e.g.*, Lee & Honoré, *The South African Law of Property, Family Relations and Succession* (Durban, 1954) p. 99 *et seq.* 365, 366.

South Africa on this point, satisfactory as it may be, is based on a misunderstanding.

But even before *Walter's* case the doctrine of constructive desertion was beginning to creep in. Constructive desertion means holding liable that person whose conduct in fact brought the marriage to an end, no matter which of the parties actually left the matrimonial home. As has been already said, logically there can be no such thing as constructive desertion until one recognises the existence of justifications for desertion in the conduct of the spouses. There are, however, clear signs in *Sutherland* v. *Sutherland* [36] of the doctrine of constructive desertion and, since this case occurred before the courts had given a decision in favour of allowing justifications in the conduct of the other spouse for desertion, it shows that the misinterpretation of Brouwer's definition in *Walter's* case is—at least in part—the result of the spirit of the times. In *Sutherland's* case, Broome J. said [37]: " Desertion is not to be tested by merely ascertaining which party left the matrimonial home first; the one who intends bringing the cohabitation to an end commits the desertion." The main authority cited was the English case of *Sickert* v. *Sickert*,[38] while the South African cases referred to offer little support for the proposition. A similar attitude, again with citation of *Sickert*, appears in *Crossley* v. *Crossley* [39] where Bristowe J. said [40]: " The question seems to me to be who is the person substantially responsible for the separation. It does not matter which of the parties actually leaves the other. The party who really deserted is the one who compels the desertion." From these beginnings has developed the whole doctrine of constructive desertion.[41] In these early decisions no part—rightly—seems to have been played by Voet's view that continued refusal of sexual intercourse was a kind of malicious desertion. This, too, however, was accepted in *Brown* v. *Brown* [42] and forms part of modern South African law. *Brown's* case was not referred to in *Sutherland* but was used in argument in *Crossley* though it was not referred to in the judgment.

To sum up: The Protestant theologians permitted a member of their Church to obtain a divorce if he were deserted by his spouse; or if he felt compelled to leave his spouse on account of her *odium religionis*. This was generalised by the German jurist Arnisaeus

36 31 N.L.R. (1910) 219.
37 p. 222.
38 [1899] P. 278.
39 1912 W.L.D. 49.
40 p. 50.
41 See Hahlo, *The South African Law of Husband and Wife* (Cape Town & Johannesburg, 1953) p. 328 *et seq.*; 1959 *Acta Juridica*, *p.* 55.
42 [1905] T.S. 415.

who, it would seem, was followed by Carpzovius. Arnisaeus would allow a deserted spouse to obtain a divorce provided he had not given good cause for the desertion. There is no sign that he would ever allow the party who actually left the matrimonial home to obtain a divorce on the ground of the other spouse's constructive desertion. The Dutch jurists, under the leadership of Brouwer, took a very different attitude and would not allow any kind of behaviour on the part of the other spouse to justify desertion. Thus, it follows that there could also be no constructive desertion. It is possible that Brouwer misinterpreted Arnisaeus, the form of whose discussion is odd and could lead to misunderstanding. In any event, Brouwer's definition follows Carpzovius' account and so it does not reflect his own views very clearly. The South African courts for some time accepted the Dutch position, but after a misunderstanding of Brouwer's definition they reverted to the view of Arnisaeus. To some extent the misunderstanding was due to the spirit of the times and English judicial influence was not altogether lacking. The courts also allowed a divorce for constructive desertion without restricting it to the guilty party's *odium religionis.*

20

The Law of Citations and Classical Texts in the Post-Classical Period

One implication of the Valentinian Law of Citations which is important for the history of juristic texts in the post-classical period seems to have been ignored [1]).

C.Th. 1,4,3, *Impp. Theod(osius) et Valentin(ianus) AA. aa Senatum Urbis Rom(ae)*; *post alia*:

Papiniani, Pauli, Gai, Ulpiani atque Modestini scripta universa firmamus ita, ut Gaium quae Paulum, Ulpianum et ceteros comitetur auctoritas lectionesque ex omni eius corpore recitentur. Eorum quoque scientiam, quorum tractatus atque sententias praedicti omnes suis operibus miscuerunt, ratam esse censemus, ut Scaevolae, Sabini, Iuliani atque Marcelli omniumque, quos illi celebrarunt, si tamen eorum libri propter antiquitatis incertum codicum collatione firmentur. Ubi autem diversae sententiae proferuntur, potior numerus vincat auctorum, vel, si numerus aequalis sit, eius partis praecedat auctoritas, in qua excellentis ingenii vir Papinianus emineat, qui ut singulos vincit, ita cedit duobus. Notas etiam Pauli atque Ulpiani in Papiniani corpus factas, sicut dudum statutum est, praecipimus infirmari. Ubi autem eorum pares sententiae recitantur, quorum par censetur auctoritas, quos sequi debeat, eligat moderatio iudicantis. Pauli quoque sententias semper valere praecipimus. *Et cetera. dat. VII id. Novembr. Ravenna dd. nn. Theod(osio) XII et Valent(iniano) II AA. Conss.*

Whether we have the constitution as it was issued in 426 A.D. or whether, as is widely believed, it was subjected to a revision in 438 A.D. does not, I think, affect us greatly and the question may be left aside for the moment.

---

1) E.g., there seems to be no sign of it in Schulz, *Roman Legal Science* (Oxford 1953) [cf. especially p. 282], nor in Wieacker, *Textstufen klassischer Juristen* (Göttingen 1960) [cf. especially pp. 156ff.], or ZSS 67 (1950), pp. 385f, nor in Gaudemet, *La formation du droit séculier et du droit de l'église aux IVe et Ve siècles* (Paris 1957) [cf. especially pp. 73ff.].

This constitution, *inter alia*, made the works of the five jurists, Papinian, Paul, Gaius, Ulpian and Modestinus, primary authorities [2]). The works of jurists cited by the five could also be produced, provided in this case that, because of the age of the works, what these jurists said was confirmed by collation of manuscripts. In the case of the five primary authorities no collation of manuscripts was demanded. Why was there this difference? There are, I submit, two possible explanations.

First, there were many good manuscripts of Papinian, Paul, Ulpian and Modestinus who were the last classical jurists and of Gaius whose work had become very popular. The works of the earlier classical jurists were not so widely read because their substance was further removed from contemporary law, and hence the manuscripts of these were uncommon and tended to be suspect. Any argument based on relative popularity and abundance of manuscripts must be concerned mainly with the age of the original works. The quality of the original writings is of secondary importance since otherwise one would have expected Julian, for instance, to have been given authority, and Modestinus to have occupied a less prominent place. Gaius, who is earlier than the other four primary authorities, is a special case. His importance is mainly due to his Institutes; and elementary books, concerned with the broad outline of the law, do not go out of date so quickly as detailed commentaries. Broad principles change much more slowly than do details. It is perhaps significant that, outside of the *Corpus Iuris Civilis*, no fragments of the works of Gaius, apart from his Institutes, have come down to us [3]), and that he is not cited by the Imperial constitutions.

Secondly, the writings of the earlier classical jurists had been corrupted to bring them up to date, hence their manuscripts were less reliable. These two possible explanations are, of course, to some degree related. But whichever is correct, the same conclusion follows, namely that there had been no large scale revision

---

2) Even before this these five had come to occupy a pre-eminent place: cf Gaudemet, *op. cit.* p. 75.

3) Cf the schema in Wieacker, *op. cit.* pp. 153f.: and cf Gaudemet, *loc. cit.*

of the works of the five primary authorities despite the intervention of about two centuries between their composition and the Law of Citations. What the Emperors want is the original opinions of the classical jurists — that is made abundantly plain by the requirement of comparison of manuscripts even if it is only for the lesser authorities. Moreover, otherwise there could hardly be a reason for designating five of the jurists as primary authorities. And yet, it is only the manuscripts of the earlier classical jurists which are suspect. If the first explanation suggested for the difference in treatment of the manuscripts of the primary and lesser authorities is correct, then the popularity of the five jurists before 426 (which accounts for the abundance of their manuscripts) must be because their works did not need substantial alteration. If the second suggestion is right, then deliberate corruption on a large scale in the texts only extended to the manuscripts of the earlier jurists.

It might be objected to the foregoing that in fact the popularity of the five primary authorities resulted in ,standard editions' of their works so that collation would not be needed for them, and hence the Law of Citations would not provide evidence against re-editing. But, first, as noted above, their popularity could only be based on the fact that they, unlike earlier classical jurists, very largely gave contemporary law and did not require large scale alteration. It is putting the cart before the horse to derive the standardisation of the manuscripts from the jurists' popularity. Secondly, there could be no such thing here as a 'standard edition' unless the Emperors designated certain manuscripts as having pre-eminent authority. There is no sign of such Imperial intervention and it can be ruled out. One can, at least in the case of the huge commentaries *ad edictum* and *ad Sabinum*, completely exclude the idea that an unofficial revised 'edition' could drive earlier 'editions' from circulation. The cost of a copy of Ulpian's 83 books *ad edictum* would be so enormous that few jurists would throw away their existing copies and rush to buy a new 'edition' for the sake of what would mainly be non-Ulpianic additions. The earlier manuscripts would continue to be used and relied on. Moreover, the smallness of the market and the enormous size of the undertaking is very much against the idea of planned multiple copying here. Rather one would expect either that a single copy would be made when the need arose or that a very few — and only a very few — would be produced from time to time. No parallels can really usefully be drawn from the republishing of, say, literary works where the economics could be vastly different either because of the smaller size of the book to be edited or because the purchasing public could be larger. Again, it is surely significant that all the writings of the five primary authorities are accepted free from the requirement of collation. If the works of these jurists had been subject to extensive alteration in post-classical times, then it would seem absolutely impossible that a 'standard edition' of all of them (or even of those at all likely to be produced in court) could have emerged.

Gradenwitz suggested that the original constitution of 426 A.D. referred only to the five primary authorities and that the constitution was revised in 438 A.D. and only then was the part inserted which is concerned with the secondary authorities [4]). This does not affect us and we need not decide whether Gradenwitz is right or not. If he is right, it is just as significant that in 438 collation of the manuscripts of the secondary authorities was felt to be necessary, but not collation of the manuscripts of the five primary authorities. It would still be difficult to attribute the difference in treatment as regards collation to oversight.

To conclude: The Valentinian Law of Citations presents very strong evidence that the works of Papinian, Paul, Gaius, Ulpian and Modestinus had not, to any large extent, been altered in the preceding two centuries. One can probably go further. If these five had not been tampered with in that time, then it is unlikely that in the same period the works of other jurists had undergone substantial revision. So any revision of the secondary authorities

---

[4]) ZSS 34 (1913), pp. 274ff. This view is widely accepted: cf the literature cited by Kaser, *Das römische Privatrecht* II (Munich 1959), p. 19 n. 3. Most recently, Wieacker tends to the view that the original constitution was the text as we have it: *Textstufen cit.*, p. 156 n. 153.

must already have occurred in the classical period. It is a priori improbable that there was such revision as early as the classical period so it is reasonable to assume that these jurists, too, did not undergo any large scale alteration at all before the Law of Citations. That is to say, collation of their manuscripts was demanded because such manuscripts were scarce (due to their lack of popularity since they were out of date) and generally neglected, and hence were suspect.

V

Law and Society

21

The Prehistory of Contracts with Especial Reference to Roman Law

Robert Feenstra, as a person and as a scholar, has been one of my heroes since I first met him in 1957 immediately before I started on my first law teaching post. A remark once overheard almost sums him up, «Er arbeitet sauber»: attention to detail, great care, balance, and, I should add, imagination. His work ranges over centuries and systems. He loves Roman law and is fond of Scotland. I hope I may offer as a tribute a paper that seeks to explain the emergence of contract law, with Roman law the primary system to be explained, in the light of social habits, with observations drawn in part from personal experience on a remote Scottish island. Naturally, I am not trying to say that social and economic conditions in early Rome and on a modern sparsely populated Scottish island are the same. Rather, instead of talking in the abstract about «what must have been done» at Rome, I prefer to give concreteness to the discussion by talking about what I have actually observed occurring.

The impetus for this paper came from a remark of the distinguished English legal historian, S. F. C. Milsom: «There were few overt decisions to be made. Custom decided what should be done, and generally who should do it... Early law does not have to cater much for choice. In the private sphere we shall see this reflected in the small part played by contracts, and the large part played by enduring relationships of a proprietary nature»[1]. However true this may be for mediaeval England, it cannot be accepted as a generalisation, because contract law was early at Rome. And my researches into customary law lead me to doubt whether there is small scope for choice in early personal arrangements[2].

In contrast to mediaeval England we shall consider a society which either uses no coined money or in which monetary transactions are uncommon.

---

[1] Historical Foundations of the Common Law^2, London and Toronto 1981, 12.

[2] See e. g. A. Watson, Sources of Law, Legal Change and Ambiguity, Philadelphia 1984, 25 ff; The Evolution of Law, Baltimore 1985, 43 ff.

For simplicity let us imagine a fairly isolated, small community which is closely knit. Most adult males will be generalists in their work: at the same time farmers, fishermen, housebuilders. Much work will be done in common, and much that is the immediate concern of individuals will be done with the assistance of others. The fisherman on his return will want and expect his neighbours to help him pull his boat on the shore; the farmer will need friends to help, both with labour and implements, in getting the harvest in before the weather turns bad; roofs of huts are much more easily put on with the labour of several men. Help is freely given, because few can be self-sufficient. Times when help is needed come frequently: often with regularity, but also often irregularly and unforeseen. Arrangements and expectations must often be flexible. For instance you may regularly, perhaps 300 days per year, help me to pull my boat on shore, but I may not perform anything like the same service for you if you fish only seldom. What will you expect from me? Nothing so definite, I believe, as a calculated equivalent. Rather, you have a generalised expectation of help. If say, in five years time, you decide to clear a field then I will, when it is convenient to me, take a day or two off fishing to help shift the larger rocks. If my boat is stouter than yours you may expect me to take you when you need to make a journey. The services rendered by one person are not treated as individual units, each to be recompensed by an equivalent unit. The services are a combined service. The expectations of those involved are even more fluid than I have as yet indicated. Each individual provides services for those who need them even if a recipient is unlikely ever to be able to match them. Without specific arrangements being made to this end there will often be a merry-go-round of help: you help me, I help another, and his son helps you. The amount of assistance given by individuals to others in the community will vary: one who habitually gives more than others will rise in status; those who do not pull their weight will lose respect.

For many situations a contract will not be wanted and will not emerge. It is the very width of choice of expectation and return that makes contract undesirable. When you ask me for a service, what I may want in return need not be a similar service. At the time of my performance in fact it will often not be known what I may expect from you. And I will not be expecting a calculated equivalent: I may in time be looking for more or less. Each service, indeed, will not be seen as a unit, separate from all other services. What I am looking for in return is often just your generalised willingness to be of help to others including me. You do not do A for me in return for X, B in return for Y, C in return for Z. The relationship is continuing and not based on a sense of a specific *quid pro quo*. You do A, B, C for me and eventually I do X for you, Y for another neighbour and Z for a widow. In no sense is X a return for A, Y for B and C for Z; nor is there a feeling that X, Y, Z should equal A, B, C.

But there will be occasions when an enforceable contract will be desirable. One may want an assurance that a specific individual will perform a particular task. A unilateral contract – which may be matched with another – like *stipulatio* may emerge and it will be marked by formalities to set it off from all other situations where legal enforcement of expectations is inappropriate and undesirable. The greater the distance in the relationship, the more desirable may appear the need for formalising the arrangement. Again, a person who has given to another physical possession of something he owns and which is not returned may want a remedy based on the deposit or loan. These, however, are the exceptional cases.

But the situation changes with the use of money. And here I want to call attention to the peculiarity of Roman law that, with the sole exception of the very anomalous (in its development) and most complex contract of partnership (*societas*)[3], every recognised Roman contract either demands that the counter-prestation be in money as in sale or hire, or be gratuitous or unilateral as in *stipulatio*, loan for consumption (*mutuum*), deposit and loan for use (*commodatum*). Moreover, money is the touchstone which determines which contract is involved; mandate, deposit and *commodatum* all become hire if a money reward is demanded; sale ceases to be a contract and becomes the legally ineffective arrangement of barter (*permutatio*) if the price is not to be in coined money. More striking still, the arrangement of loan for consumption was first recognised as an enforceable contract when money was the object of the loan: only by the subsequent *lex Calpurnia* was the action extended to cover loans of other fungibles[4].

The role of money in the emergence of contract law must be explained, and for Roman law we may begin with *mutuum* where a specific role for money in contract is first seen. In a society with an underdeveloped economy a typical major loan for consumption might be of seed-corn. One farmer is short of seed at sowing time and asks a friend to lend him some. But the term «to lend» is everywhere often used ambiguously in this context by non-lawyers. It may be used to express the notion that the recipient farmer will be bound to return an equivalent amount of corn after his

---

[3] See now WATSON, Evolution of Law 20 ff.
[4] G. 4, 19.

harvest; but equally it may be used as a euphemism for «to give», and there also may or may not be the underlying unexpressed idea that the recipient should feel himself under an obligation to do or give something eventually in return. But a loan of money of a sizable sum to the parties is different. The firm expectation is that it will be returned[5]. If it is not, the law may not be slow to intervene.

David Daube observes that «transactions originally belonging to the gift area of fellowship ‹Gemeinschaft›, tend to assume the more rigid, legalistic characteristics of partnership, ‹Gesellschaft›, when money enters»[6]. Specifically, with regard to *mutuum* he argues that the arrangement starts as a mutual service of the kind I have discussed and that the *lex Silia* making money loans – and significantly only money loans – actionable «marks a breakdown of the gift trade»[7]. Daube displays his usual acumen but I would change the emphasis. There is, I think, no breakdown of the ‹gift trade›. *Mutuum,* even of money, is very much an arrangement between friends: only that explains why no interest can be exacted in the action on the *mutuum*, and even why the separate contract of *mutuum* came into being at all[8]. Where there was no mutual trust a stipulation would have been taken for the return of the money. After the introduction of the *condictio* for a money loan, just as before, the ‹gift trade› of other obligations would continue with in some cases the return expected of an exact equivalent of what was lent, and in other cases no specific expectations. But, as Daube is aware and we shall see more fully, money is different. Eventually, the action on *mutuum* is extended to loans of other fungibles where the return was expected. But, it should be emphasised, not to other ‹loans› or ‹gifts› both because the law cannot make vague arrangements actionable, and because the parties do not want the law to intervene.

A Roman development that is a close parallel to that of *mutuum* can be found in some other contracts. *Locatio conductio,* hire, requires that one prestation be in money; where the contract involves no counter prestation and is technically gratuitous it is one of deposit, mandate or loan for use (*commodatum*); where a reward for a hiring is expected which is not to be in money no specific contract emerges. *Locatio conductio* is itself a residual

---

[5] Even in this context the term «to lend» may be used euphemistically, but almost always only where the sum involved is of little significance to the parties.

[6] D. Daube, ZSS rom. Abt. 96 (1979) 1 ff at p. 1. We are not concerned with the type of gift which is studied by M. Mauss, The Gift, London 1954.

[7] Daube 11.

[8] For the argument see Watson, Evolution of Law 8 ff.

category: all bilateral obligations involving a money prestation on one side, which are not sale, are *locatio conductio*[9]. But again we have the phenomenon that the gratuitous equivalent contracts of *mandatum* and *commodatum* emerge separately and later. *Depositum* is much older but, however it is to be explained[10], it is clearly very special. Mandate, *commodatum,* and in time many cases of deposit too, are contracts of the ‹gift trade›, belonging to ‹Gemeinschaft› rather than ‹Gesellschaft›. The *mandans* and the borrower come under non-specified extra-legal obligations. The ‹Gemeinschaft›, that is to say, continues to exist long after the ‹Gesellschaft› is in operation.

It is not at all difficult to see why the involvement of money makes a difference and to explain why money prestations play a prominent role in the emergence of Roman contracts. Money, of course, is unique as a means of exchange. Every service or object can be offered in exchange. Thus, on the one hand, when the counter-prestation is stated in money, a valuation has been placed on the service or object of which a court can easily take account. Likewise, the formulation in money terms means that the obligations are made (relatively) precise. On the other hand, for the holder money is a lasting asset which has value for him: it does not diminish if it is not used. Ten minutes regularly spent most days helping to beach a neighbour's boat ‹costs› nothing. The obligor would not be better off if he did not help, and, besides, the ten minutes offer a social occasion. A day spent clearing a friend's field when the sea is too rough for fishing ‹costs› nothing if one has nothing else urgent to do. But money not used up now remains to be used on another occasion: an obligement in money diminishes the obligor if there is no return. But setting a prestation in money has an important social consequence. It sets off the transaction as a unit which is no longer part of a continuum of unspecified obligations. It is an exaggeration, but perhaps not a great one, to suggest that the money transaction does not mark a decline in the ‹gift trade› so much as causes it. In an isolated community, the island shopkeeper creates a gulf between himself and the others. No matter how honourable and generous he is, he requires — and must do if he is himself to purchase supplies — instant payment for his goods, each purchase from him involving the completion of an obligation. However useful he is to the community, he separates himself from the ‹Gemeinschaft›. But, it must be emphasised, the ‹Gemeinschaft› continues side-by-side.

---

9 For the argument see WATSON, Evolution of Law 15 f.

10 See now WATSON, Evolution of Law 9 ff.

I have not been seeking to provide a complete view of the background to the development of Roman contract law[11]. Rather, I wanted to highlight four points. First, in an underdeveloped society where money is not used or only rarely, there is a plethora of contractual situations, and it is not the case that there is no choice. The evolution of contract law is handicapped because the law cannot cope with the imprecision and variety. Secondly, it is the case that the very imprecision of the arrangements is wanted by the parties: they are not interested in having formal legal regulation. Thirdly, at Rome, when a formal contract was exceptionally wanted, this could early be arranged by a stipulation. But many or even most transactions which in an economically more developed society would result in contracts are left outside of legal control. Fourthly, the use of money can, and in the case of Rome did, result in an upsurge in legal development. But the emergence of money related contracts does not itself involve the disappearance of the non-monetary relationship.

---

[11] In fact this paper should be regarded as supplementation to my account of the evolution of Roman contract law in Evolution of Law (n. 2). One limitation in the scope of the paper should be emphasised: it is concerned only with the intimate internal transactions of a relatively small community. It leaves untouched the whole problem of the failure to develop of a contract of barter where the parties would often be at arms length.

22

The Notion of Equivalence of Contractual Obligation and Classical Roman Partnership

IT is generally agreed that early and classical Roman law knew no requirement that the parties to a contract had to promise prestations of equal value or of value proportionate to their expected return. Nor could there, in general, have been any such requirement. The Roman jurists, as is well-known, never developed a general theory of contract but devoted their energy to the creation of individual types of contract. Some of these contractual types were unilateral, others imperfectly bilateral, and in such, equivalence of prestation is out of the question, except where as in *mutuum*, loan for consumption, the party who is not bound has brought the contract into being by an act that is in fact his prestation. *Mutuum* as a contract came into existence by the lender's physically delivering the coins or seed-corn, the borrower alone being thereafter bound, his obligation being to restore an exact equivalent. In a sense, *mutuum* is unilateral only because the Romans demanded for its creation one particular formality, namely delivery. To *mutuum* we will return.

Of greater significance in this context is the unilateral contract of *stipulatio*. This was a verbal contract; the promisee posed the question, " Do you promise . . . ? " and the promisor immediately replied, " I promise . . . , " using the same verb. Only the promisor was bound. The contract, however, should not be seen as by any means necessarily involving a gift or as being of a gratuitous nature. *Stipulatio* could be used for all sorts of transactions. For instance, it was in existence by the time of the XII Tables, the codification of around 450 B.C. and so is older than the contract of sale, *emptio venditio*, by at least two centuries in general estimation. Before the creation of *emptio venditio*, parties in a sale-like situation would create their obligations by each taking a *stipulatio* or a number of *stipulations* from the other. Each party would then be bound by a unilateral contract (which might, however, be so drafted as to be conditional on the performance of the other contract). Thus, we are in a world far removed from the present day unilateral gratuitous contract. But there is no indication—indeed the reverse is clearly true—that in a commercial situation a *stipulatio* was valid only if the corresponding *stipulatio* involved a prestation of equal worth.

Likewise there is insistence by modern scholars that in the famous consensual contracts—a great invention of the Romans—in which the contract was created simply by the parties' agreement, equivalence of promises was not demanded.[1] Of the four consensual contracts, sale, hire, partnership, and mandate, attention is naturally focused on sale, which was the most important.

For the Republic there is the long discussion in Cicero, *de officiis*, 3. 12.50–17.72. From the numerous cases discussed it emerges beyond doubt that in the absence of what the law considered to be fraud, a contract was valid and enforceable although one party had made a resoundingly bad bargain. From the classical jurists of the early Empire we have expressly general statements. Thus:

> *D. 4.4.16.4* (Ulpian 11 ad ed.) Idem Pomponius ait in pretio emptionis et venditionis naturaliter licere contrahentibus se circumvenire. (Likewise Pomponius says with regard to the price in sale that the contracting parties are naturally permitted to take advantage of one another.)
>
> *D. 19.2.22.3* (Paul 34 ad ed.) Quemadmodum in emendo et vendendo naturaliter concessum est quod pluris sit minoris emere, quod minoris sit pluris vendere et ita invicem se circumscribere, ita in locationibus et conductionibus iuris est. (Just as in the contract of sale it is naturally permitted to buy for less what is worth more and to sell for more what is worth less, and thus to take advantage of one another, so that is the law in the case of hire.)

An instructive example occurs in the context of the effect of error on the validity of a sale. Ulpian in D. 18.1.9.2 (28 ad Sab.) declared a sale void *inter alia* if bronze had been sold for gold, and that text is followed by one of Paul:

> *D. 18.1.10* (5 ad Sab.) Aliter atque si aurum quidem fuerit, deterius autem quam emptor existimaret: tunc enim emptio valet. (The case is different if it really was gold, but of worse quality than the buyer thought: for then the sale is valid.)

The text makes sense only on the supposition that, as a result of his mistake, the buyer paid more than the market price for the gold; hence, in vain, he wishes to have the sale set aside.

It is a strange phenomenon of Roman law that has never been satisfactorily explained—indeed, I have never seen it commented on—that the basic contracts of the classical system are either gratuitous (or unilateral) or else the prestation of one party must be in coined money. To this rule the sole exception is *societas*, partnership. Thus, there is no proper place in the system for a contract of barter—

---

[1] See *e.g.* among recent writers, K. Visky, "Die Proportionalität von Wert und Preis in den römischen Rechtsquellen des 11 Jahrhunderts," 16 R.I.D.A. (1969), pp. 355 *et seq.*, and for a bibliography—showing that occasional scholars hold some equivalence might have been required for sale in classical law—M. Kaser, *Das römische Privatrecht*, 2nd ed., 1 (Munich, Beck, 1971), p. 550n. 45; 2 (1975), p. 389nn. 33–36.

exchange of goods for goods—or for a contract of exchange of goods in return for services.[2] There is undoubtedly something strange here. It is quite impossible to believe that the Romans in fact did not have a need for transactions akin to barter. It must frequently have happened, too, that what was most wanted was a transfer of goods by one party now, and a corresponding delivery by the other party at a later date. The need for the contract would be diminished by the use of *stipulatio* but the limitations on this contract should be remembered. It was not only unilateral, but necessarily verbal; hence, the parties had to be face-to-face and the contract could not be created by an exchange of letters. To make matters worse, a *stipulatio* could not be made on behalf of a third party.[3] In any event, no matter how one tries to explain the absence of a contract of barter by calling in aid the existence of other contracts, particularly *stipulatio*, the problem remains that such other contracts (and notably *stipulatio*) should also have prevented the growth of a contract of sale or of deposit or of *commodatum* (loan for use). *Stipulatio* could just as well have been used in such situations as it was in barter. Reflection only increases the problem. It is hard to see why a specific contract of, say, deposit or *commodatum* should have come into existence. Take the case of *commodatum*. If the borrower did not return the thing, the lender had the action claiming ownership, the *vindicatio*, or the *actio ad exhibendum*. If the borrower fraudulently put it out of his power to return the thing, the lender had the *actio ad exhibendum*. If the borrower or any of his dependents purloined the thing, the lender had the action for theft, the *actio furti*, for double the thing's value. If the borrower or any of his dependents damaged the thing, the lender had the *actio legis Aquiliae*. The gaps in a lender's remedies that had to be filled by a contractual action were few. But in contrast the hostility towards the creation of a well-developed contract of barter was such that the Sabinian school tried to incorporate barter within sale. They were reduced to using far-fetched arguments from a misinterpretation of Homer[4] and they were unsuccessful. The Proculian view prevailed that for a sale the price had to be in coined money.[5] The Sabinian approach was impractical since on their view it would not be possible to distinguish

---

2 A very minor exception is constituted by *negotia partiaria*, that is, a form of lease where the lessor's reward is calculated as a fraction of the produce: see Cato, *de agri cultura*, c. 16, 136, 137; D.19.2.25.6; C.4.65.21; *lex de villae Magnae colonis*, Bruns no. 114; Pliny, *Epistulae*, 9.3.7.

3 See *e.g.* D.50.17.73.4. A son-in-power could take a stipulation on behalf of his father, and so could a slave for his master, but this would not anything like solve the problem.

4 See D. Daube, "Three Quotations from Homer in Digest 18.1.1.1," *Cambridge Law Journal* 10 (1949), pp. 213 *et seq.*

5 G. 3.41; J. 3.23.2; D. 18.1.1.1; 19.4.1; C. 4.64.1. It was accepted that part of the price could be a continuing obligation.

buyer from seller yet in sale the obligations of the parties differed. This makes it all the more surprising that the Sabinian style was not to attempt to improve or make fully acceptable a contract of barter. *Permutatio,* barter, did eventually emerge as one of the so-called " innominate contracts," *i.e.* it was not regarded as falling within any recognised category, but the dating of this development is quite uncertain.[6]

As for the unilateral or gratuitous contracts, it is worth emphasising that they divide into two groups. The first group contains the contracts which of necessity are gratuitous, mandate, deposit and *commodatum.* If payment is made or agreed on, the contract becomes hire, *locatio conductio.* The contracts of the second group, *stipulatio,* the contract *litteris* and *mutuum,* are not necessarily gratuitous. Thus it is true that in the action (*condictio*) brought on a *mutuum* the claim was only for the equivalent value of what had been lent, yet nothing forbade the lender taking a *stipulatio* for interest on the *mutuum,* and recovering the interests by an action based on the *stipulatio.*[7] Interest was not forbidden though at times excessive interest was regarded as illegal.

It is against this background that we should look at the consensual contract of partnership, *societas,* which alone of Roman contracts was bilateral (or even plurilateral) and not gratuitous yet did not necessarily involve a money prestation on one side; and in which also there are important traces of juristic feeling that there should be some equivalence between prestation and return.

From the beginning of the first century B.C., the earliest moment when we have evidence on this point for consensual partnership, it seems clear that all the partners did not have to make contributions of equal worth to the partnership, nor did their contributions have to be similar in kind.[8] Despite their contributions being unequal in value or different in kind the partners could agree to share the profits equally.[9] From this same time at least, the time of the jurist Quintus Mucius, there was no necessity that the profits be divided equally. What was disputed was whether the partners could agree that one of them should take a larger share of profits than he would suffer of any loss. The main text is by G. 3.149.

> Magna autem quaestio fuit an ita coiri possit societas, ut quis maiorem partem lucretur, minorem damni praestet. quod Q. Mucius (*contra naturam societatis esse existimauit. sed Seruius*

---

[6] See *e.g.* J. A. C. Thomas, *Textbook of Roman Law* (Amsterdam, etc., North-Holland, 1976), pp. 311 *et seq.*

[7] For the phenomenon see above all, M. Kaser, "*Mutuum* und *Stipulatio,*" *Eranion Maridakis* (Athens, 1963) pp. 155 *et seq.*

[8] See Cicero, *pro Quinctio* 3.12; *pro Roscio comoedo,* 10.27– 11.323.

[9] Cicero, *pro Rosc. com.* 11.32.

> *Sulpicius, cuius*) etiam praeualuit sententia, adeo ita coiri posse societatem existimauit, ut dixerit illo quoque m*odo* coiri posse, ut quis nihil omnino damni praestet, sed lucri partem capiat, si modo opera eius tam pretiosa uideatur ut aequum sit eum cum hac pactione in societatem admitti, n*am* et ita posse coir*i* societatem constat, ut unus pecuniam conferat, alter non conferat, et tamen lucrum inter eos commune sit; saepe enim opera alicuius pro pecunia ualet.
>
> (There has been a great dispute as to whether a partnership is possible on the terms that one of the partners should have a larger share in profits than in losses. Q. Mucius considered this to be against the nature of partnership, but Servius Sulpicius, whose opinion has prevailed, held that not only is partnership possible on these terms, but even on the terms that one partner shall bear no share of losses and yet have a share in profits, on the supposition that his services are considered so valuable that it is fair that he should be admitted to partnership on such terms. For it is settled law that a partnership agreement may provide that one partner should, and the other should not, bring in money, and yet that the profits should be shared; for a man's services are often as valuable as money.)

In various ways the opinion and justification of Servius are more interesting for us, but these cannot be analysed before we attempt to understand why, for Quintus Mucius, it was contrary to the nature of partnership that one party should receive a greater share of any profit than he would bear of any loss. We can be sure that it was not just a general feeling on his part that such an arrangement was unfair. The reason for saying this is partly that it is obvious that such an arrangement could be extremely fair, especially when one person is providing much of the specialised labour; partly that though even an outstanding jurist like Mucius might fail to see the equity yet, once it was pointed out, there could scarcely be the great dispute mentioned by Gaius which suggests continuing discussion.

Mucius's attitude, I believe, can be explained only within the context of early Roman partnership. The earliest Roman partnership was *ercto non cito* and came into being when the head of a family died leaving *sui heredes*, that is persons subject to his power who become independent on his death. Until they divided the inheritance they were in what Gaius calls a partnership of both positive and natural law (*legitima simul et naturalis*).[10] This partnership, at its inception at least, was not contractual. Since we are concerned with a historical period in which dependent members of a family owned no property of their own, this partnership was of all the assets and of

---

[10] G. 3.154a.

all the productivity of the partners. Succession could be either testate or intestate and there is no indication that *ercto non cito* arose only on one kind of succession or the other. At least where the partnership arose on intestacy the contributions in assets of the partners would always be equal. Where the partnership arose following upon a will and the *sui heredes* had been appointed heirs in varying shares, we would expect that any profit or loss would be divided on the basis of such shares or else the partnership on testacy would have been meaningless. It should be emphasised that *ercto non cito* would come into existence automatically on the death and that *sui heredes* had no power in early law to refuse the inheritance. When by will one heir was given double the share of the other, and the two heirs were automatically partners, a division would have to give the former twice the amount given the latter. But Roman heirs were liable for all the debts of the deceased even when they exceeded the assets; hence, in the example just given the former heir would have to bear double the loss that the latter would be responsible for.

Ercto non cito proved to be so successful that at some early point such a partnership could be set up among persons who were not *sui heredes* by using the old form of court procedure known as *legis actio*.[11] These two early forms of partnership had in common—and at variance with the later consensual partnership—that a jointly owned slave who was manumitted by one partner became free and that a jointly owned *res mancipi* transferred by one partner by *mancipatio* became the property of the transferee.[12] These rules seem to indicate that each partner was regarded as the full owner of all of the partnership assets. Partners were emotionally very close. In *ercto non cito* they were of necessity very near relatives who, if the partnership continued, had chosen to own all their property in common. In partnership by *legis actio* the partners need not have been related, but they were so closely bound in trust that they engaged in a venture involving their whole assets.

Against this background, when the new consensual partnership came into being, perhaps in as early as the late third century B.C., it was modelled on a partnership of all of the assets of the partners.[13] In such circumstances even when the consensual partnership was of less than the total assets of the partners it was to be expected that there would be discussion of the arrangements that the partners could make. Could they agree that one partner should receive more of the profits than another? Could they bargain that one partner

[11] G. 3.154b.
[12] G. 3.154b.
[13] See *e.g.* A. Watson, "Consensual *societas* between Romans and the Introduction of the *formulae*," *Revue Internationale des Droits de l'Antiquité* (1962), pp. 431 *et seq.*; above, chapter 16, pp. 175ff.

should contribute only assets, and another only labour? Though these questions might quickly be resolved, the answers were by no means entirely obvious. To point the difficulty it is enough to remember three facts. First, the old pre-consensual partnership was substantially the most complex contract of its time. It was the only bilateral or even plurilateral contract. The limits to agreement would need to be fixed, once consensual partnership was available. Secondly, unlike sale and hire, there was no requirement that the prestation of a partner had to be in money. In a money economy, even an early money economy, it is usual to measure value of goods or services in money terms. The measuring of value is more difficult when the worth of none of the prestations is fixed in cash. Thirdly, partnership, more than any other contract, involves a continuing close relationship where what was to be regarded as legally and morally proper had to be established. Partners, again unlike the parties to a sale or hire, are not at arms length.

The problem considered by Quintus Mucius—one partner taking a greater share of the profits than he bears of any loss—then does not relate directly to fairness or the equivalence of the prestations. Quintus Mucius would see that the agreement could be just. For him the issue, as the text indeed tells us, was whether such an arrangement could fall within the scope of the contract of partnership or whether it was contrary to the nature of partnership. It was, we should remember, held contrary to the nature of sale that the price consist of goods and not coined money, but the issue was not one of fairness or of equivalence of prestation. But in an important respect the problem facing Quintus Mucius was more intractable. There was no legally logical way to resolve the issue. Moreover, Mucius' answer, as we have just indicated, was in line with the situation under *ercto non cito,* and it is, I believe, plausible to suggest that Mucius' attitude was largely the result of an acceptance of what may have seemed to him to be the traditional, hitherto unquestioned, position. (In these days of purely commercial partnership, the attitude of Quintus Mucius may not seem easy to grasp. But one can produce a modern situation that is to some extent analogous, namely marriage. There is a tendency revealed in the law of many jurisdictions to treat the contributions through effort of the spouses, whatever these contributions may have been, as equal in financial terms. It is, of course, perfectly obvious that the contribution of any one spouse may well be very much greater than that of another. But an important legal trend—which varies from jurisdiction to jurisdiction in detail—seems to have as its social basis a feeling that in view of the extremely intimate and continuing nature of the marital relationship, it is contrary to the nature of marriage to investigate the respective contributions in financial terms.)

The belief that Mucius' attitude that each individual partner's share of profit had to be the same as his share of loss derived from his acceptance for consensual *societas* of inherent rules of *ercto non cito,* receives support from a detail already noticed: it was not disputed that a partner could receive different shares from his fellow partners. In *ercto non cito* following upon succession under a will the heirs could always have had different shares. If the argument is correct, then it is not the case that by the time of Mucius it was settled that profits need not be shared equally: rather the position always had been that partners could have different shares from one another. The precise scope of the dispute between Quintus Mucius and Servius Sulpicius thus is entirely explicable.

Servius Sulpicius' approach, as set out in the text of Gaius, was to cut the Gordian knot, and consider the issue on the basis of fairness. He claimed such an arrangement was indeed valid, even the more extreme arrangement that one partner should share in the profits but bear none of any loss was valid, but to justify the assertion he had to claim the arrangement was fair. " Si modo," he says; " Provided that his services are considered so valuable that it is fair that he should be admitted to partnership on such terms."

It does not emerge clearly from the text as it stands exactly what Servius' position was. There are two main possibilities. The one that seems obvious from the text is that Servius felt that such a partnership agreement was permissible only if one partner's services were so valuable as to justify it. In other words, in the event of a dispute the judge would decide if the agreement was in accord with (what seemed to be at the moment of contract) the likely prestations of the parties; if it were not the judge could declare the contract void. The other possibility is that, faced with the stance adopted by Mucius, Servius responded with an argument to the effect that such an agreement *could be* fair, and hence the partners should be allowed to fix the proportions. That is, despite their appearance as a legal rule, Servius' words from " Si modo " on are nothing more than an argument for a change in the law, with the objective of allowing the partners freedom to make their own arrangements for division of profit and loss.

In an earlier work, I had inclined to the second view mainly on the ground that the Roman courts would not have interfered with the terms of an agreement.[14] But the second view can only be main-

[14] A. Watson, *The Law of Obligations in the Later Roman Republic* (Oxford, Clarendon Press, 1965), pp. 137 *et seq.* The book contains a discussion of earlier views.

tained if we hold that the substance of a further text, D. 17.2.29.1 (Ulpian 30 ad Sab.), has been interpolated and no longer gives us the thought of Ulpian:

> Ita coiri societatem posse, ut nullam partem damni alter sentiat, lucrum vere commune sit, Cassius putat: quod ita demum valebit, ut et Sabinus scribit, si tanti sit opera, quanti damnum est: plerumque enim tanta est industria socii, ut plus societati conferat quam pecunia, item si solus naviget, si solus peregrinetur, pericula subeat solus.
> (Cassius thinks that a partnership can be formed on the terms that one party suffers no part of the loss, but the gain is shared. This arrangement is only valid, as Sabinus also writes, if the worth of the labour was as much as the loss. For often the industry of one partner is worth so much that it contributes more to the partnership than money would; likewise if he alone undertakes a voyage, if he alone travels in foreign parts, if he alone undergoes danger.)

Earlier, with others, I had held the text interpolated [15] arguing that there was confusion of subjunctive and indicative in "si tanta sit opera" and "quanti damnum est"; that "plerumque etc." does not follow on what precedes; and that "item" just does not harmonise. These arguments now seem to be of no account. Whatever we may be taught as correct Latin style, the Roman jurists in sentences with a conditional clause very frequently have a subjunctive in the conditional clause and an indicative in the main clause.[16] "Plerumque etc." makes perfect sense if it is translated, as it properly can be as "often," and not "generally." I see now that I was taking the clauses beginning with "item" as examples illustrating the previous remark (which they cannot be), and not (as they are) in apposition to it: "Similarly." A positive difficulty in holding the substance interpolated is the clause, "as Sabinus also writes." If Justinian's compilers wished to change the law they would, no doubt, do so; and if the text ripe for alteration was one of Ulpian he would be saddled with the new view. But it is not easy to see why gratuitously the compilers would support their invention by wrongly ascribing their opinion also to an earlier jurist. They had no need to bolster their opinion. And why should they pick on Sabinus?

To return for a moment to the attitude of Servius as depicted in G. 3.149. Even if we hold that he was giving an argument for a change in the law rather than stating the law as he wanted it to be, the argument itself has force only on the belief that in partnership equivalence of the partners' prestations to their rewards has a legal

---

15 *Obligations*, p. 140.

16 For Ulpian this can very easily be verified by looking at the texts of his set out in O. Lenel, *Palingenesia Iuris Civilis* (Leipzig, Tauchnitz, 1889).

worth quite different from any that might be asked for in sale or hire. The reasons for this feeling are to be sought among the factors mentioned before in this paper that made early Roman partnership such a special contract: it involved a continuing relationship between persons who had close emotional ties. But whether Servius' claim was meant simply as an argument against Mucius' position or, as seems more likely, was his view of what the law should be in contrast to Mucius' opinion, it involves a response dictated by the attitude of Mucius.

The preceding part of the text of Ulpian, D. 17.2.29 pr, enables us to take the issue rather further:

> Si non fuerint partes societati adiectae, aequas eas esse constat. si vero placuerit, ut quis duas partes vel tres habeat, alius unam, an valeat? placet valere, si modo aliquid plus contulit societati vel pecuniae vel operae vel cuiuscumque alterius rei causa.
> (If the shares were not set out for the partnership it is settled that they are equal. If, however, it has been agreed that one person have two or three shares and another person one, is this arrangement valid? It is valid provided he contributed something more to the partnership, whether money or labour, or on account of any other matter.)

It was settled law in the late Republic that partners could agree that one receive a greater share than another and there was no requirement that that partner had to be contributing more to the partnership. Otherwise Quintus Mucius could not have proceeded to discuss the more extreme case in G. 3.149. Hence the present text is often held to be interpolated and not to give the view of Ulpian or of classical law in general.[17] But our discussion of D. 17.2.29.1 makes it appear much more likely that the old view was now being questioned. If Ulpian and other jurists did hold that a partnership agreement that one partner should receive more of any profit than he would bear of any loss was valid only if he contributed more to the partnership than did another, then logically and rationally they should also have held that an arrangement by which one partner was to receive more than another was valid only if he contributed more. If in one case the arrangement can be allowed only because it is just, the same should apply in the other case.

Arangio-Ruiz holds that the original text ended with the words "placet valere," that a post-classical jurist is responsible for "si modo—operae" and that "vel cuiuscumque—causa" is Justinianic. He objects strongly to the very last part of the text both on the ground that it is ungrammatical in his view and also that it is so

---

[17] See *e.g.* V. Arangio-Ruiz, *La società in diritto romano* (Naples, Jovene, 1950), pp. 106 *et seq.;* Watson, *Obligations*, p. 142.

vague that an honest judge would always have to hold the arrangement valid. In a sense these two objections should be considered together. The phrase may appear vague but it should not be pressed to mean that the judge had absolute discretion. It refers to extra contributions of a partner that should not be counted as monetary or of an amount of labour namely the prestations spelled out in D. 17.2.29.1, " if he alone undergoes danger." The style is not felicitous, and the infelicity is brought out in the translation. But it is not ungrammatical and Ulpian is not usually highly regarded for his style. Arangio-Ruiz says " vel cuiuscumque alterius rei causa " cannot depend grammatically upon " plus contulit " or upon " si modo." But it is not intended to: the phrase depends upon " placet valere." The infelicity of the text consists in having that phrase in apposition to the very differently framed clause, " si modo—operae," and in having the phrase and the clause both dependent on " placet valere." But Arangio-Ruiz' (and others) criticism of the grammar does appear to rest on a misunderstanding.

On the view that the substance of D. 17.2.29.1 is classical, the law of partnership underwent an interesting development peculiar to itself. Thus, by the very nature of *ercto non cito* any partner's share of any credits would be exactly the same as his share of any debts; but it was not necessary that a partner have the identical share with every other partner. The criterion of apportionment was not fairness or justice, but succession. This characteristic of *ercto non cito* was sustained for consensual *societas* by Quintus Mucius on the basis of the nature of partnership. Servius responded to Mucius on the issue of fairness and held that a partner's share of profit could differ from that of his loss provided the distribution corresponded to what was thought to be his contribution to the partnership. This opinion was accepted by later jurists, and Ulpian then spelled out as law the logical consequences of introducing the notion of fairness into partnership shares, namely that the share of one partner could be greater than that of others only if his contribution was greater. Thus classical law required for partnership that, as between the partners, there had to be an equivalence of contributions and rewards. But classical law did not carry this notion of a need for equivalence over into the other bilateral contracts, such as sale and hire. Certainly there is a distinction between the two contracts just mentioned and partnership in that only partnership involves a continuing relationship among persons who have close ties, and this distinction may be relevant for equivalence of prestation being demanded only for partnership. Yet it seems more plausible to assert simply that since Roman types of contracts arose and developed individually, characteristics of one type of contract were not easily transmitted to others even when this would have been appropriate, and that this was the case here. The requirement of equivalence of prestation and reward for *societas* was not the result of a general view that valid contracts must be fair or even perhaps that fairness was a particularly important social ingredient for partnership, but arose primarily from the tradition of juristic discussion in this area where the starting point was *ercto non cito* and the law of succession.[18]

The texts for classical Roman law do not show any real working out of the consequences of the notion of equivalence of prestation and reward in partnership. Nor is this surprising since, except in the case of a disguised gift, partners would only make such arrangements when it seemed that the contribution of the favoured party justified it.

---

18 For the importance of legal tradition for legal growth see generally A. Watson, *The Making of the Civil Law* (Cambridge, Mass., Harvard University Press, 1981): for the " block effect " of Roman law see Chap. 2.

23

Illogicality and Roman Law

It is a commonplace that Rome's greatest contribution to the modern world is its law. Whether this is strictly true or not, Roman law is certainly the basis of the law of Western Europe (with the exception of England and Scandinavia), of much of Africa including South Africa, Ethiopia and in general the former colonies of countries in continental Europe, of Quebec and Louisiana, of Japan and Ceylon and so on. Perhaps even more important for the future is that International law is very largely modelled, by analogy, on Roman law. Just think of the perfectly serious arguments of a few years ago as to whether outer space (including the moon and planets) were *res nullius* or *res communes* and whether they were, or were not, susceptible of acquisition by *occupatio*. This persistence of Roman law has had undesirable consequences. First, Roman law as an academic subject has got into the hands of lawyers whose love of technicalities has frightened off classical scholars who tend not to use the legal sources. Secondly, scholars of antiquity, since Roman law is left well alone, have also been reluctant to look at other ancient legal systems.[1] So have lawyers since these other systems have no 'practical' value. Thirdly, following upon these but worse still, the usefulness of Roman law for later ages, coupled with its enforced isolation from other systems of antiquity, has often led to an exaggerated respect for it, and to its being regarded as well-nigh perfect, immutable, fit for all people. Many in "the Age of Reason" were ready to regard Roman law as "the Law of Reason".

Thus, Roman law is divorced from its context. Of course, in its natural setting it was not like that at all: it was not perfect, unchangeable or abstract reasoning. Bad rules, weak reasons, illogical arguments abound. Let me cite here only one extreme instance of a bad reason. The jurists Labeo and Paul agree that a slave who lacks a tooth and is sold without the defect being

The following abbreviations are used: C = *Codex Justiniani;* D = *Digesta Justiniani;* G = *Gai Institutiones;* J = *Justiniani Institutiones.*

[1] Nonetheless in number of publications non-lawyers have contributed proportionally more—and perhaps even absolutely more—to the study of Greek and Near Eastern legal systems than to Roman law. It should also, in fairness to Roman lawyers, be said that Near Eastern law is more immediately comprehensible to the non-lawyer.

disclosed cannot be returned to the seller as *morbosus* under the Aedilician Edict. They both give as a reason that many people lack teeth, that babies are born without teeth and yet they are not regarded as *minus sani* until teeth appear.[2] But as W.W. Buckland pointed out long ago, the argument is absurd for it is equally true that babies are unable to walk.[3]

But I do not want to discuss here weakness of reasoning by individuals. Rather I want to look at satisfactory legal developments acceptable to all or nearly all jurists where logic or strict reasoning is set to one side, where the jurists show that they are not philosophers of an eternal pure reason but hard-headed lawyers dealing with actual situations in a real world where the result is of greater importance than the way it is obtained. Developments, that is, which illustrate the famous dictum of Oliver Wendell Holmes: "The life of the law has not been logic: it has been experience".[4] The instances I will speak of are all cases where, so far as the surviving evidence goes, there was no dispute; where, so to say, there was such an overwhelming desire to achieve the end result that the illogicality was either not noticed or at least not stressed.

The first instance concerns the revocation of the kind of will known as *testamentum per aes et libram* which was the standard will throughout the classical period. This will was an adaptation of *mancipatio,* the formal mode of transfer of those things known as *res mancipi,* and as a *mancipatio* it required a transferee, five witnesses and a person known as the *libripens,* who held a bronze scale. The transferee in this case was called the *familiae emptor* and he had to declare:

> I declare that your property is subject to your command and under my control and, so that you can lawfully make a will in accordance with the public statute, let it have been bought to me with this bronze and brazen scale.[5]

He then struck the scale with a bronze piece which he gave to the testator as the symbolic price.[6] Next the testator holding the tablets on which the will was written[7] made a formal declaration called *nuncupatio* confirming the will's provisions.[8] Originally the *familiae emptor* would be in the position of heir[9], and since *mancipatio* was an immediate transfer of ownership he would become owner of the testator's property at the time of the ceremony. But now,

[2] Aulus Gellius, *Noctes Atticae* 4.2.12; D. 21.1.11.

[3] "Interpolations in the Digest" (1924) 33 Yale L.J. 343 at 347.

[4] *The Common Law* (Boston, 1881) 1.

[5] *Familiam pecuniamque tuam endo mandatela tua custodelaque mea esse aio, eaque, quo tu iure testamentum facere possis secundum legem publicam, hoc aere aeneaque libra esto mihi empta.*

[6] G. 2.104.

[7] If the will was reduced to writing, which it need not be.

[8] G. 2.104.

[9] Later he became a mere figurehead: G. 2.103.

the testator might subsequently change his mind and want to revoke the will. How could this be done? The position at civil law in the early Empire, when the picture first becomes clear[10], is that intention to revoke was not enough. Nor was it sufficient to destroy the *tabulae* of the will, even with the intention of revocation.[11] The old will was revoked only when the testator made a new and valid will by a new *mancipatio* and *nuncupatio*.[12] Destruction of the *tabulae*, it is thought by modern scholars,[13] was not enough because the will's validity derived from the *mancipatio* and the *nuncupatio*, not from the continuing existence of the *tabulae*. This opinion is, I think, correct. Logically, though, we might have expected something else. By the *mancipatio*, the testator ceased to be owner of his property. Hence, for a new will, the co-operation of the *familiae emptor* should have been required. He should have remancipated the estate to the testator for only then would the latter be owner and so capable of disposing of it once again. But this was awkward and inconvenient and not at all helpful, and the jurists did not demand so much.[14] The surviving sources record no dispute among the jurists on the requirements for revocation, and the illogicality is not pointed out.[15]

A second example involves the forms of manumission of slaves and the rights of patrons in the Republic. A slave might be freed by his master in three ways: by will, by *manumissio vindicta*, by enrolment on the census. We are concerned only with the last two.

Manumissio vindicta[16] was an adaptation of the *vindicatio in libertatem*, the procedure by which anyone could bring an action to secure the release of a free man who was wrongly held as a slave. A master who wanted to free a slave would appear before a magistrate who had *imperium*, and a friend would claim that the slave was free. The master put up no defence and the magistrate declared the slave free. In *manumissio censu*, the owner ordered the slave to inscribe himself on the censor's list of citizens. Whether the slave then became free and a citizen at once, or only when the list was issued is

10 Though Suetonius, *Divus Iulius*, 83, shows that already in the late Republic a validly made will could somehow be revoked.

11 G. 2.151.

12 G. 2.144.

13 E.g., M. Kaser, *Das römische Privatrecht* I (Munich, 1955) 578; P. Voci, *Diritto ereditario romano*, ii (Milan, 1963) 492f.

14 Possibly they did once, but if so there is no trace in the sources. The possibility does not affect the point being made.

15 It is likely that this procedure for revocation was accepted at an early date. Other theoretical problems connected with the *familiae emptor* being regarded as owner—e.g., there was no action against him if he failed to carry out the testator's instructions; and what if he died before the testator?—do not appear as practical difficulties and hence it is likely that almost from the start the *testamentum per aes et libram* was regarded as a true will.

16 See in general W. W. Buckland, *A Textbook of Roman Law*, revised by P. Stein (Cambridge, 3rd ed., 1963) 441 ff.

not clear[17] but does not concern us. What does matter is that in neither of these modes of manumission does it appear as if a slave was freed by his master. In one it seems as if the true status of a citizen wrongly held as a slave is recognized, and in the other there is no indication that the person enrolled as a citizen was ever anything else.

A master who freed a slave became the new freedman's *patronus* and as such had extensive rights.[18] The freedman owed him *obsequium* and *operae* (a number of days' labour) and, perhaps most important of all, on the freedman's death the patron might have extensive rights of succession. A master whose slave was freed *vindicta or censu* had full rights of patronage. So far as we can tell it was never even suggested that the master had not in fact freed the slave. Again the jurists reach the sensible result without apparently worrying about any illogicality. The use of a device such as *manumissio vindicta* or *manumissio censu* was essential since there was otherwise no way in which a slave could be freed during his master's lifetime.

The third instance relates to drunkenness and intention.[19] As in other systems, so in Roman law, intention was of fundamental importance in many situations. Thus, for the commission of theft there had to be an intention to steal;[20] there could be no marriage without the requisite intention of the interested parties;[21] and in the consensual contracts of sale, hire, partnership and mandate the contract was formed as soon as agreement was reached and any absence of agreement barred the existence of the contract.[22] As everyone will readily agree, extreme intoxication is able to stop the formation of intention or any agreement. British courts can provide many examples.[23] Drunkenness is common now and, to judge from literary evidence, was common in Roman times (despite the ignorance of spirits), but nowhere in the Roman sources are we told of the effects of drunkenness on intention; not for theft, not for marriage, not for contract. The text which comes nearest is D. 48.19.11.2,

17 See now A. Watson, *The Law of Persons in the Later Roman Republic* (Oxford, 1967) 185 ff.

18 See, *ibid.*, 226 ff.

19 For what follows see A. Watson, "Drunkenness in Roman Law" **Studies in Roman Private Law (London, 1991), chapter 19, pp. 243ff.**

20 *Cf.* e.g., G. 3.197; D. 47.2.23. The precise nature of the *animus furandi* and the extent of corruption in the sources do not really concern us. But see most recently J.A.C. Thomas, "Animus furandi" (1968) 19 *Iura* 1; A Watson, *Roman Private Law Around 200 B.C.* (Edinburgh, 1971) 147.

21 *Cf.* e.g., D. 23.2.2; 23.2.16.2; P. Corbett, *The Roman Law of Marriage* (Oxford, 1930), 53ff; A. Watson, *Persons,* 41ff.

22 Thus, in sale it is especially clear that error which was sufficiently grave stopped the contract coming into existence: e.g., D. 18.1.9; *ibid.*, 11; *ibid.*, 14.

23 Thus in England, *Ruse* v. *Read* [1949] 1 K.B; 377; [1949] 1 All E.R. 398 (incapacity to form intention to steal bicycle); in Scotland, *Johnston* v. *Brown* (1823) 2. S. 437 (incapacity during 3 whole days to form intention to marry).

which tells us that an injury might be caused *aut proposito aut impetu aut casu* and to illustrate injury *impetu* (on the spur of the moment), as *cum per ebrietatem ad manus aut ad ferrum venitur* (when through drunkenness it comes to [the use of] hands or iron). Strangely enough there is in general a great scarcity of Roman legal texts on conduct influenced by alcohol or on habitual or heavy drinking—only seven in all, including that just mentioned.[24] The absence of any discussion of the effect of alcohol on intention surely cannot be explained by saying that the problem did not arise in practice, and that the jurists did not think of it as a theoretical possibility. Nor because it was simply assumed that a person always intended what he did—the inability of an infant or lunatic to form an intention is continually stressed.[25] The earliest case known to me of drunkenness so extreme as to exclude intention or knowledge goes back far beyond Roman times to the story of Lot and his daughters in Genesis. Thus, 19.33: "And they made their father drink wine that night: and the firstborn went in, and lay with her father; and he perceived not when she lay down, nor when she arose". We can argue from the silence of the Roman sources that intoxication—almost always a self-induced state—was not considered legally relevant and hence did not bar agreement. Presumably it was a man's own fault if he got drunk and did something foolish.[26] The result might well be considered reasonable, but if the situation was as I have suggested then an obvious illogicality is involved. The aspect of greatest interest is, of course, the silence of the sources. I suspect but cannot prove that the jurists, satisfied with what seemed to be the legal position, were unwilling to reduce the proposition to writing lest that very fact invite contradiction.

The next example I wish to give also concerns intention. In developed classical law a person acquired possession of a thing only if he had the requisite degree of physical control over it and the right kind of intention to hold on to it. In the late Republic, apparently, requirements were not so strict.[27] This increased stress on *animus* in the Empire caused problems, for instance in the acquisition of possession by infants. Thus:

> An infant can rightly possess if he begins with his tutor's authority, for the infant's judgment is made good by the tutor's authority. This has been accepted on the ground of utility for otherwise an infant's acquiring possession is nonsense. A pupil, however, can acquire possession even

24 The others are, Aulus Gellius, *Noctes Atticae,* 4.14; D. 48.3.12pr; 24.1.4.2; *ibid.,* 25.6 *(idem);* 49.16.6.7 *Codex Theodosianus* 3.16.1.

25 *Cf.* e.g., D. 9.2.5.2.; J. 1.10 pr; D. 41.2.32.2; 50.17.5.

26 Just at we are told in sale, D. 18.1.15.1: *Ignorantia emptori prodest, quae non in supinum hominem cadit* (Only such ignorance as does not betray negligence will avail a buyer).

27 *Cf.* A. Watson, *The Law of Property in the Later Roman Republic* (Oxford, 1968) 81ff.

> without his tutor's authority. Likewise an infant can possess through a slave in respect of the *peculium*.[28]

An *infans,* we are told, can possess *auctoritate tutoris.* There are two extreme oddities in this. In the first place, we know that *auctoritas tutoris* was needed when the transaction might make the position of the pupil worse but not otherwise.[29] Now although possession did have legal consequences it would be very difficult to think of a situation—I can think of none—where *possessio,* as opposed to mere physical control, could have harmful consequences for the possessor. Almost always *possessio* brings advantages. Hence *auctoritas tutoris* should be irrelevant. In the second place, the function of *auctoritas tutoris* in other cases is not to supply an intention which is totally lacking in the pupil, but to add mature judgment to the pupil's intention. In other words it operates only when the pupil has capacity, that is, when he is *infantia maior.*[30] Hence, *auctoritas tutoris* for an *infans* seems inappropriate. The requirement of *tutoris auctoritas* here is an anomalous innovation to overcome the infant's new incapacity to acquire possession.[31] This time, though, Paul recognizes the illogicality of the decision which he says is *utilitatis causa receptum.* The argument from *utilitas* is often used when the jurists reach a solution which is dogmatically indefensible.[32]

A slave was not a legal person, and so his capacity to contract was purely derivative. W. W. Buckland says:[33] "As a slave derives his capacity from his master, it might be supposed that he could not have more than the master had. But this would have involved inconvenience, and it is clear that for a master incapable of contracting from mental or physical defect, the slave could stipulate. The rule seems illogical, but its illogicality is concealed by the fact that a slave's stipulation, as we have seen, did not require the consent or knowledge of the master." But one case seems even more illogical than the others. A slave could be a partner. The main text is D.17.2.58.3 (Ulpian 31 *ad ed.*).[34]

28 D. 41.2.32.2 (Paul 15 *ad Sab.*) *Infans possidere recte potest, si tutore auctore coepit, nam judicium infantis suppletur auctoritate tutoris: utilitatis enim causa hoc receptum est, nam alioquin nullus sensus est infantis accipiendi possessionem, pupillus tamen etiam sine tutoris auctoritate possessionem nancisci potest, item infans peculiari nomine per servum possidere potest.* On the text and for questions of interpolation see A. Watson, "Acquisition of Possession and Usucaption *per servos et filios* (1962) 78 L.Q.R. 205 at 223 ff.

29 G. 2.80–84.

30 *Cf.* e.g., W.W. Buckland, *Textbook,* 157 ff; M. Kaser, *Privatrecht* i, p. 306.

31 That in the Republic it was held an infant could acquire possession without his tutor's authority appears from D. 41.2.1.3: *cf.* A. Watson, *Property,* 82f.

32 *Cf.* J.A. Ankum, *"Utilitatis causa receptum", Symbolae* M. David (Leiden, 1968), 1 ff. D. 41.2.32.2 is discussed at 10 ff.

33 *The Roman Law of Slavery* (Cambridge, 1908) 155.

34 The others are D. 17.2.18; *ibid.,* 63.2.

> If my slave contracted a partnership with Titius and continued in it when he had been alienated, it can be said that by the alienation of the slave the first partnership was ended and also that a second was begun afresh; and likewise that an *actio pro socio* is available both to me and to the buyer; and similarly that an action can be given both against me and against the buyer on account of matters before the alienation, on other matters only against the buyer.[35]

Neither the text itself nor the fact that slaves could be *socii* (partners) has aroused much interest.[36] The language of the text (and of the others) shows that it is the slave who enters the *societas,* not his master. But more than that, in the present text the situation makes it plain that it is the slave and not the master who is the *socius.* Otherwise the alienation of the slave would not have brought the partnership to an end so far as the former master was concerned.[37] But how on earth can a slave who has no legal personality be a partner? There is no logical answer and we can say only that it was obviously convenient for the master that his slave could enter into partnership arrangements.[38] Convenience triumphed.

There are at least two illogicalities in stipulations *post mortem.* A contract of *stipulatio* to be performed after the death of one of the parties was void because, says Gaius,[39] "it was regarded as inelegant for an obligation to begin from the heir". Thus *post mortem meam dari spondes?* (Do you promise that after my death be given) and *post mortem tuam dari spondes?* (Do you promise that after your death be given) did not give rise to a valid contract, nor naturally did *Heredi meo dari spondes?* (Do you promise that to my heir be given). Neither did *Pridie quam moriar dari spondes?* (Do you promise that the day before I die be given) nor *Pridie quam morieris dari spondes?* (Do you promise that the day before you die be given) because, we are told, the day before the death cannot be told until after the death has occurred. All this so far is straightforward enough. But Gaius tells us that

35 *Si servus meus societatem cum Titio coierit et alienatus in eadem permanserit, potest dici alienatione servi et priorem societatem finitam et ex integro alteram inchoatam, atque ideo et mihi et emptori actionem pro socio competere, item tam adversus me quam adversus emptorem ex his causis quae ante alienationem inciderunt dandum actionem, ex reliquis adversus emptorem solum.*

36 See G. v. Beseler (1925) 45 *Zeitschrift der Savigny-Stiftung für Rechtsgeschichte, Romanistische Abteilung* 466; S. Solazzi (1955) 21 *Studia et Documenta Historiae et Iuris,* 306 ff. Interpolations suggested by these two authors do not affect us, and we need not consider them.

37 Even if the master was the *socius,* D. 17.2.58pr would be a totally different kind of case, and irrelevant.

38 It should perhaps be stressed again that the illogicality here is greater than in, say, sale where a slave seller could be regarded as a representative for his master, and the sale to be the master's.

39 G. 3.100.

Cum moriar dari spondes? (Do you promise that when I die be given) and *Cum morieris dari spondes?* (Do you promise that when you die be given) were valid forms and the obligation was considered to begin at the last moment of life.[40] Now no sophisticated theory of formalism will explain why this case is treated differently from the others, nor is any satisfaction to be obtained by regarding *nam inelegans esse visum est ab heredis persona incipere obligationem* (for it appeared unreasonable that an obligation should start from the heir) in G. 3.100 as interpolated.[41] The explanation, let it be said at once, has no theoretical justification, nor does Gaius give one. The easiest solution is that stipulations *post mortem* were void,[42] the rule had obvious practical disadvantages but had been in existence so long that the effect of the usual forms could not be altered. The rather absurd form *Pridie quam moriar dari spondes?* has, indeed, all the appearance of an (unsuccessful) attempt to get round the invalidity. At some stage, when the jurists were more receptive to allowing the validity of such a stipulation, a fresh attempt was made with a new formulation, *Cum moriar dari spondes?* and it worked.

A similar explanation holds true for the second illogicality in stipulation *post mortem*. An *adstipulatio* was an accessory stipulation when the *adstipulator* asked the promisor, after the first *stipulatio,* if he promised to give him the same thing. Performance by the promisor of either the *stipulatio* or the *adstipulatio* extinguished both obligations.[43] Gaius tells us that generally we use *adstipulatio* only when we are stipulating for something to be given to us after our death.[44] The stipulation itself being *post mortem creditoris* is void,[45] but the *adstipulatio,* being only *post mortem* of an outsider to the contract is valid. It is thus another device to make enforceable a *stipulatio post mortem.* But despite this apparent reasonableness Zimmern pointed out long ago[46] a theoretical, dogmatical difficulty. The *adstipulatio* is an accessory to, and dependent upon, the *stipulatio.* The *stipulatio* is void, hence so should be the *adstipulatio.*

A fascinating branch of Roman law is that known as *postliminium.*[47] This

40 G. 3.100. The literature on the text is enormous.

41 *Cf.* e.g., recently, S. Solazzi, "Sull' obbligazione a termine iniziale" (1950) 1 *Iura* 34 at 52, and the authors he cites; *contra,* e.g., J. Van Oven, "Gaius 3. 158: *mandatum post mortem mandantis*" (1956) 48 *Eos* 528, S. Di Paola, *Contributi ad una teoria della invalidità e della inefficacia in diritto romano* (Milan, 1966) p. 21 n. 46.

42 No need here to explain why.

43 *Cf.* G. 3.110–114.

44 G. 3.117.

45 G. 3.117.

46 *Archiv für die civilistische Praxis iv* (1821), 240; see more recently, V. Arangio-Ruiz, *Il mandato in diritto romano* (Naples, 1949), 148; A. Watson, *Contract of Mandate in Roman Law* (Oxford, 1961) 136.

47 On *postliminium* in general see L. Amirante, *Captivitas e postliminium* (Naples, 1950).

was, basically but by no means exclusively, the right by which a Roman who had lost his citizenship, e.g., by being captured by the enemy, regained his citizenship and recovered various private rights when he returned within Roman territory as a free man. Technically, one would expect that *capitis deminutio maxima,* i.e., by losing his citizenship and freedom, the captive would lose all his personal rights, and that these rights would not revive simply because he returned to Rome. This was, indeed, the case with those persons not entitled to *postliminium.*[48] The curious thing about *postliminium,* though, it that in classical law its effect was different on different rights. This appears most clearly in family law which is all we need look at for our purposes. Marriage was ended by capture and did not revive by *postliminium.*[49] To this there were two exceptions; first, if both spouses were captured and returned together;[50] secondly, in the opinion of some, notably Julian, where a *patronus* was captured who had married his freedwoman.[51]

When a *tutor legitimus* or *testamentarius* was captured the *tutela* (guardianship) ended but was restored, though not retroactively, if he returned.[52] *Patria potestas* was suspended by captivity and if the captive returned with *postliminium* it was as if he had never been a prisoner.[53] No amount of ingenious hair-splitting argument will make this a logical system. The explanation really is that in each branch of family law the jurists accepted the rule which would give the most satisfactory practical result. Thus, marriage was completely ended, so that if the captive's ex-wife married someone else, the status of that union and any children born to her was not in doubt. (It should be remembered that divorce was simple and without formality and hence a new marriage between the former captive and his ex-wife would be an easy possibility). For the well-being of the pupil it was essential that a tutor be there to help him, hence captivity ended the tutelage and a fresh tutor could be appointed. But since the *tutor legitimus* was his nearest agnate and the *tutor testamentarius* the person considered by the deceased *pater* to be most suitable as *tutor,* it was appropriate that their *tutela* be re-established by the tutor's return. The protection of the captive's property rights made it important that his sons were not regarded as having been free from *patria potestas* even during his absence.[54]

48 *Cf.* e.g., D. 49.15.12pr; *ibid.,* 17; 49.16.5.6.

49 *Cf.* e.g., D. 24.2.1; 49.15.12.4; *ibid.,* 14.1.

50 C. 8.50(51).1; D. 49.15.25.

51 D. 23.2.45.6. For these exceptions see above all A. Watson "*Captivitas* and *matrimonium*", *Studies in Roman Private Law* (London, 1991), chapter 4, pp. 47ff.

52 G. 3.187; D. 27.3.7.1; 27.3.8; 46.6.4.5; 26.4.3; 26.1.15; *cf.* L. Amirante, *Captivitas,* 60 ff.

53 G. 1.129; *Gai Epitome* 1.6.2; *Pauli Sententiae* 2.25.1; D. 14.6.1.1; 37.9.1.8; 38.6.15; 49.15.12.1; 49.15.22.2; *cf.* L. Amirante, *Captivitas,* 51 ff.

54 Of course, in each branch of family law particular problems could arise no matter what rule was adopted.

My last example has been chosen to leave you with a problem. The famous *lex Aquilia* of 287 B.C. regulated the law of damage to property. Its first chapter read, and was regarded by the classical jurists as reading:

> Whoever will have wrongfully killed another's male or female slave or fourfooted herd animal, whatever was the victim's highest value in that year, so much bronze let him be condemned to pay the owner.[55]

At first *occiderit,* (killed) was interpreted reasonably, but later a distinction grew up between *occidere* (to kill) and *mortis causam praestare,* (to furnish a cause of death).[56] Only the former was within the scope of the *lex Aquilia.* The line between *occidere* and *mortis causam praestare* was not always drawn in the same place but classical jurists held it was not killing to give a man poison instead of medicine,[57] or a drug to a woman which she drinks herself and from which she died,[58] to starve a slave to death,[59] to throw a slave from a bridge or river bank into the water and cause him to drown.[60] On the other hand, earlier the Republican jurist Alfenus (or his master Servius) had held that when two carts were going up the Capitoline hill, one behind the other, and the first began to slip back and the men holding it up got out of its way of their accord, and it hit the second cart which moved backwards and ran over a slave boy, the boy's owner could sue the men under the *lex Aquilia.*[61]

This classical restriction of the meaning of *occidere* is illogical and even absurd for two reasons. First the word does not usually have such a narrow meaning, and nothing in the phrasing of the *lex* necessitated or even suggested the restriction. Secondly, the jurists did not take *occidere* so narrowly in other contexts. Thus, the *lex Cornelia de sicariis et veneficiis,* the statute of 81 B.C. on murder, also used the word *occiderit,*[62] but nowhere in the surviving sources is there the slightest sign that a distinction was drawn there between *occidere* and *mortis causam praestare* or that *occidere* was interpreted narrowly.

When killing was treated merely as furnishing a cause of death, no action on the *lex Aquilia* was allowed but an *ad hoc* remedy, *actio utilis* or *actio in*

55 ***Ut qui servum servamve alienum alienamve quadrupedemve pecudem iniuria occiderit, quanti id in eo anno plurimi fuit, tantum aes dare domino damnas esto.*** D. 9.2.2pr (Gaius *7 ad ed. prov.*).

56 Apparently formulated (D. 9.2.7.6.) by Celsus (Consul for the second time in 129 A. D.); but it existed at least since Labeo, in the very early Principate (see D. 9.2.9pr).

57 D. 9.2.7.6.

58 D. 9.2.9pr.

59 D. 9.2.9.2.

60 G. 3.219.

61 D. 9.2.52.2.

62 *Collatio* 1.3; 1.3; *cf.* D. 48.8.1pr.

factum, was provided by the praetor. The problem is to know why the jurists drew the distinction. Obviously their purpose was to restrict the field of application of the statute while yet allowing the injured owner a remedy. I can offer no satisfactory explanation of their practical motivation.

It is not necessary to linger over the conclusions. I have tried to show by means of a few examples that, at least sometimes, the Roman jurists were more concerned to reach a sensible practical result than to follow the dictates of a rigorous logic, that they were not ivory-tower philosophers but sensible men dealing with contemporary problems of living. Though it may be felt that this diminishes the claims of Roman law to be a system of universal unchanging validity, it must make us accept the Roman jurists as individual human beings. And we must give credit to their sophistication.

24

Morality, Slavery and the Jurists in the Later Roman Republic

The problem I wish to discuss is the moral attitude of the later Republican jurists to slavery. The prominent jurists of the time belonged to the upper classes and, although it would be wrong to generalize from the jurists to other members of the aristocracy, we shall have a certain glimpse into the social attitudes of the period if we can gain a reasonably clear picture from the jurists. I will deal only with juristic discussion, and not with the statutes and edicts which concern slavery. No doubt the jurists would play a part in shaping these, but public political acts are less instructive for the outlook of the jurists than their legal opinions which would not be subject to the same publicity.[1] And for the purposes of this article I will say nothing about the factors which influenced the attitude of the jurists.

To begin with a very obvious point, we must not expect to find the jurists questioning the moral propriety of the institution of slavery. They were too involved in the mental attitudes of their times to speculate on that abstraction. All we can hope for is that, from their discussions of legal problems concerning slavery, certain moral perspectives will become apparent. In order to judge these discussions we must set the scene. How free were the jurists in their interpretation of the law? Were they bound to interpret provisions in laws, edicts, wills and so on in a strict way? How far could they influence the development of the law in a way which might seem contrary to logic but was consonant with their ideas of good sense? The answer to these questions is that their freedom to interpret, their power to develop, was very great indeed. A few instances will make this plain. There was an *interdictum quod vi aut clam*. This ran: "You should restore to its previous condition whatever has been done by force or by stealth and which is the subject of the present dispute, if it is not more than a year since

---

1 There seem, in any event, to be no relevant statutes. Only two edicts, so far as I am aware, throw any light on moral attitudes in regard to slaves and slavery. One of these, the edict on *operae* introduced by Rutilius, was sympathetic, the other, *de bonis libertorum*, was not: *cf.* A. Watson, The Law of Persons in the Later Roman Republic 229-36 (1967). The edict which granted an *actio iniuriarum* to a master whose slave was beaten *adversus bonos mores* or tortured without the master's authority may or may not be recognizing the humanity of the slave. The injury or insult may be to the owner.

the power of objection arose."[2] "By force or by stealth," *vi aut clam,* was the object of interpretation. Quintus Mucius Scaevola, who was consul in 95 B.C.,[3] said that something was done *vi,* by force when a person did it who had been told not to.[4] This obviously covers situations where by no stretch of the imagination can one reasonably say that force has been used. But Scaevola wishes the interdict to have a wide scope and so *vi,* by force, is deliberately given an unnatural meaning. It would be hard to imagine a case of wider interpretation. But in fact the jurist Servius Sulpicius Rufus, consul in 51 B.C.,[5] gives an even more extreme interpretation of *clam,* by stealth. *Clam* involves deliberate secrecy. But Servius held that a person acts *clam* when he does not inform someone whom he ought to think will object to what he is doing[6] "lest," says the text, "the position of fools be better than that of wise men." So Servius is prepared to change the basis of liability under the interdict. The interdict apparently envisaged only deliberate wrongful conduct, but Servius will have it given even for negligence. Another instance of extremely wide interpretation can be found in connection with the *actio aquae pluviae arcendae.* This gave a remedy to a person whose land was injured by work done on neighboring land which diverted rain water on to his property. It is hardly surprising that Quintus Mucius held that rain water meant any water which was increased by rain.[7] But Trebatius—young friend and protégé of Cicero, legal adviser of Julius Caesar and Augustus[8]—holds that the action will lie where the damage is caused by hot springs. The classical jurist Ulpian disagrees with him "for," he says reasonably, "hot springs are not rain water."[9]

---

[2] *"Quod vi aut clam factum est, qua de re agitur, id, si non plus quam annus est cum experiendi potestas est, restituas:" cf.* O. Lenel, Das Edictum perpetuum 482 (3d ed. 1927).

[3] *Cf., e.g.,* W. Kunkel, Herkunft und soziale Stellung der römischen Juristen 18 (1952).

[4] D.50.17.73.2 (Quintus Mucius *lib. sing. horon*). *"Vi factum id videtur esse, qua de re quis cum prohibitur, fecit . . . ."* Stein suggests that the definition derives from Scaevola's observation of the various cases in which the praetor granted the interdict. P. Stein, Regulae iuris 37 (1966).

[5] *Cf.* W. Kunkel, *supra* note 3, at 25.

[6] D.43.24.4 (Venuleius *2 interd.*) *"Servius etiam eum clam facere, qui existimare debeat sibi controversiam futuram, quia non opinionem cuius* [*cui*-Mommsen] *et resupinam existimationem esse oporteat, ne melioris condicionis sint stulti quam periti."* The first part of the text, as far as *futuram,* never seems to have been held interpolated. See further on the text my forthcoming, The Law of Property in the Later Roman Republic, chapter 10.

[7] Cicero, *top.*9.38.

[8] *Cf.* W. Kunkel, *supra* note 3, at 28.

[9] D.39.3.3.1 (Ulpian *53 ad ed.*). *"Idem Trebatius putat eum, cui aquae fluentes calidae noceant, aquae pluviae arcendae cum vicino agere posse: quod verum non est: neque enim aquae calidae aquae pluviae sunt."* It is possible that Trebatius is thinking of artificially heated water. On the text see my forthcoming, The Law of Property in the Later Roman Republic, chapter 7.

Thus, the jurists of the later Republic had great freedom of interpretation. They were free even to interpret literally if they wanted. For instance, the edict *Ne quis in suggrunda*[10] gave an action against one who suspended an object from eaves or a projecting roof, where the fall of the object might cause damage. The jurist Servius refused to give this action where a painter—no doubt in the hope of making a sale—hung a painting or a shield on a booth and it fell and injured someone "because the painting was placed neither on the eaves nor on a projecting roof."[11] But he did give an *actio ad exemplum huius actionis*, an action created on analogy with the action in question.

The first problem we shall examine in slavery concerns the usufruct of a slave-girl. If there was a usufruct, the usufructuary was entitled to use the object and he became the owner of any fruits, *fructus*. Cicero, *de fin.*1.4.12, tells us of a dispute between the leaders of the state:

> There was a discussion among the leaders of the state, Publius Scaevola and Manius Manilius whether a child should be included among the fruits. Marcus Brutus disagreed with them.[12]

Of these three prominent jurists, Publius Scaevola was consul in 133 B.C.;[13] Manius Manilius was consul in 149 B.C.;[14] and Marcus Brutus was praetor in 142 B.C.[15] Why should there be any doubt on this point of law? It seems difficult to find a logical reason for holding that the child was not *fructus*. A reason is given by a Digest text of Ulpian, D.7.1.68pr:

> There was an old question whether a child belonged to the usufructuary. But the opinion of Brutus prevailed, that the usufructuary had no right to the child: for a human being cannot be included in the fruits of a human being. On this

---

10 *Ne quis in suggrunda protectove supra eum locum, quo vulgo iter fiet inve quo consistetur, id positum habeat, cuius casus nocere cui possit. Qui adversus ea fecerit, in eum sestertiorum decem milium nummorum in factum iudicium dabo. Si Servus insciente domino fecisse dicetur,* [*aut noxae dedi iubebo*].
Cf. O. Lenel, *supra* note 2, at 174.

11 D.9.3.5.12 (Ulpian *23 ad ed.*) . . . *nam et cum pictor in pergula clipeum vel tabulam expositam habuisset eaque excidisset et transeunti damni quid dedisset, Servius respondit ad exemplum huius actionis dari oportere actionem: hanc enim non competere palam esse, quia neque in suggrunda neque in protecto tabula fuerat posita.*
On the text see now, A. Watson, The Law of Obligations in the Later Roman Republic 268-70 (1965).

12 *An partus sitne in fructu habendus, disseretur inter principes civitatis, P. Scaevolam, M'que Manilium ab iisque M. Brutus dissentiet. . . .*

13 W. Kunkel, *supra* note 3, at 12.

14 *Id.* at 11.

15 *Id.* at 12.

> account, the usufructuary will not have even a usufruct in him. . . .[16]

It is not clear from the Latin whether the reason given in the text for the decision is to be attributed to Ulpian or to Brutus.[17] Some light may be shed on the meaning of "for a human being cannot be included in the fruits of a human being" by a text of the jurist Gaius,[18] D.22.1.28.1.:

> But the child of a slave-woman is not included in fruits and so it belongs to the owner of the property: for it seemed absurd to include human beings among fruits since nature procured the fruits of all things for the sake of human beings.

"For it *seemed* absurd &c," *absurdum enim videbatur*, shows that Gaius thinks that this was the original reason for the decision. Indeed, I suggest, the reason for the rule would have to be along such philosophical lines. Otherwise it is difficult to imagine how the Republican jurists could ever have reached the decision—which seems contrary to principle—that a child was not among the fruits of a slave-woman.[19] We must accept, I think, that it was on the basis

---

16 (Ulpian *17 ad Sab.*). *Vetus fuit quaestio, an partus ad fructuarium pertineret: sed Bruti sententia obtinuit* [ius—*insert*, Mommsen] *fructuarium in eo locum non habere: neque enim in fructu hominis homo esse potest. hac ratione nec usum fructum in eo fructuarius habebit. quid tamen si fuerit etiam partus usus fructus relictus, an habeat in eo usum fructum? et cum possit partus legari, poterit et usus fructus eius.*

17 It is in the indicative but Ulpian frequently repeats arguments with which he agrees in the indicative. *Cf. e.g.*, Magdelain, Les actions civiles 9 (1954).

18 (2 rer. cott.). "*Partus vero ancillae in fructu non est itaque ad dominum proprietatis pertinet: absurdum enim videbatur hominem in fructu esse, cum omes fructus rerum natura hominum gratia comparaverit.*"

19 For a view of Kaser on the concept of fruits behind the reason, *see* "*Partus ancillae*," ZSS lxxv (1958) at 156-57. *But see* my forthcoming, The Law of Property in the Later Roman Republic, chapter 9.

A different explanation of the final decision reached, also based on the idea of a Roman concept of fruits, could be brought forward on account of D.5.3.27 pr. (Ulpian *15 ad ed.*), "*Ancillarum etiam partus et partuum partus quamquam fructus esse non existimantur, quia non temere ancillae eius rei causa comparantur ut pariant, augent tamen hereditatem: . . . .*" In this it is said that offspring of slave-girls are not fruit because slave-girls are not lightly bought for the purpose of producing young. Hence, it might be argued that only those new creations are fruit for whose production the bearer is typically kept (*cf., e.g.*, Kaser, *supra*); or even that only those new creations are fruit whose production can be counted upon as a normal and standard recurring event. But I think it is unlikely that such a concept of fruit (in whichever form it is expressed) explains the attitude of the Republican jurists to the question of *partus ancillae*. First, the only expression of any idea of this sort is in this text and there is no indication that it is older than Ulpian, or was shared by anyone. Secondly, there is some evidence that the Romans thought that in early times at least the birth of a baby to a slave-girl was an annual, standard event: thus, Festus says that *vernae* are those born in the spring from the slave-girls of Roman citizens because that time of year is the most natural for birth—"*vernae appellantur ex ancillis civium Romanorum* of the noble idea that a human being could not be treated as fruit for the benefit of other humans that this decision was reached. But before we give the jurists credit for their idealism, three points must be made. First, the decision is isolated and, considering the total acceptance of the social fact of slavery, moral concern on this point looks a trifle artificial. After all, masters legally had complete power of life and death over their slaves.[20] Secondly, the child born to the slave, it is held, is not fruit—but this does not mean that the child is free. It means only that it belongs to the mother's owner and not to the usufructuary. There is a certain emptiness in the application of the philosophical principle. Thirdly, and this is the most important point of all, the natural result of the decision is the immediate separation of the mother and child. The mother is under the control of the usufructuary. The child does not belong to the usufructuary who does not even have a usufruct in him. The child does not form part of the usufruct and hence the usufructuary, as such, has no liability for him. He would seem to have no legal responsibility to look after the child in terms of the guarantee normally given by the usufructuary to the owner at the beginning of the usufruct. The usufructuary, moreover, has no legal right to retain custody of the child. The person with the legal right of custody is the owner. So, looked at in legal terms, the result is that the mother stays with the usufructuary, the child goes to the owner. The consequences of the decision can fairly be said to be appalling. Of course, we cannot tell how frequently in practice the usufructuary might nonetheless keep the child in his household at his expense. But it must often or even usually have been the case that the child would be sent back to its owner. Apart from the

---

vere nati, quod tempus anni maxime naturalis feturae est;" and elsewhere, "*vernae, qui in villis vere nati, quod tempus duce natura feturae est &c.*" (*cf.* 2 H. Wallon, Histoire de l'esclavage dans l'antiquite 17 (2d ed. 1879). Incidentally there is a certain paradox in Ulpian's argument in that certainly in the Empire the bearing of children by a slave woman was regarded as advantageous. Thus, for instance: (1) the writers on agriculture say that the fecundity of female slaves is to be encouraged; *e.g.*, Columella, 1.8.19 (cf. H. Wallon, *supra*): (2) Horace counts the swarm of young slave children among the wealth of a house; *epod.*2.65f; *serm.*2.6.65ff. Ulpian himself indicates in D.7.7.6.1 (45 *ad ed.*) that work could be extracted from slaves at five. See now above all for the view that in the Empire the Romans did not regard slave-breeding as unprofitable, Brunt, JRS xlviii (1958) at 166, and the references he gives. One cannot meaningfully say that Ulpian's point in D.5.3.27pr is that *ancillae* were not *primarily* kept for the production of young. Animals, such as sheep, could give a number of different products but nowhere is it suggested that only those things for which they were primarily kept were *fructus*. All in all, it is difficult not to agree with Buckland that the reason given by Ulpian in D.5.3.27pr expresses "somewhat obscurely, the real reason, which is respect for human dignity, rather than any legal principle.": F. Buckland, The Roman Law of Slavery 21 (1908). The respect for human dignity is, of course, limited: it does not extend to abolishing slavery.

[20] *Cf.* F. Buckland, *supra* note 19, at 36.

initial misery of the separation of mother and child, there is the further consideration that the owner would often regard it as troublesome to have to bring up a slave child without its mother. One would imagine that, inevitably, it would sometimes happen that the child would simply be exposed and left to die and that it would often happen that the child would be sold to a slave owner who was prepared—on account of the later profits—to buy it and bring it up. If it had just been accepted without question that the child was *fructus*, there would still have been a question of separation of mother and child when the usufruct came to an end when the mother would return to her owner and the child would not. But under this rule the separation might not occur for many years, the usufruct in the slave-woman would frequently end only with the death of the slave-woman herself, and the chances of the slave-child being reared would be considerably enhanced.

The conclusion to be drawn from these three points, and particularly from the second and third, is that the jurists' decision was based on abstract philosophical principle and did not take into account the practical moral questions of the welfare and happiness of the slave-mother and child.[21] Incidentally, the decision which holds in an artificial way that children of slave-women are not fruit is in itself an example of the freedom which the Republican jurists had to develop the law.

I should mention before we leave this topic that it is from time to time suggested, with differing emphasis, that the real reason for the decision is economic.[22] Thus for instance, Arangio-Ruiz says, "Much more probably, the decisive reason was that, in the conflict between the proprietor and the usufructuary of the slave, it appeared that the little slave was too valuable to be given to the latter." And, of course, as I have stressed, it is by no means certain that we have textual evidence for the philosophical or moral argument in the Republic. Still, I think a short answer can be given to those who take this economic viewpoint. In the discussion which Cicero mentions between the leaders of the state, arguments for the different opinions must have been given. The jurists cannot have relied simply on their authority. And these arguments must have been juristic in nature. And it is not a juristic argument to say in a dispute that the property must be attributed to one party rather than to the other because it is so valuable. The arguments adduced must have been different. This is not to suggest, of course, that

---

[21] *Cf.*, *eg.*, O. Lenel, *supra* note 2, at 538; 1 M. Kaser, Das römische Privatrecht 378-79 (1955).

[22] *Cf.*, *e.g.*, V. Arangio-Ruiz, Instituzioni di diritto romano 166 (14th ed. 1960); G. Grosso, Usufrutto e figure affini nel diritto romano 202 (2d ed. 1958).

behind the arguments adduced there may not have been an unexpressed economic viewpoint, but the discussion did not turn on that and its existence can only be a matter of conjecture. Further, if this economic viewpoint was important in the decision, the decision would still show—though in a different way—a totally heartless and callous attitude to slaves.

The second problem I want to look at concerns a legacy left to a slave by his master.

> D.35.1.40.3 (Iavolenus *2 ex post. Labeonis*). An owner left a legacy of five *aurei* to his slave: "Let my heir give to my slave Stichus, whom I have ordered in this will to be free, the five *aurei* which I owe him according to my account books." Namusa writes that the reply of Servius was that nothing was given as a legacy to the slave, because a master could not owe his slave anything. I think that following the intention of the master a natural rather than a civil debt is to be looked for. And that is the law in force.[23]

It may be that the text has not come down to us absolutely in its pristine form[24] but the accuracy of the substance, especially for the view of Servius, cannot really be doubted. Justinian's compilers, certainly, would never have invented the opinion of Servius which they would then be dismissing as erroneous. And one cannot really allege that a careless scribe was responsible for the view attributed to Servius, which is then contradicted by a later jurist in the text. Thus, we have Servius holding that a legacy by his master to a slave whom he has freed under the will of the five *aurei* owed to him according to the master's account books is void because a master can owe his slave nothing. Technically, a master could owe his slave nothing. But the master's intention is clear. There can be no dispute about what the master wanted. And Servius' decision is totally against the master's intention. There are about 139 texts concerning legacies which can be isolated as going back to Republican decisions. The great majority of these concern the question of the content and extent of provisions of the will. Not one other of these 139 shows a decision contrary to the master's clear intention.[25] We have even a text where Servius himself says that regard must be had for the intention of the testator.

---

23 *Dominus servo aureos quinque eius legaverat: "heres meus Sticho servo meo, quem testamento liberum esse iussi, aureos quinque, quos in tabulis debeo, dato." nihil servo legatum esse Namusa Servium respondisse scribit, quia dominus servo nihil debere potuisset: ego puto secundum mentem testatoris naturale magis quam civile debitum spectandum esse, et eo iure utimur.*

24 *Cf. Index Itp.*

25 D.32.29pr. (Labeo *2 post. a Iavoleno epit.*) does not: *cf.* for the reasoning behind the decision, G. Garrido, Ius uxorium 125-26 (1958). Neither does D.30.63 (Celsus *17 dig.*): Servius there excludes the dead slave-woman's child from the legacy because he regards the child *accessionis loco legatus.*

D.33.10.7.2 (Celsus *19 dig.*). Servius declares that the intention of the person who left the legacy must be examined to see the category in which he placed the object in question: but that if someone is accustomed to ascribe something of which there is no doubt but that it belongs to a different category, for instance, silver tableware or woolen cloaks or togas, to the category of furniture, these things ought not on that account to be contained in a legacy of furniture. For words should be understood according to common usage, not according to the idea of individuals.[26]

The text goes on to say that Tubero disagrees with Servius but that Celsus himself agrees with Servius. Servius' principle is one accepted today: the intention of the testator must be examined but words which are generally unambiguous are to be given their ordinary meaning. Even before Servius the principle was established that the testator's intention was to be taken into account. Thus, we are told that Quintus Mucius knew a Roman senator who wore women's dinner dresses. If he were to leave a legacy of "women's clothing," it is said, he would not be thought to have intended those which he wore as if they were men's clothing.[27]

Thus, Servius' decision in D.35.1.40.3 that the legacy to the slave of the five *aurei* which the master owed him is void is very strange. I do not know how one can explain it other than on the basis that Servius is being unfair to the freed slave. He is stressing the social difference between the master and his slave. The master cannot be in the debt of the slave.

The third instance also involves Servius. It concerns a rule, to which we will be returning, that if a slave was ordered by will to be free, but under a condition, and the heir obstructed the fulfillment of the condition, the *statuliber*—that is the name given to a slave conditionally to be freed—would get his freedom. The text, D.40.7.3.2, comes from Ulpian's 27th book *ad Sabinum*.

---

[26] *Servius fatetur sententiam eius qui legaverit aspici oportere, in quam rationem ea solitus sit referre: verum si ea, de quibus non ambigeretur, quin in alieno genere essent, ut puta escarium argentum aut paenulas et togas, supellectili quis adscribere solitus sit, non idcirco existimari oportere supellectili legata ea quoque contineri: non enim ex opinionibus singulorum, sed ex communi usu nomina exaudiri debere.*

Cf. now on the text, 2 Voci, Diritto ereditario romano, parte speciale 835 (2d ed. 1963).

[27] D.34.2.33 (Pomponius *4 ad Quintum Mucium*). *Inter vestem virilem et vestimenta virilia nihil interest: sed difficultatem facit mens legantis, si et ipse solitus fuerit uti quadam veste, quae etiam mulieribus conveniens est. itaque ante omnia dicendum est eam legatam esse, de qua senserit testator, non quae re vera aut muliebris aut virilis sit. nam et Quintus Titius* [*Mucius*—S] *ait scire se quendam senatorem muliebribus cenatoriis uti solitum, qui si legaret muliebrem vestem, non videretur de ea sensisse qua ipse quasi virili utebatur.*

For an explanation of this passage see L. Wilson, The Clothing of the Ancient Romans 172 (1938).

> Hence the question arises, if by chance money is owed to this slave either by the heir, because he had spent money on behalf of his owner, or by a third party, and the heir does not wish to sue the debtor or pay the money to the *statuliber*: ought the *statuliber* to get his freedom on the score that he suffers delay due to the heir? Now the *peculium* was either left to this *statuliber* as a legacy or it was not. Servius writes that if there was a legacy of the *peculium* he has suffered a delay in achieving liberty on this score because something was owed to him under his master's accounts and was not given to him by the heir. Labeo also accepts this opinion. Servius holds the same even if the heir causes a delay because he does not exact the money from the debtors. For he says he will get his freedom. I also think that what Servius says is correct. Since, therefore, we think the opinion of Servius is correct, let us see whether the same should be said even if there was not a legacy of the *peculium* to the slave. For it is settled that a *statuliber* ordered to pay to the heir or another can pay from the *peculium* and if the heir stops him giving it, the *statuliber* will get his freedom.[28]

For Ulpian in such circumstances, it is irrelevant whether or not the slave was left a legacy of the *peculium*. But a distinction had been drawn between the case where there was a legacy of the *peculium* and where there had been no such legacy; and it was apparently drawn or accepted by Servius. We are only given Servius' opinion for one side of the distinction but whether he explicitly stated his opinion on the other part or not, we can deduce from the text that according to Servius the *statuliber* would not in the circumstances here become free if he had not been left a legacy of his *peculium*. This means that where a slave was left his freedom on condition of paying a certain sum to the heir—a common situation—but was not left a legacy of his *peculium*, he could not pay from his *peculium*. This seems rather strange and it was certainly not accepted later. It means in effect that most slaves in that position would never get their freedom. Only if some indulgent outsider paid the money to the heir would the slave become free. Again we

---

28 *Inde quaeritur, si forte debeatur pecunia huic servo vel ab herede, quod in domini rationem plus erogaverat, vel ab extraneo, nec velit heres debitorem convenire vel statulibero solvere pecuniam: an debeat ad libertatem pervenire, quasi moram per heredem patiatur. et aut legatum huic statulibero fuit peculium aut non: si legatum peculium fuit, Servius scribit moram eum libertatis passum ob hoc ipsum, quod ei aliquid ex ratione dominica deberetur nec ei ab herede praestaretur: quam sententiam et Labeo probat. Idem Servius probat et si in eo moram faciat heres, quod nolit exigere a debitoribus: nam perventurum ad libertatem ait. mihi quoque videtur verum quod Servius ait. cum igitur veram putemus sententiam Servi, videamus, an et si non fuerit praelegatum* [*legatum*—Mommsen] *peculium servo, idem debeat dici: constat enim statuliberum de peculio posse dare vel ipsi heredi iussum vel alii: et si eum dare impediat, perveniet statuliber ad libertatem.*
The text has been held interpolated in substance, but see now A. Watson, *supra* note 1, at 204-05.

have a Republican decision which is very hard on the slave. It is, one might think, also contrary to the intention of the testator, though this is perhaps not so clear as in D.35.1.40.3.[29]

The fourth case comes from Alfenus Varus, who was a pupil of Servius and who was *consul suffectus* in 39 B.C.[30] It concerns a different matter and I cite it for a very different purpose.

> D.44.7.20 (2 *dig.*). Not in all situations is a slave who obeys his master free from penalty, for instance if a master ordered his slave to kill a man or to steal from someone. Therefore, although it was at the order of his master that a slave committed piracy, an action ought to be given against him after he has been freed. And he ought to pay the penalty for whatever he did by force, where the force was connected with evil-doing. But if some quarrel arises from a law-suit and controversy, or some force was used for the sake of retaining a right and villainy was absent from these occasions, then it is not right for the praetor, since the slave acted at the order of his master, to give an action on that account against him when he is free.[31]

The text originally formed part of Alfenus' discussion of the *lex Aquilia*[32] and it is mainly concerned with civil, not with criminal, liability. Since the master had power of life and death over his slaves it was reasonable enough to develop a rule that a slave who, acting under the instructions of his master, committed a delict would at times not civilly be liable after he became a free man. The examples given in the text where the slave, now a free man, is not accountable are a brawl developing from a law-suit, presumably one to which the master who gives the command was a party, and violence for the sake of retaining a right. The principle underlying these examples seems to be that in these cases the slave is ordered to do something for what may appear to be the protection of the master and also to be not unreasonable. [Incidentally, the choice as an example of the brawl developing from a law-suit is evidence of the text's genuineness, which has been doubted. It has a slightly

---

29 It may be worth observing that where the *peculium* was the object of a legacy to the slave, Servius could regard as due to it what had been paid out for the master: *cf.* A. Watson, *supra* note 1, at 208.

30 *Cf.* W. Kunkel, *supra* note 3, at 29.

31 *Servus non in omnibus rebus sine poena domino dicto audiens esse solet, sicuti si dominus hominem occidere aut furtum alicui facere servum iussisset. quare quamvis domini iussu servus piraticam fecisset, iudicium in eum post libertatem reddi oportet. et quodcumque vi fecisset, quae vis a maleficio non abesset, ita oportet poenas eum pendere. sed si aliqua rixa et litibus et contentione nata esset aut aliqua vis iuris retinendi causa facta esset et ab his rebus facinus abesset, tum non convenit praetorem, quod servus iussu domini fecisset, de ea re in liberum iudicium dare.*
On the text, now see A. Watson, *supra* note 1, at 174-77.

32 *Cf.* 1 O. Lenel, Paligenesia iuris civilis 40 (1889).

comic flavor, a human interest element. It is one of Alfenus' characteristics that his legal discussions are often based on cases which have elements which will appeal to his readers. Thus, we find in the same book of his *Digesta,* a breach of servitude resulting from planting pots and kettles in land,[33] a man making a dung-heap against his neighbor's wall,[34] a groom having his leg broken when his stallion sniffed a female mule which kicked out,[35] a brawl over a lantern which a shopkeeper (or probably better, tavern or brothel keeper) placed on a stone to light customers to his place of business and which was removed by a passer-by whose eye was put out in the struggle,[36] and a *servus dispensator* spending his master's money on a "little woman."[37] The proportion of this kind of case in the book cannot be due to chance.[38]] The first point to notice about our present text is that it was only in very limited circumstances that at this time a freed slave would avoid being subject to an action for delicts committed at his master's command. The second point to notice—and this is, I think, more significant—is the phrasing of the opening of the text: *Servus non in omnibus rebus sine poena domino dicto audiens esse solet,* "Not in all situations is a slave who obeys his master free from penalty." So in a few cases, it implies, he will be liable to a penalty. The phrasing of the text suggests that the general rule was that a civil action did not lie against a freed man who, when a slave, had committed a delict at the order of his master. In fact, as we learn from the text, the position was very different. Except in limited circumstances the freed slave would be liable. The form of the text implies great magnanimity toward the slave, and an understanding of his weak position in respect of his master's commands. The substance of the text shows a much harsher attitude. The difference between the form and the substance is illuminating for the attitude of the jurist—he thinks that the slave is very generously treated.

Other texts—indeed the great majority—show a logical approach to problems involving slaves. Sometimes the decision is logical but harsh. When we remember the freedom to interpret and to develop the law which I mentioned at the beginning of this lecture we might feel that the jurists were not prepared to put themselves out to help the underdog. One example, again from Alfenus Varus, is particularly clear.

> D.40.1.6 (*4 dig.*). A slave agreed on a sum of money for his freedom and he gave it to his owner. The owner died before

[33] D.8.5.17.1.
[34] D.8.5.17.2.
[35] D.9.1.5.
[36] D.9.2.52.1.
[37] D.11.3.16.
[38] On all this see A. Watson, *supra* note 1, at 174.

> he manumitted him, and by his will he ordered him to be free, and he left him a legacy of his *peculium*. He asked whether or not the heirs of his patron should return to him the money which he had given to his owner for liberty. He [*who may be Alfenus or his master Servius*][39] replied that if the owner after he received the money entered it in his own accounts, it had immediately ceased to be part of the *peculium*; but if, in the meantime, until he manumitted him, he had returned it to the slave it was regarded as part of the *peculium* and the heirs ought to restore the money to him when he was manumitted.[40]

The decision seems to turn on the idea of the *peculium* as a fund separate from the accounts of the master, so that if the master considered the money among his own funds it immediately ceased to be part of the *peculium*. The decision seems to be legally unimpeachable, but it is very rigid. If they had wished, the jurists would have been able, without too much trouble, to reach a decision more sympathetic to the slave.

At times, though, the jurists may seem to pass over an opportunity to deal hardly with a slave. Thus, Alfenus Varus himself in D.33.8.14 (*5 dig.*):

> A person had written thus in his will: "When I die let my slave Pamphilus have his *peculium* and be free." The question was raised whether there seemed to be a proper legacy of the *peculium* to Pamphilus, because he was ordered to have the *peculium* before he was free. He [*again this may be either Alfenus or his master Servius*] replied that there was no order in things conjunct, and it did not matter at all which of them was said or written first. Therefore the legacy of the *peculium* seemed valid just as if he were first ordered to be free, then to have his *peculium*.[41]

But it should not be thought that Alfenus or Servius is leaning over backwards to be generous to the slave. It would have been

---

[39] *Cf.* U. von Lubtow, 3 Studi Betti 369.

[40] *Servus pecuniam ob libertatem pactus erat et eam domino dederat: dominus prius quam eum manumitteret, mortuus erat testamentoque liberum esse iusserat et ei peculium suum legaverat. Consulebat, quam pecuniam domino dedisset ob liberatatem, an eam sibi heredes patroni reddere deberent necne. respondit, si eam pecuniam dominus, posteaquam accepisset, in suae pecuniae rationem habuisset, statim desisse eius peculi esse: sed si interea, dum eum manumitteret, acceptum servo rettulisset, videri peculii fuisse et debere heredes eam pecuniam manumisso reddere.*

See now on the text, A. Watson, *supra* note 1, at 178-80.

[41] *Quidam in testamento ita scripserat: "Pamphilus servus meus peculium suum cum moriar sibi habeto liberque esto." consulebatur, rectene Pamphilo peculium legatum videretur, quod prius quam liber esset peculium sibi habere iussus esset. respondit in coniunctionibus ordinem nullum esse neque quicquam interesse, utrum eorum primum diceretur aut scriberetur: quare recte peculium legatum videri, ac si prius liber esse, deinde peculium sibi habere iussus est.*

difficult to reach the decision that the legacy was void. To do that, one would have had to hold, first, that the provisions were disjunct, not conjunct as they obviously are, secondly that provisions in a will are not to be interpreted with regard to one another, thirdly that the position of provisions in a will is to be understood as having a temporal significance and fourthly, that the testator's intention, even where it is obvious, is not important.[42]

At this point one question demands to be put, namely are there no texts which show the late Republican jurists giving even a slightly strained interpretation in order to help a slave? The answer, so far as I am aware, must be that there are none. There should perhaps be a qualification to that. The texts show that in the later Republic there was a rule that if it was due to the heir that a *statuliber* could not fulfil the condition set upon his freedom the *statuliber* was to become free.[43] This may be a generalisation by the jurists of a provision of the XII Tables that a slave who was ordered to be free on condition that he paid a certain sum to the heir, if he were sold by the heir, gained his liberty by paying the sum to his purchaser.[44] But it should be observed, first, that the provision of the XII Tables may itself reflect the already existing rule that the *statuliber* becomes free if it is due to the heir that he is unable to fulfil the condition. The XII Tables' provision may be explaining the working of the rule in a particular and slightly complicated situation which might otherwise give rise to difficulties. Difficulties such as, did the very fact of the sale mean that the heir was bringing it about that the *statuliber* could not fulfil the conditions? Even if the *statuliber* had no money? Or had the sale no effect on the status of the *statuliber* who still had to pay the heir to gain his freedom?[45] Secondly, if the rule is a generalization of the XII Tables' provision, it is a very natural generalization and

---

42 Exactly the same arguments apply to the more complex D.32.30.2. (Labeo *2 post. a Iavoleno epit.*): *"Cum testamento scriptum esset: 'Sticho servo meo heres quinque dato et, si Stichus heredi meo biennium servierit, liber esto', post biennium legatum deberi existimo, quia in id tempus et libertas et legatum referri deberet: quod et Trebatius respondit."* ["Let my heir give five to my slave Stichus and, if Stichus serves my heir for two years, let him be free." When such a clause had been written in a will, my opinion is that the legacy is due after two years because both the freedom and the legacy should be referred to that time. And Trebatius replied the same.] See now on both these texts, 2 Voci, *supra* note 26, at 807.

43 D.40.7.3.2, 11 (Ulpian *27 ad* Sab.): *cf.* A. Watson, *supra* note 1, at 204-08.

44 XII Tab.7.12: *Epit. Ulp.*2.4; D.40.7.29.1; *h.t.* 25: *cf.* M. Kaser, Das altromische Ius 160-61 (1949). Doubts on the accuracy of the tradition are expressed in 1 Voci, Diritto ereditario romano, introduzione, parte generale 73 (1960).

45 For silence on important topics in the XII Tables and provisions on less usual ones see Daube, *Texts and Interpretation in Roman and Jewish Law*, 3 Jewish Journal of Sociology 3 (1961).

it would have been surprising if it had not occurred. Thirdly, the generalization might have been much earlier than the period we are concerned with. Fourthly, the classical law was much more favorable towards the *statuliber*. There the general rule was that the *statuliber* was to be free where it was not due to him that the condition was not fulfilled.[46]

This fourth observation brings us on to a rather different point of general application. In classical law there was a well established rule of *favor libertatis*. Where a provision in a will was doubtful, it was to be interpreted in favor of liberty. There is not the slightest sign of the existence of *favor libertatis* in the decisions of the jurists of the later Republic despite the richness of the surviving sources on the *statuliber*.

A striking contrast to the attitude of the jurists here can be found in certain old rules of procedure. Under the *legis actio* procedure one could not sue on behalf of another, except in a very few cases. One of these few cases was the *vindicatio in libertatem*,[47] an action brought on behalf of someone whom, it was alleged, was wrongfully held as a slave. Again, one of the peculiarities of this action was that the rule *ne bis de eadem re sit actio* did not apply: any number of *adsertores libertatis* could sue in succession.[48] Moreover, in such an action the praetor ordered that the object of the dispute be considered a free man until the final decision.[49] These three provisions are certainly very old. A fourth rule in favor of the person treated as a slave was in the XII Tables. Under the *legis actio sacramento*, the two parties gave a penal oath of either 500 or 50 *asses*: 500 where the suit concerned matters worth 1,000 *asses* or more; 50 in matters of lower value. But where what was in dispute was a man's freedom, the XII Tables provided that the *sacramentum* would be for 50 *asses*, no matter how great the value of the man might be.[50] The explanation of the generous approach of these rules is that the person treated as a slave may turn out not to be a slave at all, but a free man.

To conclude: the attitude of the jurists in the later Roman Republic in developing and interpreting the law when it affected slaves was unsympathetic. There is no indication that they ever went out of their way to find an interpretation helpful to the slave but, on the other hand, we have a few texts which show that at

46 D.40.7.3.10 (Ulpian *27 ad* Sab.).

47 G.4.82; J.4.10pr: *cf.* G. Franciosi, Il processo di libertà in diritto romano 150 (1961); M. Kaser, Das römische Zivilprozessrecht 46 (1966).

48 Cicero, *de dom.* 29.78.

49 Livy, 3.44.5.12; D.1.2.2.24; (Pomponius *lib. sing enchiridii*); *cf.* now, M. Kaser *supra* note 47, at 74.

50 G.4.14.

times they took up a position positively contrary to the interest of the slave. In the one situation which we know of where moral issues were raised as such in connection with slavery, the discussion was apparently purely abstract and not concerned at all with the welfare of the slaves.[51]

---

51 A very different matter—which cannot be gone into here—is that of the protection by the praetor of slaves who were informally manumitted. This protection almost certainly dates from the Republic though it is not directly evidenced; *cf.* A. Watson, *supra* note 1, at 196-98.

Probably D.28.5.21pr. (Pomponius *1 ad* Sab.) is not relevant to this paper. Though in circumstances where Labeo holds valid the appointment of a slave as heir, Trebatius regards the appointment as void, Trebatius' decision almost certainly is not influenced by the fact that the person named is a slave; *cf.* my forthcoming, The Law of Succession in the Later Roman Republic, Chapter 4.

25

Roman Slave Law and Romanist Ideology

HISTORICAL OBJECTIVITY is no easy task. David Daube has shown there is no scholarly effort independent of fashion (by which he understands a cultural trend) and idiosyncracy (by which he understands a personal bent).[1] A further element obscures the truth: the self-selection of scholars. Independently of fashion and idiosyncracy, those scholars who choose to work in a particular field will share some common features. Scholars who choose to specialize in Roman law will tend to admire the Romans and their achievement in law-making. They will want to approve of the rules they find in the legal sources, hence they become blind—or at least excessively short-sighted—to some obvious blemishes.

I should like to discuss three aspects of the law of slavery which have been widely misunderstood, and where the misunderstanding makes Roman law more decent than it was. Roman slavery may be condemned by later scholars but they neglect or misinterpret information on some of its most distressing features.

I

The starting point for the first example is W. W. Buckland's famous book, *The Roman Law of Slavery* (Cambridge 1908). He says (36): "During the Republic there was no legal limitation to the power of the *dominus*: *iure gentium* his rights were unrestricted. It must not, however, be supposed that there was no effective protection. The number of slaves was relatively small, till late in that era, and the relation with the master far closer than it afterwards was. Moreover, the power of the Censor was available to check cruelty to slaves, as much as other misconduct." Others, too, write of censorian intervention as protecting slaves against cruel masters. Thus A. H. J. Greenidge simply writes: "The slave was unprotected by the civil law, and until the introduction of the *Lex naturalis* into Roman jurisprudence, there were no rights of men as such which might safeguard him. But the cruel punishment of a slave was visited from the earliest times by the censors."[2] But how effective was the protection of the censors? It should be stated straight away that it is mentioned by Dionysius of Halicarnassus in his comparison of Athens and Rome. At Athens, he says, any man was free to act inside his own home as he liked. At

[1]"Fashions and Idiosyncracies in the Exposition of the Roman Law of Property," *Theories of Property*, ed. A. Parel and T. Flanagan (Waterloo, Ont. 1979), 35 ff.

[2]*Infamia: Its Place in Roman Public and Private Law* (Oxford 1894) 63 f. He cites no evidence. See also M. Kaser, *Zeitschrift der Savigny-Stiftung* 58 (1938) 73 ff.; *Das römische Privatrecht*[2] (Munich 1971–75) 1.114, 284; at 284 he says that censorian intervention is credible, even if there is no sure evidence for it; J. A. C. Thomas, *Textbook of Roman Law* (Amsterdam 1976) 393.

Rome, in contrast, every house, even the bed chamber, was open to the authority of the censor: "For the Romans believed that neither should a master be cruel in the punishments doled out to his slaves, nor a father be too severe or gentle in training his children, nor a husband unjust in his partnership with his wife, nor children disobedient to their aged parents" (*Roman Antiquities* 20.13), and so he goes on. It is not obvious that much weight should be attributed to this passage. In the first place, Dionysius gives no specific example of censors' punishing cruel masters. We need take out of the passage only that censors could punish cruel masters—which no one would doubt—not that they actually did so. Secondly, how much Dionysius really understood of the work of the censors may be doubted. He mentions as if open to the censors' authority children who were disobedient to their parents. But the nature of the censorian mark of disapproval was such that it could be used only against a *paterfamilias*, a male who had no living male ancestor to whose power he was subject.[3] Thus, children who disobeyed their aged father could not be disciplined by the censors and any mark of censorian disapproval would be put against the aged father who was held responsible for the children's behavior. At the very most, sons in power might be rebuked by the censors. If Dionysius could be misleading here, it is not clear that he would necessarily know much about censorian disapproval of cruel masters. Perhaps more significant than this weak passage of Dionysius is the total silence of the Roman writers on any specific instance of censorian intervention against a cruel master, a silence that can scarcely be the result of chance.[4] One might add that the Romans relished stories about rigid censors, so the silence here is particularly noteworthy.

The issue, of course, is not whether the censors could, or even occasionally did, punish cruel masters. It is whether the censors' power could and did effectively check cruelty to slaves. The answer must be a resounding no.

First of all, censors were appointed only at intervals of four or five years, five being more usual, and at times there were much longer gaps. The maximum period for which they could hold office was fixed according to tradition in 434 B.C. by the *lex Aemilia* at eighteen months.[5] This means that in general for three and a half years out of every five there were no censors to mark their disapproval of cruelty. Only the most notorious instances would even have a chance of being remembered.

Secondly, slaves had no access to censors, or other elected public officials or judges. They had no standing, and no legally recognized avenue of approach to anyone in authority. No machinery was created by which their complaints could be heard. In addition, they were in the physical control of the master who could ill-treat even more those who might be tempted to complain of ill-treatment. If any complaint was to be made to the censors it would have to be

[3] Kaser (above, n. 2) 75.

[4] See T. Mommsen, *Römisches Strafrecht* (Leipzig 1899) 24 n.1.

[5] See, e.g., T. Mommsen, *Das römische Staatsrecht*[3] (Leipzig 1887) 2.349.

made by a citizen. It seems impossible to believe that such complaints could ever have been frequent or meaningful. To begin with, unless the cruel treatment of a slave was public and blatant, another citizen would have had no direct experience of it. Again, class or group solidarity, a component in every society, would make it very rare for one citizen to inform on another for ill-treatment of his slaves. However kind and close to his own slaves a citizen might be, outside of his family his ties were with the other citizens (especially those of similar wealth and social standing), not with the slaves of other people. Further, unless the cruelty was public, evidence of it would be almost impossible to obtain. Slaves would not be questioned by the censors about their masters; and if they were their word would be suspect.

Three apparently unconnected details will illuminate the difficulties for believing that the censors' *regimen morum* could have been effective in controlling cruelty to slaves.

The first relates to the *lex Aelia Sentia* of A.D. 4 in the reign of Augustus. Gaius in his *Institutes* (1.13) tells us:

> By the *lex Aelia Sentia* it is provided that slaves who have been put in bonds by their masters by way of punishment or who have been branded, or who on account of wrongdoing have been questioned under torture and who have been found guilty of that wrongdoing or who have been handed over to fight in the arena with sword or with wild beasts or who have been cast into a gladiatorial school or prison, and are subsequently manumitted, whether by the same master or another, become free men of the same status as surrendered enemies.[6]

Under the statute some freed slaves are not to acquire citizenship but are to be placed in the lowest possible category of free non-citizens, and these slaves are those who have been severely punished by their master or tortured by the state. But the statute draws an express distinction: where the freed slave had been questioned under torture he now has this lowly status *only if he had been found guilty*; where the freed slave had been put in bonds or branded by his master he now acquires this status *whether he had been at fault or not*. Whatever else we may conclude from the distinction, there could be no greater evidence of a lack of interest in the rightness or wrongness of a master's savage treatment of his slave. To his dying day the slave, if freed, would carry the burden of his punishment, merited or not. The law dates from the early Empire, but it is unlikely to incorporate changed attitudes to cruelty by masters. D.20.1.27 (Marcellus, 5 *dig.*) also illustrates this same lack of concern. A master pledged a slave, then put him in chains for a very trivial offense (as we are expressly told). It is made obvious that for the jurist the slave's market value has been

[6]*Lege itaque Aelia Sentia cauetur ut qui serui a dominis poenae nomine uincti sint, quibusue stigmata inscripta sint, deue quibus ob noxam quaestio tormentis habita sit et in ea noxa fuisse conuicti sint, quiue ut ferro aut cum bestiis depugnarent traditi sint, inue ludum custodiamue coniecti fuerint, et postea uel ab eodem domino uel ab alio manumissi, eiusdem condicionis liberi fiant, cuius condicionis sunt peregrini dediticii.*

reduced. The sole question is whether the creditor has an action for the harm done to his security.

The second detail—which I have never seen mentioned—encompasses both the Empire and the Republic. To the best of my knowledge, not one single surviving legal text refers in any way whatever to sexual abuse of slave children by a master. This cannot be accidental and requires explanation. The leading alternatives must be either that such abuse did not occur or was rare, or that it was not a matter that interested the law or the jurists. General knowledge of human nature might suggest that the former alternative is implausible. This is supported by D.47.10.25 (Ulpian, 17 *ad ed.*) which gives the master the action for damage to property against a person who raped (or seduced?) his immature virgin slave girl. But if sexual abuse of slave children by the master did not excite juristic comment, it seems unlikely that ill-treatment of slaves by masters would often in the Republic attract the moral indignation of the censors. I hope to show later in this paper that legislation, when it came, which protected slaves was not primarily moral in character.

The third instructive detail is found in the well-known, even famous, text of Seneca, *De Ira* 3.40.1–3:

> To chide a person who is angry is only to incite his rage. You should approach him with various gentle appeals, unless you are such an important person that you can reduce his anger just as the deified Agustus did when he was dining with Vedius Pollio. One of his slaves had broken a crystal cup. Vedius ordered him to be seized and to be put to death in an unusual way. He ordered him to be thrown to the huge lampreys which he had in his fish pond. Who would not think he did this for display? Yet it was out of cruelty. The boy slipped from the captors' hands and fled to Caesar's feet asking nothing else other than a different way to die: he did not want to be eaten. Caesar was moved by the novelty of the cruelty and ordered him to be released, all the crystal cups to be broken before his eyes, and the fish pond to be filled in.

Apparently Vedius Pollio believed masters could treat a slave as they wished, and he did not expect to be interfered with for feeding a slave to his lampreys. Augustus' response was extra-legal but was permitted by his position of power. Augustus, it may be recalled, was later to restore the censorship.

II

The next example of the failure of scholars of Roman law to appreciate the cruelty in the Roman law sources is found when we link two well-known and universally accepted propositions. The first is that slaves were widely used in commerce to the great financial advantage of their masters. The second is that, even in a civil suit, slaves could only give evidence after torture. When the two propositions are put together, it emerges that when a slave's evidence was permissible at all in connection with a contract that he made, then he could only testify to the existence of the contract or any aspect of it under torture.

Suddenly the widespread use of slaves in business that has seemed to indicate, among other things, a recognition of slaves as human beings is revealed as having horrifying undertones. I do not recall ever seeing the two propositions linked in any textbook of Roman law. Indeed, the two Roman texts which expressly show for contract law that slaves could be interrogated—under torture, of course[7]—are not mentioned in the best-known current textbook, that of M. Kaser,[8] or the most outstanding recent one in English, that by J. A. C. Thomas.[9]

Pauli Sententiae 5.16.1: Reasons of equity show that a slave can be interrogated about his own act. For it ought not to be an obstacle to someone who lent for use or deposited something through a slave without a written document.[10]

C.9.41.15. (Diocletian and Maximian, A.D. 294): There is no doubt that slaves can be interrogated about their own act not only in a criminal case, but even in one involving money (for example when things are delivered by them to other people on account of deposit or loan for use or in other cases recognized by law).[11]

The reason given in the first text for torturing a slave, namely fairness, should be noticed. The contracts specifically mentioned are deposit and loan for use, and in both texts delivery has been made by the slave. Since these contracts are imperfectly bilateral and the action lies to the depositor or lender it follows—as, indeed, is express in *P.S.*5.16.1—that it is the slave's owner who is the plaintiff. In other words, the slave's owner, suing to recover the value of his property can and will in the absence of other fully satisfactory evidence, submit his slave to interrogation by torture. The slave is tortured as a witness for his master. We have no textual evidence as to whether in contract cases a slave could be a witness against the master, but general principle evidenced for other matters indicates the answer is negative.[12] The wording of *P.S.*5.16.1 might but need not be taken as implying that the contract was directly made by the master and the slave was merely used as a delivery man, but the wording of C.9.41.15 clearly shows that torture could be applied where the contract was made by the slave. Slaves were not competent witnesses in all kinds of civil law suits and we have direct evidence, from these texts, only for *depositum* and *commodatum* among contracts. But in both texts *depositum* and *commodatum* are

[7] A few of the texts that make it plain that slaves' evidence was allowed only under torture are: C.9.41.12 (A.D. 291); 9.41.18 (529); D.22.5.22.1 (Arcadius)

[8] *Das römische Privatrecht*[2] (above n. 2).

[9] Above, n. 2.

[10] *Servum de facto suo in se interrogari posse ratio aequitatis ostendit; nec enim obesse ei debet, qui per servum aliquid sine cautione commodat vel deponit.*

[11] *Interrogari servos de facto suo non solum in criminali causa, sed etiam in pecuniaria (veluti quando per eum depositi vel commodati nomine vel in aliis causis legibus cognitis res praestitae sunt) posse non ambigitur.*

[12] See, e.g., C.9.41.1; h.t.2.

expressly given only as examples and it is difficult to see why slaves' testimony would be permissible here, but not in other cases of contract.

What is revealed by those texts is of great practical importance. Slaves were extensively used in commerce. Their testimony was permitted only for some types of action, but always only if there was otherwise insufficient evidence. A slave making a contract, therefore, would have the greatest possible incentive to make sure that there was always good evidence for it and for its terms. The master, too, would have an incentive to ensure that the slave appreciated the need for good evidence: it would be difficult to trade successfully when it was known one tortured one's slaves. If the slave could not be a witness against his master, the other contracting party would have a practical burden imposed on him and would insist on a sufficiency of witnesses or written evidence. The outcome is that there is a gulf—to the best of my knowledge also overlooked by modern Romanists—between the famed ease with which a Roman contract could be made, and the practical requirements that would be insisted on when one of the parties was a slave.[13]

The very small number of texts on torturing a slave for evidence of a contract may indicate that in practice the use of slaves for evidence was rare. But equally it may simply be indicative of the Roman jurists' well known indifference to all questions of what actually went on in court, including how issues of fact were proved.

Interrogation of slaves in civil suits was not restricted to contract cases nor need they have been active parties. One text will suffice:

C.9.41.12 (Diocletian and Maximian, A.D. 291): Whenever it is a question of ownership of slaves, if the truth cannot be uncovered by other proofs, the legal authorities approve the view that the slaves themselves can be interrogated, with torture.[14]

Finally on this issue I will raise but not answer the question why the Romans insisted that slaves' testimony be always accompanied by torture. It was not because they believed that in this way, and this way alone, would truth be elicited. Thus, from the field of criminal behavior:

D.48.18.1.23 (Ulpian, Book 8 of the *Duties of the proconsul*): It is declared in imperial rescripts that not always, but also not never, should trust be given to torture. For it is a delicate and dangerous business and one that may be deceptive. For many people by reason of endurance or toughness are so contemptuous of torture that the truth can in no way be extracted from them: others have so little endurance that they will tell any lies

[13]In modern French law, for instance, the formalities required for proving some contracts are different from and more rigorous than those for the making of the contracts. Of course, informality in business dealings is not particularly desirable.

[14]*Quotiens de dominio mancipiorum tractatur, si aliis probationibus veritas illuminari non possit, de se ipsa esse cum tormentis interroganda iuris auctores probant.*

rather than suffer torture; thus it happens that they confess in various ways so that they incriminate not only themselves but also others.[15]

The answer to the question must lie in the psychology of slave states in general or of Rome in particular. Certainly it is difficult to believe that the Romans regarded as trustworthy evidence elicited by torture from a slave, with respect to a contract made on behalf of the master by the slave, when the torture was applied with the approval of the master, and when the evidence was needed on behalf of the master, and when the master was the plaintiff.[16]

III

For the third example we will return to the issue of restraints on the master's power to ill-treat his slaves, this time specifically to the question whether from the time of Constantine this power was more restricted. It is widely held that from this time legal limits on the master's power to punish were more strictly imposed,[17] and C. Dupont goes so far as to suggest that this was possibly due to the influence of Christianity.[18]

Restrictions were first introduced in the early Empire. The *lex Petronia*, of uncertain date but before the eruption of Vesuvius in A.D. 79, took from masters the right to give their slaves to the beasts without the approval of the judge.[19] The law was not entirely satisfactory and *senatus consulta* and a rescript were passed in support.[20] Close in time was an edict of the Emperor Claudius, which is reported by Suetonius[21] and to which we will return, apparently to the effect that if sick and worn out slaves were exposed by their master they became free and did not revert to his control if they recovered; but if a master killed rather than exposed his slave this was murder. Domitian forbade the castration of slaves,[22] and so later did Hadrian.[23] Hadrian also, we know, expelled from the country for five years a matron called Umbra who had atrociously treated

[15]*Quaestioni fidem non semper nec tamen numquam habendam constitutionibus declaratur: etenim res est fragilis et periculosa et quae veritatem fallat. nam plerique patientia sive duritia tormentorum ita tormenta contemnunt, ut exprimi eis veritas nullo modo possit: alii tanta sunt inpatientia, ut quodvis mentiri quam pati tormenta velint: ita fit, ut etiam vario modo fateantur, ut non tantum se, verum etiam alios criminentur.*

[16]For the facilities for torturing slaves, at the order of private master or public magistrate, to be provided by the holder of the public office of funeral undertaker, see lines 8–14 of the inscription from Pozzuoli published by L. Bove in *Labeo* 13 (1967) 22 ff.

[17]See e.g. Mommsen (above, n. 4) 617; Kaser, *Privatrecht* (above n. 2) 2. 126.

[18]*Les constitutions de Constantin et le droit privé au debut du IVe siecle: les personnes* (Lille 1937) 31 ff.

[19]D.48.8.11.1.2 (Modestinus).

[20]D.48.8.11.2 (Marcian).

[21]*Claudius* 25.2; D.40.8.2 (Modestinus); C.7.6.1.3 (A.D. 531).

[22]Suetonius *Domitian* 7; D.48.8.6 (Venuleius Saturninus).

[23]D.48.8.4.2 (Ulpian); 48.8.3.4 (Marcian); *P.S.* 5.23.13.

her slave woman for slight reasons.[24] Of more general importance was a rescript of Antoninus Pius which is recorded in Justinian's *Institutes*:

J.1.8.1: Therefore slaves are in the power of their masters. This power indeed comes from the law of nations; for we can see that among all nations alike masters have power of life and death over their slaves, and whatever is acquired through a slave is acquired for the master. (2) But nowadays, it is permitted to no one living under our rule to ill treat his slaves immoderately and without a cause known to the law. For by a constitution of the deified Antoninus Pius whoever kills his slave without cause is to be punished no less than one who kills the slave of another. And even excessive severity of masters is restrained by a constitution of the same Emperor. For when he was consulted by certain provincial governors about those slaves who flee to a holy temple or to a statue of the Emperor, he gave the ruling that if the severity of the masters seems intolerable they are compelled to sell their slaves on good terms, and the price is to be given to the owners. For it is to the advantage of the state that no one use his property badly. These are the words of the rescript sent to Aelius Marcianus: "The power of masters over their slaves should be unlimited, nor should the rights of any persons be detracted from. But it is in the interest of masters that help against savagery or hunger or intolerable injury should not be denied to those who rightly entreat for it. Investigate, therefore, the complaints of those from the family of Julius Sabinus who fled to the statue, and if you find they were more harshly treated than is fair or afflicted by shameful injury, order them to be sold so that they do not return to the power of the master. Let Sabinus know that, if he attempt to circumvent my constitution I will deal severely with his behavior."[25]

The text is taken from Gaius who, however, does not quote the rescript[27] and who gives a rather different explanation for it: "for the same reason prodigals are interdicted from the administration of their property."

[24]*Coll.* 3.3.4.

[25]*In potestate itaque dominorum sunt servi. quae quidem potestas iuris gentium est: nam apud omnes peraeque gentes animadvertere possumus, dominis in servos vitae necisque potestatem esse, et quodcumque per servum adquiritur id domino adquiritur. (2) Sed hoc tempore nullis hominibus qui sub imperio nostro sunt licet sine causa legibus cognita et supra modum in servos suos saevire. nam ex constitutione divi Pii Antonini qui sine causa servum suum occiderit, non minus puniri iubetur quam qui servum alienum occiderit. sed et maior asperitas dominorum eiusdem principis constitutione coercetur. nam consultus a quibusdam praesidibus provinciarum de his servis qui ad aedem sacram vel ad statuas principum confugiunt, praecepit, ut si intolerabilis videatur dominorum saevitia, cogantur servos bonis condicionibus vendere, ut pretium dominis daretur: et recte; expedit enim rei publicae, ne quis re sua male utatur. cuius rescripti ad Aelium Marcianum emissi verba haec sunt: 'Dominorum quidem potestatem in suos servos illibatam esse oportet nec cuiquam hominum ius suum detrahi. sed dominorum interest, ne auxilium contra saevitiam vel famem vel intolerabilem iniuriam denegetur his qui iuste deprecantur. ideoque cognosce de querellis eorum qui ex familia Iulii Sabini ad statuam confugerunt, et si vel durius habitos quam aequum est, vel infami iniuria affectos cognoveris, veniri iube, ita ut in potestatem domini non revertantur. qui Sabinus, si meae constitutioni fraudem fecerit, sciet, me admissum severius exsecuturum.'*

[26]G.1.52.53; D.1.1.6.1.

[27]But Ulpian does: D.1.6.2.

The reasons given for restricting the masters' power are revealing. Not a word is said about the well-being of slaves, and this is true also for the texts that refer to earlier restrictions. But Gaius makes a correlation with prodigals. They are interdicted from administering their property in the interest of the relatives who will inherit their estate and who will suffer if it is squandered. Likewise masters who ill-treat their slaves reduce their value and this should be prevented in the interest of their relatives. The rescript of Antoninus Pius that is thought worthy of quotation by Justinian in the *Institutes* and again in the *Digest* actually stresses that masters should have unlimited power over their slaves, and the claim is that it is in the interest of masters that help against savagery should not be denied to those who entreat for it. Presumably "masters" here means the slave-owning class in general rather than the individual masters who abuse their slaves. If this is so, then Antoninus Pius is referring to an eternal tension in slave-owning communities—between protection of slaves from cruel masters and the authority of masters—which will be discussed shortly.[28]

There is, incidentally, an interesting sidelight on the rescript of Pius. Protection was afforded an ill-treated slave if he fled to the statue of the Emperor. But it was standard practice in buying a slave to demand a guarantee that he had not fled to the statue.[29] Such a slave was obviously thought to be not the kind one wanted to buy.

To come now to Constantine:

C.Th.9.12.1 (A.D. 319): If a master beat a slave with a rod or whip or put him in chains to guard him, and the slave dies, the master need have no fear of prosecution. Distinctions of time and questions of interpretation are abolished. He should, of course, not use his right immoderately, but he will be charged with murder only if he killed the slave intentionally, by a blow from the fist or a stone, or by using a weapon he inflicted a lethal wound, or ordered him to be hanged by a noose, or by a wicked order instructed that he be thrown from a high place, or administered the virus of a poison or tore his body by public punishment, that is by tearing through his sides with the claws of wild beasts, or by burning him with fire applied to his limbs, or if with the savagery of monstrous barbarians he forced the slave to leave his life almost in the tortures themselves, with the destroyed limbs flowing with black blood....[30]

[28]On this rescript see also W. Williams, "Individuality in the Imperial Constitutions," *JRS* 66 (1976) 67 ff., at 76 f.

[29]D.21.1.19.1 (Ulpian, 1 *ad aed. cur.*).

[30]*Si virgis aut loris servum dominus adflixerit aut custodiae causa in vincla coniecerit, dierum distinctione sive interpretatione depulsa nullum criminis metum mortuo servo sustineat. Nec vero inmoderate suo iure utatur, sed tunc reus homicidii sit, si voluntate eum vel ictu fustis aut lapidis occiderit vel certe telo usus letale vulnus inflixerit aut suspendi laqueo praeceperit vel iussione taetra praecipitandum esse mandaverit aut veneni virus infuderit vel dilaniaverit poenis publicis corpus, ferarum vestigiis latera persecando vel exurendo admotis ignibus membra aut tabescentes artus atro sanguine permixta sanie defluentes prope in ipsis adegerit cruciatibus vitam linquere saevitia immanium barbarorum.*

The rescript is retained in Justinian's *Code*, 9.14.1. "The claws of wild beasts" appear to have been instruments of torture which were made out of metal. The reference to "distinctions of time," etc., suggests that there had been earlier rulings which drew distinctions based on the space of time that elapsed between the punishment and the death. A decade later the same Emperor issued another rescript on the subject:

C.Th.9.12.2: Whenever such chance accompanies the beatings of slaves by masters that they die, the masters are free from blame who, while punishing very wicked deeds, wished to obtain better behavior from their slaves. Nor do we wish an investigation to be made into facts of this kind in which it is in the interest of the owner that a slave who is his own property be unharmed, whether the punishment was simply inflicted or apparently with the intention of killing the slave. It is our pleasure that masters are not held guilty of murder by reason of the death of a slave as often as they exercise domestic power by simple punishment. Whenever, therefore, slaves leave the human scene after correction by beating, when fatal necessity hangs over them, the masters should fear no criminal investigation.[31]

It is these two rescripts that are cited to demonstrate that the law was becoming more humane to slaves.[32] Against that view it is enough, I believe, to point to the rescript of Antoninus Pius which has already been quoted. But Dupont, for instance, draws two distinctions.[33] First, under the rescript of Antoninus a master is guilty who kills his slave without cause; under that of Constantine the question is different, namely it is enough to know if the master used or did not use punishments which were prohibited and barbarous. Secondly, she says that the main innovation of Constantine lies in the use of the phrase "then he will be charged with murder." She admits that under Antoninus the master who killed without cause suffered the same penalty as one who killed another's slave and that the owner of a slave whom someone had killed could ask for a criminal prosecution which carried the capital sentence. But, she says (with others), the courts were indulgent in such cases, more so than if the victim had been a freeman.

We may dispose of part of Dupont's second point fairly quickly. It is reasonable to assume that the courts would be more indulgent to the killer where the victim was a slave, but we cannot tell whether this attitude changed once the

[31]*Quotiens verbera dominorum talis casus servorum comitabitur, ut moriantur, culpa nudi sunt, qui, dum pessima corrigunt, meliora suis adquirere vernulis voluerunt. Nec requiri in huiusmodi facto volumus, in quo interest domini incolume iuris proprii habere mancipium, utrum voluntate occidendi hominis an vero simpliciter facta castigatio videatur. Totiens etenim dominum non placet morte servi reum homicidii pronuntiari, quotiens simplicibus quaestionibus domesticam exerceat potestatem. Si quando igitur servi plagarum correctione imminente fatali necessitate rebus humanis excedunt, nullam metuant domini quaestionem.*

[32]But M. I. Finley does cite them as rulings protecting masters who had beaten their slaves to death: *Ancient Slavery and Modern Ideology* (London 1980) 122.

[33](Above, n. 18) 33.

Empire became Christian. In other respects, the two rescripts of Constantine and the interpretation of them that has just been described raise serious questions—also for Roman law in general—not all of which can be answered.

We may begin with the assertion that for the first time it has become murder to kill one's slave. The earlier rescript of Antoninus does not name the offense and whether or not it was called murder does not seem of great significance. What matters is the treatment of the crime and its punishment. We are told that the penalty is the same as for killing another's slave. What is in issue cannot possibly be the civil action for damages: the master cannot be suing himself. Hence it must be the crime, for which the punishment is capital. If this argument is correct then Constantine's rescripts do not necessarily seem to mark an advance towards a more humane regard for slaves. Actually Suetonius, discussing the edict of the Emperor Claudius (above, 59 with n. 21), does in fact say *caedis crimine teneri* ("liable to the charge of murder") of masters who kill their slaves. It is sometimes suggested[34] that Suetonius, not being a very precise writer, may have given too early a date for the rule that it was murder to kill one's own slave. Perhaps the reason for this view is the contrast between the two parts of the edict: one that permits a master to allow a slave to die; one that charges with murder a master who kills a slave. But there is no psychological conflict: the absence of a duty to provide care may easily co-exist with a duty not to kill.

Secondly, Dupont's argument in favor of the increased mildness of the law towards slaves under Constantine is that the question is whether or not the master used forbidden means of punishment. This is inaccurate even if we consider only C.Th.9.12.1. According to the rescript two questions must be asked. First, were prohibited modes of punishment employed? If the answer to that question is positive, but only then, does one ask the second question, did the master kill intentionally? Thus, for criminal prosecution of the master, Constantine in C.Th.9.12.1. is adding an extra requirement.

A third problem is whether the two rescripts of Constantine, C.Th.9.12.1 and C.Th.9.12.2, are to be taken as a unitary statement of the law or whether the latter may be regarded as a substantial modification. C.Th.9.12.2 could be read as excluding all criminal investigation where a slave dies at the hands of his master even when there was evidence of a deliberate killing; or it could be understood as being restricted to deaths following upon permitted punishment. The rescript does not say that there will be an investigation if forbidden punishment is applied and the slave dies. The problem for removing the ambiguity comes from the nature of imperial rescripts as a legal source. Until rescripts were issued as a collection, as in the *Theodosian Code*, it was not easy

[34]For instance by Buckland, *Slavery* (above, 53) 37, who accepts that Antoninus Pius' ruling on the subject restated existing law.

for persons other than the addressee to know their contents. This was so even when, as here, the rescripts were apparently issued to public officials.[35] The office of Maximilianus Macrobius, the addressee of C.Th.9.12.2, is unknown, and we cannot tell whether he could have had knowledge of the contents of C.Th.9.12.1. Even if it can be assumed he had, we still would not know whether in the later rescript Constantine was adopting a modified stance. Since the compilers of the Theodosian Code were instructed by Theodosius II in 429 to collect all general laws enacted from the time of Constantine and were expressly told to retain obsolete laws (C.Th.1.1.5), we cannot tell even for the early 5th century whether or not the two rescripts are thought to be in harmony. It may be significant that C.Th.9.12.2 with its—at least apparently—more lenient view towards masters does not reappear in Justinian's *Code*. It is certainly significant that C.Th.9.12.1 does at C.9.14.1, and that the rescript of Antoninus Pius is also retained, even more prominently in J.1.8.2, and in D.1.6.2. For Justinian at any rate, the rescript of Antoninus Pius and the first rescript of Constantine are to be regarded as being in harmony.

A final question, perhaps the most important of all, admits of no easy answer. How, in practice, were cruel masters to be brought to justice? There is an inevitable tension, in states where the slave population is extensive, between protection of the slaves from cruel masters and the authority of masters. Protection of slaves is not just a humanitarian issue: it is also important for the state. The rescript of Antoninus Pius claims that it is in the interest of slave owners—presumably as a whole—that cruelly treated slaves have the possibility of relief. Otherwise slave frustration may lead to slave revolt. On the other hand, masters would find it intolerable if slaves could continually challenge their authority by threatening to haul them into court for misbehavior. The Roman solution was to deny the slaves access to the courts except where the action was a claim that a slave was really free, and (by the rescript of Hadrian in *Coll.* 3.34) where the slave's complaint was that he had been castrated. In addition, as we have seen, if the slave took refuge at a shrine or imperial statue, then by the rescript of Antoninus Pius the slave's complaint would be investigated but the slave was not regarded as an accuser. If the slave was killed, obviously he was in no position to bring a criminal charge against his master; nor—at least from the time of Constantine—could his fellow slaves be of assistance since it was forbidden under pain of death to act as informer against one's master:

C.Th.9.5.1.1 (A.D. 320–323): Also in the case of slaves or freedmen who try to accuse or inform against their masters or patrons, the assertion of such atrocious

[35] See, e.g., H. F. Jolowicz and B. Nicholas, *Historical Introduction to the Study of Roman Law*[3] (Cambridge 1972), 371 ff.

audacity shall be repressed at the very outset . . . , a hearing will be denied them, and they will be crucified.[36]

Nor is much improvement to be found in the next half century of Christianity:

C.Th.9.6.2. (Valens, Gratian, and Valentinian, A.D. 376): When slaves thunder forth as accusers of their masters, none of the judges is to await the outcome; it is settled that no inquiry is to be made, no investigation to be heard, but the authors of the wicked accusations are to be burnt along with the statements of the accusation, with all the instruments of the writing and of the intended criminal charge. We make an exception of attempted high treason in which betrayal is honorable even for slaves, for this crime too is directed against *domini* [i.e., the Emperors].[37]

Consequently masters who killed a slave deliberately would be brought to justice only if fellow citizens laid complaint or if there was spontaneous investigation by the authorities. Neither practice seems likely to have been common.[38]

The above examples are from the Roman law of slavery. But the problem of the self-selection of scholars leading to a bias in interpreting the materials of their chosen field must be general.

[36]*In servis quoque vel libertis, qui dominos aut patronos accusare aut deferre temptaverint, professio tam atrocis audaciae statim in admissi ipsius exordio per sententiam iudicis conprimatur ac denegata audientia patibulo adfigatur.*

[37]*Cum accusatores servi dominis intonent, nemo iudiciorum expectet eventus, nihil quaeri, nihil discuti placet, set cum ipsis delationum libellis, cum omni scripturarum et meditati criminis apparatu nefandarum accusationum crementur auctores: excepto tamen adpetitae maiestatis crimine, in quo etiam servis honesta proditio est, nam et hoc facinus tendit in dominos.*

[38]Though a failed prosecution after a complaint by a fellow citizen seems to be the background of a rescript of Diocletian of 285: *Coll.* 3.4.1.

26

Legal Transplants and Law Reform

EARLY in 1974, a few months before the publication of my slim volume, *Legal Transplants*,[1] appeared the important and fascinating article of Otto Kahn-Freund, " On Uses and Misuses of Comparative Law." [2] Our aims and approaches were very different. Professor Kahn-Freund was concerned with comparative law as a tool of law reform; I was attempting to set out guidelines for comparative law as an academic discipline in its own right. Professor Kahn-Freund's approach was more sociological, mine was more historical. Yet even when these factors are taken into account it must be confessed that our conclusions differ more than just in emphasis. I was of the opinion that successful borrowing could be made from a very different legal system, even from one at a much higher level of development and of a different political complexion. What, in my opinion, the law reformer should be after in looking at foreign systems was an *idea* which could be transformed into part of the law of his country.[3] For this a systematic knowledge of the law or political structure of the donor system was not necessary, though a law reformer with such knowledge would be more efficient. Successful borrowing could be achieved even when nothing was known of the political, social or economic context of the foreign law.

Kahn-Freund, on the other hand, begins with the opinion of Montesquieu that it was only in the most exceptional cases that the institutions of one country could serve those of another at all. For Montesquieu, law was very closely linked with its environment because of factors such as climate, fertility of the soil, the size and geographical position of the country, the kind of life led by the people, their wealth, density, trade and so on. Kahn-Freund accepts Montesquieu's accuracy for his own time, but contends that things are now rather different, that environmental factors are now much less important as barriers to transplantation but that " the political factors have equally gained greatly in importance." Kahn-Freund's principal thesis [4] is that the degree to which any rule can be transplanted depends primarily on how closely it is linked with the foreign power structure. He sets out his conclusion [5]: " All I have wanted to suggest is that its use [*i.e.* the comparative method]

---

1 (Edinburgh: Scottish Academic Press; Charlottesville: University Press of Virginia, 1974.)

2 (1974) 37 M.L.R. 1 *et seq.*

3 *e.g. Transplants*, p. 17.

4 " Uses and Misuses," p. 12 *et seq.*

5 *Ibid.* at p. 27.

requires a knowledge not only of the foreign law, but also of its social, and above all its political context."

The question whether either of these views is right—or more nearly right—has very considerable implications for the status of comparative law and the role of the comparative lawyer in law reform, and I should like to look at it a little more closely in two stages: legal borrowing up to and including the age of Montesquieu; recent legal borrowing.

First, at the outset it should be noted that, as Kahn-Freund rightly points out,[6] Montesquieu did regard *l'esprit des lois* as partly contained in political factors. Kahn-Freund further observes that in what, in his view, is a decisive passage [7] Montesquieu formulates the political factor in terms of principles rather than of institutions. One should perhaps also mention another passage of Montesquieu which seems to bring his opinion of legal borrowing in the eighteenth century rather closer to that of Kahn-Freund for the twentieth.

> "*Comme les lois civiles dépendent des lois politiques, parce que c'est toujours pour une société qu'elles sont faites, il seroit bon que quand on veut porter une loi civile d'une nation chez une autre, on examinât si elles ont toutes les mêmes institutions, et le même droit politique.*" [8]

Here, it would appear, Montesquieu does formulate the political factor in terms of institutions and he suggests that for borrowing legal rules it is a good thing to have knowledge of the foreign political context.

With all his insights into the factors which militate against the transplanting of legal rules, Montesquieu badly—very badly—underestimated the amount of successful borrowing which had been going on, and was going on, in his day. It is enough to draw attention to the Reception of Roman law in Western Europe. Of course, not every Roman legal institution was adopted at all, and many of those which were were profoundly modified in the process. Yet the Reception involved such a massive transfusion of Roman legal rules into the states of Western Europe that one simply cannot accept Montesquieu's claim that it is "*un grand hazard*" if the rules of one nation can suit another.[9] Moreover the Reception shows that legal rules may be very successfully borrowed where the relevant social, economic, geographical and political circumstances of the recipient are very different from those of the donor system. Indeed,

[6] *Ibid.* at p. 7.

[7] *De l'Esprit des Lois*, Book XIX, Chap. 4.

[8] *Ibid.* at Book XXIX, Chap. 13.

[9] If Montesquieu's claim had been about all the legal rules—considered as a unit—of a nation, then the matter would be other. It is, of course, almost impossible for all the legal rules of one nation to suit another.

the recipient system does not require any real knowledge of the social, economic, geographical and political context of the origin and growth of the original rule. How otherwise could one explain the use made of Roman law by fifth-century Germanic tribes, the acceptance of so much Roman law dating from different periods and different political circumstances in the Middle Ages and later by so many diverse States in Western Europe, in monarchies, oligarchies and republics alike? How can one account for the influence of the twelfth-century Provençal work *lo Codi* on the law of so much of Southern Europe and Palestine?[10] For instance, in the *Livre des Assises des Bourgeois*, which was written at Acre in the mid-thirteenth century, 63 of 237 chapters are a straight translation from *lo Codi*, and a further 59 show some influence. In its turn, the *Livre des Assises des Bourgeois* was made applicable in Cyprus.[11] One of the facts which emerges most clearly from the influence of Roman law is that legal rules can be adopted from a system which is politically or economically (or both) much more highly developed.

Of course, where a rule of Roman law was inimical to the political, social, economic or social circumstances of a later state, its chances of being borrowed by that later state would be greatly diminished. But this reduced possibility of being borrowed existed, it seems to me, usually only when the rule was inimical and not also when the Roman context of the rule was simply different from the circumstances prevailing in the later state. Indeed, from the influence of Roman law—even without looking at further supportive evidence—one might deduce the proposition: "However historically conditioned their origins might be, rules of private law in their continuing lifetime have no inherent close relationship with a particular people, time or place." [12]

As for modern times, the great extent and importance of borrowing in law reform is well-known.[13] Without hesitation one can accept the proposition that a foreign legal rule will not easily be borrowed successfully if it does not fit into the domestic political context. The word "political" is used—as Kahn-Freund uses it—with a rather wide meaning, with reference not only to the structure of government and governmental institutions but also to powerful organised groups such as the Catholic hierarchy in Ireland or the

---

10 On this and for further reading, see *Transplants*, p. 61 *et seq.*

11 See Philippe de Mézières (1327–1405, Chancellor of Cyprus), *Le Songe du vieil Pelerin*, Livre 2, fo. 141r. 2.

12 Further reflection has shown me—rather belatedly—that this was the main point I was trying to make in *Transplants*. The proposition will be further investigated in a forthcoming book, provisionally entitled *The Divergence of Law from Society*.

13 See *e.g.* Kahn-Freund, " Uses and Misuses," p. 2.

TUC. It is, I hope, one of the services performed by Kahn-Freund's article that it will not be so easy in the future simply to accept the argument "The United States (or Germany) could achieve this by legislation, therefore so can we."

But where I disagree with Kahn-Freund is with his view that the degree to which any rule can be borrowed depends on how closely it is linked with the foreign power structure and that the use of the comparative method requires a knowledge not only of the foreign law but also of its political context. One illustration may serve to explain this. The Irish rejection of divorce as Kahn-Freund states,[14] can only be explained in terms of the political power of the Catholic hierarchy. And he rightly says "But does not for example the staggering contrast between the English and Irish attitudes show the central importance of the power factor as a determinant of assimilation and differentiation?" Now, should an attempt be made to introduce English-style divorce law into Ireland, it would be enough on my view to look at the Irish power structure to know that the attempt would fail. For that success or failure in Ireland, the power structure in England and any knowledge or appreciation of it is quite irrelevant. A similar example can be found in the Industrial Relations Act of 1971.[15] The prospects for its success or failure were determined by the power structure in British industry. The knowledge would not have been particularly helpful that in America, a major source of influence on the Act, the industrial power structure was different from in Britain.

A rather different point may also be made here. When a legal rule is firmly established and working efficiently in one country it is not always easy to see how closely it is linked with the power structure. This will be particularly true when the rule in question is of some considerable antiquity. But on the other hand, when a legal change is suggested for a particular country it is not so difficult to spot the factors which would favour, or militate against, the success of the reform.

That in the modern world legal rules deeply embedded in their political context—using "political" still in the same wide sense—may be successfully transplanted to a country with very different traditions is clear from the example of Japan in the late nineteenth century. French law served as the model for the Japanese Penal Code and Code of Criminal Procedure which were enacted in 1882. After some initial difficulties a Civil Code was adopted in 1898. This contained what was in all essentials the German law of contract,

---

14 "Uses and Misuses," p. 15 *et seq.*

15 See Kahn-Freund, "Uses and Misuses," p. 23 *et seq.*

delict and property: The first three books of the Code are virtually a translation of the *Bürgerliches Gesetzbuch.*[16] German succession and family law were accepted only with considerable modifications and were not, at least in the short run, a complete success. What counted for the speedy success of this transplant in general was the Japanese desire for it, not their knowledge of the French and German political context of the legal rules, or any similarity of that political context with what existed in Japan.[17]

On a different matter, I am not entirely persuaded by the opinion that environmental factors are now less important, political factors more important, in determining the difficulties for a legal transplant.[18] In Catholic German states of the sixteenth and seventeenth centuries divorce would be just as inconceivable—despite the example of their Protestant neighbours—as in modern Ireland, and for similar reasons. Moreover, Montesquieu in underestimating the extent to which transplants occurred necessarily overestimated the extent to which environmental factors hindered legal borrowing.

On this last point a little more should be said. When a law of general application is passed in a particular jurisdiction, say England and Wales, it is in most cases meant to apply both to a city like London and to remote mountainous districts of Wales; to the very rich and to the poor. Hence it ought to cope with very different environmental factors. Within the range of its application, climatic conditions, fertility of the soil, the life led by the people, their wealth, density, trade and so on may vary greatly. Hence such a general

---

[16] See, *e.g.* W. J. Sebald (transl.), *The Civil Code of Japan* (Kobe, Thompson; London, Butterworth, 1934), p. ii.

[17] See, *e.g.* Yosiyuki Noda, *Introduction au Droit Japonais* (Paris, Dalloz, 1966), p. 49 *et seq.*; R. David and J. E. C. Brierley, *Major Legal Systems in the World Today* (London, Stevens, 1968), p. 454 *et seq.*; Kahn-Freund, "Uses and Misuses," p. 8 and notes 66, 67. For further instances of large-scale transplants to a very different kind of society see J. Zajtay, "La Réception global de Droits étrangers" in *Études de Droit contemporain* (*nouvelle série*) [VIIIe Congrès International de Droit comparé, Pescara 1970] (Paris, Editions de l'Épargne, n.d.), p. 31 *et seq.* The acceptance of a code (or codes) based on developed Western law by a developing country with the aim of modernising the society (or aspects of it) is a very particular type of transplant which deserves much fuller treatment than is proper here. Famous instances, in addition to the Japanese, are the Turkish Civil Code of 1926 and the Ethiopian Civil Code of 1960. That the law in these codes may remain "law in books" rather than "law in actual operation" is not necessarily synonymous with rejection of the transplant. It may take a long time for the law in the codes to be fully operational just as the Reception of Roman law in Western Europe required centuries. Moreover it is possible to exaggerate the extent to which the codes are not operational: see, *e.g.* J. Starr and J. Pool, "The Impact of a Legal Revolution in Rural Turkey," *Law and Society Review* (1974), Vol. 8, p. 534 *et seq.*

[18] But I freely admit that I know of no way to measure the effect of these factors, especially since the word "political" is used with a wide meaning. If the arguments were to be developed further than appears necessary for the purposes of this note it would at once become essential to attempt to define or describe fully terms such as "power factor," "political factors," "political context."

statute may in many cases not be so very closely tied to any one particular kind of environment, and thus will be transplantable with greater ease. Naturally the smaller the jurisdiction, the more closely linked with a particular environment a law might be. In the France and Germany of Montesquieu's time, when small jurisdictions abounded, it may just have been the case that environmental factors were more of a handicap to transplants than they are now.

27

The Justice of the U.S. Constitution

There are many notions of justice, and at least three separate conceptions of justice have been found or have been argued for in modern Western systems of law.

One notion of justice insists that the inequalities of people should be reflected in the law, that persons should be grouped in accordance with their possessions of particular attrributes that are held to be intrinsically relevant, and that an individual's rights and duties should be made to depend on his inclusion in the group. This notion of justice amounts to an assertion that superior and inferior persons should be openly recognised and legally designated as such. The attributes that are to determine superiority or inferiority vary from society to society, but for this notion of justice they must be such as can be used to place individuals within a group. To avoid misleading or even leading terminology this may be termed the notion of justice number One.[1] This system, be it noted, is not necessarily inconsistent with a goal of individual justice.

A second notion of justice in law insists that persons should all be treated as formally equal in their standing before the law. This notion involves great respect for the individual who, with regard to law, is always to be treated as no different from any other person. To avoid misleading or even leading terminology this may be termed the notion of justice number Two.[2] It, too, is not necessarily inconsistent with a goal of individual justice.

The third notion of justice in law insists that persons must be treated as individuals – certainly not as members of a group, losing personal identity in group identity – and that all individuals should be treated equally, not formally as in notion number Two, but in actuality. Thus, to avoid inequality of treatment, benefits should be given to those at a disadvantage, financially, intellectually or in some other way. to avoid misleading or even leading terminology this may be termed the notion of

[1] The notion of justice here can be, and often has been, cynically abused. But that does not exclude its being honestly held by well-meaning human beings.

[2] The notion of justice here can be, and often has been, cynically abused. But that does

justice number Three.[3] Again the system is not necessarily inconsistent with a goal of individual justice. The politicised reader may wish to substitute his own terminology for notions One, Two and Three.[4]

The respect given in the United States to the notion of justice number Two can scarcely be more clearly expressed than in the first paragraph of the preamble to the American Bar Association's *Model Code of Professional Responsibility* (1981):

> The continued existence of a free and democratic society depends upon recognition of the concept that justice is based upon the rule of law grounded in respect for the dignity of the individual and his capacity through reason for enlighted self-government. Law so grounded makes justice possible, for only through such law does the dignity of the individual attain respect and protection. Without it, individual rights become subject to unrestrained power, respect for law is destroyed, and rational self-government is impossible.

Upon the recognition of the concept of justice number Two, we are told, depends the continued existence of the United States as a free and democratic society. Only through this concept of justice in law is justice at all possible and only thus does individual personal dignity attain both respect and protection.

Most systems of the law, of course, incorporate a combination of two or more notions of justice. For instance, even under number Three, it is often impracticable or uneconomic in law to take account of differences in individuals who in many regards come to be treated as if they were formally equal under notion number Two; and some advantaged persons are given special legal rights, whether as members of the party or as high-ranking military officers or whatever, so that to some extent the notion number One of justice in law is accepted. Again, in systems corresponding to all three notions particular groups such as infants and lunatics may often be given special protection. The issue here is that observedly weaker persons who form a recognisable group will be given help. Moreover systems corresponding to all three notions may, in order to reward individuals for meritorious service to the state, give all members of a particular group such as veterans certain standard benefits. What above all matters in practice and in theory is not the exclusive use of one notion of justice, but the relative preponderance of one notion. Even the United States, which we have seen to be addicted to notion number Two,

not exclude its being honestly held by well-meaning human beings.

[3] The notion of justice here can be, and often has been, cynically abused. But that does not exclude its being honestly held by well-meaning human beings.

[4] A fourth notion of justice is to be found in the law of the East European socialist states, namely that individuals' rights must be exercised in conformity with the material and cultural interests of the socialist society.

partakes at the highest official level in notion number One. This is most apparent in the – admittedly rather special – concept of affirmative action, in so far as it is enshrined by law.[5] Under this concept, women or members of minorities are for some legal purposes classified as members of a particular group, and given legal rights as members of that group. With regard to these rights, what counts is the status of the person as a member of the group, not her or his specific experience or talents as an individual. In exactly the same way, in eighteenth century England for example, any peer of the realm could claim the legal rights of peers on the basis that he was a peer even though he did not have the wealth or talent or bravery that was thought to be typical of peers. But the notion of justice number One in the instance of affirmative action is special in that it only confers relative, not absolute rights. Only when the relevant qualifications seem to be otherwise equal, is it the case that in law the benefits are to be given to the woman because she is a woman or to the member of the minority group because he or she is a member of the minority group. The theory behind this seems to be that the merits of the individual as a member of the group are greater than appears because the group as a whole has been disadvantaged.[6] The experiences of the individual may not be typical of those of the group.

It will not, I hope, be suggested – as it has been to me in discussion – that this analysis is wrong; and that the United States' exception belongs to notion number Three of justice precisely because the difference between number One and number Three notions of justice is that the former but not the latter envisages the distinctions in law to be permanent: that under notion number Three of justice each, with the passage of time, will have the standing of an individual, though he or she is now treated properly as a member of a group. On this basis individuals will be treated as members of a group with the expectation that the standing of the group will not be permanent but, by present differences in treatment, past differences in treatment of the groups will be cancelled out, all groups will merge and disappear, and the members of all (past) groups will be treated

5 'Affirmative action' is a term used with a variety of meanings, and is a rather hazy notion. In brief and non-technically it is usually used to express the idea that in any context where qualifications are equal, priority is to be given to blacks, members of other minority groups, and women. See e.g. *University of California Regents v. Bakke*, 438 U.S. 265 (1978); *United Steelworkers v. Weber*, 443 U.S. 193 (1979); *Fullilove v. Klutznick*, 448 U.S. 2758 (1980); *Teamsters, International v. U.S.*, 431 U.S. 324 (1977).

6 As is often the case there is here a great discrepancy between theory and practice. In practice, on the one hand, the bulk of women and blacks are illegally discriminated against; on the other, some elite women and members of minority groups receive preferential treatment probably beyond that permitted by law in admission to college, professional school and in obtaining high-status employment. It should be noted that for this second alternative also no attention is paid to the personal relevance for the individual or membership in the group.

as equal, not in actuality but formally. To treat this approach as number Three involves the logical absurdity of holding that a set of rules designed for a specific end, where neither the rules nor the end touch at any point on the number Three notion of justice, and where the rules conform to the number One notion of justice (treatment of individuals not as such but as members of a group) and the end conforms to the number Two notion of justice (individuals to be treated as equal not in actuality but formally) is nonetheless in reality number Three. Under the number Three notion of justice, the insistence here would be that individuals had in the past been treated, with injustice, as members of a group to the general detriment of the group considered as a whole; and that to right the wrong thus imposed, individuals should now be treated as individuals in the consciousness that, in so far as they had participated in the group experience, they had suffered.

Nor will it be suggested I think – though the possibility must be made express – that, because affirmative action is constitutional in the United States the view of justice has undergone a fundamental change and the dominant view of justice in the United States is now notion number One. In fact the precise categorization of affirmative action among the three notions of justice need not detain us so long as it is accepted that the United States very strongly retains notion number Two as its fundamental conception of justice.

The citizens of the United States have widely different ethnic, cultural, religious and other roots. They may be African, American Indian, Arab, Asian, European and so on, and they may be of the Buddhist, Christian, Hindu, Islamic, Jewish, or other religious faith. But they have one thing in common. They have the legal right under the United States' Constitution to be treated equally.[7] This equality under law has been enshrined in American thinking since the famous claim in the Declaration of Independence in 1776: 'We hold these truths to be self-evident, that all men are created equal, that they are endowed by their Creator with certain unalienable rights, that among these are life, liberty and the pursuit of happiness.' On the day in 1963 when two black students were first admitted to the University of Alabama, President John F. Kennedy declared in a speech: 'This nation was founded by men of many nations and backgrounds. It was founded on the principle that all men are created equal, and that the rights of every man are diminished when the rights of one man are threatened.'

The equality that is envisaged under the Constitution is that corresponding to our notion of justice in law number Two. All are to be

[7] See e.g. Equal Protection Clause of Fourteenth Amendment to U.S. Constitution; also *Brown v. Board of Education*, 347 U.S. 483 (1954), *Bolling v. Sharpe*, 347 U.S. 497 (1954), *Craig v. Boren*, 429 U.S. 190 (1976); *Frontiero v. Richardson*, 411 U.S. 677 (1973); *Massachussets Board of Retirement v. Murgia*, 427 U.S. 307 (1976); *Graham v. Richardson*, 403 U.S 365 (1971).

treated as formally equal. This high-minded notion is – with the exception of affirmative action above mentioned – so central in law that even well-intentioned laws proposed by moral persons to allow different rules to apply to different groups would be declared void as unconstitutional. There cannot be within a state, for instance, a law permitting the requirements for a valid marriage to be different according to the religion of the parties, as Roman Catholic, Mormon or Moslem.[8]

Yet the fact that different notions of justice in law can be held should prompt the question whether we have the ideal approach.

There are many different legal traditions: such as Islamic, Jewish, Chinese, Japanese, Western (i.e. European, though not in a geographical sense); and many subdivisions, such as for Western law, common law and civil law systems, each subdivision of which can be further subdivided. And we must not forget the customary systems of African or American Indian tribal groups. Yet the American legal system is entirely, or almost entirely, Western law. This is obviously the case; it has, to the best of my knowledge never been questioned, and hence it will not be argued for here. Suffice it to say that comparative lawyers never group it elsewhere. Thus René David and John E. C. Brierly list it along with English law under the heading of 'The Common Law' thus splitting it off even from continental European civil law systems![9] And Konrad Zweigert and Hein Kötz likewise treat it as part of the 'Anglo-American Legal Family'.[10] Just as definite are Mary Ann Glendon, Michael W. Gordon and Christopher Osakwe in their book appropriately entitled *Comparative Legal Traditions*.[11] Equally specific are John H. Barton, James L. Gibbs, Victor Hao Li, and John H. Merryman: 'In this course, however, we treat the West as a single cultural area which includes European civil law and the Anglo-American common law as well as the socialist law of the USSR and Cuba and the Capitalist law of the U.S.A. and, for example, Argentina'.[12] The book of these last-named authors has an even more significant title, *Law in Radically Different Cultures*.

Thus, the citizens of the United States who come from a non-Western background are, by the very fact of the Constitution, deprived of their legal tradition. They cannot even make use of their legal rules except where these do not conflict with the system of Western law that is in force. A few examples may help to make plain the extent of their deprivation.

Marriage law offers a first example. There can be no polygamous

[8] But in the absence of a compelling state interest which requires the imposition of uniformity, the Free exercise Clause will protect 'unconventional' religious practices: see e.g. *Sherbert v. Verner*, 374 U.S. 398 (1963); *Follett v. Town of McCormick*, 321 U.S. 573 (1944); *Pierce v. Society of Sisters*, 268 U.S. 510 (1925).

[9] *Major Legal Systems in the World Today* (London, 1978).

[10] *An Introduction to Comparative Law*, trans. T. Weir, I (Amsterdam &c, 1977).

[11] *Comparative Legal Traditions* (St Paul, Minn., 1982).

[12] *Law in Radically Different Cultures* (St Paul, Minn., 1983), p. 5.

unions even for those such as Mormons and Muslims for whom it is traditional and religiously sanctioned, so long as members of other groups in the state are restricted to monogamous marriage. Yet other countries may allow polygamy even for particular groups when it is excluded for other groups: for example, in Hong Kong (and also elsewhere), the Chinese, but not others, may legally have 't'sip', concubines or secondary wives.[13] In each United States' state the consent of parents is not required at all or is not required when the bride and bridegroom are above a particular age even for members of cultural or religious groups (such as Muslims) that require that such respect for parents be shown. The same law of incest applies to all within a state, thus, for example, depriving Jewish women of their right to marry their uncles or nephews. Many states have a minimum age requirement for marriage, thus preventing citizens of, for example, Nepalese origin from contracting child marriages. The consent of the bride to her marriage is a fixed requirement in the United States, but the requirement is foreign to many from other cultures: for instance, to Shaf'i Muslims no matter how old the bride may be provided she is a virgin. Divorce is permitted in all states of the United States and one cannot by contract before marriage take away from either husband or wife the right to initiate divorce proceedings even if they belong to a non-Western culture which forbids divorce entirely or forbids a wife to divorce her husband. Nor are traditional non-Western inhibitions on divorce given legal recognition here. Yet traditional Vietnamese law forbids a husband to divorce his wife who has mourned his parents for three years: and divorce is forbidden to a couple who married poor but have become rich.

Similarly, the rules of intestate succession are the same for all the inhabitants of a state. But many non-Western cultures rank the degrees of kinship very differently. Also women may be excluded from inheriting on intestacy; or eldest sons may receive a double share of the inheritance. And in some of these cultures testate succession is excluded. To show both that the rules of intestate succession in another culture may be very different from those of the United States and that other countries permit legal rules to apply to one group but not to others, we may consider the rules of intestate succession that apply to Parsis under the Indian Succession Act, 1925, sections 50-56. The other rules in the Act regulating the devolution of the estate on intestacy do not apply to Parsis. On the death of a male Parsi, sons inherit double the share of daughters, and widow inherits the same share as a son; if the deceased leaves a parent or parents as well as a child or children or widow and child(ren), the father inherits one half the share of a son, the mother one half the share of a daughter. Parents do not succeed to a daughter (at least when there is a widower or child), but each child and widower receive equal shares.

[13] See, e.g., L. Pegg, *Family Law in Hong Kong* (London, 1981), pp. 22ff.

Indeed, the whole notion of the family may be in sharp contrast to that of the West. One need only think of the common African and Indian concept of the extended family. But benefits established by law are given only to those who in the Western tradition count as family. Pensions awarded to the dependents of United States marines killed in action will not be given to those for whom a marine was financially responsible in his own culture; not to first cousins for example, and not even to his children who by Western tradition are deemed illegitimate.

One could go on with examples from other fields: the holding of property by, say, an African tribal group from which an individual cannot withdraw and at the same time take his property share is not possible in the United States; legal rules on witchcraft and magic are determined according to standard Western views; as are those on traditional non-Western medical treatment, and on attitudes to surgery. But enough has been said to establish the point.

It may, however, be suggested that it is no serious thing for citizens to be deprived of their legal tradition by the United States' Constitution. The response to that suggestion, were it made, should be in two steps.

First, legal traditions and legal rules have direct practical effects. For instance, child marriage, even if not consummated for several years, cements social and economic ties and creates legal bounds between families. These social and economic ties, through legal connections, may be vital in a low level economy and yet may have to be delayed for years. The rules of intestacy may create dire hardship for those who would traditionally inherit, but do not. Individuals may even have acted in a way that made their position worse because they relied on an inheritance that was then withheld from them. If it be suggested at this point that everyone is presumed to know the law or should know the law, the answer is that *they* knew *their* law but not the law imposed upon them because it is Western law. The burden imposed, above all on those who speak poor or no English, is immense. Further examples of the practical impact of legal rules need not be given. Everyone knows that legal rules have practical effect.

Secondly, law develops in large part through culture and is part of culture.[14] A legal tradition plays a large role in a group's culture. In so far as a group's identity is delineated by a shared culture, the forced deprivation of part of it and the forced acceptance of alien culture has, obviously, serious effects. If, as is often tellingly maintained, minority groups are at a distinct disadvantage because they have to live and perform within alien cultural parameters, how much greater this disadvantage must appear once it is realised that the alien culture includes the legal tradition and it is enforced by law.

[14] See, e.g., A. Watson, 'Legal Change: Sources of Law and Legal Culture', 131 *University of Pennsylvania Law Review* (1983), **above, chapter 7, pp. 69ff.**

It is, moreover, not just individual legal rules that are imposed. The whole world view inherent in the Western legal tradition is also imposed. Non-Western groups may have very different views of the role of law in society, of the strict legal separation of religion and the State, and of the value to be accorded by law to the concept of personal liberty. But even within their own group their ideas are not permitted to prevail at law. The strict and definitive solutions that are entrenched in Western legal thinking and the obvious appeal to force that is inherent in Western law are objectionable to Chinese legal thought. The disregard in most Western lawsuits of a search for a compromise that will enable the parties to save face is horrifying to those accustomed to African customary law. Again, 'Law, in classical Islamic theory, is the revealed will of God, a divinely ordained system preceding and not preceded by the Muslim state, controlling and not controlled by Muslim society.'[15] Though this view may be unhistorical, the Islamic legal tradition is one in which separation of religion and the State is irreligious and immoral.

The point of this paper is to indicate that in the name of equality, in the aim of justice in law according to notion number Two, those citizens whose legal tradition is not the Western tradition have been deprived of their own legal tradition by the United States' Constitution. Despite my best efforts I have not been able to uncover any evidence that those who imposed and who impose this Western legal tradition have noticed that they deprive others of their legal tradition or have thought at all of the consequences of this deprivation.

One should perhaps go further and suggest some reform. There are at least two possible ways to alleviate the worst effects of the total dominance of the Western legal tradition under the Constitution, one being much less complete than the other. The much less complete way is to draft laws always to be as permissive as possible. A marriage statute for instance would permit polygamy and polyandry, establish no minimum age for marriage and permit groundless divorce. But this approach is by no means satisfactory. First, it will not work in all situations: for example one could not frame general provisions of intestate succession that would correspond to all of the regimes that are favoured in different traditions. Secondly, sometimes a legal tradition itself demands narrow expression of a rule. Thirdly, one common function of legal rules is to provide some degree of social and economic predictability. If one invites a business associate home for dinner and includes her spouse in the invitation, one expects her not to turn up with seven lawfully wedded husbands. Some of this predictability would be lost if legal rules were framed so as to be as permissive as possible. Fourthly, this approach would in any event not really address the problem: non-Western legal traditions still would not

[15] N.J. Coulson, *A History of Islamic Law* (Edinburgh, 1964), pp. 1f.

be enshrined in the United States and given legal effectiveness by non-Western courts.

The other way is in fact quite simply to allow persons to live in accordance with their own legal tradition. All adults would opt, with their dependents, for membership in a group which would have its own law. Where this was appropriate under particular legal traditions individuals could opt out of one tradition and opt into another. A Constitutional change would be necessary. It might be thought that plurality of legal traditions would cause problems, especially of conflict of laws. So it would, but not problems that have not occurred elsewhere and been found to be soluble. A plurality of personal laws operating together within a defined territory is and has been a common phenomenon.[16] Bishop Agobard of Lyons is reported to have held around 850 A.D. that 'it happened constantly that of five people meeting in one room, each followed a law of his own.'[17] Some contemporary African states allow persons to live according to their tribal customary law, and also to opt for a Westernised national system.[18] France by its Law of 7 May, 1946, proclaimed that all nationals of overseas territories (including Algeria) would have the quality of citizens on the same basis as French nationals whether of metropolitan France or of the overseas territories, and particular statutes would establish the conditions in which they exercised their rights of citizen. In France d'outre-mer French citizens may have their rights and duties determined by Western (French), Islamic or customary law courts, in accordance with their status. Indeed, an expert on legal pluralism has recently pointed out 'that situations of legal pluralism are the norm rather than the exception particularly in Asia and Africa'.[19] If other countries can deal with it so can the United States.

Another approach to the problem is available, and will probably appeal to many. To do nothing. After all, it may be claimed, the individual who foresees a problem may do some state-hopping. A United States state must have the same legal rules for all its inhabitants, but states need not have the same rules as other states. The individual may change his

[16] See, e.g., M.B. Hooker, *Legal Pluralism; an Introduction to Colonial and Neo-Colonial Laws* (Oxford, 1975); *The Personal Laws of Malaysia* (Kuala Lumpur, 1976). These works give examples of the difficulties in conflict of laws.

[17] See P. Vinogradoff, *Roman Law in Medieval Europe*, 3rd ed. (reprinted Hildesheim, 1961), pp. 25f.

[18] See e.g. J.F. Holleman, *Shona Customary Law* (Manchester, 1969); S.M. Seymour, *Native Law in South Africa*, 2nd ed. (Cape Town, 1960) (conflict of laws is discussed, pp. 25ff); V.V. Palmer and S.M. Poulter, *The Legal System of Desotho* (Charlottesville, 1972) (the place of customary law in the legal system is discussed, pp. 96ff).

[19] See Hooker, *The Personal Laws of Malaysia*, p. xxxii.

domicile or even his temporary residence. For instance, typically a marriage that is valid in the place where it is celebrated is valid elsewhere. It now seems even that a marriage that is not incestuous where it is celebrated, but would be so regarded in the place of domicile of the parties, will be treated as valid in the latter state.[20] Still, state-hopping is not a full answer: no state may have the rules wanted within a particular non-Western tradition, the state-hopping may be excessively inconvenient, the legal result is not always certain, and will become much more uncertain if the state-hopping is treated as *fraus legis*. The do-nothing approach is not satisfactory on this ground. It still requires justification. Perhaps the justification should be that the Western legal tradition, particularly that branch of it accepted in the United States is, first of all, the best possible, and, second of all, is ideally suited for all people irrespective of their culture or tradition. This approach will appeal especially to those who are steeped in the United States' legal tradition, and who are insiders in the United States' legal culture.[21]

[20] See e.g. F.P. Storke, 'The Incestuous Marriage-Relic of the Past', 36 *University of Colorado Law Review* (1964), pp. 473ff. Interestingly, the author concludes that 'uncle-niece and aunt-nephew marriages should be prohibited everywhere, with no special dispensations or exemptions on religious grounds', p. 499.

[21] It will be noticed that a system of personal laws does not correspond to any of the three notions of justice set out at the beginning of this essay, but may contain elements of them all.

Index of Texts

I. LEGAL SOURCES

A. PRE-JUSTINIANIAN WRITERS AND COLLECTIONS

F. CASES

II. NON-LEGAL SOURCES

A. *GREEK AND ROMAN AUTHORS*